WITHDRAWN

D1604516

Continued on back

A SOCIAL PSYCHOLOGY
OF DEVELOPING
ADULTS

A Social Psychology of Developing Adults

Thomas O. Blank
Lehigh University
Bethlehem, Pennsylvania

A WILEY-INTERSCIENCE PUBLICATION

JOHN WILEY & SONS

New York · Chichester · Brisbane · Toronto · Singapore

Library of Congress Cataloging in Publication Data:

Author's name entry.
Blank, Thomas O., 1947-
    A social psychology of developing adults.

    (Wiley series on personality processes, ISSN 0195-4008)
    "A Wiley-Interscience publication."
    Includes bibliographical references and indexes.
    1. Life cycle, Human.   2. Social psychology.
3. Developmental psychology.   4. Personality.
I. Title. II. Series.
HQ799.95.B55   305.2′4   81-19835
ISBN 0-471-08787-4   AACR2

Printed in the United States of America

10 9 8 7 6 5 4 3 2 1

To Ilene—

Let us grow old together,
You and me.

Series Preface

This series of books is addressed to behavioral scientists interested in the nature of human personality. Its scope should prove pertinent to personality theorists and researchers as well as to clinicians concerned with applying an understanding of personality processes to the amelioration of emotional difficulties in living. To this end, the series provides a scholarly integration of theoretical formulations, empirical data, and practical recommendations.

Six major aspects of studying and learning about human personality can be designated: personality theory, personality structure and dynamics, personality development, personality assessment, personality change, and personality adjustment. In exploring these aspects of personality, the books in the series discuss a number of distinct but related subject areas: the nature and implications of various theories of personality; personality characteristics that account for consistencies and variations in human behavior; the emergence of personality processes in children and adolescents; the use of interviewing and testing procedures to evaluate individual differences in personality; efforts to modify personality styles through psychotherapy, counseling, behavior therapy, and other methods of influence; and patterns of abnormal personality functioning that impair individual competence.

IRVING B. WEINER

University of Denver
Denver, Colorado

Preface

The decade of the 1970s saw a great deal of movement in both social psychology and the collection of subdisciplines interested in adult development and aging. For one thing, social psychologists moved far in the direction of social cognition, with the great emphasis on attribution theory. As this approach took hold in social psychology, however, a group of personality and social psychologists, discontented with the stranglehold of universalistic, mechanistic models and experimental methods, have forged a set of new models and methods for social psychology. Kenneth Gergen, Brewster Smith, Rom Harre, and many others have emphasized the importance of sociocultural contexts and of the historical processes of development within those contexts to the form and process of social behavior and social thought. They have also stressed more naturalistic and phenomenological research paradigms.

Contemporaneously, the areas of social gerontology, life-span developmental psychology, and the psychology of aging have been making great strides in both methodological and conceptual orientations to adult development. Paul Baltes, Warner Schaie, Gisela Labouvie-Vief, and many others, especially the late Klaus Riegel, have advanced adult developmental psychology toward a thoroughly contextual, dialectical model radically different from the maturational and social structural models that have dominated developmental psychology and social gerontology, respectively.

These two revisionist perspectives have much in common, and both areas of psychology and social science have much to offer to each other. Yet, surprisingly, there have been no attempts to bring together the dynamic new approaches in personality and social psychology and the kind of orientation in life-span development that could combine with those approaches to transform our approach to understanding adult personality and social psychology and, indeed, social psychology in general. Equally important, many of those in the forefront of the new approaches have, inadvertently, closed off possible avenues of communication and greater awareness of development and adulthood issues on the part of personality and social psychologists who have not given their allegiance over to the radical reconstructionists. That is, by emphasizing methodological and conceptual sophistication and the inadequacies of current methods and models, these innovators have had the effect of denying entry into developmental approaches to personality and social psychology through less pure, but still adult-oriented, pathways.

This book is designed to bridge several gaps just outlined. It is an initial attempt to combine innovative approaches in life-span development with issues and research areas in personality and social psychology, such as attributions, ecological-environmental aspects of social life, stereotyping and prejudice, and other content areas. It is designed to combine basic and applied, theoretical and empirical, dialectical and traditional mechanistic orientations into a broader perspective on social psychology; one that allows for emphasis on and exploration of both change and stability, structure and process. It is designed to help make life-span developmental psychology and social gerontology more social psychological and personality-social psychology much more developmental and adult-oriented.

I aim to do this by describing and discussing the value of *both* innovative and traditional models, traditional and innovative methods, basic and applied perspectives, and behavioral and cognitive components of social psychology. I include both conceptual exposition and speculation (Parts 1 and 4) with detailed description of research—my own and others'—in several content areas of interest to social psychologists regardless of orientation. Part 2 is a detailed discussion of attributions about achievement across adult age groups. In it I focus on what I already mentioned as a major area of social psychology, looking at both self- and other-attributions across adult age groups, including a preliminary chapter on a meaning analysis of attributional language by young, middle-aged, and older persons. Part 3 concerns ecologies of social activity, satisfaction and affect, and environmental cognition in various age groups.

By moving across and among a number of areas and perspectives I hope to give to all of the parties essential to the development of an adult-oriented, development-sensitive personality-social psychology—and that certainly includes life-span developmentalists, psychologists of aging, personality and social psychologists of every persuasion, and social gerontologists, sociologists, and other social scientists—a set of paths to common work on issues of common interest. I hope to engender a marriage of interests in adult development and patterns of long-term change and stability in the lives of individuals, while respecting differences in approaches, models, and assumptions.

In that regard, the book is directed first of all to professionals in the array of disciplines noted above, and secondly, to graduate students and advanced undergraduates in those and other areas of psychology and social science. Although it is not designed as a text, it certainly would be useful as part of the readings in such courses as "Current topics in psychology," "Developmental approaches in social psychology," and a range of life-span development/aging special topics courses. In fact, I have used elements of the book and many of the ideas in advanced undergraduate and graduate courses in life-span development, psychology of aging, social psychology of aging, and environmental psychology of aging.

As noted previously, the book is divided into four major parts. Part 1 is an exposition and conceptual appraisal of current personality and social psychology in regard to adult development and of current work in adult development relevant to social psychology. Chapters include detailed consideration of several alternative approaches to a social psychology of developing adults. Parts 2 and 3 are detailed considerations of topical areas already noted, including much original work. Part 4 of the book is more speculative, concerning the relationship of an adult-oriented, development-sensitive social psychology to issues current in social psychology (especially "crises" in the field and the relationship of sociological and psychological orientations to social psychology), social gerontology, and life-span development, as well as several other content areas. That section, and the book, closes with a brief conceptual discussion of stability and change in individual social development, in historical societal development, in the developmental changes in physical environments, and in the relationship of those developmental progressions.

My debts of acknowledgment are many and varied. Although I was dimly aware of the issues I discuss in graduate school at Columbia University—and I wish particularly to thank two then-faculty-members there in the mid-1970's, Phillip Shaver, now at the University of Denver, and Howard Hunt, now at Cornell University Medical Center, for their guidance and encouragement—I began in earnest to develop most of the ideas contained in the book while a postdoctoral trainee in social gerontology from 1976 until early 1979. The program, funded by NIMH through the University of Missouri (PHS 5-T32-MH14681), gave me many things—the sense of ambiguity and marginality that a postdoctoral position appears to be good at engendering, but, more positively, exposure to a range of disciplinary and subdisciplinary orientations to both social psychology and adult development, and a time to ruminate and sort out what it means to me to be a social psychologist interested in adult development and aging. I am grateful in particular to the then-Director of the program Ellen Horgan Biddle, now at the University of Louisville, and many faculty and students in the program, especially Jane Rankin, now at Drake University. As part of that postdoctoral program I was fortunate to be a member of the Midwest Council for Social Research on Aging, which also greatly broadened my horizons and interests. Many individuals in that seminar program from 1976 to 1979 have influenced my work. Although they are too numerous to mention I must, of course, single out Warren Peterson, Training Director, for a special thanks. During that period I also performed the research reported in Chapters 10 and 11. The Older Consumer Study was completed with research money from my training grant and with the outstanding assistance of Cindy Piedimonte in design, execution, and analysis of all components of the study. The work on housing for the elderly was supported in part by Social Security grant HEW SRS 10-P-90151 to the University of Missouri, Warren Peterson, Principal Investigator. I particularly want to acknowledge the efforts of Ruth Kuhar, Teresa Bleir, and, especially, Linda Phelps for their part in the housing study, in which I was only a peripheral partner.

As I moved from my postdoctoral experience to a research appointment at the Institute for Community Studies, University of Missouri–Kansas City, I continued to benefit from many of those relationships already noted and from interactions with Paul Bowman, Frank Neff, Carolyn Kieffer, Elena Bastida, and other colleagues. The support of the National Science Foundation Social and Developmental Psychology Program (NSF BNS78-26378) was invaluable in furthering the research program on attributions reported in Chapters 5, 6, and 7; and I gratefully acknowledge that support and the assistance of first Kelly Shaver and then Robert Baron as Program Directors. Of course, any opinions, findings, and conclusions or recommendations expressed in this book are those of the author and do not necessarily reflect the views of the National Science Foundation. Cindy Piedimonte also assisted in this research, as did Joyce Burr, and Bernard Weiner was a valuable consultant. Their input was indeed major. The academic job search study reported briefly in Chapter 8 was facilitated by a grant-in-aid from the Society for the Psychological Study of Social Issues to Ilene Staff and myself. More generally, I have also profited from the expertise and interest of Lawrence Wrightsman, of the University of Kansas, while I was in Kansas City and since.

More recently, I have benefited from an appointment in one of the few multidisciplinary Social Relations departments in the country, at Lehigh University. The University's unsponsored research program provided assistance in manuscript preparation; several secretaries assisted ably with typing the manuscript.

I feel fortunate to be able to acknowledge several other debts of gratitude. One set of thanks goes to Brewster Smith, Kenneth Gergen, Douglas Kimmel, Kelly Shaver, David Chiriboga, Stuart Albert, Paul Baltes, Harold Orbach, Bernice Neugarten, Gisela Labouvie-Vief, and the late Klaus Riegel for the impact they have had on me in brief personal encounters and in my extensive reading of their work. Their ideas are an inspiration I have not as yet been able to fulfill fully in my own work. A second set of thanks is specifically for those who have graciously read and critically analyzed this manuscript. My new Lehigh colleagues Robert Rosenwein and Roy Herrenkohl and other colleagues already mentioned have helped me on various portions of the manuscript. George Banziger of Marietta College performed the greatly appreciated function of reading the entire manuscript in draft form. His cogent comments and wide range of knowledge, and the comments of the others, greatly improved the organization and preparation of the book. At the same time, as authors often note, the errors and omissions that remain are my own responsibility.

I also would like to acknowledge the impact students in my classes have had on my ideas and research directions. One example, but one of many, is the work by Barbara Hildner mentioned in Chapter 8. Two other students—Lynne Green in Kansas City and Nancy Yaeger at Lehigh—searched the manuscript for copious citation errors, corrected those, and provided general bibliographic assistance.

The lyrics to the song ''Circles'' are copyright by American Broadcasting Music, Inc., and used by permission. The figure that portrays M. P. Lawton's environmental model is adapted by permission of the American Psychological Association. The figure first appeared in ''Ecology and Aging,'' by M. P. Lawton and L. Nahemow in C. Eisdorfer and M. P. Lawton (Eds.), *Psychology of Adult Development and Aging*, American Psychological Association, 1973. My thanks to the publishers for their permission to reproduce their copyrighted material.

The guidance and support of Herb Reich, Senior Editor in the Wiley Professional Group, and the editorial and production staff there have been invaluable throughout the course of my first book publication effort.

Finally, I have a difficult task to adequately thank Ilene Staff for support, ideas, critical analysis, and assistance in virtually all that I do. The impact of her contribution is nowhere yet everywhere throughout my professional work; her caring, insights, and encouragement are central to all phases of my life, as she, I, and our relationship change and yet remain.

THOMAS O. BLANK

Bethlehem, Pennsylvania
February 1982

Contents

A SOCIAL PSYCHOLOGY
OF DEVELOPING
ADULTS

PART ONE

Current Incompleteness and Potential Paths Toward Completion

CHAPTER 1

Current Personality and Social Psychology: The Gray Snapshot

To be alive is to undergo an unavoidable, continuous process of development, undergoing exposure to a vivid, moving panorama of events and experiences and their integration with personal events and perspectives. As we proceed through life we play a balancing act of changes and stabilities, of continuity and discontinuity. Over time, we are what we were, but we are also different. From at least the moment of birth to at least the moment of death, every living organism is part of that interwoven process of development at every level from the societal to the cellular and in whatever mode of reality we choose to consider—biological, social, personality, cognitive. Furthermore, each of those levels and each of those realities is, in turn, coexisting and coterminous with some state of all of the others. Life is intimately grounded in relationships.

This interplay is all the more evident at the levels of social behavior and social cognition. At every point in the life-span, at every phase of the life course, from infancy to old age, we as persons can ill afford to ignore our embeddedness in all of the changing, developing levels of existence that influence our social actions and our modes of approaching our relationships to others.

We are immersed in a changing, modifiable world and we traverse through it with changing, modifiable bodies and minds. In such a world, quite obviously, to stand still is to change, to remain stable in relation to a set of changing physical and social environments requires the ability to change with them. Since some of the changes in our worlds are (at least phenomenologically and, often, demographically) quite orderly and progressive, some of the changes demanded of us are able to be ordered and predicted. However, other changes are (again phenomenologically and/or demographically) disordered, almost chaotic; to maintain relationships and some sense of stability in them requires flexibility and fluidity in the levels of reality which are most distinctly ours—our bodies, our personalities, our behavioral repertoires.

None of the foregoing is at all surprising. People know it. They go through life working out for themselves their relationship to the world in which they find themselves at each moment. They try to attain a mix of stability and change that is *relatively* comfortable, *relatively* challenging, and—most important—that makes sense. In that process people are sometimes bound to act the same way over and over but at other times to act differently in the superficially and externally "same" but internally "different" world of two points in time.

These basic ideas about the nature of life and the intermingling of change and stability in physical existence and, especially, in social life are neither new nor hidden from the view of the lay public or the scientific community. Indeed, they are part of the foundation of much ancient and modern philosophy and literature. For example, Heraclitus is renowned in every basic philosophy course for his metaphor of the river and for the description of reality it expresses—the instability and change inherent in life and relationships: "Nothing endures but change," and thus "you cannot step twice into the same river." Yet he did not ignore the dialectical complement to that instability, for he also remarked that "the road up and the road down is one and the same." It is equally true to say that the river—and the road—constantly change—and thus they are never the same at two different occasions, and the river and road are yet always the same, for they travel through the same territory and the same general configuration. Change and stability are *both* real.

As we proceed through centuries of philosophy and literature we can find many more statements of one or both sides of the change-stability relationship. Abraham Cowley noted that "The world's a scene of changes, and to be/Constant in Nature were inconstancy" (from "Inconstancy"). Alphonse Karr reminded his readers that "the more things change, the more they stay the same."

These statements typify the attitude to life, change, and stability that characterize a complete view of the individual's relationship to nature and to other persons. More recently, popular songwriters have continued to reflect a social reality that is in contemporaneous flux and stability, change and constancy. One of many examples is the lyric statement in a recent song by Harry Chapin, "Circles":

> All my life's a circle, sunrise and sundown.
> The moon rolls thru the nighttime, 'til the daybreak comes around.
> All my life's a circle, but I can't tell you why.
> The seasons spinning 'round again, the years keep rolling by.
> It seems like I've been here before, I can't remember when,
> But I've got this funny feeling that I'll be back once again.
> There's no straight lines make up my life and all my roads have bends.
> There's no clearcut beginnings, and so far no dead ends. . . .
> I've found you a thousand times, I guess you've done the same,
> But then we'll lose each other, it's just like children's games.
> And as I see you here again, the thought runs thru my mind
> Our love is like a circle, let's go 'round one more time.[1]

While poetry, song, literature, and philosophy have spoken well and clearly to persons interested in these issues, sometimes, to make their sense of themselves and their worlds, people may look to personality and social psychologists, developmental psychologists, and other social scientists for a modicum of guidance, for some understanding. And when they do so, what is it they find?

ON BEING A NAKED EMPEROR

What do we tell them when they ask? How do we portray their lives? Even though as people ourselves we know as much as other people the "facts of life" described above, you could not tell it by what we do—the theories we produce, the methods we use to investigate them, the samples we employ to explore the vast regions of social behavior and social thought, even the areas of interest we pursue. None of them give many clues that we know what people know without us, much less that we know more than they. Rather, what we present to the world are bits and pieces of responses, behaviors in laboratories or other structured environments by college students or other highly captive, controlled populations. These bits and pieces, further, are treated by us as though they are ageless and timeless, that is, as though if accumulated sufficiently and placed together according to some universal, timeless template, they will form a mosaic that describes all people, at all times of life and all seasons of the world. The picture we give to those who look to us is a monochrome snapshot; a dull gray picture of a person poised between late adolescence and early adulthood, told to stand in front of a bare white wall, frozen and unmoving. But like the Emperor of the fairy tale, we ask people to believe us when we point to our nonexistent clothes. We tell them about the shades of coloring, the nuances of tone, and the flash of movement. Unfortunately, like the emperor, we are naked. We really do not have a lifespan, development-sensitive psychology of social behavior and social cognition at all. Instead, we have sacrificed a vivid depiction of everyday reality for the sterile controllability and convenience of having college students do relatively strange things in artificial situations (as has been discussed often by others and will be discussed later in this chapter).

These are bold statements which must be examined further before the way is laid for any different approach. The reality of this state of affairs must be established, reasons for it explicated, and its impact on social psychology and on understanding of social life evaluated prior to development of alternatives and presentation of examples of a few faltering steps in a new direction. The latter themes and elements comprise the body of this book; a brief examination of the state of the field, reasons for that state, and results of it upon social psychology's role in society is the central focus of this chapter.

CURRENT AGELESS SOCIAL PSYCHOLOGY

The approach of personality and social psychologists to adult developmental issues of changing relationships in changing contexts has been what might be best termed benign neglect.[2] I think it is fair to say that no social psychologist decides that adult-hood is not important; that aging processes and changing relationships to others based on age identification are irrelevant; that people are nothing more than passive receptacles into which attitudes, beliefs, and behavior systems are poured; or that people's conceptions of their worlds are hardened and fossilized by the age of 25. Nor was it vicious prejudice that led to a "snapshot social psychology" of college students doing what comes naturally in unnatural surroundings, far removed from the flesh and blood, multidimensional, unfolding drama of the social life of adults. Yet the result does not look substantially different from what it would be if the incompleteness were intentional and malicious.

I will be going into detailed consideration of a variety of aspects to this sterility and incompleteness in social psychology and will consider theories, methods, areas of interest, and samples as they all share in the constriction of current ageless social psychology. Prior to that detailed exposition, the reader may wish to stop for a moment and reflect upon his or her own areas of interest in social psychology. I challenge the reader to produce more than a handful of studies in *any* major research area of current social psychology—attributions, attraction, aggression, attitude structure and attitude change, group dynamics, environmental use, persuasion, conformity—that use noncollege student adult samples, that use developmental research strategies (even rough ones such as cross-sectional age comparisons), that test development-sensitive theories, or that explore adult-oriented areas of interest within their broader area (e.g., divorce, childrearing, or other family matters, retirement, business, or other work matters). Of course, isolated examples of all of these can be found—and some of those will be discussed in this and succeeding chapters—but the search is neither easy nor very productive in relation to the number of studies that are explicitly college-student-age-oriented (e.g., on exam-taking, dating, teacher-student relations), much less in relation to those that are supposed to be general, but are regularly examined only in restricted contexts.

The subject matter of social psychology is intrinsically relational, for it is the study of the relationship of an individual's interior life (cognitive processes, personality,

---

[2]For the time being I am going to ignore a group of personality-social psychologists to whom much of this does not apply. Marjorie Fiske Lowenthal and associates (1975), George Valliant (1977), Daniel Levinson (1978), Erik Erikson (1959), Bernice Neugarten (1977), and others have, in fact, spent considerable time delineating aspects of development in personality factors beyond childhood. These views are important and will be considered and evaluated later in the book, especially in Chapters 13 and 14. Unfortunately, as will be expanded upon then, some of the objections raised here—and others to be considered later—do apply to those approaches, particularly to the organicist stage model (psychoanalytic) orientation of most of those personality psychologists. Other of the complaints to be laid out in the following pages, obviously, do *not* apply to these theorists and researchers. In any case, for the present, the group "personality and social psychologists" is used primarily to typify those who publish in outlets such as *Journal of Personality and Social Psychology, Journal of Social Psychology* and *Journal of Experimental Social Psychology, Research in Personality* and the like (and who dominate both psychological and sociological social psychology) rather than to those more comfortable with *Journal of Personality* and with more classically psychodynamically oriented work and to those in the Piagetian tradition (also considered in Chapter 14). In other words, most of the current criticisms are directed rather explicitly to those who consider themselves to be primarily social psychologists.

motivations, recollections) and influences external to him or her (physical objects and environments, institutions and organizations) and, most dramatically, the interior lives of those with whom the person has contact (*their* cognitions, *their* personalities, motivations, and recollections, *their* attitudes toward and expectations for that individual, *their* actions toward and with him or her). It is also concerned with the relationship of the individual's inner life and outer life actions, behaviors, and coordinations with others. Its subject matter is intrinsically in flux, but its realization of the subject matter is not reflective of those realities. Rather than understanding social psychology as a flow of relationships, most social psychologists—including most revisionist critics of the traditional definitions of the field (for example, see Armistead, 1974; McGuire, 1973; Smith, 1974; and many others to be cited later), have chosen to crystallize the subject matter into a series of vignettes, and have masqueraded that crystallization with terms that imply the flow and form and relationships they have taken pains to excise.

In answer to an objection that well may be forming in the reader's mind, I must hasten to add at this point that social psychologists, indeed, constantly speak of change. In some ways it is their stock in trade. Yet the "change" is of a severely limited sort, not much like what most people mean by change, and certainly not at all what they mean by development. The area of attitude change theory and research typifies what I mean. Think of classic research programs by Hovland, Janis, and their followers (1953) or by Festinger (1957) and other cognitive dissonance researchers.

Researchers in this area are, in fact, obsessed with studying change. Stability of attitudes indicates nothing more than failure on the part of the experimenter, for change is what is "supposed" to result from experimental intervention. But the "change" studied is merely a manipulation of events over an extremely short span of time, events thrust upon an essentially passive recipient. That is, the person—the "subject"—and the contextual surroundings, in both immediate and larger-scale terms, *are* defined to be and expected—in fact, *required*—to be otherwise static. It is the manipulation that *induces* change. Indeed, if the recipient brings too much of himself to the situation, he is likely to be excluded from the sample—"after all, he had had a bad day or was sick or. . . ." And perish the thought of really trying to find out if the "change" was real, that is, if it becomes internalized and *used* in the process of acting as a social being! There is no recognition of constant change, of ebb and flow, that is, of *development* in persons, places, or things. There is assumed to be a state of no change until an experimental manipulation (or a real-world experience that replicates it) occurs. We are obstinate in our emphasis on enforced change, but equally obstinate in disregard for free, self-motivated, internally directed change. Individual change that is not explicable in the restricted terms of the research paradigm becomes the basis and core, not of attempts to understand it, but of the "error" term in statistical analysis.

Attribution theory affords another example of these phenomena. Spurred on by the provocative *phenomenological* observations of Fritz Heider (1958) and by the evident importance of perception of causality as a mediator of social relationships, personality and social psychologists turned to the study of attribution *processes*. Again, the term strongly implies a concern with fluidity and movement, with temporal and contextual embeddedness. But that, too, becomes something quite different in the hands of the social psychologists. The study of attribution processes becomes miraculously transformed into thousands of studies, almost all of attributions as though they were static schemata applied in mechanical fashion to situations. The structures themselves are believed to exist and to be changeable only by external manipulations (as in attitude change) or by the plodding accumulation of experiences, incrementally heaped one upon the other with no more active reconstruction and individualization, no more *development,* than is to be found in attitude "change" by experimental manipulations.

The list can go on. As will be discussed throughout this book, virtually every area of social psychological investigation is formulated and explored in ways that are likely to minimize the possibility of "real" (i.e., not experimentally controlled) change or development, to play down the input of the individual and his or her "personhood" (the dreaded individual differences factors to be discussed shortly), and to take active, interactive processes of everyday life and make them over into clean, crisp, pacified mechanisms.

Interestingly, this style of study coexists with an extreme interest in statistical interaction. Is it in these interactions that we can find our sense of involvement and active construction of social behavior? Hardly. The interactions of interest bear the marks of the methods and models noted above. The interactions do not seem to be of the same kind as life gives us—they are not interactions of the tension of relationships, the balance of factors which typifies life. Rather, they are the interactions of static, controlled elements. They are ballistic, billiard-ball kinds of interactions (see Buss, 1979; Howard, 1979; Harre & Secord, 1972). Further, interest in interactions seldom includes treating the person as the ultimate interactor. No, he or she, once again, is the recipient, the manipulated, the composite of structures in mechanical relation to one another.

Before proceeding further, I perhaps should spend a moment clarifying what I mean by several terms I have so far cavalierly brought into the conversation, since their level of precision is important throughout the book.

I have described how the "change" that social psychologists consistently examine is not developmental. In that discussion I tried to show that "change" as a term is broad, embracing both short-term, manipulated differences over short periods of time and transformation of structures over long periods (within the individual or across individuals, generations, and even societies). "Change" simply points to a lack of equivalence on some dimension from Time A to Time B. I will often use if contrapuntally to its complement—stability. Again, stability may be short or long term; it simply implies equivalence on some dimension across times of observation. I will use these terms in this manner, avoiding important but involved and peripheral arguments concerning the meaning—possible and operational—of equivalence, given imperfect measurement instruments, varying contexts, and so on (see Baltes, Reese, & Nesselroade, 1977; Labouvie, 1980; and many other methodological sources in life-span development and/or measurement).

At the same time, I have juxtaposed to the position of social psychology, in which changes that take place—at least those of interest to the researcher—are invariably short term and externally determined, the concept of development. In many ways, this term, too, is broad and, therefore, has multiple, situationally determined content. In general, by "developmental" I simply mean processes of change and stability—actually of the relationship as it can be described in terms of change and stability—over *relatively* long periods of time. I know that description is vague, but I feel that most people, most of the time, would not have much trouble differentiating development from "nondevelopmental change." For one thing, we have fairly clearcut images of development: most persons would call differences found over a time measured in years "developmental" in terms of an individual's life, but not necessarily see it as "developmental" in terms of a religion or a culture. Secondly, development would imply activity from the point of view of that which is developing; such activity is often missing from social psychological studies of "change."

I do not think it is wise to get too far astray into some of these issues (or others, such as the differentiation between history in the sense psychologists often use it, e.g., history of experiences, and development). I will, however, point out one more aspect of the definitional issues. As I proceed through the book I will quite explicitly use two very different definitions of "developmental" when applied to both theory and research in social psychology. One sense, the weak sense, is a reference to age comparisons and/or to study of issues that are intrinsically related to periods of the life-span other than late adolescence-young adulthood, the undisputed favorite for social psychologists. In this concept there is no *necessary* linkage of age differences to change processes, although I will argue, especially in Chapter 2, that thorough consideration of "weak developmentalism" will be beneficial to a social psychology of developing adults.

The other sense of developmental, what I will for convenience call "strong developmentalism," does entail a concern with process and with the relational nexus of change and stability that is developmental even from moment to moment. This is a concern with flux and instability, with tension and conflict in constant interplay with stability and consistency and balance. It's a different conception of the present—as constructed and relational—from current social psychology. I will concentrate on it in Chapter 3.

The problems catalogued, and therefore the possibility for solutions, lie at several levels. Some of the deficits in current social psychology are rather superficial; they can be erased by application of fairly easily realized renovations. Critics who differ with the status quo at this level are likely to propose that a new method be applied or a new area of interest included in the field (see, for example, McGuire, 1973; Schlenker 1974). But it is also possible to see the problems as far from superficial, to see flaws throughout the fabric and into the base of the discipline, flaws which most likely cannot be corrected by renovation. Those who believe the problems in the field lie at this level are likely to speak of reconstruction, not renovation—of revolutions, not renewal (see Gergen, 1973, 1978; Archibald, 1976, 1978; Harre, 1977a, b, 1979).

Criticisms of aspects lying closer to the surface tend to revolve around discussions of methods or areas *within* traditional boundaries—new ways to analyze experimental data, for example, or new areas into which to thrust basic social psychological theories and concepts, or new types of samples to study. To a large degree, the research portions of this book will be attempts to begin to answer criticisms of personality and social psychology at this level, and this level is discussed more fully in Chapter 2.

Although the research discussed in Parts 2 and 3 is primarily research designed to overcome rather superficial problems in the field and superficial "correctives" for them, that should not be taken to imply that I do not espouse the more radical criticisms, which center on theory construction and conceptual design of research rather than on specifics of the method. In fact, major sections of the book are discussions of the need for a radical reorganization of the social psychological enterprise, a reorganization demanded by the unresponsiveness of social psychologists to the pulse of change over the life span, to the dialectic of development, to the interplay of individual change and stability within a world of change and stability. Rather, the lack of progress made on the front in the empirical portions of the book is because of the requirements of the task and the long-term commitments involved in exploring a reconstructed social and personality psychology.

I have two aims in this book, directed to the two levels of development noted above. I believe in radical surgery, because I believe the problems lie deep within the discipline and its lack of concern with the multidimensional, constructive flow of social life. At the same time—and perhaps inconsistently—I believe much can be accomplished even at the more superficial levels to make social psychology considerably more responsive to the realities of social living, to open it up to "weak developmentalism" to relieve the nonage, nonadult nature of the field. I am caught in a tension between wanting to proceed with the investigations of social psychological phenomena while simultaneously wanting to go beyond what tools for empirical, "scientific" research allow me to do. Whereas that position may be somewhat uncomfortable, it is hardly unusual (see, for example, Brewster Smith's discussion of his position in the 1979 Nebraska symposium—Smith, 1980), and I believe a case can be made for the overall healthiness of such a state of constant tension and challenge, as I will discuss in later sections.

In any case, since the more superficial set of problems is more amenable to fairly quick "fixes" and progress of a sort, I will present a point of view on dealing with those aspects more fully in Chapter 2 after giving more detailed descriptions of the core criticisms of social psychology at all levels in the remainder of this chapter. Chapter 3 and Chapter 12 deal much more specifically with the assumptional and methatheoretical aspects of current social psychology and its critics.

As will be discussed in considerably more detail in those chapters, the views espoused in this book resonate well with recently formulated critiques of social psychology-as-history and with dialectical social psychology. Since those views have been widely and thoroughly expounded by many "revisionist" social psychologists (e.g., Armistead, 1974; Elms, 1975; Gergen, 1973, 1978a, 1979; Harre, 1977a; Harre & Secord, 1972; McGuire, 1973), I will not detail the arguments again. Especially in Chapters 3, 12, and 15 I will try to explain how my views relate to my understanding of those positions.

FOUR LEVELS OF CRITICISM

The variety of criticisms can be broadly categorized into four types of critiques: assumptions and theoretical approaches, theoretical issues, areas of interest, and methods. The latter includes issues of design of the research model, methodological tools of analysis appropriate to various designs and goals of social psychology, and sampling. Each category will be discussed briefly, followed by criticism more specifically related to development. All of the issues will continue to reemerge throughout the book as the pattern of discussion shifts and progresses.

ASSUMPTIONS

Social psychology as a discipline has been built on the belief that there are transpersonal and transsituational regularities of social behavior and cognition and, further, that these regularities are brought about, at least in large part, by the existence of universal psychological (and/or social structural) mechanisms. These mechanisms are presumed to be orderly and predictable. In other words, the goal of social psychology is to reveal orderly, predictable regularities of social behavior and cognition, regularities that rest upon a set of universal mechanisms. Regularity and universality, or stability, are basic assumptions underlying social psychological models of individuals and their relationships with other individuals.

Whereas this set of assumptions can lead to a fairly wide variety of metamodels of development (organic stage, social structural stage; these will be considered at later points in the book), most of these have been eschewed in favor of a rather simple linear accumulation model of development. Development is seen as quantitative variation, making it easy to measure—and easy to manipulate—individual development or, more precisely, change. If social behavior at a particular time is merely a reflection of an accumulation of experience of a particular sort (reinforcement history, socialization experiences), then developmental exploration is of minor interest, at best, as I will discuss later.

Unfortunately, for social psychologists, it is unlikely that life is such a simple matter, fitting such a simple model. This is true even where the model appears to have its greatest applicability. For example, one might feel that surely vocabulary increases as the number of words available increases. As it does, the child gains more and more ability to communicate. Therefore, the argument may proceed, if anything happens to adults it *must* be the same thing. This simple linear transformation of child development to adult development is not necessarily legitimate, as Labouvie-Vief and Chandler (1978) and many others (including, for example, all stage theorists) have cogently argued. However, even given that, the accumulation model of even a straightforward accumulation of words is hardly as simple as it seems.

First of all, it tends to ignore half of its own thesis -- more of and less of. Each "more of"—words, roles, and so on—is also a "less of." Children do not merely add new words to their vocabularies; they drop off a variety of old sounds used in child babbling (Jakobson, 1972). They may lose the efficiency and effectiveness of many preverbal gestures. It is the same with adults. One who goes to graduate school does not merely add on knowledge through simple accumulation. Rather, he or she exchanges some knowledge for others. Does the new psychology Ph.D. know poetry as well as she did in college? Does the newly trained master electrician know the rules and terms of childhood games as well as when a child?

But, of course, loss of function—debiting as well as crediting—certainly can be fit into an accumulation or continuity model. And with or without it, the larger fallacy of seeing *change* as merely *transfer* remains. More crucial is something an accumulation model is not well equipped to handle: changes. Additions, subtractions, and so on are always *in relation to* other things and other changes. The meaning of a new word, a new role, an added bit of experience, depends fundamentally on where it is used and with whom it is used. A child does not merely add new vocabulary items—he or she learns how to adopt a perspective that goes along with vocabulary, but transforms the use of a word, as Krauss and Glucksberg (1977) and others have illustrated.

The "somethings lost and somethings gained in living day by day" change the relationship of all those things still there. To reduce the flux of life to a model of accumulation (with or without disaccumulation) is an illegitimate transformation of reality.

Yet, a simple accumulation model is the most common in personality and social psychology. And this model of reality leads to a model of investigation of reality that emphasizes regularity and seeming universals as it directs the research enterprise at its most basic levels of theoretical and empirical investigation. Research is guided into areas which are likely to support, or, at least, unlikely to falsify, that assumptive base, the belief that social psychological investigation is a matter of uncovering universal psychological laws of social behavior reducible to a formula of "more of. . .less of." In other words, social psychology is destined and designed to be a nomothetic science, because deepest reality is assumed to be commonality—universal mechanisms. Within this approach, differences are in their essence only a veneer upon the core of constancy. Everyone is different, of course, because their experiences have been unique, but underneath those differences is the reality—the commonness of the mechanisms (which are, unfortunately, usually observable only through all those layers of experiential encrustation).

Obviously that position implies much about the nature of social psychology. For example, it clearly downplays the study of individual differences as an end in itself. Rather, individual differences, though they may be useful to practitioners, are really not legitimate as the central subject matter of a discipline or subdiscipline (Zajonc, 1976). Differences simply are not recognized as elementary or natural. Yet, age and developmental stage notions are necessarily an introduction of individual differences, since the modal subject category of social psychological research is the college student, a point to be discussed shortly. Therefore, opposition to individual differences, age-related or not, encourages an antidevelopmental (or adevelopmental) stance.

Furthermore, the position necessitates the view that the individual is in any event essentially passive. He does not actively construct reality; reality is there, it is immutable, it is the natural order of things. Once again, insofar as people are different, they are accidental, not modal; when they are homogeneous is when they begin to be available as representatives of the reality of the social psychological mechanisms, because then the essential regularities are not masked by "unwanted" variance, such as may be brought about by subjects acting as personally involved origins of the structure of their behavior and its relationship to external events. The assumptive base is essentially nonindividualistic.

As noted previously in passing, this assumptive base is essentially antidevelopmental as well as nonindividualistic. Developmental change is merely a series of veneers, it is not part of the essential nature of social life. Regularity and order are believed to be the way of nature; thus, regularity and order are elementary, whereas change, at least nonexperimental change, is secondary. Change of *any* sort is suspect unless it can be controlled strictly by the experimental change agent. Change of the magnitude of *historical* development; that is, change over the long term—a major part of an individual's lifespan or a generation of a society—is particularly to be avoided. If dramatic changes on that level are consistently discovered, the discovery means one of two equally distasteful possibilities for the clean accumulation of scientific wisdom about social psychology. On the one hand, long-term change may be simply an even messier form of the encrustations of accident hiding the reality at an even larger distance from the surface. On the other hand, perhaps the assumption of a stable base underlying reality, and the subsequent structuring of social psychology, is misguided.

Both conclusions are far reaching; both are possible. However, they have very different implications. If the first is true, then the study of long-term development is particularly to be avoided. That is what mainstream social psychology has done for many years. If the second is true, as at least a visible minority of social psychologists, such as Gergen (1973, 1977, 1979), Smith (1980), and Harre and Secord (1972; Harre, 1977a, 1979) believe, then a revolution is critically necessary. The similarities and differences between those positions and mine will be discussed in succeeding chapters, especially Chapters 3, 12, and 15. It is important at this early stage to recognize that the assumptions steering social psychology are clearly opposed to the idea of long-term change, development, as an object of concern. Thus, those who espouse a development-sensitive social psychology are likely to take a radical position vis-a-vis current social psychology in the area of assumptions.

THEORIES

Problems in other areas such as theories, areas of interest, method, and sampling are in important ways independent and yet follow quite directly from the assumption structure of the field. Theories, of course, are formulated to be theories of stabilities of behavior and cognition and to be nonindividualistic at their core. Theoretical formulations may include a stage model of child development (although even that within social psychology is quite rare), but they rarely, if ever, have anything more than a simplistic, accumulation view of social behavior and social cognition of adults. Only one of many examples (partly useful because it is more explictly framed than most formulations, which simply ignore discussion of development, and partly because analyses related to it are discussed in detail in Part 2 of this book) is theory in the area of attributions. Bernard Weiner (1972), in passing, defines the extent of developmental processes in attributions about achievement as follows:

> It is postulated that general ability is inferred from the number, percentage, and pattern of success experiences at prior achievement activities, considered in conjunction with the perceived difficulty of the attempted tasks. . . .This outcome is merely one more bit of evidence in the entire life history of the organism—all of which is used to infer ability level. (p. 357)

Unfortunately, this brief statement is one of the *most complete* references to development in attribution theory. It is clear, though, that attributions are conceived to be processes related to a simple linear accumulation of experiences into the receptacle which is the human mind; each incident is a "bit of evidence." The stepwise, accumulative idea of scientific investigation finds its counterpart in the stepwise, accumulative model of "development." How those simple experiences may be radically restructured or reorganized by life events or by individual searches for meaning *behind* the externals of the event are questions which are ignored or, more properly, ruled out of order; it is the recording and storage of accumulated experiences which defines the schemata and becomes the determinant of personal use of attributions in the future.

Thus, the form of the theory is bounded by the assumptions. And that form usually excludes individual developmental factors, certainly past childhood (that also is usually ignored, although Weiner, 1972, p. 405 seems to feel a stage model is appropriate for preadulthood and he [e.g., 1979; Weiner & Peter, 1973] and other researchers have done a limited amount of child developmental research in the attribution area).

At the same time, there is nothing in the general assumption outlined earlier which *requires* that theories exclude age and developmental factors. Indeed, the assumption of stability can still leave room, for example, for a stage model of the development of attributions (or aggressive responses or personality integration or other areas). The assumptive base does not *disallow* theories that include development; rather it restrains those theories so that development becomes redefined into a stable, universal regularity of reality or as merely a natural-world manipulation of the sorts of external controls usually manipulated in the laboratory. That is to say, theories of social psychology, even if the assumptions remain intact, need not be as bereft of developmental issues and age as they are.

Thus, objections to the state of theory of social psychology vis-a-vis adult development need not be based exclusively in an attack on the assumptions as such. There is much room for at least some types of development-sensitivity *within* the assumptive model of universal regularity, but it is room, space for exploration, that has been consistently ignored in current theoretical development. There is unexplored space, and exploration of those areas can be fruitful without forcing social psychology to undergo a radical reconstruction (although such a reconstruction may hasten such exploration). These issues will be explicated in later chapters.

AREAS OF INTEREST

Virtually identical concerns can be voiced about areas of interest that social psychologists have included in (or excluded from) their purview. Areas have regularly been defined with reference to presumed mechanisms such as attitude structure and personality structure, or to a particular type of behavior such as conformity, altruism, aggression, coalition formation, person perception, and social facilitation. That virtually none of these areas has been explored among other than college student groups is a recognized problem and will be discussed shortly. But the other side of the coin is also important. That is, the areas of interest studied by social psychologists have by and large been defined by theories which are in turn based in the assumptions previously discussed. Stable structures and the universally applicable lawfulness of their dynamics, or superficial behaviors interpreted as outcomes of this operation of simple universal psychological mechanisms, have been the rule. Areas of interest explicitly rooted in development or change, in the relationship of actively formulated individual mechanisms to varying, active contexts, have not fared nearly as well, nor have content areas defined by social or personal relevance to persons other than college students. Whereas the first is an important area-definition problem, I will deal more directly with the latter at this point; that content areas particularly relevant to development and to adult age groups have been understudied.

I should hasten to add that it is certainly the case that researchers (and perhaps even more so text writers) recently have turned to a different conception of what is interesting to social psychologists and of what should be studied by them (a social issues approach to be discussed in more detail in Chapter 12). New texts (e.g., Goldstein, 1980) and recent editions of older ones (e.g., Wrightsman, 1977) have placed increasing emphasis on application and on "unusual" areas. In doing so, these social psychologists have increasingly centered research and speculation around a number of social issues: social effects of drug use, social psychology of sexual behavior, effects of television on children's social and cognitive development, alternative life styles, and sexism and sex roles. These concerns are important, and a social psychology which includes such areas of interest is certainly more likely to be important and relevant to a large segment of the adult population. But, interestingly, even the choice of such socially relevant issues seems quite clearly to have been made with one age group—young adults—in mind. Much less interest has been shown thus far for areas of interest likely to be more relevant to adults and older persons (and, at least sometimes, less interesting to young adults)—communication patterns in marriage, meaning of divorce, widowhood, work identification in relation to self-esteem, retirement, parenting and grandparenting, ageism and age-based discrimination, coping with change from a pretelevision, precomputer age to one permeated by advancing technologies in those areas, psychological effects of crime, urban decay, bureaucracy. More explicitly, developmental studies of the evolution of a relationship, of changes in context, of beginnings and endings (Albert, 1980) and what comes between those, and of the constructive nature of reality that have found favor among sociologists interested in social psychology (Goffman, 1967; Gubrium & Buckholdt, 1977; Berger & Luckman, 1966), but little recognition or use in most of the content areas of social psychology have also been ignored or isolated on the fringes of the field.

Of course, it is improper to leave the impression that there has been no research in these areas; there is some, and some of it is excellent. For example, Levinson and his associates (Levinson, 1978) and Sarason (1977) have examined the relationship of work roles to psychological and social psychological life; various topic issues in the *Journal of Social Issues* have dealt with divorce, parenting, and other areas. A number of researchers, discussed in detail in Chapter 8, have looked at control and competence in elderly populations. Yet, clearly, the amount of attention paid has been small compared to the magnitude and importance of the issues in the lives of many adults. Little has been done in relative terms, and little of that which has been done has been closely coordinated with theory and research in the "mainstream" areas of social psychology. As will be discussed later, much of it is not fully developmental.

One of the major sources of impetus to research on adult development, in fact, has come from outside the discipline, in the form of Gail Sheehy's (1976) tremendously popular treatment of the life events of middle age, which led many adults to query social psychology on its specialized knowledge of those areas. That request has spurred social psychologists to legitimize midlife work and to begin to examine those issues more systematically.

In any case, areas of interest have not typically been chosen to be representative of the areas of social psychology which impinge most directly on the daily lives of adults. Rather, they have too often been chosen to reflect assumptions which may well not be warranted, and are in some ways systematically biased *against* "relevancy" to everyday life, or to match with interests of the college students involved so fully as subjects and as primary recipients of research results in the form of courses. Once again, though, the point must be made that ignorance of the areas of interest mentioned is not a necessary concomitant of belief in universal psychological laws, even though it follows from that belief. Areas of interest have been ignored both because of those assumptions and independently of them or any other systematic set of assumptions.

METHODS

The demand for interpretable results (main effects and the sort of lower-order interactions discussed earlier) and for clear-cut statements about causality seem inevitably to necessitate the reduction of complex, real-world relationships to simple, statistically controllable situations. The overwhelming and overweening weight accorded to gathering replicable data, even if it be of trivial behavior in artificial settings, makes generalizability a secondary issue for many social psychologists. The ease of availability of college students as subjects for this sort of research further militates against heterogeneity in sampling. Thus, the typical methods of social psychology—experimental manipulations on homogeneous samples—follows from a scientific need to be "productive." These methods allow for little exploration of developmental change and of relationships. Interestingly, even trenchant, outspoken critics of the methods of social psychology (e.g., Harre, 1979; Harre & Secord, 1972; McGuire, 1973) seldom note the relevance of the developmental issues and of the adevelopmentalism of the methods they criticize (or of the new ones they advocate).

Yet, once again, the restrictions in methods are not free-standing problems or issues. The assumptions of mainstream social psychology and the belief that there are stable universal laws of social behavior lead to precisely the sorts of methods that are apparent in the field. The assumptions place a premium on methods that maximize the likelihood of finding those regularities that are presumed to exist, to have ontological reality. That is, the assumption leads toward controlled experimentation in artificial settings, since it is there that as many as possible of the layers of individual and group difference can be stripped away to get a glimpse at the "real" mechanisms.

The assumptions also provide a rationale for nondevelopmental methods. That is, if in fact it is the case that the subject matter of social psychology is a set of universal mechanisms, then situational variation and individual differences are extraneous, and interpretations which use them are likely to be erroneous. Alternatively, interpretation of results gathered in the most basic settings, a bare laboratory, and on a set of persons selected to be as homogeneous as possible are not only the easiest to obtain, they are actually the cleanest and best examples of social psychological science in action.

Use of one age (sex, race, etc.) group is not only permissible, it is preferable. A college student is as good as any other to study since the subject matter is universal in nature, just as a laboratory setting is as good an environment as any. If one type of subject or one type of setting is as good as any and is easier to control or to homogenize, then using that type is the method of choice.

An extreme belief in the universality assumption supports and leads to the kind of methods which are prevalent and which are decidely antidevelopmental. But the belief in stable, universal laws does not *necessarily* lead to the extreme poverty of research design used in social psychology. Just as college students and laboratories are in some senses and situations as good as any other theoretically and better practically, so in other circumstances others may be equally usable and equally proper. As will be discussed in Chapter 2 and at several other points, even without proceeding beyond the universality assumptions of social psychology there may be many researchable questions that could be better addressed by a social psychology which was adult-oriented and which used a wide range of participants (and settings).

Further, it can be argued that, even if there are universal psychological laws, we can only be sure of what they are *after* studying the phenomena in question over a range of settings and types of subjects. Since the layers covering the universals are deep, and since social structures are not homogeneous, one could not be sure, staying within one culture, whether what was found was, in fact, one of those universal laws or only one last deep layer of encrustation. Harry Triandis (1976, 1978) and others have placed great importance on cross-cultural research, not because they feel there are no social psychological laws of universal breadth, but precisely because they believe there *are* such laws. Triandis clearly argues for changes in methodology, especially sampling, even as he does not argue against the general ontological and epistemological approach of traditionally noncomparative social psychology. His argument, in turn, echoes Brunswik's (1956) earlier plea for representative sampling of stimulus situations and contexts and Barker's (1968, 1977) more recent ecological approach (see also Berry, 1979; Triandis & Lambert, 1980).

By the same token, many who would not be willing to argue for the strong form of the universality assumption use the methods of standard social psychological research just the same. Thus, the methods are and should be critically considered separately from the assumption, in their own right, not simply as a logical extension of a particular set of assumptions.

Samples

One area within the broad category of methods which has obvious implications for the ability of social psychology to be adult-oriented, much less developmental, is the area of sampling already noted. Reliance on experimental and survey measures—both open to criticisms of artificiality and triviality—is well documented (see, for example, Fried, Gumppert, & Allen, 1973; Helmreich, 1975; Sommer, 1977), as is reliance on (mostly white male) college students (Carlson, 1971; Higbee & Wells, 1972; Blank, 1979). Examination of various journal and text sources for various years using various methods of content analysis consistently shows that two-thirds to over four-fifths of all subjects in social psychological research are college students. The implications of that heavy reliance for interpretation of findings have been described well; the lack of generalizability (on a surface level at least) seems clear.

BREAKING THE COLLEGE STUDENT NORM

Whereas college students may be appropriate for some purposes, even most traditional social psychologists would agree that they may be less appropriate for many other purposes. In fact their qualities, often recognized as positive—generally intelligent, curious, self-analyzing—can make them particularly illegitimate for a wide range of studies. In many ways they are uniquely unsuitable populations from which to derive general laws. They are most likely self-selected to be more achievement-oriented, more introspective, and more ''intelligent'' than the average population, and they are certainly in a setting which emphasizes those characteristics and a rationalistic, intellectualizing approach to tasks. The problematic nature of that kind of sample is usually not even noted by researchers generalizing from their data. However, occasional note is taken of the fact; for example, the editors of an important book on attribution (Jones, Kanouse, Kelley, Nisbett, Valins, & Weiner, 1972) mention that the use of college students is likely to bias attribution results. Yet both they and other attribution researchers have seldom strayed beyond that group to a more "normal" population.

Of course, there are also other differences between college students and the general population. They are clearly and obviously more educated than most adults, and they tend to have different racial, ethnic, and sex composition. Yet theories are based entirely on the observed behavior of college students.

One major difference between college students and others that has not often been discussed by the critics of over-reliance is the central one for this discussion. That is, college students are, quite obviously, from a narrowly selected range of ages and experiences. The modal student is in his late teens or early twenties, a period which is usually regarded as transitional from late adolescence to early adulthood. In fact, Carlson (1971) referred to this age group as "not quite completed adults" (p. 207). Interestingly, apparently Carlson feels that somewhat older persons, say 30 year olds, would be "completed" adults, a point of view that has almost as little developmental sensitivity as the use of college students to represent "adulthood." Only rarely have college students lived through a variety of life events such as marriage, death of a loved one, divorce, stagnation in a career, retirement, that are characteristic only of later development, but are quite common occurrences over a full life-span. Only about 20 to 25% of those researched are even possible representatives of those who have experienced or are experiencing such life events.

Yet the lack of truly adult subjects is even more dramatic than the percentages of college students indicate, since the next highest percentage is children and adolescents. According to Higbee and Wells' calculations, 9% of the samples used in studies in *JPSP* for 1969 were "normal adults"; Carlson had found 6% in 1968 *JPSP* and *Journal of Personality*. My own analysis (Blank, 1979) of over 5000 articles published in *JPSP, JSP, JESP,* and *Sociometry* for 1965 to 1977 indicated that only about 2% of the articles could be identified as having adult samples on the basis of their titles, that is, by scanning titles for such words as "adult," "child," "age," "aged," "elderly," "development," and "maturation." Also, I found that most textbooks in social psychology made no reference to adult age comparisons of any sort.

Even more alarming than these figures are the types of "adults" which comprise that 2% (or the other percentages found by other researchers). Carlson, for example, noted that all of the adult samples were "special" populations, such as racetrack patrons for a study of gambling, pregnant mothers, aboriginal tribesmen, and so on. Many of the "adult samples" did not even indicate age of subjects or use age as a variable in analysis.

My analysis of "adult" populations adds emphasis to Carlson's point about types of adults. Researchers in most of the studies made no attempt to analyze age differences; in fact, most did not even give any clear indication of the age of subjects. Most of the subjects were likely to be *young* adults at best such as parents of elementary school children, spouses of college students, military personnel, and so forth. In fact, many of the samples were chosen to represent the special "captive populations" of prisoners and mentally ill or retarded. Detailed examination of those studies in which

Table 1.1.   Breakdown of Articles with Adult Subjects, 1965-1977
(from survey of 5240 articles—see text for details about sources)

Age clearly secondary to purpose of study	
Specific interest in mentally ill or retarded	26
Specific interest in criminals or prisoners	7
Subtotal	33
Age important to study	
No specific ages or range of ages given	
"Parents" (usually of school age children)	9
"Adults," no ages specified	5
"Aged," versus young	4
General age range in correlational study	6
"Specific categories"—spouses of college students, teachers, business executives, office managers, auto salesmen, arthritics, Wallace supporters, three-generation families, military personnel, accident victims, institutionalized old people (one or two each)	12
Subtotal	36
Mean or range of ages given in "subjects" section	
Institutionalized older persons—mean ages of 75.3, 73.1, and 77.2 years	3
Black South African businessmen—mean age 37.6	2
Normal Americans—includes studies with mean ages of 48, 35 (mothers), 29 (mothers), ranges of 18–49, 25–45 (women), 19–50 (female undergraduates), 18–31 (couples), 20–77 (American and Greek adults), up to age 55, up to age 44, and 1964 college graduates	12
Other cultural groups—rural Indians (45 and above), Indians (20–75), and Mayas (40–50 and an older group)	3
Subtotal (ages clearly given)	20
Total (adult studies)	89
Total (age as important variable)	56
Percentage of articles dealing with adults (89)	1.7%
Percentage of articles with age as an important variable (56)	1.1%
Percentage of articles with "normal" Americans, including some over 30 years old (48)	0.9%
Percentage of articles with "normal" Americans, including some identified as over 50 years old (4)	0.1%
Percentage of all articles with older adults (including other cultures and institutionalized) (13)	0.25%

an age range *was* given and was found to have included middle-aged or older persons showed that most were members of other cultures or were institutionalized in nursing homes (< 5% of all post-65 Americans). As shown in Table 1.1, overall less than 0.2 of 1% of the studies available clearly used middle-age or older adults, and most of those were from other cultures or a select (captive) sample! A handful of studies are likely to give any reasonably useful information about the general population of post-college-age Americans.

Other potential sources in social psychology, such as the *Handbook of Social Psy-*

chology (Lindzey & Aronson, 1968) also contain few references to adulthood and aging research. Yet another potential source or outlet, gerontology journals, turned out to be slightly better as a source of social psychological information on aging (see Abrahams, Hoyer, Elias, & Bradigan, 1975; Blank, 1979).

Thus, these data on sampling reinforce the general points made about the consistently antidevelopmental, nonadult orientation of social psychological assumptions, theories, areas of interest, and methods. Social psychology has been treated as though it were an "ageless" science, able to be studied without reference to age relationships or to developmental change in persons, situations, or societies. By ignoring age as a factor and by ignoring temporality as an *essential* component of social life, by focusing on stability and universality, by using samples homogeneous in age and in a host of characteristics related to age and status (education, amount of experience, developmental perspective, exposure to environment in which studies are done), and by reducing the subtle, complex, interwoven textures of reality into simple, passive elements blindly banging against each other, social psychologists have left themselves as naked as the Emperor, and their portraits of social psychology are without depth or meaning. They have perseverated in trying to capture the manifold subtle shades of what it means to people to be social beings into little gray snapshots of a narrowly defined set of people, all posed motionless before an unchanging, unrelated gray background. There is little depth, little meaning, and even less variety; there is virtually no sense of movement, of becoming and having been as well as of being. Social psychology is nondevelopmental, in both senses of that term. It avoids the reality of life as process and development at the same time as it neglects those who are not amenable to study by restricted methods in restricted settings. Both nondevelopmentalisms keep social psychology in a perpetual state of adolescence—its subject matter, samples (and typical adolescent belief that it has found the truth) are all less and less appropriate as it tries to expand to adulthood and to developmental concerns.

The thesis of this book is that there are other ways of trying to capture those shades and meanings, the movement, the drama and the drudgery, the constant interrelationships of changes and stabilities, of commonality and diversity, of "now" and "then." The ways—methodological, conceptual, theoretical—to be explored are not to be interpreted as perfect or as anywhere nearly approaching the texture of social psychology. But maybe they are steps in some directions that could add a little color here, a little motion there, a little depth, and a little clearer focus on the interrelationships of the elements in the pictures.

If we are naked in what we can show to the world and would like to be clothed; if we agree that all we have are dull gray snapshots when what we want to be able to show people with pride are color shots and even some three-dimensional movies of social psychology, how are we to proceed? If social psychology now is not developmental or adult-oriented, what would a social psychology of developing adults look like? More properly, what would a few social psychologies that are development-sensitive and adult-oriented look like?

Discussion of those questions—and of those social psychologies—is the essence of this book.

CHAPTER 2

A First Step: Multiple Black and White Snapshots

Are older people different from younger and/or middle-aged people in the way they react to social situations, in the kinds of behavior choices they make in a particular situation, in the cognitive processes they use to understand, deal with, and make sense of their lives? Do they act differently; do they think differently? Do they change themselves as they move through time? Does age make a difference?

If so, why? Are there biological stages of social psychological processes? Are there different mechanisms at different periods of the life span? Are there differences bound up in social roles—social stages—or in other historically developing changes in society that make today's middle-aged (old, young) persons different both from what they were and will be and from what their elders were and their children will be at the same age?

In Chapter 1, I discussed in detail why we as social psychologists should be paying attention to questions like these and indicated how seldom we do so. In this and the next chapter I will expand upon several approaches I think we should be taking to enable us to find answers to some of these questions about every topic of interest to social psychologists such as social perception, attributions, attitudes, group dynamics, choices and social decisions, aggression, and attraction.

As I indicate here, the sorts of general questions just posed can be fruitfully asked about every topic of interest for current social psychology, as well as about the sorts of issues I mentioned in Chapter 1 as having received short-shrift from social psychologists—marital and family relations and major disjunctures in them—divorce, death of spouse, children growing into adults, middle and later life roles and decisions. It would probably be best for you as an individual to think in terms of your own areas of interest—how those questions would fit into them and how answers may be already developed or could be developed in that area with the tools and approaches we will be considering.

However, to help provide a handle to you I will adduce examples in a range of areas. Many of these, as you will see, do not come from social psychology in a formal way, but from cognitive psychologists of aging, social gerontologists, and personality researchers. Whereas that fact may enable us to build bridges to other areas more easily, the result is that often the studies have been peripheral to the researchers' interests and, thus, have not had an adequate follow-up examination of ideas and further questions raised by the results. I will also ''preview'' some of the research programs and results that have been focused on the area of attributions; the research is discussed in detail in the five chapters that comprise Part 2 and in the Appendix. For purposes of initiating that example, I must note, as I mentioned in Chapter 1, that attribution research, even though it has been a central area of interest in social psychology, has proceeded with at best a primitive understanding of attributions as developmental, phenomenological, or processual. Research has centered instead on exploring experimenter-induced change in attributions; reactions using restrictive response formats to a restricted, artifical set of stimuli; and correlation with personality measures. Whereas all of these approaches have been productive in some limited ways, they have kept attributionists occupied while conceptualization even of what attributions are assumed to be (and of what use they are normally put to) have remained unexplored and vague (see Buss, 1979; Hamilton, 1980). Additionally, for present purposes, virtually all of the studies have retained the "grand traditions" of social psychology—college student samples, situational variation restricted to situations college students would be interested in, and little application to "normal" life attempted (there are exceptions, of course, to be considered fully in later chapters).

This chapter in particular involves the discussion of an approach that is quite prosaic and yet essential, one that is developmental, but only in a weak sense. I will argue that the step is neither as big or revolutionary, or as hard to take, as that which I will consider in Chapter 3 nor as little or self-defeating as some critics may find it to be at first glance.

Early in Chapter 1 I proposed that current social psychology provides only a collection of relatively unrelated gray, dull snapshots to reflect the color, movement and multidimensionality of social psychology as it is lived. I will take this opportunity to describe and defend one avenue of supplementation to current social psychology. Even though it is by no means a perfected implementation of the social psychology of developing adults, it can provide a greater variety of snapshots that will broaden the range and applicability of social psychological research and theory.

What, exactly, is this step? It is straightforward—the treatment of adult age group differences as independent variables, in a procedure analogous to use of other group differences and individual differences as factors in personality and social psychology. Conceptually, it is a recognition that persons of various ages (and, as we shall see, of various cohorts) are systematically different from those of other ages, and that those differences are likely to reveal useful information about how development and age, as well as group membership, affect individuals and their social behaviors and cognitions. Methodologically, the step is simply to examine adult age groups when focusing on topics of general interest to (non-adult-oriented) social psychologists. This simple step has rarely been taken up to this time in the history of social psychology, as the review of research in the preceding chapter showed.

As those data reveal, individual differences with or without an age component are little regarded in social psychology. At the same time, other individual differences, and certain kinds of demographic differences treated as group differences, are considered to be legitimate by most social psychologists. For example, Weiner and others in attribution research (e.g., Weiner, 1974, 1979, and many other sources) have made extensive use of personality factors, such as achievement motivation and failure/success orientation, to classify people by attributional style. Others have examined an array of social psychologically relevant personality factors—locus of control (Rotter, 1966, Phares, 1976, and many other sources), pawn-origin (deCharms, 1968), self-monitoring (Snyder, 1974), and self-awareness (Wicklund & Duval, 1972). Other often used personality descriptors have been authoritarianism (Kirscht & Dillehay, 1967), Machievellian personality traits (Christie & Geis, 1970), and sensation-seeking (Zuckerman, 1978). The list could easily be expanded upon, and the validity or degree of merit of these various factors is not at issue at the moment. Rather, it is clear that certain types of personality-measure-based individual differences have been admitted into traditional social psychology circles on a regular basis. Even those opposed to individual differences, because of the supposed lack of ontological reality in such factors, have allowed these variables as long as it has been made clear that the factors are merely summary statements of differential experiences (see Mischel, 1968; Zajonc, 1976).

Many social psychologists have also allowed demographic, group-differences factors such as sex, race, and status into social psychological conceptualizations and research in much the same way. This has more often than not been the result of demands on the part of society in general and of a minority group in the field itself rather than a need on the basis of theoretical conceptualization or an overriding concern to reflect reality. The latter comment is not meant to indicate doubt as to the sincerity of the researchers involved, but to restate what others have described as the "faddish" nature of social psychological research efforts and the choice of group differences primarily on the basis of social issues. In fact, I would assert that choice of topics on the basis of social relevancy is at least as valid as choice on the basis of theoretical necessity. Further, those reasons, as well as more theoretical ones, apply to examination of age differences as fully as to group differences that have been explored.

Examples of group differences or subgroup research, as with personality factors, could go on indefinitely. Clearly, there has been at least a segment of social psychologists who have felt that research on sex differences (e.g., Maccoby & Jacklin, 1974) and race differences (see, for example, Chapter 15, in Wrightsman, 1977) are important. Many also feel that establishment of specialized varieties of theory to fit a particular group has been well worth the effort and loss of homogeneity involved. By and large, these social psychologists have been less concerned with explication of the relative contribution of, for example, genetic determinants, biological differences, social role and status, and historical placement factors in etiology of differences than with the effects of different status characteristics on the individual's cognitive and behavior style. Nor have they been deeply interested in whether or not differences are at the deepest levels of mechanics and structure (genotypes) or only at the phenotypic levels of some more superficial basis for differences.

When research of this kind has been done, often rather large differences have been uncovered in a range of social behavior and social cognitive processes. But whether differences or similarities have resulted, the central focus consistently has been on delineation of differences and/or similarities among the groups involved.

Explication and exploration of differences in groups of adults who differ in age is likely to be at least as important and at least as rewarding as the other kinds of group/individual differences investigations. That is, comparisons of persons in different ''stages'' of the life cycle may be of considerable value in the understanding of and relevance to the everyday lives of a wide range of persons; the information thus gathered may also feed back to and enrich more general social psychological theory and research (as well as social development theory and research in preadult stages).

AGE DIFFERENCES PSYCHOLOGIES: GUIDEPOSTS AND CAUTIONS

It is one thing to assert the value of this aspect of the ''maturing'' of social psychology; of course, it is quite another to marshall evidence in support of the thesis. Support can be given, I believe, but it is not likely to come from within traditional social psychology, since virtually no adult age group research has been done there (except as will be discussed in later chapters). In later portions of the book I will adduce evidence from recent research which encourages deeper penetration into the social psychology of adult development, but prior to that it may be useful to strike out in several directions for illumination on points made thus far. This foray away from social psychology as such is partly in the nature of an aside, but partly is an essential step in my argument. In the remainder of the chapter I will concentrate on the strengths and weaknesses in two distinct branches of research: the (nonsocial) psychology of aging and the (nonpsychological) social psychology of aging. Both indicate the value of the sort of perspective espoused here (and both illustrate the shortcomings of the perspective as well). Consideration of the two clarifies the gap which a social psychology of adult age differences could fill.

Psychology of Aging

Psychologists within most major areas of psychology besides social have already seen the value of researching adult age differences. There are many sources for this work (notably major reviews such as are found in the American Psychological Association-sponsored *Psychology of Adult Development and Aging,* Eisdorfer & Lawton, 1973; the recent *Handbook of the Psychology of Aging,* Birren & Schaie, 1977; and Poon, 1980) and in a wide range of texts in the psychology of adult development and aging (e.g., Botwinick, 1978; Elias, Elias, & Elias, 1977; Kimmel, 1980a). Thus, the areas of learning, motivation, memory, cognition, sensation, perception, motor performance, decision-making, and psychopathology will be used here as indications that adult differences and aging have proven to be useful on both descriptive and explanatory levels. Specific findings will play a part in development of several other chapters (e.g., sensation, perception, and motor performance in Chapters 9–11 concerning environmental relations; motor performance, decision making, and motivation in relation to achievement orientation and performance differences in Chapter 6; psychopathology in Chapter 8). In the *Handbook* cited above, Baltes and Willis (1977) place social psychology with several other subdisciplines of psychology as areas of greatest neglect in the psychology of aging.

Sociologists and Personality Psychologists Studying Aging

At the same time as psychologists have explored adult age differences in most areas of psychology besides social behavior and cognition, there has been an active group of sociological social psychologists and personality psychologists who have carved out an area within social gerontology called the social psychology of aging (see Bengston, 1973; Bortner, 1967; Havighurst, 1968; Lowenthal, 1977; for expositions of the point of view). Obviously, an area called "social psychology of aging" can be expected to have a great deal in common with the social psychology of developing adults to which this book is devoted.

Surprisingly, the relationship is not as clear and direct as might be expected. To be sure, there is overlap between the two areas and, as will be argued in Chapters 12 and 14, the development of greater common exploration of common interests could benefit both adult-oriented social psychologies. But, at present, the social psychology of aging is solidly within social gerontology, a field which is often described as interdisciplinary, but which in reality is virtually a subdiscipline of sociology, as is clear from even a cursory glance at major texts in the area (e.g., Atchley, 1980; Hendricks & Hendricks, 1977). Most of those involved in social gerontology who were trained as psychologists and continue to have ties with psychology (e.g., Bernice Neugarten, Douglas Kimmel, Marjorie Lowenthal, Robert Havighurst) are clearly personality psychologists rather than social psychologists.

The differences between the social psychology of adult development propounded here and the social psychology of aging, then, are in large part the same differences which have led to and perpetuated the independent and sometimes competitive relationship between what are often called psychological social psychology (PSP) and sociological social psychology (SSP). These differences, their bases in disciplinary organization and departmental competition, and the impact they have had on the two main types of social psychological investigation have been discussed elsewhere by other social psychologists and myself (see, for a sampling, *American Sociologist,* 1977; Archibald, 1976; Blank, 1978; House, 1977; Stryker, 1977; Wilson & Schaefer, 1978), and will also be considered in Chapter 12. However, for readers who may not be familiar with the issues, I will briefly explain the basic differences, since they are important to later stages of my discussion. Those sources cited above should be consulted for details.

To most sociologists social psychology is the study of the relationship of individuals to social structures and/or the relation of indivduals to other individuals *as members of society* and as *representatives* of role requirements and role enactment. It is the study of *relationships* of certain kinds structured in certain ways. Further, most SSP proponents tend to examine these essentially extraindividual relationships by using surveys, scales, or participant observation and by analyzing the gathered data in correlational and descriptive terms. Social psychological theories, in this view, are tied more or less tightly to sociological theories; this social psychology is directly related to other subdisciplines of sociology such as deviance, marriage and the family, and socialization.

The extraindividual nature of this sociological approach is well illustrated by two quotes from sociologists, one a social psychologist of aging. In his aging-related book, Bengtson (1973) described a "microlevel" of interpersonal behavior analysis, including changes in the number, kind and quality of interpersonal contacts. These *are* areas of interest to a PSP advocate as well as to one identified with SSP. But Bengtson immediately continued by redefining this psychological microlevel into a sociological one, by stating that these changes "can be analyzed in terms of events that alter roles, norms, and reference groups (Bengtson, 1973, p. 14)." In a similar vein, Erving Goffman stated that his interest is "not the individual and his psychology, but rather the syntactical relations among the acts of different persons mutually present to one another," and thus his emphasis is placed on "not, then, men and their moments. Rather, moments and their men" (Goffman, 1967, p. 2).

A psychologist studying social behavior, on the other hand, is likely to be focally interested in precisely the mirror image of Goffman's description, in the study of "the individual and his psychology" and of persons behaving in their moments. To most psychologists, social psychology (PSP) is the study of social behavior and cognition, an exploration of cognitive-psychological mechanisms of social life. Social behavior and thought are assumed by these social psychologists to be guided by and explicable in terms of more general psychological principles and mechanisms; thus, social psychology is distinctly viewed as a part of general psychology. PSP theorists tie their approaches into such general psychological theories as are used in learning, memory, motivation, and cognition rather than to extrapersonal sociological concepts. The preferred locus of "cause" of behavior is intraindividual. This view has been held by many social psychologists over a long period of time (e.g., F. Allport, 1924; G. Allport, 1968; Berkowitz, 1975). Those who view social psychology in this way, furthermore, tend to use experimental designs in laboratory settings, striving to uncover universal psychological mechanisms of social behavior and social cognition. This social psychology, in particular, has paid extremely little attention to aging; those few studies that have been done will be described below and in later chapters.

I should note that these two conceptions of social psychology are not inherently in conflict, although there has been relatively independent development of the two traditions and they have relatively separate major characteristics as just outlined on methodological, theoretical, and level of analysis grounds. These differences are both developed from and exacerbated by disciplinary identification and the strictures of sometimes stifling disciplinary boundaries. Again, the interested reader is referred to other sources more focused upon these issues, as cited earlier.

This state of the field—separate traditions of social psychology, sometimes at odds and seldom acting in concert—has been problematic for the development of a single, unified social psychology and for the coordinated development of many interest areas, including aging. In fact, this situation has particularly affected the area of adult development and aging, since it has combined with the consistent identification of social psychology of aging with social gerontology, and thus with sociology, to insure that social psychological investigation of aging has had little to do with the aims of the social psychology of adult development proposed in this book. The social psychology of developing adults would be tied closely with the mainstream area of social psychology within psychology.

In the social psychology of aging, experimental approaches and even systematic behavioral observations have been distinctly eschewed; major theories in PSP, attribution, social learning, cognitive dissonance, and so on, are seldom mentioned, and PSP areas of major interest, self-perception, social motivation, aggression, attraction, altruism, attitude change, persuasion, and others, are virtually unresearched in aging. Rather, almost all research and theory are sociology-oriented and, therefore, are concerned with extraindividual, social structural mechanisms, role relations, or adjustment to normative demands. Also, methods are almost totally restricted to scales and surveys, with a modicum of relatively unstructured observation as an occasional supplement. When intraindividual, psychological factors have been considered, they are usually framed in more or less traditional personality theory terms rather than in more mainstream social psychological ones (see, for example, Havighurst, 1968; Neugarten, 1964, 1973; Lowenthal, 1977).

As a result, a large part of the reason why a more clearly cognitive and behavioral social psychology of adult development has not been formed up to this time is the disciplinary competition between SSP and PSP and the historical accident of social psychology of aging having developed within what is clearly an SSP tradition. I will discuss this and several points to be made in the following further in Chapters 13 and 14.

Yet, it is not entirely correct simply to categorize the social psychology of aging as a direct application of SSP to adulthood either. The typical SSP emphasis on external causes of social action has been apparent, but it has regularly been supplemented by a more individual focus derived from personality theories. That is, social psychologists of aging have often bypassed the PSP approaches more likely to be relied on by major SSP theorists when they include an individual emphasis (see Homans, 1961; Burgess & Bushnell, 1969). In this way, the social psychologists of aging differ from SSP as well as from PSP.

The personality orientation in the social psychology of aging deserves some further consideration at this time, although a more detailed discussion of it will be deferred until Chapter 13. Many readers may have quite justly been noting my own oversight of personality theorists in my earlier discussions of the lack of regard aging has been shown in social psychology. Personality psychologists such as Neugarten (e.g., 1964, 1970, 1973, 1977) and Lowenthal (1977; Lowenthal, Thurnher, & Chiriboga, 1975) certainly deserve—their work demands—a fuller consideration. I have painted a picture of an almost total vacuum concerning adult development in social psychology. That picture is true with a particularist definition of social psychology, but it is not as true if personality is included within "social psychology," which is a reasonable way to proceed. Indeed, the researchers noted above and Gould (1978), Levinson (1978) and others have been directly concerned with adult development and, in some cases, particularly concerned with later adulthood for many years.

The contributions these psychologists have made should be considered very seriously, to be sure. There are, however, several reasons why I have given less attention to this body of literature than some readers may feel I should. First of all, whereas I am concerned with social behavior and social cognition (social psychology as defined by the mainstream) these writers have all been centrally concerned with individual personality, with the inner life. Of course, that is not to deny their relevance to the present discussion, since there are clear social aspects to the development of an individual's personality, nor is that sufficient reason to ignore their work, since personality and social psychology should be more rather than less related to each other.

Rather, the major reason I have sidestepped consideration of these views is because I feel they are really not useful for the kind of work I am trying to develop. All, in fact, have a common core and base, and that is in a stage-theory model of development, based predominantly in early life. That is, all these theorists discuss adult development as the expression of a set of universal stages. In fact, they share a base in one particular type of stage theory; not the cognitive stage model of Piaget, but the psychodynamic stage model of Freud and the neo-Freudians. Adult stages are portrayed as essentially biological (or, in some less psychodynamic views, social structural); they are placed upon the essentially passive individual as they are called forth by advancing years. Implicit, and sometimes explicit, in the models is this unique combination of biological determinism overlaid by structural functionalism. There is a great deal of emphasis on *the* stages of adult development. As just one cogent example, Lowenthal et al. (1975) entitled their monograph *The Four Stages of Life*.

There has also been a great deal of emphasis on personality types formed early in life and thenceforth interacting in predictable ways with life events (as made explicit in Sheehy's, 1976, title—*Passages: Predictable Crises of Adult Life*). At the same time, there is little emphasis on personality as an outgrowth of social communication, as an interplay of stability rooted in instability, as a set of relationships constructed in daily life. In a way very different from the sterility of much in mainstream social psychology, these views arrive at a common point; they include remarkably little of the social or the situational as a transcendent force in formation and maintenance of one's personality and of one's social cognitions.

One important aspect these theorists quite consistently ignore is an aspect of social psychology of both types that I have not explicitly mentioned. That is, although both major types of social psychologists look for distinctive, characteristically different mechanisms as underlying behavior, they both emphasize a situationism of thought and action; they explicitly recognize the influence of the current situation as it interacts with their primary concern—internal psychological processes in PSP, and social structural and role requirements in SSP. Whereas the emphasis on situations has sometimes been lost in PSP's haste to reduce situations to their minimal elements (see Bowers', 1973, critique of social psychology) and in SSP's reaction against behaviorism, situationism is a major element in the historical development and conceptual base of both social psychologies. It is perhaps best exemplified in Barker's (1968, 1977; Wicker, 1979) ecological psychology. But personality theorists (of the type found in the social psychology of aging, not such situationist theorists as Sullivan, 1953, and Angyal, 1941) tend to ignore situational influences except in their extreme forms (these points, as noted earlier, will be considered further, in Chapter 13).

Another problem with this body of work is the cross-sectional or simple longitudinal nature of the measures used to examine personality development. Often the re-searchers have begun with persons in their forties and fifties and followed them into later periods of adulthood. Whereas this is an advance in method beyond much of the cross-sectional research prominent in most areas of social psychology, it becomes a problem in that the data thus collected, from one cohort (or a very restricted set of co-horts) are used to identify the supposedly universal stages inherent in the model. The data are biased in their interpretation into a maturation explanation, when the validity of that explanation is by no means necessarily the case, given the data. I would refer you to Kimmel's (1980a,b) discussions of this issue, as well as to more consideration in Chapters 13 and 14.

In other words, personality development approaches that bear upon a social psy-chology of developing adults are rooted in a stability model, with the determining forces in social life considered to be inner-biological or external to the individual; in either case, the person is characterized as a relatively passive element in his or her own development. As a result, those approaches are of limited usefulness for a social psychology of developing adults.

The foregoing, and further criticism in Part 4, should not, however, be interpreted as grounds for ignoring these approaches. To the contrary, the stage models of Erikson, Neugarten, Lowenthal, Gould, Levinson, and others are useful; they are particularly valuable—invaluable—as descriptions of current expressions of adult personality within a highly technology-oriented society and as evidence for the per-sistence of stability in one's self and one's orientations even in a rapidly changing world. They are strong evidence for the stable result of what may, however, be inher-ently unstable forces. They are, however, of less value as explanation (although, it should be noted, as good as many) and may well be powerfully influenced by the unique span of life shared by almost all of the theorists currently writing (that is, most of them are members of a particular cohort, coming into its own in the years after World War II; see Kimmel, 1980b).

One other personality aspect of the social psychology of aging as presently consti-tuted that is of interest is the inordinate emphasis in it placed upon *adjustment*. In fact, the social psychology of aging has distinctly and obviously been a social psy-chology of persons *adjusting*—to intra-individual (biological) decline and extraindividual (social structural) reductions in social importance. As Gubrium (1973) has pointed out, even what is labeled in social gerontology as "activity theory" is rooted in decline concepts more evident in its alter ego, disengagement theory. Both rely heavily on the aspects of stage theories noted a few paragraphs ago—a passive model of the individual as recipient of social and biological forces fundamentally beyond his or her control. Insofar as the individual is only a re-actor and not an actor, the best the individual can do is to adjust to "the facts." There is reason to doubt that helplessness resulting from biological decline or loss of roles is either as factual as it is taken to be or as overriding a concern in the social behaviors and thoughts of persons as they grow older as must be predicted from the model. These issues, too, will be discussed again in Chapters 13 and 14, and additional discussion can be found in other sources (e.g., Gubrium, 1973; Marshall & Tindale, 1978; Kuhn, 1978).

In any case, the relationship of social psychology of aging to the types of social psychology and to a model of adjustment has resulted in the social psychology of aging having little effect on reducing the antihistorical bent of nonaging social psychology. At the same time, research done within the psychology of aging makes it clear that a social psychology of adult development—of age differences—is possible and is likely to be a positive contribution to understanding the social psychologies of adults.

At this point a few examples may illustrate the potential of the approach, whereas fuller consideration and description of research that bears upon a social psychology of age differences will be considered in Parts 2 and 3.

In 1972 Klein compared conformity in an Asch-type experiment across adult age groups. He had young and old subjects join young confederates in a line-judging task, with the confederates giving incorrect judgments on some trials. He found that older persons were more readily conformist in the situation; that is, they were considerably more likely to agree with incorrect judgments by stooges than young persons were. Thus, Klein described an important difference among age groups. Further, to move toward explanation—the "how" and "why" questions posed at the beginning of the chapter—Klein hypothesized that older persons are typically less sure of themselves in such an artificial task and that they, thus, are more ready to accept judgments of others.

Klein's study was flawed and incomplete in several important ways, making interpretation ambiguous. He used young confederates, leaving unanswered the question as to whether older people are conformist in a general way to others, even when they are incorrect, or if they only feel a need to conform to *young* others. Furthermore, by using only one task, Klein did not explore generality; further, that one task is one that depends on one of the key problem areas of older persons compared to younger ones—visual acuity. It is not surprising they felt unsure of themselves with such a task. Also, the task situation was considerably more unusual for the older participants than for young students accustomed to doing strange things on cue for authority figures. Finally, Klein's notion that older persons conform more *because* of being insecure about their abilities could have been examined further by manipulating the level of confidence of young and old. Hypothetically, younger persons who were manipulated to be low in confidence in relation to old should then act like untrained, "normal" older persons; alternatively, older persons manipulated to be high in confidence should have ceased to act "old" and to be more conforming. This research strategy is strongly propounded by many experimental aging researchers (e.g., Birren & Renner, 1977; Baltes, Reese, & Nesselroade, 1977). Unfortunately, Klein apparently did not perform the further experiments necessary to test these notions.

However, this idea was supported by and elaborated upon in several studies by Jack Botwinick (1966, 1969). He found that older persons indeed were more cautious in responses in a risky shift paradigm under some circumstances (low confidence), but he also showed that carefully designing the situation so that risk was the most "acceptable," conforming behavior led older persons to make riskier decisions than younger ones.

This isolated study by Klein and related work by Botwinick provide at least some evidence that adult age differences are likely and that examination of them, especially by using hypothesized mediational mechanisms to simulate ''old'' behavior in nonold and ''nonold'' behavior in older persons, could well be theoretically and empirically meaningful. Such notions, and a large number of studies of cognitive and motor performance in relation to training and related factors (see major reviews of psychology of aging already cited, Baltes & Schaie, 1976; Schaie & Labouvie-Vief, 1974; and a brief review in Chapter 4), together support the contention that differences among age groups in a wide range of behaviors, including social ones, are both real and amenable to systematic investigation. In terms of our earlier discussion of personality vis-à-vis social psychology, it is interesting to note that emphasis is placed upon ''replacing'' age with situational manipulations so as to examine developmental phenomena without ultimately relying upon organic factors, whether universal stages or idiosyncratic biological pressures. This again indicates how a social psychology of developing adults will be quite different from the personality psychology of aging in social gerontology.

UNAVOIDABLE WEAKNESSES IN ADULT
AGE DIFFERENCES STUDIES

Although the results of these few studies and of ones to be considered in later chapters indicate the value of conducting adult age differences research on social psychological processes and thereby serve as guideposts as to how to proceed in a social psychology of developing adults through a social psychology of adult age differences, they also serve to illustrate the shortcomings inherent in this kind of research.

First of all, if we refer back to the analogy of color three-dimensional movies introduced in Chapter 1, we must conclude that age differences research is not necessarily of any more depth or any more color than research which centers on college students and ignores adults. That is, age differences research does not change the snapshot from gray to color, from two dimensions to three. It does little or nothing to add texture to the background and the context, and it does little to add movement, flow, change, or relationships. Rather, age differences research results in offering to the interested adult a *set* of dull gray snapshots; the person is told to pick the one closest to himself or herself in age in precisely the same way that members of minority groups and women are being given the option in race differences and sex differences research to find a picture more to their liking, more like themselves. The face may be more familiar—and that in itself may be of considerable value—but the essence of the snapshot remains the same.

These weaknesses are important to consider. Only after doing so can we answer the question, ''Is it worth it, then?'' As with other group differences, furthermore, age differences research and theories that include age differences in a conceptual way have another major drawback that severely limits their value. As with other demographic research, simply finding age differences is merely descriptive. Even more crucially, it is intrinsically time-bound. Thus, interpretation and dissection of the components of differences are equivocal at best. It is not possible to state whether the differences are caused by differences in mechanics—in central processes and structures—or are only reflections of different shades and depths of patina. It is still not known whether differences are differences because of age or because of something else extraneous to individual development, whether they are constitutional or only functional, elementary or reactive.

Such weaknesses will be clear in data to be presented later, such as research on attributions across age groups (see Chapters 4 through 6). Even though I and others have found some evidence of age differences in self-perception, the relative contributions of age, status differences, and differences resulting from stereotypes that persons of all ages have about persons from different age groups (also found) cannot be fully examined with the kind of analyses allowed by the data.

These problems and shortcomings of an age differences approach have been explicated in detail by K. W. Schaie, Paul Baltes, and a host of other life-span developmentalists, social gerontologists, and psychologists of aging (e.g., Baltes, Reese, & Nesselroade, 1977; Schaie, 1965, 1977). Social psychologists, however, have not begun to face up to such questions, since they have virtually ignored even the possibility of precisely those factors which are essential to separate conceptually and methodologically. They must be faced by social psychologists of developing adults.

A reader familiar with developmental design may safely proceed past the next rather elementary section, but it is essential that all readers understand the following points, therefore, I will briefly describe the issues involved.

Life-span developmentalists speak of three elements contributing to age differences: age itself (maturation), cohort (generation, subgroup), and time of testing (historical context of the studies). Typically, age differences research is done *cross-sectionally;* that is, the time of testing is essentially the same for all subjects, regardless of age group. However, age and cohort are both uncontrolled. Obviously, there can be no independent assignment to an age-cohort combination at one point in time. That is, a young person cannot be randomly placed in a cohort born 70 years ago.[1]

Thus, differences are unavoidably differences among members of two or more age-cohort combinations. This is clearly and simply illustrated by the research by Klein (1972) discussed earlier in this section. We can not tell if Klein's differences in conformity are the same as differences that will be found in similar comparisons now or 20 years from now, whether they are general or specific to the combination of age with time of testing. Yet such knowledge is obviously important; it is quite a different story, with different implications, if the effect is general or specific.

Cross-sectional studies of age differences, then, may or may not reveal effects of aging or of being old (or middle-aged or young); no amount of ratiocination or of

---

[1]That is, there cannot be independent assignment to real cohorts. However, several social psychologists have experimentally manipulated cohort (usually called generation in their research) by controlling duration in a small group which has members moving in and out on a schedule. For example, recent investigations by Weiting (1977) have in fact related microgenerational differences crossed with "actual," chronological age generations. This body of provocative research is, in effect, a manipulation of cohort independent of actual age of subject. These researchers have found microgeneration effects remarkably similar to age stratification effects on actual groups and cohort relationships in society. However, the work is not likely to be recognized as authentically developmental in scope because of its emphasis on manipulation and its obvious artificiality. It is, however, close to the concept of experimental manipulation of age referred to previously.

data-manipulation can insure an unambiguous interpretation. Because of these insurmountable problems, some of the more methodologically sophisticated lifespan developmentalists have declared simple age differences research to be essentially worthless and intrinsically uninteresting (see, for examples of extreme judgments, Schaie, 1965; Riegel, 1978; Baltes, Reese, & Nesselroade, 1977). They would deny the validity and value I have given to the snapshot series approach.

As an alternative, they have proposed a matrix research design, called the General Developmental Model, which includes cross-sectional slices, longitudinal measurement of each original cohort, and cross-sequential measures (of persons of equal age at several different times of testing). Of course, they recognize that longitudinal time sampling confounds age with time of testing while holding cohort constant and that cross-sequential comparisons confound time of testing and cohort, but hold age constant. By continued use of this model, Baltes, Reese, & Nesselroade (1977) and others feel that the weaknesses and confusions of each method separately can be counterbalanced by the other comparisons possible in the entire matrix.

Objecting to the Objectors

Although I share their concerns, as will be more evident in Chapter 3, I disagree with their conclusion and remedy on two levels. I feel they go too far and not far enough at the same time.

First of all, it should be kept in mind that the extreme statements against age differences research by Riegel, Schaie, Baltes, and others concern the extremely limited value of age differences research *as a way to examine explanations of developmental change*. That is, cross-sectional or simple longitudinal adult age differences research yields results which are conceptually equivocal.

That is indisputable, as my discussions of conformity and attribution research indicated. Thus, their objections on that level are clear and justified. What is not clear, however, is that the level of explanation of developmental change is the only one to consider at this point, as they seem to feel, that weakness and ambiguity there necessarily mean that the constricted methods and their results are worthless. The objection, however valid on one level, should not be generalized to mean that data gathered using simplistic methods are strictly uninterpretable or, even more so, that they are not useful. Just as sex differences, race differences, and personality differences research models are useful in many ways, even though they are flawed in other ways; so will age differences research be useful. The important point is that they be taken to be what they are and not something else; that is, they be interpreted, insofar as they can be, in a matrix of results rather than isolated as universally applicable facts. Social psychologists of developing adults, even more than other social psychologists, must beware the trap of universalism and transhistoricity assumptions. At the same time, I would argue that they should avoid rejection of data on grounds that do not justify rejection, only caution.

I would argue that limited information of limited value can still be useful and informative. If that were not the case, research would become stultified, and only a few topics of long-standing interest to researchers and with instruments for measurement which are likely to be transhistorically and transculturally valid would be researched.

Perhaps the intelligence measures that Schaie, Baltes, and their colleagues have been exploring fit these requirements. Even that is certainly debatable (see, for example, Labouvie, 1980; Labouvie-Vief & Chandler, 1978; Riegel, 1978); in any case, it is clear that few other areas would come close to meeting those requirements.

The net result of requiring strict adherence would not be a strengthening of understanding adult development, but a profound constriction of areas of interest to the few which are most tractable and concurrent restriction of research to the few centers that can sustain long-term research efforts. Further, such a blanket condemnation of the value of adult age differences research is especially likely to entail continued exclusion of studies of adult social development, since especially in that area the necessary long-term validity of measurement tools simply does not exist. To dissuade social psychologists from doing manifestly overly simple age differences research is effectively to discourage them from doing adult development-sensitive research of any type. The result is a paralysis of attempts to gather even descriptive information on adult differences.

Can *you* commit yourself to an involved, long-term set of studies on your area of interest, with measures that you can assure yourself will be equally valid 10 years from now as they are now, that will be "state of the art" conceptually 10 years from now, and that will be fundable 10 years from now, in a field as faddish and transitional as social psychology? I doubt your answers will be "yes." If not, are you willing to abandon the study of adults and of adult development? If your answer here is "no," then I feel you must proceed the best you can with what you have, constantly trying to make it better, but using it for what it may be worth.

To give encouragement to social psychologists to do development-sensitive, adult-oriented research, even if it is only simple, superficial, "trivial" age comparisons (as I am doing myself) is likely to get social psychologists involved directly in the same issues upon which Schaie and Riegel base their pessimistic conclusions. As my personal experience indicates, a social psychologist who approaches adult development as an age differences social psychology soon begins to have an appreciation for the tensions of cohort and time of testing and maturation factors, begins to have a measure of frustration and dissatisfaction with his or her flawed data even as the simplistic descriptions tantalize. The social psychologist of developing adults is led into a fascinating, but in some ways overwhelming new world, in which superficial here-and-now data are manifestly colorless and motionless, but latent with the richness and color and depth of being an historically developing individual in a web of temporal and spatial textures and relationships. Exploration of those areas is the goal of a development-sensitive, adult-oriented, relational social psychology as I envision it; that the means are prosaic and distorted and ambiguous does not necessarily mean they are not steps in the right direction.

The Value of Description

I do not think the value of an age differences social psychology as an introduction to adult and development-sensitivity is the only value that that social psychology will have, either. I feel that age comparison research, on its surface and in and of itself, is of considerable value. Again, the analogy to race and sex differences work is apparent. The value of adult age group comparisons made at one point is not simply to be measured by their representativeness for understanding developmental change and the relative contributions of what in child developmental theory is often labeled "nature and nurture." Judged by that standard, it must be admitted, adult age difference comparisons are indeed limited.

The value of comparisons, however, can be seen in a different light, as nothing more—but nothing less—than subcultural factors similar to ethnic identification, social class, and culture. That is, consideration of development can be placed in the background for the moment; age group differences are convenient indicators of a complex of environmental and historical events that differentiate the groups at least as clearly as place of residence or color of skin. Racial and sex differences in social behavior and cognition are interesting whether or not we can convincingly "prove" them to be biologically based. Indeed, as I noted at the beginning of the chapter, social psychologists interested in those differences often are not concerned with that level of understanding or usefulness. The same applies to our interest in age as a differentiator among adult groups.

It is quite clear that older persons (and middle-aged ones and younger adults) collectively have a wide range of commonalities of experience, interests, and life orientation which separate each "generation" or cohort from the others. Indeed, social gerontologists have regularly used age categorization as a means to identify separate subcultures (Rose, 1965) and have debated whether the elderly should be classified as a minority group in relation to nonelderly adults (Neugarten, 1974; Streib, 1965). The array of systematic subcultural and environmental differences, of course, makes interpretation of cross-sectional data even more risky and confusing than may otherwise be recognized. On the other hand, they make attempts at understanding differences in those terms that much more important.

The theory of age stratification within sociology (for example, Riley, Johnson, & Foner, 1972), analogous to class stratification and stratification of roles based on sex, lends validity to seeing age differences research as a legitimate and useful study in group differences. As I will argue later, psychological social psychology investigation of age differences may illuminate role analyses of age and subcultural analyses of age stratification. In terms of the present argument, the recognized validity of those ideas lends validity to adult age differences research in a social psychology of developing adults. Older persons have clearly differentiable group identification, conciousness, and even housing siting (see Chapter 9) from persons of other ages. Thus, their problems and their concerns are often (but not always) different in important ways. A delineation of when age group differences are and are not regularly used as differentiators is a part of what is urgently needed in social psychology.

The social psychology of members of each generation and each age group, because it is in its essence embedded in different concerns and current contexts as well as in mechanisms which developed in different historical contexts and educational structures, is bound to be unique and meaningful. If examination of adult age differences is disallowed, these differences will not be revealed. That has been the state of social psychology because of its antidevelopmental, adultless nature; I do not feel that has been productive. Unfortunately, it would also be the result of insistence on developmental methodological sophistication and condemnation of anything less than that as a "halfway" measure.

Adult age group differences are real and important, whether or not we can give a statistically clean answer to the question as to whether they are true developmental changes or "merely" systematic differences at this time. Rather than requiring a prohibition against such "unsophisticated" research, the latter issue—an important one—should goad social psychologists interested in adult development to be constantly unsatisfied with their results, to be looking beyond, to be striving to overcome their weaknesses by combining empirical investigation and careful, well-informed reasoning. That their social psychology is clearly historical and limited can disabuse them of the notion that they are revealing universal truths (but the fact that they are moving beyond typically ageless studies toward age-awareness indicates that they probably have already been disabused of that notion). It should lead to questioning of what has been gathered, what it means, and where it can go, and a healthy skepticism and humility. However, it should not lead to paralysis. It can and should propel the researcher-theorist into a search for more adequate ways to capture the tones and textures, movement and brilliance of social living.

That last set of statements leads to perhaps the most important reason to avoid premature entrapment in a no-win situation of total dissatisfaction with adult age comparison research. I think it would be wise for social psychologists to be wary of a too-great identification of propriety in research with the General Developmental Model and its abilities, an identification with which some lifespan developmentalists appear to feel comfortable. In many ways, the brilliance of this methodological sophistication can hide the reality of the design and its strength. It is in essence still a way to gather snapshots. Better in tone, yes; more precise and interpretable, yes; and in an array which can be arranged spatially and/or temporally, within persons and across them, but snapshots nonetheless. The investigation done to its fullness can statistically separate major factors in the causal structure behind the behavior; but the fact remains that the topics researched, the assumptions underlying the work, the theoretical formulation tested, and the methods themselves have no guarantees with them. They do not guarantee that the topics studied are topics of change and development, of relationships and of what Riegel designated "relations of relations (1978)." The interactions and main effects are transhistorical only within the range studied; whereas constancies across several cohorts and times of testing raise the likelihood of transhistorical value, they do not restrain the forces of change and tension, which may make the findings invalid at some later time, appreciably differently from basic models of psychology. They contain within themselves severe problems of interpretation that underlie all longitudinal and cross-cultural research, the virtual impossibility of full meaning-correspondence of measurement tools from one time to another, from one place or context to another (see Labouvie, 1980). That is to say, as Riegel (1978) and Gergen (1979) have previously argued, the General Developmental Model does not—cannot—go far enough. It is bounded by the characteristics of its components. It is not relational.

None of this criticism should be taken to imply that a general developmental scheme, separating age and cohort and time of testing effects, is anything short of a major contribution to developmental research. Certainly, a full analysis of this kind is a far leap beyond simple age differences comparisons. The question is not one of its value; the question is one of effect. If the effect of pressing for such a model is a warning to exercise caution and humility in interpretation of one's own age differences data, then the value is positive. But if the effect is one of discouraging simple adult age comparisons because they are inevitably "mushy," then the result may be less than benign, especially as far as social psychology is concerned. It means that social psychology will continue to ignore development and change, likely retreating back to the pristine simplicity of ignoring adult age groups and using college student and other captive populations rather than making the sacrifices needed to do what one social psychologist (a dialectical revisionist, in fact) referred to as "fiendishly difficult" and "dreadfully boring" (Thorngate, 1976, p. 406).

If the effect of discouraging reliance on simple adult age comparisons and disdaining *any* potential value in them means that potentially interested social psychologists will not be led to proceed into and then past simple age comparisons to exploration of the depth and meaning of adult social psychology because a relatively painless, relatively traditional entry point was closed to them by the uncompromising pronouncements of some life-span developmentalists, the price is far too high. That would be a loss for social psychology *and* for a well-rounded understanding of adult developmental processes that includes social behavior and social cognition. Further, if it seduces the few researchers who may be able to afford to proceed with a full General Developmental Model investigation of some sort of social performance—for instance effects of presence of others on motor performance or conformity to group decisions—into believing they automatically have data incomparably better than anything other researchers could possibly produce, that, too, would be a disservice to the field.

If, however, knowledge of the General Developmental Model, of the weaknesses of age comparison research, and of the implications of the various time sampling methods can aid and enable social psychologists interested in adult development and aging to carve out research topics, theories, and methods with development and change and relationships clearly in mind; if it goads them toward always doing better than they have so far; if it epitomizes a certain kind of research point of view so that it can both be aimed for and (as will be discussed in Chapter 3) aimed beyond, then it can serve a valuable purpose indeed.

CHAPTER 3

Beyond Age Differences: Three-Dimensional Color Movies

The last chapter was in many ways a defense of a relatively simple (though cautiously applied) adult age differences addition to social psychological investigation, in recognition of the fact that social psychology needs that added type of subgroup research. I also emphasized recognition of the reality of adulthood and the pattern of differences and similarities that may underlie membership in different age groups at a point in time and movement through various age group memberships on the individual level. That, however, is only part of a social psychology of developing adults. Within it is contained the seeds for an argument that social psychology in fact *must become a different sort of enterprise* if it is to be really development-sensitive.

In this chapter I will develop a point of view for a revolutionary social psychology of developing adults, a social psychology of interrelationships of changes and stabilities. The point of view will be discussed in more detail in Part 4 of the book, after consideration of research topics and more specific areas of interest. In turn, the discussion shares much with ideas developed by others in social psychology and elsewhere. Especially important influences are the social-psychology-as-history and later aleatory model approaches of Kenneth Gergen (1973, 1976, 1977, 1978a, b, 1979, 1980) and the radical dialectical orientation of the late Klaus Riegel (1976, 1978, 1979). These, in turn, are clearly related to broader categories of theoretical and conceptual orientation by a range of dialectical psychologists (e.g., Buss, 1979; Baumgardner, 1977) and to the developmental contextualism of Bronfenbrenner (1976, 1977) and Weisz (1978).

For readers who may be unfamiliar with those positions I hope this brief statement can be an introduction to those lines of thought and spur you to further reading in the stimulating works cited. At the same time, I hope this discussion is more than a restatement of those positions; certainly the discussion is more focused upon cognitive-behavioral social psychology than the presentations others have made.

Before I move to that "revolutionary" approach mentioned above, I will recapitulate what we have considered thus far, using somewhat more formalized terminology. There are several ways to conceive of the value and treatment of temporality—the essence of development —in any scientific investigation, including social psychology. The simplest of these methods of treatment—and the one that best describes traditional and most current social psychology—is *achronic*. The term, literally meaning "without time," is obviously accurate as a description of the sort of social psychology practiced rigorously within the field—one snapshot, usually of a person in his or her late teens or early twenties, with no indication of temporality of either the subject or the background in the picture. In fact, such indications are fastidiously and often ingeniously excised from both the subject and the background; seldom is the research report accompanied by a warning that "the picture presented here is likely to be reflective only of a very specific set of actors in a very particular place and time."

Of course, as we have considered earlier, the assumptive base in a scientific investigation of regularity and stability explicitly disallows the validity of a sense of time. Time is not only ignored, it is to be avoided. As we have further seen, even without an explicit or conscious commitment on the part of an investigator to the lawfulness of stability and the "illegitimacy" of change and irregularity, the methods of investigation and the theoretical constructions militate against temporality. It is either on the periphery and deemed irrelevant, or the deck is stacked in favor of stability and regularity so that the impact of change becomes statistically and conceptually trivial. In a circular fashion, the reality of change and movement—and, even more so, the possibility of meaningful interplay between change and stability—is denied. Investigations are framed so that those will not be discovered, and the subsequent lack of change or maturational developmental effects in results is taken as verification of their irrelevance. The obvious effects of the manipulated variables and their stability are taken as proofs of the ageless, universal, pantemporal character of the findings, when in reality the investigators seldom have allowed for the relevance of anything other than stable factors. Both standard psychological investigations and age differences research focused solely on age group identification as a social structural characteristic are of this achronic mold.

A Step Toward Temporality

I will borrow from Riegel (1978) a phrase, *synchronic* research,[1] to indicate age differences research of the type discussed in Chapter 2. The research to be reported in Parts 2 and 3 is primarily of this type. It is the classical kind of "developmental" research, in which current age differences are used as a "stand-in" for developmental differences. As opposed to achronic research, development is of interest, however the researcher uses a pseudo-time factor to represent what he or she believes to be a

---

[1] I should point out, however, that I feel this label is somewhat misleading, since at a later point Riegel (and I) will speak of synchronization and asynchronization in a discussion of a very different model and methodology of development. The term literally means "same time," and thus Riegel feels it is appropriate to describe cross-sectional studies, that is, models and research that look at age differences, but take all measurements at one point in time, at the "same time." I do not feel the terminology is ideal, given what I noted above and will discuss in more detail later, but because it was used by Riegel (who is turn took it from usage in linguistics) and is, therefore, likely to be recognizable by lifespan developmentalists and others who have read his work, I have decided to retain the usage here. Riegel did not consider nor use a word for the kind of research I have delineated above, that which is without *any* age relationship involved, but I believe the term I have used, "achronic," fits in well with his usage for this and other types of developmental models.

universal developmental process. In fact, the approach might better be called "pseudo-chrony" to clearly indicate the fact that there is no tracking of processes during time actually involved, that all measurements are taken contemporaneously. Instead of only looking at self-perception and attributional decisions in college students we might (and we have! see Chapters 4 through 6) gather several age groups and compare and contrast how they make attributions and how they use attribution information to influence their actions and expectations; that entails using a synchronic approach.

This model of development and method of approach is an advance beyond achrony in many ways, as we already considered in Chapter 2 without using this terminology. It opens up areas of interest ignored by perseveration on one element frozen in history. It is likely to provide a set of descriptions—snapshots—at least one of which may have characteristics more similar to the characteristics of the interested inquirer than the typically used "ageless" model. It makes consideration of development and qualitative changes throughout life more logical and simpler than the achronic measurement approach (especially since it usually includes an implication of universal applicability of the single snapshot) allows. Finally, it provides a concept of and the means for at least limited investigation of the interplay between levels of progression; for example, individual development and social change.

On the other hand, as has been described in detail in Chapter 2, a synchronic psychology of social behavior and social cognition, like all synchronic investigations and models of development, has major drawbacks. In many ways it is not much of an advance over the achronic approach. Regardless of the number of samples taken or the sophistication of measures, it is essentially static and two-dimensional in concept and operation. It yields no more than a series of snapshots and usually involves a conception of change, insofar as it exists, only within one element (persons, in the case of cross-sectional studies; time of testing in cross-sequential). For example, many developmental psychologists in the past interpreted adult age differences in intelligence, showing lower intelligence test scores for older subjects, as revealing maturational change. Only recently have investigators using more sophisticated methods shown the error of that view, a view that influenced practical approaches to old age and, possibly, encouraged negative stereotypes of aging for many years (see Labouvie-Vief, 1977, for one of many reviews of that whole body of research; also see Baltes & Schaie, 1976, and Horn and Donaldson, 1976, for a lively "debate" on some related issues).

Sociologists and the mass media provide another example of confusion in use of synchronic data. They regularly interpret differences between the same kind of age samples (e.g., changes in polls) as examples of change brought about by current events, external contexts, or cohort differences, even though alternative psychological and/or maturational models may be just as likely to be correct. Social psychologists of aging tend to see changes from age 60 to age 70 in life orientation as resulting, for example, from retirement or declining health, disregarding other life events and ontogenetic factors, especially psychogenic ones (e.g., life review—see Butler, 1963—or terminal drop, a sort of backward causality from time of death—see Riegel & Riegel, 1971).

It is clear from these and other examples that synchronic social psychology is bound to have major weaknesses built into its very nature, making it less than ideally suited to be used to further understanding of social behavior and social cognition as lifespan developmental (in this case, adult developmental) processes.

A Social Psychology Moving Forward in Time

A third major way of looking at development is the *diachronic* approach, what is often called *longitudinal* research. It is similar to synchronic social psychology in that it is limited to providing a set of snapshots of different ages; the difference is that here the snapshots are all of the same person, taken at different "sittings." Thus, this is the first approach that is really developmental in its essence; it proceeds "through time," as the root of the name indicates. The same persons are followed through several points in time. One might, for example, have people make attributional decisions about their lives each year for five years and get "change" measures, which could then be related to differences in experiences, roles (preretirement and postretirement, for example), and biological changes (loss or gain of acuity).

Even though this approach has a great advantage—it follows time in reality, instead of ignoring it or merely using surrogate variables—in many ways it, too, is incomplete. Simple longitudinal measures, of course, confuse age-maturation (the personal factors) and time of testing, since there can be no random assignment of a particular age to a particular time of testing. Added to this are the major problems inherent in giving the same measures to persons at more than one time, as is a problem in all longitudinal research (see Campbell & Stanley, 1966). Whereas some of those methodological, and therefore interpretive, ambiguities can be resolved in one way or another (see Baltes et al., 1977), the conceptual problems remain. Age flows along and is measured at different times, but each point of entry is but a frozen frame, a slice of time, as it is in synchronic designs. A diachronic social psychology of adult development is not likely to be a social psychology of interrelationships nor is it likely to reveal relationships of change and stability. Diachronic psychology, typified by stage approaches, concentrates on stability, regularity, and universality even as it allows for change in the sense of movement from one stage to another. The flow of time is a linear, chronological progression, assumed to be "paced" approximately the same for everyone (I will discuss this further in Chapter 14).

In the social psychology of adulthood, perhaps the closest model to a completely diachronic one is Erikson's (1959) stage model, although many elements of social gerontological theories sometimes labeled as social psychology, for example, activity and disengagement (see Chapter 13 for more discussion), have an implicit stage orientation and diachronic perspective. In each case, development is conceived to be internally and/or externally controlled, essentially a universal and sequential progression through a set of stages. Most of the models are either heavily biological-maturational or heavily social structural; few are dynamic analyses of the interrelationships of those and other factors. Another current example is represented by Gail Sheehy's (1976) book *Passages,* subtitled "Predictable Crises of Adult Life."

Polychrony: Multidimensional Temporality

A fourth conception of the scope, assumptions, and methods of social psychology is that which Reigel calls "dialogical psychology." In keeping with the "-chrony" designations for the other approaches, I will call this "polychrony" (or "polysynchrony," since the concept of synchronization is an important part of it). It is this sort of social psychology that is truly revolutionary in that it represents a clean break from the whole set of universality assumptions that underlie all of the other approaches, including virtually all social psychological investigations. This perspective involves a combination of dialectical and social-psychology-as-history approaches (cited earlier) with a consistent emphasis on individual development and the individual as active participant in the ongoing construction and dissolution of relationships. It is thus a model for a development-sensitive social psychology. However, with the exception of several of Kenneth Gergen's recent papers (e.g., 1977, 1979, 1980) and Brewster Smith's presentation at the 1979 Nebraska Symposium on Motivation (1980; see also Smith, 1977), and a few other scattered, sketchy discussions (e.g., Secord, 1976), the dialectical-historical approach has not been applied to the organization of a development-sensitive, adult-oriented *social* psychology.

In approximately the same period, ecologically oriented social psychologists (e.g., Barker, 1968, 1977; Bechtel, 1977; Wicker, 1979) have developed theoretical statements about the relationship of persons to contexts—behavior settings—which change over time. They have created and finetuned means to examine the interrelationships of social behavior to physical environments. Because of the centrality of contexts of behavior, these views are important to the perspective being developed here, but review of them will be deferred until Chapters 9, 10, and 11. They can provide a point of correspondence between person and context and the changes that both are constantly undergoing.

Dialectical approaches to social psychology and the social-psychology-as-history approach have forced social psychologists to face up to the importance of temporally defined social contexts as well as the physical ones noted by the ecological psychologists. Gergen has been in the vanguard of those who stress the historical embeddedness of social structures, institutions, and cultures, and who place great importance on variation in those structures and contexts over time as they influence social behavior.

As I proceed further along these lines of concern, I will be increasingly concerned with a "dialectical emphasis," as I will call it. That term, however can be taken to indicate a number of different ideologies and approaches and, thus, it is important to clarify the way in which I will be using the term. I am not primarily concerned with proposing an ideology for social psychology, and certainly I am not using the term "dialectics" in the sense of materialistic dialectics, as Baumgardner (1977), Buck-Morss (1977), Archibald (1978), and others use it. Rather, like Riegel (1978, 1979), Smith (1977), and Buss (1979), I am more concerned with dialectics as representative of an emphasis on tension and imbalance as being fully as central to social behavior and thought as stability and balance are. I am interested in the constant interplay of change and stability, the one as an antithesis to the other, and particularly in the *relationship* of change and stability as the irreducible synthesis of those superficially opposing forces. I am concerned also with a developmental dialectics, the view that there are a set of progressions (each of them containing both change and stability) over time, interacting with one another in ways varying moment-to-moment from a multidimensional synchrony (harmony) to asynchrony (chaos). The resolution of these progressions into synchrony is neither common nor optimal; rather, the placement of progressions in juxtaposition to each other is in fact an affirmation of the validity of social living.

I will discuss these issues in more concrete terms as I develop my argument in this chapter. For the moment I will return to exposition of the views in social psychology and lifespan developmental psychology which can be placed under the heading of "polysynchronic."

All of the emphases I have been citing are deeply critical of the status-quo orientation of most of social psychology. That is, the critics have often vociferously attacked the assumptions behind most of social psychology—beliefs that it is possible to formulate universal psychological laws of social behavior and social cognition, that experimentation and control are the preferred mode of investigation, that balance is to be valued most highly, and that individual differences are irrelevant or worse. The assumptions noted, of course, all center around the belief that stable, universally applicable mechanisms form the core of social life across history, across place, and across cultures. The revisionists likewise attack the traditional theories of the field, theories that are essentially concerned with the effects of stable structural elements on other stable structural elements. They are concerned with deficiencies, many of which are, at their root, antidevelopmental and/or anticontextual.

The impact of these revisionist, nonuniversalistic models of social psychology (both the discipline and the subject matter) is open to question, although it is telling that many major figures in the field of social psychology have been at or near the forefront of the revisionist movements whereas others, even those committed to more universalistic models, have included at least some elements of the criticisms into their recent work. Examples of the former include William McGuire (1973, 1979), who has led an attack on the tendency of social psychologists to be content with linear models and with main effects or low order interactions. Brewster Smith has in fact stated that "it seems to me to require a heavy dose of dogmatic blindness not to agree with Gergen (1973) and Cronbach (1975) that the central problems and relationships to be dealt with are heavily cultural and historical. . . .We should make a more serious try to find models that better fit our own historical, cultural, meaningful domain (Smith, 1980)." These and other prominent social psychologists join Gergen (1973, 1978a,b, 1980) and Paul Secord (1976; Harre & Secord, 1972).

Examples of those who have recently begun to integrate new models and approaches with their more traditional approaches include Lawrence Wrightsman (1980) and Harry Triandis (1978). The latter has been particularly emphatic in the necessity of cross-cultural comparative research (relevant to my exposition of age-differences research in Chapter 2), whereas Wrightsman has turned toward adult developmental psychology of personality for guidance into adult-relevant areas of concern. The list, hopefully, will have grown by the time this book reaches the reader. In any case, many elements within social psychology appear to be ready for an approach that combines contextual and cultural-historical developmental notions with social psychological questions, even though, as I noted earlier, there have been few attempts to do so thus far, even by those revisionists noted above.

Concurrently, theorists in lifespan developmental psychology and other developmental researchers also have found new cause for including the importance of historical development into their work. Some of this direction has arisen from the recognition by Baltes, Schaie, and others (e.g., Baltes & Labouvie, 1973; Baltes & Schaie, 1976; Schaie & Labouvie-Vief, 1974; Baltes, Reese, & Nesselroade, 1977) that intelligence and other aspects of cognitive development appear to be more closely related to social structural elements, notably common experience factors of a particular historical group—that is, cohort—than to individual ontogenetic processes, at least in older adulthood. Several of these developmentalists and others (e.g., Labouvie, 1980; Labouvie-Vief & Chandler, 1978; Riegel, 1976) have spoken of major qualitative discontinuities in cognitive processing over the life span. That is, they feel that descriptions of cognitive development as stepwise and progressive or as simple accumulation are simply invalid. They emphasize that the "same" set of actions or operations when done by different aged actors may mean, and therefore be, different things.

Perhaps the most extreme form of the life-span developmentalists' point of view is that proposed by Riegel, especially in several posthumously published books (1978, 1979). For example, Riegel states that our conceptualization of psychology should recognize that "there is thus never anything static and fixed" (1978, p. 49). Coordinate with the revisionist social psychologists, the life-span developmentalists emphasize the influence of nonbiological, nonontogenetic factors at the same time as they oppose the belief of most psychologists in orderly and regular stabilities and progressions.

Riegel proceeds even further, by developing his dialogic approach to the major areas of psychological investigation, clearly including, but not emphasizing, social psychology. Dialogical—polychronic—psychology is unequivocally relational and temporal; it is centrally concerned with the interstices between a set of progressions, four of which Riegel feels can be relatively easily differentiated in common sense terms. The idea of a set of progressions is not new, since it is contained in the conception of the independent influences of maturation, cohort, and time of testing. Reigel's formulation, however, both makes the progressions and their meaning clearer and, most critically, moves from consideration of independent effects of the progressions to a focus on the interrelationships of them.

Riegel (1978) describes a set of four progressions: (1) inner-biological, (2) individual-psychological, (3) cultural-sociological, and (4) outer-physical. The first and second progressions form the "inner dialectics" of development, and the latter two compromise the "outer dialectics." Each of these is constantly in a state of dramatic change, and each pair is, therefore, in tension, or conflict, within itself. A progression in one sense is development (as in social development, moral development, etc.); in another way, however, it is an aspect of development, the latter being the relationship of the totality of the progressions. In this perspective, Riegel clearly introduces the "balancing act" idea referred to in the first several pages of this book as inherent in real social psychological relationships. "Balance" in social life is an act, both in the sense of a performance and in the sense of active involvement on the part of the individual and his or her contexts.

Before further discussion of polychrony it may be time to reflect on what Riegel's four progressions conception means vis-à-vis the major dimensions of social psychology we have considered up to this point: assumptions, theory, areas of interest, and methods. Riegel's work (and that of Vygotsky, 1962; Rubinstein, 1958; and other Soviet dialecticians that have clearly informed his conceptualization) are major advances toward a more realistic psychology (and, specifically at this point, social psychology) than the psychologies of the so-called realists. It also represents a needed reemphasis on both individual and social after the extenalizing, often materialistic, dialectical conceptualizations of some of the revisionist social psychologists and life-span developmentalists (who, for their part performed an equally necessary and valuable role as respondents to the undue emphasis on intraindividual causality of more traditional psychologists).

Riegel stresses the reality of all four factors, which in turn can be placed into several dimensions. He is as vehement as other revisionists in decrying the lack of consideration given to external factors, especially external historical ones, by behaviorists, organicists (e.g., Piaget, Chomsky), and humanistic-individualistic personality psychologists alike. Whereas the organicists place stress on biological unfolding and the humanists on intrapersonal psychological determinism, neither makes more than passing reference to the active construction of reality from without; the external world is but a stage upon which the internally determined patterns of actions are performed. In that regard, Riegel places great stress on the workings of the external forces surrounding the life of the individual. At the same time, he criticizes the simplistic externalizations of the behaviorists who allow only for the current, immediate environment without reference to history and broader contexts.

Thus, Riegel forcefully argues against points of view that entail ignoring external factors as well as against those that lead to a gross externalization of development and of behavior devoid of intraindividual and broader historical factors. He certainly finds comrades in the revisionist social psychologists when he attacks behaviorism, but he finds less comradeship when he equally finds fault—as he must, to be consistent—with materialistic dialectical approaches and social structural-cultural explanations common to both sociologists in general and to many of the critics of psychology and social psychology. Dialectical materialists fail to acknowledge the importance of internal factors as part of a dialectical process with those things convention leads us to call "external." The dialectical materialistic argument often proceeds from the obvious misuse of biological causality and biological reductionism in many psychological and social psychological interpretations of behavior and the concurrent lack of recognition of context typical of the developmentalism of past years. Riegel fervently believes, and I with him, that only an approach that recognizes both organisms and contexts as equally active and constructive have any hope of being representative of reality.

At the same time, Riegel performs another needed service, that of differentiating between factors within the contextual constellation and within the personal sphere. By contextual constellation I mean those factors of physical and sociocultural environment that surround and help define the individual. The abstractive, but apparently necessary, duality of Person and Environment is mirrored by a duality within each. At the risk of implying a separatistic dualism between mind and body which is not intended by Riegel or by me, it is clear that biogenetic development and cognitive-personality development are often quite distinct and, sometimes, at odds. That is the case with sociocultural and physical environmental aspects of the extrapersonal sphere as well. The former includes a bewildering array of roles, institutions, and bureaucratic structures, other persons and their activities and internal states. The latter—the physical environment—includes a wide range of physical elements. In most cases, though, what is sociostructural or cultural is relatively well differentiable from what is physical-environmental.

You can, I am sure, make these differentiations concrete by thinking about your own "life space" and personal situation. You seldom confuse the physical and social characteristics of your neighborhood with each other or either of them with your body or your conception of yourself. At the same time, you can unite various ultimately separable characteristics of the progressions in which you find yourself for a wide array of purposes. For example, you can combine both other people and rules of conduct with physical characteristics of the environment and call *that* your neighborhood, an approach congenial to ecological-social psychology.

Most theories of the determinants of social behavior blur the boundaries among at least some of the four elements or progressions. Some of these have been mentioned in passing already. Behavioral, social learning approaches, concerned only with factors external to the person, nevertheless confuse contingencies of the natural world and of more or less purely physical aspects of the made world (for example, architecture) with contingencies imposed by the will of other individuals and collections of individuals—laws, regulations, age stratification and resultant differential role expectations, and cultural ethos. At the same time, all aspects of inner determinism are seen as equivalent in their lack of utility and merely epiphenomenal nature.

Those who use stage models of development of social behavior and personality avoid detailed consideration of external factors; the environment is but a stage, or rather a set of passive objects to be manipulated in a certain way at a certain stage of development. Little differentiation is made between other persons as external factors and physical objects. Likewise, cognitive unfolding is seen as essentially the result of biological unfolding, happening in front of the inexorable and unchanging structure of the world as it really is—an almost platonic idealized stability of the physical world. Social and moral development are defined as following from cognitive development, which in turn is but the necessary concomitant of structural changes in ontogenetic, intraindividual evolution. Alternatively, social behavior is considered to be the necessary result of intrapsychic progression through personality stages; once again, the external world becomes a blur.

Many critics of current social and developmental psychology have done a different sort of blurring, confusing both aspects of inner dialectics with each other. As a result, they have dismissed internal determination as being "merely biological" and, therefore, given the problems obviously inherent in biological reductionism, as inadmissible in ways not dissimilar from what behaviorists have done. In several of his earlier writings on social-psychology-as-history, Gergen (e.g., 1973) certainly left the impression that he believed explanation in terms of individual factors to be faulty because he felt such explanation was necessarily biological. Some of the dialectical and social-psychology-as-history critics have been much more vehement in their denial of internal processes than Gergen, who, to be sure, has made clear in his later work that he does not hold to that position.

In any case, Riegel, more than other related writers, has consistently placed emphasis on the meaningfulness and critical importance of each of the four sets of factors and the essential contemporaneity of all of them. He raises the level of argument in much other revisionist writing by accepting their insistence on the importance of a particular factor, but refusing to accept a corresponding de-emphasis of any of the others. Constantly Riegel is saying, "Yes, this is *and* so is that," rather than "this, instead of that."

The most valuable aspect of a dialectical formulation such as Riegel's is the total commitment to time and change within each of the progressions or spheres of life that impinge on social behavior and social cognition and make the person what he or she is. That is, each progression is a sequence of events, of actions. The constant factor in development is activity and movement. This is accompanied by the resultant necessary correlate—a deemphasis of static structuralism accompanied by the ascendance of historicism and development. His emphases on historicity, on the inevitability of change, and on the preeminent status of *progression* mirror the historical arguments of others in developmental and social psychology. Combined with his ecumenism in regard to the range of progressions, this emphasis forces one interested in development to be interested in relationships first and foremost. The core question immediately shifts from "What are the universal regularities of social behavior that form the core around which individual and group differences form their encrustations?" to "How is it that there are regularities at the surface, given the uniqueness and flux at the core?" The answer, quite clearly, must lie in analysis of relationships, not of structures and objects. Theories must be theories of relationships between and within each and all of the progressions of life. These relationships are both stable and unstable, change and stability.

The central assumption of a dialectical model such as this is the reality of relationships as those form objects and events, not vice versa. This is diametrically opposed to the overriding emphases in social psychology on stability, equilibrium, and balance apparent in virtually all models of all content areas (of course, forming the core of balance theories of attitudes, persuasion, and attitude change). It involves a different conception of the relationship of the individual to place and time, to his or her own biological development and to culture, to his own personhood and her environment.

Thus, adding new areas of interest and age comparisons, dispensing with the universality and stability assumptions of social psychology, and establishing historical models of context, although all important and essential, are all only beginnings of a development-sensitive social psychology. Beyond and behind and informing that sort of housecleaning must be a conception of development that turns the ontology of social psychology on its head. Virtually all previous social psychology, even contextual approaches such as ecological psychology, are based on the assumption that regularity and constancy are to be found below the surface of change and difference. All developmental models, insofar as they are considered in social psychology, are based on an assumption that there is a goal to be attained, a particular relationship of person to environment, of individuals to others, a state of balance or quiescence. But the dialectical model centers on the idea that "reality" is to be found wherever change and conflict and tension are, that balance and stability are unusual. In fact, Riegel (1978) states quite clearly that he feels a state of balance *as a goal* is unhealthy, since it consigns growth and change to the status of necessary evils.

Stability is *not* the normal characteristic of social life; change is. Development and change are the universal, ageless core of behavior and thought, including (perhaps especially) social behavior and thought. The relationship of cognition and action to contexts—physical, social, and individual-historical—is the key to understanding. At the same time, though, all the contexts are fluid and changing as are behavior and thought. In this conception, the search for regularity and linear causality and continuity is invalid and doomed from the start. *Relationships* as they change, adapt, adjust, and influence each element of the relationship should be the focus of social psychology. Interplay and interaction are the *simplest* elements of social behavior and thought. Linear methods, age-specific designs and theories, and psychological or sociostructural monism are at best only rough approximations to the understanding of these interactions. Change is at the core of understanding.

If lifespan developmental social psychology is seen in this light it is both highly revolutionary and, paradoxically, very traditional. It is revolutionary, for it summons personality and social psychologists to abandon the hope of finding and explicating stable, universal psychological laws of social behavior and instead requires them to strive to understand relationships that are changing and growing, coming to life and dying. A stable endpoint of research and theory, even as only a working assumption, is no more acceptable than a belief in a stable endpoint of individual or social development. This new formulation leads to the inclusion of "individual" differences—not only in persons, but also in places and times—into models of behavior and cognition. It is thoroughly ecological and thoroughly personal at the same time (and similar in many ways to Angyal's (1941) approach to a Gestalt theory of personality).

Yet curiously, the kind of social psychology involved in a developmental perspective such as this one is in some ways more akin to traditional perspectives that ignore age as a factor than to personalism and individual differences research on the one hand or to dialectical social structuralism, on the other. For, in the final analysis it is not age or biological determinism which produces most changes in social behavior and thought; age is "merely" a measure of opportunity to experience a variety of environments, a variety of life events, a growing multitude of stimuli and responses and relationships. The personal reality of "age" mirrors the methodological one stressed by Schaie, Baltes, and other experimental psychologists of aging and development. Thus, ultimately, taking age into consideration as a variable, finding the relationship of age differences or age changes to social behavior and to cognitive processes, mechanisms, and performance (and to environmental and societal changes) leads to an emphasis not unlike that of traditional experimental scientists, who in their laboratories try to induce changes in behavior or in cognitions. Indeed, some life-span developmentalists are thoroughly behavioristic (e.g., Ahammer, 1973; Baer, 1973) and see age differences research primarily as an important and convenient opportunity to study behavior change over long periods of time.

In another way this perspective is also more traditional than some other approaches with which it shares revisionist characteristics. It does not externalize the locus of behavior to physical or social structural environments as completely as some revisionist models do. It does not entail a denial of regularity and stability or even of the search for universals, as some models do, although it does point to different directions in which to continue the search—into regularities of change, the stability of relationships that can come about only by each element changing in synchrony, and the universality of the close connection of individual behavior and thought to context.

Each element in every relationship is affected by its relationship with other elements. It is not a simple matter of one progression controlling the others or of linear causality in any sense, as would be the case in traditional approaches. Thus, it is both traditional and radically different from tradition. Each relationship, each dynamic of development, is transforming all of the progressions, forming the base from which a new relationship will spring, in turn to transform and modify every progression anew. The progressions may, at some points, be ballistic, with internal logic, but they are *also* ultimately lifeless without the base of their relationships to others. Even at the most basic levels of description of mechanisms, the simple laws of either-or break down and the cooperation and competition, the thesis and antithesis, of forms and elements combine into a logic of their own; they form a new relationship.

Further, these relationships and this inexorable demand for change are embedded within the sometimes independent, ballistic processes of sequences *within* each progression. Since there are at least four of these semi-independent progressions, each with an internal logic as well as a set of interfaces with other progressions, the rule of relationships is conflict and tension; asynchronization, not synchronization and rest, is the norm. Riegel (1978) gives a good summary of this position when he states that "development and history are never completed. At the moment when completion seems to be imminent, new questions and doubts arise in the individual and in society. The organism, the individual, society, and even the outside world of nature are never at rest. And in their restlessness they are rarely perfectly synchronized " (p. 169). More radically, he stated, as cited earlier, that "there is thus *never* anything static and fixed" (p. 49, italics added).

This formulation, obviously, requires a new approach, new theories, and new methods. Prior to his untimely death, Riegel was beginning to proceed from his manifesto for a dialectical psychology (1976) to the construction of new methods, primarily historical and primarily ethogenic (that is, toward meaning of events within natural life), to explore relational, dialogical psychology. Indeed, he was researching dialogues and interactions shortly before his death (as discussed in his 1978 book), as a way to represent the logic of research design for the future as he envisioned it.

It is obvious that if the nature of life has a dialectical, relational quality as its essence—and it appears to be the case—then current methods, theories, and assumptions must all be put behind us. Methods set up to find stability and theories devised to idealize consistency and balance are doomed to failure. They are literally unreal. In terms of social psychology specifically, the revolution must be dramatic, the break with all that has gone before must be clean. Even most critics of social psychology may be underestimating the task at hand. That was graphically illustrated to me in a reaction by Kenneth Gergen to an early paper I sent him concerning my emerging view of adult developmental psychology. After all was said and done, he noted, I still had been unable to bring myself to really ''bite the bullet'' when it came to empricism and the model of science contained in most of social psychology (see also Gergen's published works, especially 1978b, 1980, for what he means by ''biting the bullet''). And indeed I had not done so; indeed, the revolution is to be bold and dramatic if it is worth doing at all.

At this point, though, I think we must move back to a critical question *and* to the discussion of the traditional aspects of the approach I am outlining which was presented a few pages ago. Does embrace of a dialectical, relational, polychronic social psychology really entail essentially throwing out all that has come before? Does it mean, as Riegel stated, ''since human beings are changing all the time they cannot be appropriately described by instruments that are supposed to reflect universal and stable properties'' (p. 149), that the conclusion about the imperfection of the basic models of analysis (cross-sectional, etc.) ''does nothing less than invalidate all the developmental data reported in the literature'' (p. 71)? Is the picture of the world Riegel and other dialecticians give us full and complete? Is it the case that ''there is *never anything* static and fixed'' (Riegel, 1978, p. 49, italics added)?

It is at this point that I believe Riegel and his adherents must be judged carefully, and I believe it is here that they often go too far because of the awareness they have of the incompletenesses and even erroneous judgments to which traditional methods and models have led us. It is here that Riegel, too, has forgotten some of his own arguments and the logic of development. He dismisses weak conceptions, weak methods, and weak theories as essentially anachronisms. In even more striking fashion than Baltes and Schaie and their colleagues (although statements as positive and unequivocal as those cited above can also be found in their writings), Riegel insists that stability is but an illusion; it is the gloss that hides the reality of change and indeterminacy and asynchrony. He speaks of the importance people place on change and transition when asked to characterize their own development, and he concludes that because of this dialectical psychology is ''primarily concerned with how groups and individuals succeed in overcoming their tranquility and balance. Consequently, dialectical psychology looks on crises, catastrophes, and revolutions and reinterprets them in positive terms'' (Riegel, 1978, p. 217).

Yet is it not the case that the concerns of persons as often as not run to stability—trying to remain the same, trying to ''be themselves''? Is it not true that many of our behaviors, concerns, and approaches to life *are* consistent and continuous and that we work to make them that way? The attribution data reported in Chapter 8 indicate persons are not afraid of change, but at the same time they see themselves as continuous in many ways from their pasts and in fact see transgenerational transmission of values about achievement as important. Neugarten's (1964, 1968, etc.) basic approach, as well as those of many other social gerontologists, as we have already noted in Chapter 2 and will be discussing in much greater detail in later chapters (especially Chapter 14), leans heavily toward stability and continuity. The fact that we criticized the magnitude of the emphasis and its shortcomings in not recognizing change and tension does not obviate the findings or the validity of stability as well as instability.

In fact, if it is true that ''synchronization denotes a balance structured in time which can be understood only if the state of imbalance is also taken into consideration'' (Riegel, 1978, p. 59), must it not also be just as true that for change to exist there also must be stability, that the state of imbalance can also only be understood if balance is taken into account, that discontinuity and continuity are *equally* real? Is not stability the necessary thesis for change as antithesis? Indeed, is not a stability-oriented, balance-seeking social psychology a necessary thesis, an essential part of the relationship that is the ongoing construction of social psychology?

Certainly, Riegel is correct; stability is only likely to be maintained by changing each progression to make it correspond with—move in synchrony with—other progressions. However, that does not and cannot make stability less real than change. Instead, both change and stability are contained within their relationship and the relationships of the progressions or sequences that are the nature of biological organisms, personalities, societies, and physical environments alike. To deny a role to stability that is coequal with that for change and discontinuity is an ideological action not unlike the acts of the majority of psychologists who have used the ontological reality of stability to disregard change and history (the latter, of course, is an ideological act Riegel and other dialecticians lament). The full dialectic of development is the interplay of change, *and* stability of nonlinearity *and* linearity, of continuity *and* discontinuity. It is the interwoven fabric of individual structures and individual development with social and physical environmental change and stability. Traditional social psychologists (and, I might add, psychologists of aging) have ignored far too much in their search for stability and universality and their psychologizing of the basis for action. But, although I am certain most dialecticians would not take issue with my recognition of stability in the abstract, in their conceptualizations and in their proposed methods and their willingness to discard *anything* and *everything* based in static models using static methods, many dialecticians, including Riegel, have downgraded regularity and stability to the vanishing point.

They fail to deal in a clear and unequivocal fashion with the equality of change and stability. They have failed to keep in mind that any model of social behavior and social cognition, any idea of development, that relegates stability and constancy to a subordinate position to change and imbalance and conflict is as misleading, as unreal, as those models and ideas that have subordinated conflict and change to the place allocated to equilibrium and regularity.

If those further ideas are correct, if a complete approach to the social psychology of developing adults is to be historical and developmental, social and individual, sensitive to change and to stability, then the construction of that social psychology will require hard work and a broad inclusive perspective. It will, however, not be a total abandonment of our past nor will it be obstinate in its decertification of either change-process social psychology or stability-structural social psychology.

CONCLUDING COMMENTS FOR PART 1

Before I proceed to a discussion of research programs in adult development, virtually all of which are a step backward from the sort of relational social psychology defined here to the sort of social psychology described in Chapter 2 (I will give a rationale for that move in the Introduction to Parts 2 and 3), I want to give one brief example of where I think this approach to social psychology would take us. I believe, first of all, that it would inevitably make us more clearly historians, philosophers, and poets than we have allowed ourselves to be. It would require us to pull back from a conception of our data as useful simply because it is scientific and would instead force us to examine what we produce in the light of its value, as information, as a guide for action, and as a guide for living. It would require us to make sure our construction of reality made sense in the same way as people's constant construction of their own realities did. It would demand of us that we abandon some of our fictions so that we could better understand particular experiences, particular events, and particular causes and effects as fictions. We are as naive as the ''lay psychologist'' in many ways in our assumptions about the world.

I cannot point to such a social psychology. Indeed, one of the earliest criticisms of the positions explicated by Riegel, Gergen, and others, is that they are not amenable to research. That is true, but I think to some degree the understanding of our search as in fact requiring static models and an emphasis on uncovering balance as theses for the antithesis of change models and conflict theories is a healthy place to begin. We can recognize our incompleteness and strive to transform it even as we need not flog ourselves for our inconsistencies. Can we not recognize and live with our own inconsistencies?

However, I will give one illustration. I will be discussing attributions in the next five chapters and have mentioned that research area as an example at several earlier points. Only in Chapter 7 of Part 2 do I even begin to show much progress into a social psychology of relationships and meanings. Even there the beginnings are rudimentary. I do believe, though, that in that direction attribution research can be made more relational and must be made more so to be maximally useful in the ways outlined above.

How, then, may we proceed in that direction? We must move beyond the notion that people carry stable attribution schemata around with them and apply them as they go through life. We must instead assume that attributions, like other social psychological events, are constructions for the moment, are relationships hammered out as needed. Some of these ideas are obviously close to the self-perception scheme outlined by Bem (1972), in which he asserts that attitudes are formed *ex post facto* upon demand, to "cover" oneself in explanations about behaviors already done. These ideas, though, go further than Bem in the direction of seeing each attribution and each act and outcome to be explained as bound inextricably together with the progressions as we have discussed them, the relationships that are currently available. To understand attributions as social psychological phenomena we must delve deeply into their use, beyond cavalier statements that determinations about stability affect future expectations and those about locus of causation influence affect (Weiner, 1979). We must explore the natural range of attribution use, the meanings individuals give to words and concepts in successive times and places, and the ingredients persons see as crucial in forming a clear idea about causation in a particular instance. We must examine how that information is formed and used in particular relationships to others (role expectations, others' needs, etc.). Furthermore, that sort of information must be gathered across the widest range of persons possible. The stabilities and changes in elements and in their relations over time and over place must be vigorously pursued.

Such an approach to attributions has not been attempted (at least not since Heider, 1958, pointed us in that direction), but it is possible with means at our disposal. Those means include the ethogenic approach discussed further in Chapter 12 and explicated in detail by Harre (1977a, 1979; Harre & Secord, 1972) and phenomenological sociology and many aspects of symbolic interactionism (see Psathas, 1973; and Gubrium & Buckholdt, 1977, for the former; Stone & Farberman, 1980, for the latter).

A relational social psychology of attribution use and of the meaning of causality and responsibility will be a fitting antithesis to the thesis of traditional, experimental explorations. Both are required before they can together lead to a newer, yet still inevitably imperfect, synthesis.

First Steps Toward a Social Psychology of Developing Adults

RESEARCH EXAMPLES

Implementation of a social psychology of adult development will neither occur overnight nor be accomplished without hard work. It will require both a sense of vision and a willingness to proceed toward that vision in small, faltering steps. The central section of this book is the record of a number of attempts to take such steps.

Part 2 is a detailed consideration of what is clearly the most major area of interest in social psychology today: attributions. In Part 2 I will be discussing issues and problems in that area that bear upon development and change. I will rather exhaustively cover both theory and research that others have done which are relevant to adult development and aging. Those are primarily research studies on attributions *about* older persons and work on achievement across the life-span. In the three chapters that follow that initial discussion I will proceed into detailed accounts of an original research program I have been conducting that explores not only attributions about older persons, but also attributions about middle-aged persons, attributions *by* young, middle-aged, and older adults about themselves, achievement orientation across those age groups, and an analysis of attributions and achievements from a somewhat different, more ethogenic perspective: that of meanings. In the latter chapter I discuss the elements that persons of various ages consider important in their use of attributions for self-concept information and maintenance and for direction of future behavioral attempts. In Chapter 7 I also briefly touch upon future research directions concerned with adulthood and with more general attribution work which are likely to be productive. Finally, in the last chapter of Part 2, I discuss the meaning these findings may have for application to several problems and issues of adulthood and aging

In Part 3 I bring evidence from others' theory and research and from my own work in two relatively different areas of environmental psychology of aging to bear upon the relationship of older persons to their neighborhoods and the interrelationships among biological, psychological, social, and physical environmental factors that bind and direct social activity within home and neighborhood. Part 3 includes detailed exposition of an ecological-environmental model and discussion, specifically, of design factors in housing for the elderly and of shopping behaviors of older persons

(and adults of other ages). Although these studies are clearly less "social psychological" in a mainstream social psychology sense than those in Part 2, I try to show how
that apparent shortcoming works to their advantage in forming linkages with areas of
interest in social gerontology and lifespan development and I indicate how these concerns with ecology are inextricably bound up with an understanding of social behavior and social activity. In fact, they are linked to the areas of interest in Part 2 through
the mediation of control as a changing, developmental matter.

In many ways the exposition in these empirical research portions of the book is a
retreat from the sort of social psychology of adult development proposed and explored in the last chapters, especially Chapter 3. But, as I have indicated already at
several points throughout the book, especially at the end of Chapter 2, I do not agree
with some radical critics of current social and developmental psychology that age differences research, even with fairly superficial measures, is worthless in itself, nor do
I believe that discouraging research of that sort will benefit social psychology or the
study of adult development and aging in the long run.

For the foreseeable future, a social psycholoty of developing adults must include
adoption of an uncomfortable position, poised straddling the fence between traditional social psychology—with its achronic, ultimately shallow methods and models
as well as its empirical base and precision—and a radically new social psychology
more in tune with dialectical and historical social psychologists and, of course, with
the tone I adopted in the earlier part of this book, especially Chapter 3. The position
demands resolution in favor of the new (since the old social psychology has done
such an inadequate job of dealing with development and with being adult). Only with
a new approach is there a chance that comfort and rest may be found.

But we must remember what we have been saying about living as an adult (actually, living), about what kind of world we want our social psychology to reflect and
influence. That which is comfortable, that which contains no tensions and no contradictions, that which is perfect is not by any means that which is most vital. Why
shouldn't a social psychology of developing adults contain in itself that which it seeks
to explore? If we really believe that life is constant change, is built on tension, and,
indeed, allows us no resting place; if, that is, we "bite the bullet" of developmental
dialectics; then it is clear we must also admit contradiction, tension, lack of resolution, and maximum variety into our discipline.

This is not an apology for the incompleteness and weakness of the research to be
reported. Nor is it a defense, for there is much room for improvement in my research
programs, even as traditional social psychology. I do not ask the reader to accept
them as the apex toward which they must strive or as the epitome of what a social psychology of developing adults should be—far from it. I only wish that the reader use
them for what they are worth (examine them as merely rough approximations), and
that he or she not use their weaknesses to reject the striving that will lead toward a social psychology of developing adults.

It is my hope that the weak, clearly achronic and diachronic research investigations described in Parts 2 and 3 will serve as guides into an increasingly stronger
commitment to a social psychology concerned with adult issues, with development
and   sensitivity   to   the   possibility—the   likelihood—of   change,   progress,

interrelationships and tensions *and* stability and a sense of rootedness. They may be taken as illustrations of a social psychology of developing adults which does not wait for radical reorganization of the field, but which can begin to provide information and insight now. Flawed and restrictive though that information may be, it would make social psychology more generally useful, more humanized and relevant, broader, deeper, and richer than it has allowed itself to be.

On the other hand, it should be clear that the value inherent in these studies is not in any way a denial of the need for radical reorganization. Though some social psychologists may find this set of approaches sufficient for their purposes—and I will consider some of those valid purposes, especially practical ones, in the course of Parts 2 and 3—most will probably proceed on this level *at the same time* as they continue to be dissatisfied with their models, their methods, and, most importantly, their results. Some radical reconstructionists, however, may decide, with Riegel, that this type of research is too inadequate and too far removed from reality to be useful for their purposes. That is, of course, their privilege. *You* must judge for yourself.

But remember that to side with the extreme revisionists is likely to mean losing contact with the majority of empirical social psychologists, not just those entirely committed to static conceptions, but also those who find such conceptions useful or have not yet been able to proceed past them; it means cutting off from mutual relevance most social gerontologists and developmental psychologists. It may mean almost total paralysis in gathering empirical data with *any* relevance to adulthood. My choice is to proceed *now* with what I have to offer. The work of others summarized here and the original research described are meant to show that, even if we cannot jump from here to there, we *might* be able to make our "here" a bit more compatible with our vision of "there." If we do that long enough and are always mindful of the similarities as well as the differences between the two locales at each successive point in time and space, we may begin to "be there" more and more.

PART TWO

Achievement and Attributions

CHAPTER 4

Attributing, Achieving, and Self-Concepts Across the Life-Span

The study of attributions and attribution-related behavior has certainly been the most prominent, most researched area of personality and social psychology in the 1970s, and it promises to retain a central role in the field in the 1980s as well. Literally hundreds of journal articles with an attribution focus are published each year. A number of recent books (Frieze, Bar-tal, & Carroll, 1979; Jones et al., 1972; Harvey, Ickes, & Kidd, 1976, 1978; Shaver, 1975; Weiner, 1972, 1974) have been wholly devoted to advancing a data base and theoretical concepts in this area. Considerable space has been devoted to the topic in virtually all new editions of texts, and, indeed, Harvey and Smith (1977) wrote an introductory social psychology text in which they discussed all standard social psychological topics in terms of attributions. At the same time, Bernard Weiner (1979) has proposed that attributions may be the basis for a general theory of motivation. Thus, it is an understatement to assert that a knowledge of attribution processes and uses in all age groups, including adults, is a core prerequisite for a personality-social psychology of developing adults in the 1980s.

At least part of the reason for the appeal of attributions and the resultant mass of research and theory in this general area is that attributions are phenomenologically important elements of daily life. That is, people do spend time and effort in trying to reveal information about why things happen the way they do, and they at least sometimes use those ideas and determinations to decide how to approach further similar situations (in the case of self-attributions) and/or how to deal with others as the behaviors of those others are played out and have effects (other-attributions). Beyond the importance of lay use of attributions, it is clear that attribution-making is phenomenologically processual and contextual. That is, attributions—the use of information to decide causality and the subsequent use of those decisions to direct future actions—are part of processes of interacting with other persons and of reconciling one's own needs, perceptions, and actions with experienced outcomes. This was made clear in the one source most likely to be named by social psychologists as the origin of attribution theory (or at least the origin of any considerable amount of interest in attribution processes within established social psychology): Fritz Heider's 1958 book, *The Psychology of Interpersonal Relations*. The book is relentlessly phenomenological, naturalistic, and contextual; the framework for attribution studies is intrinsically relational and dynamic.

Additionally, attribution theory is closely related, conceptually and organizationally, to theoretical conceptions of personality variously labeled as locus of control (Rotter, 1966, 1975), pawn-origin (deCharms, 1968), perception of choice, and feelings of mastery (White, 1959). Those, in turn, are considered by many personality theorists to be central elements in self-conception (White, 1959; M. B. Smith, 1980). Furthermore, self-conception is prominent in discussions of the stages and tasks of adulthood by a wide range of theorists from Erikson (1959) to Lowenthal, Thurnher, and Chiriboga (1975), Levinson (1978) and Neugarten (1977), indicating a link to adult developmental psychology. Quite a bit of data, to be reviewed in Chapter 6, has been collected on responses of adults and older persons to locus of control and related scales, which are presumed to be related both to attributions and to self-conception.

The data, both in regard to adult development and, more generally, in regard to exploring linkages of the above and other intuitively related concepts—self-monitoring, self-awareness—to each other and to attribution patterns and processes have been weak, confusing, sometimes contradictory, and generally rather unsatisfying to workers in this area (see Bradley, 1978; Buss, 1979; Elig & Frieze, 1979; Ickes & Layden, 1978, for reviews of some of the problems). Surely the problems stem in part from tendencies to overextend from rather specific concepts to general applications of scales by persons with different orientations and aims from those original concepts; that is certainly the case with locus of control. However, these issues will not be dealt with in this book except as they relate to adult developmental research on attributions. In fact, clarification of the problems and resolution of at least some of them that has been done thus far has taken place only *after* the narrowly defined, laboratory-based, achronic studies of age-, sex-, and race-biased samples of college students were supplemented by comparisons to other groups and examination of data from successive cohorts of college students. This process has been especially apparent in locus of control research (see Rotter, 1966, 1975; Lao, 1975; Joe, 1971). There is reason to believe more clarity may be gained after age-related biases are eliminated (or comparatively examined) as well.

From the foregoing it is apparent that the application of theory and the direction of research on attributions to adult development is an important component of a social psychology of developing adults. It is also clear that a process-oriented, phenomenological approach—perhaps including components such as we have discussed in detail in Chapter 2 and Chapter 3—should be an essential aspect of attribution research, regardless of age or other characteristics of samples.

Yet, despite the almost incredibly large number of articles and studies produced, the inherent processual and contextual nature of attributions, and the central place of attribution-related concepts in personality and social psychologies, there has been an almost total vacuum in the area of attributions insofar as adult development is concerned. This is true at every level, from descriptive data on attributions of adults and older persons to exploration of the phenomenology of attribution processes in adults (or college students, for that matter!) and to use of attribution theory to gain insight into problems of adults and older adults—work and retirement, marital relations, areas such as those noted in Chapter 1 of this book in more general terms. There has been little coordination of related gerontological and life-span developmental concepts (to be reviewed briefly later in this chapter) with the most predominant general organizing principle of current social psychology. The few exceptions to those generalizations will be noted in this and the next few chapters.

This failing has led to unanswered questions and to problems with attribution work that correspond closely to those already outlined in the early chapters of this book.

Since attribution theories have at least the potential of being general models of social behavior and of motivation, and since they are also related to personality organization and development, it is essential that the generalizability of the models be examined well beyond the college students on whom virtually all the work has been done. It is essential that the phenomena of attributing and the process of change in attributional mode across large segments of the life-span be given high priority, along with more structural analyses of attributional schemata and their application in a particular instance.

Quite early, attribution theorists recognized both of these points. As mentioned several pages ago, Heiders's (1958) approach to attribution processes was explicitly phenomenological and relational. As noted in Chapter 1, the editors of the influential 1972 volume on attributions recognized a danger in their concentration on college student attributors. Heinz Heckhausen (1967), in his major review of achievement orientation, a review closely related to Weiner's achievement attribution work, pointed out the importance of work on adulthood as follows: "The growing research on human life course and especially old age will be faced with a large number of questions (i.e., to mention just one, the achievement-related crisis of the aging person)" (p. 161). He then decried the total lack of research directed that way. The failure of subsequent researchers to heed those words of caution and encouragement to broaden their samples has been clear and its results obvious; attribution theory—especially, perhaps, achievement attribution work—has been the study of the kinds of causes students mention most when asked to explain the results of taking school examinations. Forays beyond those strictures have certainly occurred (for example, Frieze's, 1976, consideration of a social situation, and much of the work reported in the recent, application-oriented volume edited by Frieze, Bar-tal, & Carroll, 1979, as well as some work on adults), but they have been few compared to the continuing emphasis on the limited set of situations and samples brought about by concentrating on captive audiences of students.

GOALS FOR THIS PART

This chapter and the following four are an attempt to provide a compilation of research and theory in attributions that may reasonably be related to adult developmental changes and stability and, conversely, of issues and data in adult development and aging that, whereas usually not explicitly attributional in the same sense as most social psychologists use the term, bear upon unresolved issues and shortcomings in current attributional work. In particular, I will concentrate on one prominent subarea of attributions—achievement attributions. Each of the three chapters following this will include a review of work others have done and detailed exposition of recent and on-going work with which I have been involved. In the course of those reviews and re-ports, a number of major issues will arise and will be considered as they do. In the re-mainder of this chapter I will first briefly review the area of achievement attribution, then discuss what I see as three cross-cutting definitions of "attributions" and corre-sponding methods of approach to studying attributions (and the problems of commu-nication among persons working in the areas, who often do not recognize their differ-ences because of the common attribution terminology and/or do not recognize their similarities because of the different loci and different methods each entails). Finally, I will describe on a general level the sample of adults I have used in several studies to explore each aspect of achievement attributions across adult age groups.

Before beginning this section I should reiterate what I pointed out in the Introduc-tion to Parts 2 and 3 and in various points in Part 1 of the book. A reader particularly oriented to life-span methodology and to the shortcomings of research using straight-forward, linear designs with cross-sectional time of measurement may find much to be disappointed with in the research to be considered. Indeed, the studies—my own and others—are all cross-sectional and based in relatively superficial measures of "the attribution process." The samples, although broadened on the dimension of age, are certainly not optimal for precise analysis of age changes versus cohort differ-ences, and the sampling techniques are not sensitive to many of the developmental research issues discussed, for example, in Chapter 3 of this book and in many other reference works (e.g., Baltes, Reese, & Nesselroade, 1977; Riegel, 1978).

To those readers I give my apology, not to ask forgiveness, but rather to give my defense. I reiterate what I said in the introduction to the empirical section of the book. I *agree* with the critics that the methods and the data to be reported in the next several chapters are far less than what the social psychological investigation of adult devel-opment requires and aspires to. Insofar as that is the case, the data will necessarily be limited and limiting. At the same time, the methods are certainly not worse than those consistently used within a restricted age range. The value, low though it is in relation to a mature social psychology of adult development (is maturity a possibility for such an approach to social psychology?) is high in relation to more traditional social psy-chological investigations that have ignored both the concern with change *and* the more limited concern with age I have portrayed in Part 1 of the book. Thus, at the first level, I continue to see value in such research even as I see its apparent and, I agree, serious problems.

At the second level, I hope that even those critics who most adamantly insist that nothing of value can be found doing what I am trying to do, that trying to get light into a dark room by opening a door into another only slightly less dark room is an exercise not worth the effort of finding and opening the door, will be patient. Perhaps I can persuade them the studies discussed in the next two chapters have some value beyond what was available before; even if not, I certainly hope that I can show them, in Chapter 7, that the kinds of simple, age differences studies discussed initially both can lead and are leading to an attribution model and research technique that is more directly phenomenological, change-oriented, and developmental.

BASIC CONCEPTS IN ACHIEVEMENT ATTRIBUTION THEORY

Within the broad range of attributions, that subarea which concerns attributions about success and failure outcomes—that is, achievement attributions—is one particularly relevant to many aspects of adult social psychology. It is centrally involved in the relationship of attribution decisions to self-conception and, particularly, to ongoing feelings of mastery and control (or, alternatively, lack of mastery and feelings of being prey to external determinants of the direction of one's specific actions and one's life course). Thus, we may turn to theoretical statements and research related to achievement attributions for further analysis relevant to the social psychology of adults and the social psychology of development.

Bernard Weiner and his associates (for example, Weiner, 1972, 1974, 1979; Frieze & Weiner, 1971; Elig & Frieze, 1975, 1979; Frieze, 1976) and Heinz Heckhausen and his associates (Heckhausen, 1967; Heckhausen & Weiner, 1974; Meyer, 1970) have been major figures in the development of the area of achievement attributions. The basic model used by Weiner will be used as a point of departure for this discussion and for the empirical research to be described, although, as will be obvious in the later portions of this chapter and in the other chapters of this part, the range of attributional elements will be expanded and modified in light of the research. Although this work may be familiar to many readers, it is an important base for further discussion and, therefore, I will briefly review Weiner's basic model and some related recent criticisms and subsequent modifications.

Weiner bases his model in Heider's (1958) discussion of "can" and "try." He places four factors with which Heider explicitly or implicitly dealt in his discussion—ability, effort, task difficulty, and luck—into a 2 × 2 matrix.[1] Two of these factors are stable and two are unstable; one of the stable and one of the unstable factors are personal, and one of each is extrapersonal. The matrix thus has a locus of causality (internal-external) dimension and a stability (stable-unstable) dimension. The stable personal factor, roughly identified with ability, is similar to skill or to Heider's personal part of "can." Effort, generally associated with motivation and involvement, is categorized in earlier presentations as solely an unstable personal factor, although Weiner has since realized and noted (e.g., 1978) that effort attributions to a stable personality factor (lazy, industrious) are often made and are more properly placed with ability in those cases. In any case, certain sorts of personal attributions are more or less stable, others more or less unstable (the "more or less" nature will be discussed later).

---

[1]Rosenbaum (1972), one of Weiner's students, has pointed out the value of including a third dimension—intentionality—and others have discussed additional factors (such as globality-specificity or controllability from the point of view of the person doing the causing—see Abramson, Seligman, and Teasdale, 1978; Wortman, 1976). Although these points are well taken, Weiner (1979) and I both feel that the fourfold classification is still conceptually and practically worthy of future investigation, with its limitations noted. At least one study, by Wiley (1979), leads to the conclusion that, in any case, personal control and locus are highly correlated and, thus, either is quite sufficient for most purposes.

Table 4.1.   Modified Version of Weiner's Model of Achievement Attributions[a]

| Stability | Locus of causality | |
	Personal (internal)	Extrapersonal (external)
Stable	Ability	Task Difficulty
	Also skill, personality, traits, long-term effort, age, strength	Also social structures, role requirements, influence of stable others
Unstable	Effort (short term)	Luck
	Also mood, attentiveness, interest	also others' help or hurt, ambience of environment, short-term cooperation or competition

[a]Also interaction terms—Person X Task, Person X Others, which are usually unstable.

The other two factors are outside the person's direct involvement. "Task difficulty" is the label given to stable characteristics of the situation and/or the task, whereas "luck" is an unstable external factor, the fluctuation of correspondence between personal and extrapersonal, transitory contextual influences. Thus, Weiner arrives at a matrix that looks like that presented in Table 4.1. As I have completed the figure, the matrix is not limited to the four broad attribution types Weiner has used as important in each cell—ability, task difficulty, luck, and effort. Rather, those are archetypes of a particular combination of locus of causality and stability. The expansion of the list, however, is not without its difficulties, as will be discussed.

Prior to that discussion it should be added that Weiner and his associates feel that the kind of attribution made, on the one hand, is dependent on a personality type and, on the other hand, results in differential reactions to success and failure. In particular, Weiner has identified two categories of persons. One type of person, labeled success-oriented, tends to ascribe success outcomes to personal stable factors and failure outcomes to a mixture of personal and external causes. The other category of person is the failure-oriented one, who sees failure as resulting from personal causes, mostly stable ones, and success as resulting from external factors. The personality typology will be discussed further in a later section of this chapter and again in Chapter 6.

Furthermore, Weiner and his colleagues (and other researchers) hypothesize that the kind of attribution that is made will affect both one's expectations for future success and one's feelings about the outcome. In particular, expectations are linked to stability dimension determinations, whereas affect is linked to the locus dimension. Details concerning these formulations and data bearing upon their value are contained in several other sources, such as Weiner (1972, 1974, 1978); Ickes and Layden (1978); Abramson et al. (1978), and Frieze (1976), and will not be further reviewed here. The data do, however, present a mixed picture, particularly in regard to the linkages between personality types and actual specific attribution decisions, affects, and expectations. That mixed picture illustrates some of the need for caution in use of the model.

PROBLEMS WITH THE ACHIEVEMENT ATTRIBUTION MODEL

Before I discuss the use to which the model will be put, it is important to detail and examine some of the other problems that have been noted in regard to the model I propose to use as the base for further exploration of the attributions of adults and older persons. The model is, in fact, open to criticism on several levels, not the least of which is that it is not amenable to developmental concerns. What then are the problems? Again, they have been reviewed in detail in other sources (e.g., Buss, 1979; Ickes & Layden, 1978; Elig & Frieze, 1979) and what follows is a noninclusive list.

Conceptually, the two dimensions do not appear to be adequate for all purposes. As was noted in footnote 1 above, various additions to the dimensions have been proposed. Another, more important and striking incompleteness in this and other attribution models, superficially surprising in light of the status accorded to attribution theory in social psychology, but really intrinsic to the mechanistic aspects of the models and their development within the kind of personality and social psychology prevailing in the mainstream of the discipline, is the lack of explication of external factors into those that are social and those that are not. Surely it makes a difference whether the external cause of a failure is seen to be the action of another, the physical environment, or the nature of the task. All these kinds of factors can be operative, yet one usually is predominant both in "reality" and in the subjective estimates of the observer. This differentiation is likely to be at least as crucial as whether the cause is seen to be internal or external. The distinction has been made in some of the more detailed taxonomies already cited (e.g., Elig & Frieze, 1975; Meyer, 1980), but it has not been made a major concern of research or a central element in the theoretical framework. It is tempting to place part of the reason for this in the steadfast reliance of all but a few researchers on academic success and failure and of virtually all on college students in academic settings as the sole source of responses. At the same time, the problem is present even in those restricted situations and samples, as indicated in frequency data by Meyer (1980) and Falbo and Beck (1979).

Furthermore, the attributional model is severely restricted in that each dimension is seen as a dichotomy, although it is fairly obvious that each dichotomy is a false one. Seldom are the causes of success or failure purely personal or purely nonpersonal; similarly, causes are seldom clearly stable or unstable. Rather, whatever value each dimension has is primarily as a continuum. Sometimes attributions closer to one or the other end of that continuum predominate and, indeed, the manner of elicitation of responses (having people allocate causality among factors or having them rate the importance of each one and then comparing the strength indicated in the ratings) is more appropriate to a less dichotomized interpretation of the dimensions. However, the fact remains that the model does not do a good job of allowing for discrimination among degrees of "personalness" or "stability"; it does not recognize the inherent "more or less" nature of each of the categories.

Some theorists have moved away from the simplistic dichotomous nature of the categories, particularly in the direction of including interaction factors (e.g., ability × task difficulty, ability × other's help or hurt). Although this approach may be advantageous, it is hardly a solution to the problem. This treatment of the dynamic, open nature of the factors in actual situations is open to criticism raised in Chapter 1 in regard to interaction analysis that fails to place relationship and interaction at the center of a dynamic model. That is, interaction terms become merely another few categories equally as nondynamic and nonrelational as the original "main effects" categories.

The reductionist abstraction from the continuous nature of both dimensions is particularly apparent and problematic when explaining development, and age-related differences become important. The potential for expansion of general attribution theory that may occur on the basis of an adult developmental orientation is illustrative of the value of adult developmental social psychology to personality and social psychological theory, a point to be discussed in detail in later chapters. In any case, the gross dichotomization of potential causal explanations into stable and unstable factors ignores the progressive, more-or-less character of virtually all phenomenologically valid "attributions."

This leads to a major *methodological* concern, the relative value of using a closed, inherently artificially limited list of potential responses, for which subjects are to assign ratings, or to use an open-ended response format. The tension is between a set of causes chosen so as to meet the needs of the researcher, but not necessarily reflective of reality, versus an array of possibilities which are unmanageable and imprecise. The debate concerning this issue continues, as does the previously noted one concerning the number and type of dimensions, to which it is related. Frieze (1976) and others in the Weiner tradition have found what they feel is clear verification of the importance of the closed set of factors they have often used at the same time as they encourage future researchers to use an open-ended format when feasible and especially when new situations and/or new types of respondents are matters of interest (Elig & Frieze, 1975; Weiner, 1979). In this way, they hope to insure that all valid, regularly used attributions are included and accounted for. At the same time, they clearly feel that the open-ended responses fit rather well into the original dimensions and that, in fact, the original set of factors, plus a few more interactive ones, are those which are predominant in people's minds. Others, however, do not see consonance in the sorts of causes that people give in free situations and those supplied to individuals when they are asked to participate in attribution studies. Eskilson and Wiley (1979), and Falbo and Beck (1979), for example, have done various classifications of attributions they elicited in an open-response format and concluded that the factors do not fit well into Weiner's classification scheme.

That argument may continue, and a few observations should be made concerning its relation to matters more closely at hand. First of all, the critics appear to feel uncomfortable both with the idea of having a restricted set of causes available *and* the external validity of the causes used in closed-ended studies. Criticism in the first regard is certainly well taken, as Weiner (1979; Weiner, Russell, & Lerman, 1978), Frieze (1976; Elig & Frieze, 1975, 1979) have been free in admitting. Constant verification of the validity of the set of attributions that most clearly fit the dimensional matrix can only be done by including a wider range of possibilities with the traditional ones and seeing which are used most regularly. The preferable method is to leave the choice open; alternatively, various researchers, such as Locke-Connor and

Walsh (1980) and Meyer (1980), have pretested a broad list and then used the most often mentioned from that in a subsequent closed-format study.

The other half of the criticism, however—that the factors Weiner pinpointed in his original classification into ability, effort, task difficulty, and luck are faulty—must be examined more closely. The question is not, as Falbo and Beck (1979) and others would have it, a simple one of whether or not persons spontaneously use the specific words. Rather, it should be a question of whether those words convey the ideas people most often use. That is, each of Weiner's words is really a name for a category or family of causes. Each is a shorthand for a set of conceptually related factors. "Ability" stands in for "ability-type factors," that is, ones which have a set of characteristics most people include in the meaning of that single word, "ability." That is, most people would accord to ability characteristics of being personal and relatively stable; they would also accord those characteristics to other causal words, such as skill, personality traits, and physical limitations. The same sort of analysis can be done for each "type." "Luck," for example, has the characteristics in people's minds that it is transitory and that it is seen as an external event that happened to come along at that time.

In other words, what should be focused on is whether the causal words people use regularly and consistently fall into natural groupings. If they do, then the characteristics of those natural groupings should form the basis for the dimensions and for characterizing additional causes. This, in fact, is what Weiner did on what was admittedly rather subjective grounds. He decided that there were four major types of attribution statements people made; he further decided that one was best characterized by the commonly used word "ability," another by the common word "luck," and so on. Whether or not he correctly identified the best particular word is certainly a valid consideration, especially when only those words were supplied to subjects without a full statement of their archetypal nature, but it is not the basis upon which to decide whether or not his dimensional matrix is correct. Unfortunately, some researchers have taken what they see as lack of adequacy on the first ground to be a major failing on the second.

The confusion on this point, however, does indicate a major problem, one that has the potential of being answered only by extensive use of a broad range, not only of causes available, but of situations and respondents, as is being proposed here. That is the real fact that any particular word is not really easily classified; that different people in the same situation, and the same person in different situations, invest a particular word with different meanings, different relations to the outcome and, therefore, different implications for future expectations and affect. That fact leads, I believe, to much of the confusion in the discussion as to whether Weiner's choice of words was correct and whether his choice of dimensions is correct. It also produces real difficulties for those who would like to develop a taxonomy of causal words (e.g., Cooper & Burger, 1980; Meyer, 1980). Those efforts are important, yet they appear doomed to failure or to constant idiosyncracy of particular groups of subjects, situations for which attributions are made, and so on. It is simply the case that almost all of the causes given in free formats, and all the causes used in closed-ended measures as though they are clearly this or that sort of cause, can easily fit into at least several of the major dimensions. Thus, severe questions concerning where to place a cause do and will continue to arise.

Several specific cases clearly make this point. It is well known that Weiner originally conceived of effort as the archetype of unstable personal factors, only to find out that many of his subjects saw effort as a stable personality trait—that is, "this is the sort of person who did his typical good job because of his typical expenditure of a burst of energy at the right time." In subsequent research, effort was specifically defined to be short-term, whereas another term (long-term effort, tenacity) was supplied to allow persons to indicate that other sort of effort.

Another of Weiner's original archetypal factors can even cross both dimensions at the same time. "Luck" is not always believed to be an external, unstable force operating in a highly transitory, random way. Rather, it is often seen as a stable personal trait—being lucky is a state of the actor, often representative of a trait characteristic. Saying that "he was lucky" to succeed, then, can mean either that this was a highly unusual, externally caused outcome *or* that it was a verification of the belief that "he" is a characteristically lucky person.

The lack of clarity becomes even more apparent when a wide range of causes, approximating the number available to users of the English language, is available as is the case in real situations. Causes such as "not having the proper tools," "prejudice" on the part of an employer, "interest," and "luck" mean too many things to too many people to be placed into a particular category by coders of the statements with a high degree of confidence. Indeed, it is quite possible that they cannot be placed into a category with any degree of confidence by the attributor, although that disarming possibility has not been examined thus far.

A particularly striking case in point will be important in the next several chapters. The cause "age," quite regularly given as an explanation of the outcome, particularly failure, of an older person, can be conceived of in a number of ways and, in fact, there is disagreement among social psychologists as to where it should be placed. Susan Green (1979) makes a case for placing it into the category of an external, uncontrollable factor; that is, she sees "age" to mean a host of ailments and limitations thrust on the person from the outside and/or as a stereotype indicating prejudice on the part of the observer. In either case, she sees age as uncontrollable and external (although to see one's body as external, as she appears to do in regard to the first interpretation, seems strange). Banziger and Drevenstedt (1980; Banziger, 1979) on the other hand, place age into the unstable personal category, with the idea that the individual is changing and whatever is changing about her or his body and its abilities is, therefore, unstable. Elig and Frieze (1975), although they do not discuss age as such, see physical limitations as fitting into a personal stable place in the schema. As will be seen in the discussion of my data, I have followed that idea and have scored age as both personal and stable, recognizing that "stable" is a relative matter, but that the age-related impact on ability is certainly considerably more stable than it is unstable; it is likely to endure for the rest of a person's life. Green (1981) provides a further review of this critical issue.

What is the upshot of this sort of difficulty? Does it mean the abandonment of the dimensional classification? I think it does not. That is, even though any particular attribution can fit into almost any pigeonhole, depending on what was in the attri-butor's mind at that time—what he or she *meant* by the use of that word—I believe there is considerable evidence that people do interpret causes as personally based or not and as likely to endure over long periods of time or not and that those sorts of de-terminations influence how they will act and how they will understand the meaning of that outcome.

The lack of clarity in the research attempting to make linkages between attributions and affect or between attributions in the past and expectations may be the inevitable result of the constructed nature of a cause (or reason; the debate about the similarity or difference in those two words will be discussed in Chapter 7). People use causes on an ad hoc basis, and a major part of the challenge to attribution theorists must be to determine the degree to which the situation, the "characteristic center of gravity" of the person doing the attributing, the characteristics of the actor, and the outcome it-self come to determine or codetermine the meaning of this or that causal word as it is used at that time. Do people consistently use a particular word, imbuing it with dif-ferent meanings at different times and situations (e.g., consistently referring to effort or lack of effort as a major cause, but using it as a stable factor for some persons and an unstable one for others; as stable for success, but unstable for failure, etc.), or do people consistently use (that is, mean) a particular sort of attribution (e.g., personal stable) even though they may sometimes call it ability, other times skill, other times personality, other times effort, or other times luck, depending on the other aspects of the attribution event? These sorts of questions are challenges unanswered by attribu-tion theorists who have acted as though a particular word has a particular meaning—have fallen into a fallacy of stability in vocabulary—and can be easily and unequivocally classified into one or another type.

The Static Nature of the Attribution Model

The difficulty of assigning a causal word to a category, with which we have dealt in the last few pages and will deal in detail in the Appendix, is overshadowed by an even more severe problem with the attribution model typically used in this body of theory and research; the model is entirely a static, nondynamic, and therefore, ultimately limited model. It is not even in principle reflective of reality, of life as it is lived and attributions as they are made. The taxonomic approach, important though it is within the kind of modeling of attributions that has taken place, nonetheless shares the static nature of the model with the cruder, earlier forms of the model. Therefore, they too are limited in their usefulness to guide research and to lead to understanding. It is not only the case that the "same" attribution may mean different things in different situa-tions or to different people, it is likely to mean different things to the *same* person at different times and, indeed, could mean something different to the actor/attributor in just a moment between the time he makes it as an observer and uses it to internalize that judgment about himself. Causal statements are not likely to take up residence in one's head as a set of schemata ready to be brought into action when an outcome is noted; rather, they are likely to reside in the situation (that is the process of combining all elements available into an attribution) itself, as part and parcel of the awareness of the outcome. The great value of the attribution model (Kelley's, 1972; and Shaver's, 1975, general models as well as the more specific achievement model by Weiner, 1972, 1974, 1979) and the body of supportive evidence in a host of studies must be balanced by these underemphasized concerns.

A TRICHOTOMY OF ATTRIBUTION STUDIES

To be sure, the kinds of objections outlined above are major, and it is clear that analysis of the social psychology of developing adults using an attributional model will require that the model be modified and expanded. At the same time, though, the area of attributions is so central to current social psychology, and the task or act of making attributions about causality and using those attributions to decide about further actions in the social sphere is a common and important activity in daily life, that we can hardly ignore it in a social psychology of the 1980's. To form an adult-oriented, development-sensitive social psychology without it would reveal a significant gap in that social psychology; to include it, however, is a challenge to go beyond the sort of attribution theory developed up to this point.

In any case, as we have been required to do before, we must for the moment place aside some of these concerns and use the current model for what it may reveal in a preliminary way about adult social and personality development within the lifelong contexts of intertwined change and stability. At many points, the model as it is now developed will be lacking in that regard, and the issues discussed above—and others equal or larger in importance—will arise again as we proceed through the discussion of research results and as we consider the implications of the data which have been collected using the static, limited tools available at present. By the end of this part of the book, hopefully, the reader will see that what has been done using the static model may be useful in some regards in and of itself and, further, that the act of using the static model to try to deal with the dynamics of actual attributing at various vantage points in the life-span may lead to a more dynamic model of attributing. That model may then fruitfully be used to examine the meaning and processing of attributions—and the possibly general mechanisms underlying them—at all points of the life-span.

Thus far we have considered the characteristics and some of the problems with the model of attributions about achievement proposed by Weiner (1972) and explicated in hundreds of subsequent studies. One issue we have not discussed is the rather basic definitional ambiguity of the area itself; there are in fact at least three different sorts of research going under the designation of attribution research. Although some aspects are shared, to be sure, the types have developed rather independently of each other, and most practitioners of one type or another have self-designated their type as "true" attribution research. Interestingly, as with personality and social psychology of aging in general, the social psychology of aging has included quite a few studies identified as attributional which have, almost invariably, used a different, minority, definition of attributions from that for which the term has come to be used in mainstream social psychology.

Several theoretically oriented attributionists have discussed the different types of attribution research (see, for example, Shaver, 1975, Buss, 1979, and a text by Worchel & Cooper, 1979), but I am not aware of *researchers* who emphasized placing combinations of these perspectives into a single program, as will be presented in the next three chapters (although, as I will discuss later, the research on actor-observer differences is in some ways a bridge between two of the three). The three areas that I will consider, simply labeling them Type I, Type II, and Type III attributional studies, are really a pair of types differing primarily on direction of concern and a third type that is distinctive from both of the first two types in that it has a different methodological thrust.

Type I—Attributions as Perceptions of an Actor

One major area of attributional analysis is clearly within the more traditional area of social perception. That is, attribution schemata are interpreted as internal representations of generalized expectations for others (and for oneself *as though* one *were* an other, as Bem's, 1972, earlier analysis makes clear). They are concerned with relatively static objects—attributes. In this sense, attributions are closely related to stereotypes and, when attributions *about* various differentiable groups of persons are concerned, the attributions about—the assignment of *attributes to*—are, in fact, likely to be the stereotypic depiction one has of the group within which the particular person is placed. The typical, and appropriate, approach to the sort of attribution research labeled Type I is the provision to the subject of a performance by a particular actor resulting in a particular outcome. Although hypothetical situations have been the norm, for ease of presentation and experimental control (for the moment we leave aside the questions raised in the first chapters of this book concerning the value, and reality, of experimental "control"), having people make attributions about real situations would be more revealing. Possibly archival analyses of reports of successes and failures—of sports teams, of national and international figures, of politicians, and so on—could be used for this purpose. Indeed, several such analyses have been reported; Lau and Russell (1980) analyzed descriptions by sports managers and others for wins and losses, and Carroll (1979) analyzed reports by parole boards of their decisions, which could be seen as estimations of the success or failure of the prisoner to be paroled.

Some research in the Type I mold has concerned attributions about old versus young targets, and it will be discussed further in Chapter 5, along with data from my research program that bears upon this sort of attributional analysis of adult age differences. Banziger (1979) discusses other possibilities in this type of research. Social gerontological studies of attributes and stereotyping are also relevant and will be considered in Chapter 5.

Type II—Attributions as Effective in One's Own Achievement Behavior

The second major type of attribution study is best typified by Bernard Weiner's use of the attribution model to understand achievement motivation and achievement-related behavior. In more general terms, this kind of attribution research is the study of the mechanisms of processing information about performance so that it can be used to make decisions and determine actions in particular circumstances. It is an examination of the use of attributions to give formal meaning to events that can be classified as success and failure and that are personal from the point of view of the attributor. At the same time, it treats attributions more as a process—attributing them as a product, an attribute, as is more common in Type I analyses.

Most of the achievement research has had this goal: to understand the matrix of attributions contained in a person's head and used by that person to understand personally experienced outcomes of his or her own performance. As such, the Type II analysis is closely related to more explicitly personality psychology concerns with achievement motivation and achievement orientation. It is at this point that it is concerned with individual differences, both as measured by achievement motivation and other personality scales and by factors such as race and sex. This interest is quite unique in the broader area of attributions.

Curiously enough, though, Type II concerns with personal attributions have often been researched through the entry point of methods appropriate to Type I, but not to Type II attributions. That is, subjects have been given hypothetical situations, usually of a hypothetical actor similar to oneself or without any limiting characteristics, and have been asked to make attributions for that performance. The data have then been interpreted to represent attributional inclinations which have behavioral effects in terms of one's own approach to achievement situations, performance, and so on. The hypothetical measures are presumed to be projective tools to get at general schemata. Obviously, the underlying assumption is that one's manner of attributing is a general personality characteristic that reveals itself whenever attributions are made. There seems to be some evidence for this, at least when the judged person is similar to and/or liked by the attributor (Snyder, 1976). This presumption is not necessarily a good one, however, given actor/observer differences as noted below, and for other reasons, chiefly the static nature of the proposed schemata.

Additionally, germane to the research to be reported in Chapter 8, there has been virtually no research of this sort concerned with Type II attribution patterns of adults, although there have been a limited number of achievement motivation studies across age groups, and studies of related measures such as locus of control. Those related studies will be discussed in Chapter 6, along with original data examining attributions across age groups using a Type II approach.

Linking Other- and Self-Perception: Actor/Observer Differences

One seeming link between Type I and Type II attribution studies is the area of actor/observer differences, an area which I will not review in any detail for several reasons. First of all, it has been the topic of several detailed presentations (e.g., Jones & Nisbett, 1971; Miller & Ross, 1975; Monson & Snyder, 1977; Snyder, Stephan, & Rosenfield, 1978); secondly, it is somewhat beside the point from our interests.

Most often, the typical actor-observer differences—greater linkage of personal attributions and success outcomes by actors rather than by observers—has been laid to one of two root causes. The first of these, an *information processing* difference (for example, the actor having greater knowledge of his or her internal motivations and greater information about his or her past experience and, therefore, being able to have better information on consistency and distinctiveness) (e.g., Jones & Nisbett, 1971, Miller & Ross, 1975) would lead to a belief that actors would be more likely to attribute failures as well as successes to themselves. The second explanation, a *motivational* one (e.g., Snyder et al., 1978) is based on the belief that persons, in various ways, try to maintain self-esteem and feelings of control over their outcomes. One good way to do that is to take credit for success and at the same time to place blame for one's own failure on something or someone external to oneself. The data in regard to the last point, unfortunately, have not been clear enough to make a definite decision (of course, the data are likely to never be clear enough, since it is likely that both of those sorts of factors, perhaps plus others, as will be noted shortly, are differentially available and differentially effective in particular sorts of situations).

In any case, consideration of Type I and Type II attributions together highlight this set of issues. Most of the research on self-esteem maintenance by attributional biases, quite naturally, has been of a Type II nature, that is concerned with self-attributions. It is here that individuals are expected to work to protect their own interests, and thus it is here that motivations are expected to play major parts. In that sense, some of the motivational explanations given for the kinds of differences noted make little sense when studied as "observer" differences. Type II attributions are, theoretically, used by people to direct their own actions and to understand the outcomes of those actions. Type I attributions, on the other hand, are devices to bring order to the world around oneself, to understand the actions of others, and to use that understanding in further dealings with them. Put in that way they may seem quite different, but are they?

If there is an elemental difference in attributions—if the bases for the differences in actor and observer roles are caused by different motivations—is it logical to continue to talk about a person's *mode* of attributing? Doesn't that person have several, independent modes, at the minimum one for self and one for others?

One point in this issue that has seldom been explored is the kind of self-relevant motivations that may come into play in *both* Type I and Type II attributions. That is, Type I attributions could also be motivated by self-esteem and defensive needs. As we will see in the data to be presented later, one regularly makes attributions about others that bring oneself in as a controlling agent in others' successes and failures. That is, they feel that they *share* in the outcome with the other. This obvious point has been missed by researchers and theorists in both traditions, for reasons discussed earlier. Attribution research has seldom been socially oriented, and little has been done recognizing the social nature of both one's own and others' outcomes, a point already discussed in regard to the kinds of attribution possibilities which are made available in closed-ended research. Attribution researchers have seldom used real situations—and often used unreal hypothetical ones—in both Type I and Type II research, and this artificiality has made it unlikely that the interlocking aspects of the two types would be revealed in the data, including that on actor/observer differences. Attribution researchers have rarely placed both types of attributions side by side within a design, but instead have relied on group differences brought about by differential instructions.

One area of research has considered in some detail the self-relevance of attributions about the performance of others—the attributions made by teachers about their students (see, for example, Cooper & Burger, 1980). These researchers have found that teachers did involve themselves—their motivations and skills—in many of their explanations of pupil behavior. And, in fact, they made attributions for those others almost as though they themselves were the actors. Persons who participated in my studies, to be reported below, regularly reported events such as a child doing well and being happy, a friend losing her shyness, and so on, as their own success (and, I might add, corresponding problems as a failure). These sorts of mixed cases, blurring the lines between personal and nonpersonal situations, are important ones, but they are consistently overlooked by attribution researchers, including those who are ostensibly centrally concerned with actor-observer differences. They are overlooked in the dangerous act of setting up a dichotomy between Type I and Type II, by considering one to be "social perception" and the other to be personal motivation.

One other aspect that is missing in both the main body of research and in the studies concerned with teacher evaluations is the importance in self-attribution of the placement of oneself in a particular subgroup to which certain sorts of attributions are regularly made by "passive" observers. That is, in our case, it is likely that persons of various ages use the stereotypes they—and others—have about their kind of person, their generation, as a touchstone from which to proceed in making personal attributions. Again, the boundary between personal and nonpersonal, between Type I and Type II, becomes blurred, as blurred as the boundary between personal and external causes themselves. Rather, the embeddedness of *all* attributions has often been ignored—in attitudes and personality as well as in information processing principles and motivational needs, in specifics about the situation and specifics about the actors, in definitions about every component of the process (What is success? What is failure? How is ability a part of the person? How does ability differ from effort or mood or adequacy of direction given to oneself by others? How independent and self-reliant are actors? How independent and reliant should they be?). The list can go on. These are the sorts of questions that are at the core of the act of deciding why something happened the way it did, and these are the sorts of questions that have been all but ignored and avoided in Type I and Type II attribution studies and in the actor-observer studies that held promise of bridging some of the gaps.

Type I and Type II attributions, it seems, are both more similar and more different from each other than they have appeared to be. Indeed, the search for a stable set of characteristics of each, differing from a stable set of characteristics of the other, is doomed to failure. Every personal attribution is based in and made in relation to how the actor would have analyzed the outcome if it had happened to someone else. Conversely, every attribution about others is rooted in and made in relation to the kind of attribution conclusions the observer would have made if he or she had been in the other person's shoes. Both "personal" and "other" attributions are made with considerable amounts of motivations and needs—of the attributor and what is presumed to be in the mind of the actor, if that is not the same—guiding the information processing (that may itself be nonmotivationally biased, as all perception and cognition is, since the mechanisms are limited and limiting). To avoid some of the baggage attached to the terms "actor" and "observer" I will use the terms personal and nonpersonal, or self-relevant and other-attributions, throughout the remainder of this section of the book. At the same time, I will attempt to bring some light to bear on many of the issues raised and, in a preliminary way, examine the questions asked above.

Is there guidance for looking at the sorts of questions raised? Certainly, there is not a great deal of guidance in the standard Type I and Type II attribution literature. Rather, I will gather Type I and Type II data across age groups to use it to highlight some of the inadequacies built into those data, as well as to add the increment of knowledge they may contain. There is, however, an area of attribution study, much less recognized and much less prominent than the types mentioned above, one that *is* oriented toward answering the kinds of questions I have raised. Although the label of Type III attribution study for this approach to the question may be somewhat misleading, since it does not fit into a simple trichonomous classification with the others, I will refer to it that way as a shorthand to distinguish it from the two types already discussed. I will briefly describe the approach here and will make more use of it in Chapter 7.

Type III—Attributions as Socialized Meanings for Events

Although actor-observer differences research and, to some degree, Type II research itself, raise some questions about the social meaning of outcomes and action, those explorations have generally avoided detailed consideration of meaning in favor of precise operationalization and quantification. Consideration of the vocabulary of attributions has been left to more philosophically oriented psychologists, some of whom have taken up Heider's (1958) original phenomenological concerns through analysis of attributional language, using the philosopher's tools of ordinary language analysis and the ethogenic approach promulgated by Harre and Secord (1973; Harre, 1977a, 1979) and others. Prominent in this group have been Harre and Secord themselves and Allan Buss (1978, 1979b). Their discussions have centered around types of causes, the differences between causes and reasons, and other conceptual topics. This has been an important counterbalance to the rather externalized, bloodless attribution research we have thus far discussed.

At the same time, these analyses, it seems to me, have carried with them their own set of flaws. Because the basis of these analyses have been in philosophy, the investigations have often been limited to what is sometimes sneeringly referred to as "armchair theorizing." Although I oppose the sneer in that reference, that is, I disagree with the obvious negative tone of the empiricists' references to the application of thought and of philosophical-linguistic analysis to the issues at hand, I find it disarming that the core of the ethogenic method—if you want to know what people think, why not ask them?—has often been bypassed in favor of asking no one but oneself. Powerful analyses of the nature of attributional cognition could indeed be performed by detailed interviewing—questioning—of a wide range of persons. Important insights into the everyday use of language could also be gained by systematic mining of the rich veins of archival data—the explanations of important successes and failures given in the media, for example. Above all, an emphasis on attributional meaning related closely to the kind of research and the kind of orientation discussed in Chapters 2 and 3 would be very much in keeping with an adult-oriented, process-oriented social psychology.

Yet, as I mentioned, most of this work has been *ex mente* rather than a qualitative, meaningful analysis of systematically gathered natural language. It has not considered either individual differences in use of attribution language or the lack of precision in normal usage. One example may illustrate the difficulty I see with this. One prominent debate in this group of attributional analyses has revolved around the differences between causes and reasons; for example, Buss (1979) feels that lack of recognition of those crucial differences in basic attribution research is a major factor limiting the value of that basic research. However, these critics have not tried to ascertain whether, in fact, persons normally make the sorts of distinctions the philosophers and linguists feel they should make. Data, to be considered in Chapter 7, indicate that in reality people do *not* make the kinds of classifications the philosophers feel they should. In fact, the information presented in that chapter is some of the first data on relatively broad definitions of attributional terms and on the development of an achievement attribution dictionary in any group, including college students.

In any case, the third sort of attribution work, a meaning analysis of attributions, is an essential element in anything that could be called a complete model of attribution and the use of causal information and decisions. At the same time, a meaning analysis that does not take into account the usage people actually make of attributional language misses the mark, even as it in itself provides a counterbalance to the relatively naive empiricism of the vast majority of attribution studies. In my analysis of the earlier elements of my research program I will concentrate primarily on standard Type I and Type II attribution data and analysis, and as we proceed through these materials the cautions discussed throughout this rather lengthy section must be kept in mind without, I trust, invalidating the work and its usefulness. In later analysis, in Chapter 7, I will develop an analysis of meaning that I hope will fulfill some of the strengths of the Type III work just outlined while giving it an empirical, but not empiricist, flavor that it has lacked and relating it to individual and group, especially age group, differences. In the end I hope that we will arrive at the foundation for a body of knowledge about attributions that contains elements of all three types and that recasts the conceptions of all those types into a more developmental, relational, dynamic, and realistic model of attributing.

ACHIEVEMENT ATTRIBUTIONS: BRIEF OVERVIEW OF RESEARCH

Before proceeding to direct consideration of adulthood and aging in attributional terms I want to spend a few pages giving a groundwork in general achievement attribution findings.

Heinz Heckhausen (1967) spoke of each person having a ''characteristic center of gravity'' in his or her process of abstracting attributions from ongoing situations and events. A number of studies—all sharing at least some of the problems and inconclusiveness just discussed—have found relationships of a characteristic placement of causes for success and failure—of attributional schemata—to other cognitions, affect, and behavior. It appears that some persons, sometimes labeled success-oriented because of the presumed tendency they have to link success to personal stable causes, tend to be positively oriented toward achievement-related tasks and settings; they are likely to approach such tasks, especially those of intermediate difficulty, and to continue at the task in the face of both success and failure. Others, termed failure-oriented because of their presumed bonding of failure to personal ability, avoid achievement-related settings and are negative in affect toward them; they may be more likely to try tasks which are very hard or very easy (although Weiner, 1979, notes that this tendency may be overestimated in some studies), spend as short a time as possible on the task, and are neither encouraged by success to continue nor spurred by failure to persevere.

The corpus of data collected to test these hypotheses has been far from unequivocally supportive of the theoretical specifications, but a fair amount of those data provide at least partial support. The interested but less informed reader should consult several sources, such as Atkinson (1964), Atkinson and Feather (1966), Mehrabian and Bank (1975), and Weiner (1974, 1978) for detailed presentations of the data for these generalizations as well as discussions of inconsistencies.

Weiner and his colleagues have interpreted these data in attribution terms, especially in relation to the four factors and two dimensions already discussed. They emphasize the hypothesis that affect is dependent on the locus of causality dimension (see also Klein, Fencil-Morse, & Seligman, 1976; Abramson et al., 1978; and others who have found support for this within the learned helplessness paradigm), whereas expectation of outcome is more closely related to beliefs about the stability dimension. Both failure-oriented and success-oriented subjects sometimes make objectively unlikely attributions, of course, based on the characteristic center of gravity noted by Heckhausen. Failure-oriented persons are more likely to ascribe failure to stable, personal factors (even when the task is in fact random). The attribution to ability and other stable personal causes, whether warranted or not, is likely to result in negative affect. Further, since the cause of the failure is seen to be stable and permanent, expectation of future outcome success is low. There is no sense in trying again (or in approaching future achievement-related tasks) if the same failure-producing ability level will still be there (in fact, it would lead to further self-concept damage if failure once again resulted.)

This side of the attribution coin for failure-orientation has been fairly well supported by Type II research. The other side of the coin, that success would be interpreted as externally caused, and thus have little positive influence on affect or expectations of future success, has not received much support.

Success-oriented persons show a far different pattern of affect and behavior (at least in their idealized state), again presumably because of linkages with attribution schemata. They tend to attribute success to both ability and effort and failure to the personal, but unstable factor of effort. Thus, they can pride themselves on success, but at the same time can respond to failure without severe negative affect by trying harder. Attribution for failure to an unstable factor particularly means that outcome expectations are relatively independent of the particular past outcome, and the fact that the factor is also personal means that affect and orientation to the task can remain high—the person remains in control and effective. As a result, these persons would be expected to approach achievement-related tasks, persevere at them, have high affect, and choose maximally informative tasks of intermediate difficulty. Most of these predictions have been borne out in research.

It should be noted that these behaviors are as likely to be based on distorted information as behaviors associated with failure orientation. Both sets of biases are assumed to develop as relatively adaptive responses to what is *perceived* to be a certain kind of characteristic *outcome*. Thus, it is reasonable, and not biased, for someone who, in fact, regularly fails to avoid performance tasks and so on (Weiner's use of the term "disengagement" to label such a possibly appropriate response invites comparison of these results to the massive gerontological literature on "disengagement theory," a comparison which will be discussed in detail later). It is also reasonable for someone who in fact regularly succeeds to search out tasks, persevere at them, and feel good about performing. Problems arise, however, when one overgeneralizes (biases attributional schemata) or bases the decisions on inaccurate data (i.e., misperceives one's actual success/failure rates or ratio). Yet, small biases at some time may induct an increasingly strong tendency to further bias attributional decisions.

ADULTHOOD, AGING, AND ATTRIBUTIONS

Although some of the conceptual problems and failures to replicate with which the field has been plagued are important, to say the least, again it is not central to the discussion and data to follow and, in fact, not relevant to the application of achievement attribution theory and method to adulthood and aging until a considerably later stage of research programs in that area. That is to say, in many ways the most basic, and most supported, assertions in the formulation provide considerable avenues for application to adult-relevant issues, at least within the sphere in which Type I and Type II attribution research has its value.

At the same time, critiques of the model (in Buss, 1978, 1979b; Ross, 1977; Miller & Ross, 1975; and in Weiner's own later work [1979; Weiner, Russell, & Lehrman, 1978]) should be kept in mind, and I am hopeful that at least some of the data produced—and some of the methods used to produce those data—in the original research to be reported in succeeding chapters will be an advance not only insofar as it includes middle-aged and older persons, but also as it contributed to general achievement attribution theory and methodology.

As I mentioned earlier, there have been several Type I studies related to aging. They will be reviewed in Chapter 5. Yet, in comparison to the body of research in the area, the amount of effort devoted to considering age as a factor in attribution processes and determinations is small indeed. There have been a number of studies of the development of attributions and related variables in children (e.g., Ames, Ames, & Felker, 1976; Crandall, Katkovsky, & Crandall, 1965; McGhee & Crandall, 1968;

McMahan, 1973; Weiner & Peter, 1973) and, of course, the primary group of concern has been college student-age young adults. But virtually no research in the area of adult achievement attributions had been developed until 1978; since then approximately 10 studies, to be reviewed in the next chapter, have appeared, mostly as unpublished papers or presentations at professional meetings. For example, Banziger and Drevenstedt (1980), Connor, Walsh, Litzelman, and Alvarez (1978), S. Green (1980), Locke-Connor and Walsh (1980), Reno (1979), and Smith (1979) have all reported Type I attribution research, usually concerned with the perceptions of old people by college students. Banziger and Drevenstedt (1980) also included Type II analyses. McCarthy (1977) used Weiner's categories to get attributions from older persons (Type II), but the situations were restricted primarily to reminiscences about long past events, and the analysis was more focused upon clinical applications than on understanding attribution processes. Those studies, and research being developed more recently by some of the researchers noted above, is the extent of the few minor gestures toward post-college-age in the attribution literature. Shaver (1978) made some general observations on the basis of previously collected survey data.

Because of this paucity of studies, we simply do not know whether relatively clear-cut findings of attribution theory and research, especially in regard to Type II attributions, are true about adults beyond college age or not. We do not have data concerning whether the general adult population, and/or older persons specifically, respond in similar ways to how college students do, whether they tend to overascribe to motivational, internal factors, especially in regard to others (Ross, 1977; Jones & Nisbett, 1971), tend to take more credit for personal success than blame for bad outcomes (Weiner, 1974, and many others), tend to sort and use information in ways similar to "a good scientist" (Kelley, 1972; Frieze, 1976), tend to overemphasize the cost of negative factors over the benefit of positive ones (Kanouse & Hanson, 1972), or show the so-called actor-observer differences already discussed. Generalization of these basic findings to adults will *not* be proper if there are systematic differences in assumptions behind and circumstances for use of attributions even if the mechanisms and general processes themselves remain constant over time and over the circumstances of advancing chronological and functional age. And, although psychologists like to think they are researching universal mechanisms, as we have discussed in detail, it is possible that the mechanisms themselves change over long periods of time and/or over major life events. Both the change and stability of mechanisms and the change or stability of specific assumptions applied to the mechanisms are important; neither has been systematically examined.

Some aspects of the studies in this research program add the same sort of information to the Type I attribution studies about aging just noted. The studies also are expansions on the basic Type I theme. The hypothetical actors described include middle-aged persons as well as young and old for the first time, and the situations are broadened to a wider range of situations, including social situations along with both academic and other nonsocial situations. In other aspects of the research I highlight Type II self-attributions and explore the relationship of those to attributions about others similar to and different from oneself, a type of research which has recently been noted by Monson and Snyder (1977) using characteristics other than age as defining similarity. Still another aspect of the research within the Type II area is examination of the relationship of attributional differences and of age differences to a recently developed measure of "achievement motivation," the Work and Family Orientation Questionnaire developed by Helmreich and Spence (e.g., 1978). This measure promises to be much more usable for wide age-range comparisons and for developmental analysis than the exclusively academic or job-oriented measures of the past (such as scales developed by Mehrabian, 1968, 1969) and the complex projective devices advocated by McClelland (1953) and his followers. Finally, although the research program is at an early stage of development and in measurement terms is achronic or quasi-diachronic, the program includes aspects of a relational, dynamic, intrinsically developmental approach to the meaning of attributions and the language of outcomes, causes and reasons, and their effects; that is, it includes exploration of Type III attribution areas.

SAMPLE FOR THE STUDIES

Issues in Sampling for Adult Developmental Social Psychology

An issue which must be faced in the earliest stages of any adult developmental research program is that of method of sampling. The problems are in some ways unique and in other ways similar to those faced in all group comparison research. Members of different ages, as of different races or subcultures, are likely to be systematically at variance on a wide variety of factors, making interpretation difficult, since this variation is often caused in some way by the people being members of those different groups and yet is not necessarily caused by being "that sort of person." Obvious examples abound. For example, much of the discussion of the question of the racial impact on intelligence test scores concerns the relative importance of race as such, which can hardly be separated from the current statistical factors concerning differential income distribution, locus of housing, educational opportunities, and social structures across the races.

It is the same with age group membership. Old people may be different from middle-aged and young—and, on race or sex, from one another—because of systematic variation in educational opportunity, experience with the particular task, sensory acuity, orientation to the task or compliance or motivation, or a host of other factors which are somehow correlated with but not the same as being old.

Those differences, in turn, may well be more properly considered cohort differences than age differences. On the other hand, of course, it is possible that the differences on performance as measured *may* be because of the criterion variable itself—age, in the case of developmental studies. It is the responsibility of the researcher to do her or his best to separate these factors as much as possible. At the same time, it is patently impossible to do so unambiguously, as we discussed briefly in Chapter 2 and Chapter 3. Thus, the researcher is always caught on the horns of a dilemma, having to choose among potential sets of trade offs at the earliest stages of research, knowing full well that each choice leads to its own sort of restrictions in the latter stages of analysis and interpretation.

That is, wherever one lies in the continuum from belief that all "age" differences are intraindividual (for example, biological determinism) to belief that they are all caused by extraindividual factors—and, of course, responsible social scientists are likely to place themselves somewhere between those extreme points of view—he or she must make tough choices concerning sampling. What choices one makes has major effects on the sort of interpretation which is then possible based on those data. Thus, it is crucial to an understanding of the data to be presented in succeeding chapters to understand clearly the choices I have made in this research program in regard to sampling.

Representative Versus Comparable

Two different approaches may be taken. On the one hand, the researcher can choose to try to get "normal" representatives from each age group, from each cohort in the case of a cross-sectional design. In the case of old versus young, at the present time this choice will mean that the groups will differ widely on education level and recency of familiarity with testing situations, on activity level, health, family role, and on many other factors. This approach will maximize the likelihood of finding differences, but it will also minimize the possibility of interpreting those differences or, at least, of separating cohort and extraindividual (nonintrinsic) factors from more personal, elementary characteristics having to do with inner biological and individual psychological development.

On the other hand, a researcher can choose to obtain a set of groups that differ *primarily* in terms of age, but are as similar as possible on the more extra-personal and experiential levels. Thus, the research can "control" for level of educational attainment, experience with test situations, familiarity with the task, sensory acuity, or whatever other factors are likely to be relevant since they are likely to be independently associated with both age and task performance. In this case, sometimes the method of control is prior to the measurement time by choosing samples to be as equivalent as possible on those factors; at other times some of the subjects of each age group are given special instructions or training sessions designed to equalize them in familiarity with the task and the way to approach it (for example, see Labouvie-Vief & Gonda, 1976). In the latter case, a control group that has retained cohort and current experience differences, because it has not received training designed to reduce those factors, can be directly compared to the group given special pretask experimental manipulations and to the other age groups. The effect of this sort of sampling, of course, is that it minimizes the likelihood of finding adult age differences (or other subgroup differences), because it means elimination of the covariance of the nondevelopmental, age-related differences. The price to be paid for that result, however, is that each group is differentially representative of its cohort. In this case, the older adults who are highly educated and open to test experiences are (or certainly may be) less like others of their cohort than the young are of their own cohort, since educational opportunities have increased through each cohort and since younger people in active academic settings are a larger proportion of their whole cohort than middle-aged and older persons are.

The major differences in data produced by the two methods and the debate on the "proper" methodology to use are apparent in the work on intelligence differences in adult development (e.g., Baltes & Schaie, 1976; Horn and Donaldson, 1976; Labouvie-Vief & Chandler, 1978) and are discussed in detail in several sources, including Baltes, Nesselroade, and Reese (1977), and Banziger (1979). As with many other debates, both sides have a great deal of merit, because both approaches are both useful and informative at the same time as they are open to criticism for being incomplete solutions. As a result, both may be usable, but neither can be used incautiously, for on its own it may be dangerously misleading.

It is certainly important to know about the impact of large-scale cohort differences and smaller-scale current experience ones on social behavior and social cognition. It is essential to be aware of the interaction of experience with current context and physical environment. Knowledge of cohort differential opportunities for experiencing certain environments and certain tasks can be especially valuable in terms of devising short-term policy. Equalization of opportunity may depend on knowing the systematic differences that accompany membership in a particular cohort at a particular moment in time. Thus, population representativeness is particularly appropriate to such needs.

The other side of the coin is also true. It is important to understand the effects of growing older, of developing, of taking a different perspective in relation to comparison groups, of experiencing inner biological and individual psychological progressions over increasingly longer periods of time. Recognition of developmental effects, especially as they interrelate with nondevelopmental, but age-related ones, may be more important for long-term policy decisions, decisions leading to building-in differential support as well as equal opportunity.

Yet, some of the sources of differences, some of these key factors, are revealed better with one sort of sampling; others with the other sort. The choice must be made by each researcher on the basis of personal interest and goals for the research.

Although it should be noted that Baltes et al. (1977) have taken a rather firm stand in favor of representativeness and proportional sampling, in this particular case, I felt it was important to try to minimize the effects of extraneous sources of difference and to examine potential differences in attribution modes, relationship of attributions and performance, and meaning of attributions without the confounding elements of educational level, verbal fluency, current experience, and peripheral motivational differences. I felt it was crucial to see if the common interpretations of adulthood and aging as times of retreat from achievement and activity, from concern with attributions, were any deeper than the superficial level of cohort differences and unequal opportunities within society. I thus aimed for comparability across several factors which are in fact "naturally" related to the cohort and historical differences that are in turn inextricably interwoven with age in a simple cross-sectional design such as this. I should hasten to add, though, that the word "naturally" is not, of course, meant to imply a necessary or essential relationship between, for example, cohort and average education level attained by early adulthood or cohort and recency of experience with academic settings, but only in the sense of commonness of cooccurrence. Indeed, there is a recent upswing in the number of persons beyond "normal" college age who are enrolled in college, and the education level curve appears to have peaked. We may even see a time a few generations into the future when the average education of the older generations will be higher than that of younger cohorts. It was not, in fact, difficult to locate individuals across wide age ranges who are relatively comparable on these factors.

Having made that choice and, I hope, defended it well, I must, of course, remind the reader once again that this choice, like any other, has weaknesses. Rather than hiding those weaknesses, I intend to discuss them and the impact they may have on the validity of various interpretations of the data, and I intend to show that the studies to be reported are of value in themselves and can serve as signposts to point to more adequate study of the aspects of attributions central to social perception and self-analysis.

Approach to Gathering Participants

Toward the end of revealing age differences in groups comparable on salient covarying factors, I have drawn all of my subjects from lists of current and recent *participants in continuing education* opportunities at the college level. Those participants include young, traditional college-age persons who are going to college part-time while working full-time and who are, thus, less likely to be caught up in the overcognizing and rather unusual activity patterns of the full-time college student direct from high school. It also includes middle-aged men and women, some with college and professional backgrounds, some not, who are also going to school part-time. Finally, it also includes older, retired persons—again some from professional-level backgrounds and some not—who are attending college-level classes in their communities. All subjects thus have relatively similar (high) levels of interest in education and in self-enrichment and a relatively similar current acquaintance with test and other task-oriented situations.

Of course, this method of selection carries with it the problems noted above concerning the choice of comparable samples across ages. It is, of course, likely that the students from the different age groups are in fact enrolling in the same courses for different reasons (or are enrolling in a different mix of courses through continuing education auspices). These motivation-for-education differences may have subtle and undetected effects on responses. In particular, postretirement education may be less laden with the job advancement aspects of education, which are major elements in the careers of the young and middle-aged continuing education students.

Of course, general cautions about this type of sampling and about cross-sectional studies must always be borne in mind. Beyond this is one other concern. The sort of sample I have used has been criticized by one reviewer of some of my work as, in effect, the same old tired choice in slightly different clothing. That is, I have found myself using college students, even though I have criticized the overuse of college students in attribution research. A full defense of such a choice cannot be made, although preliminary results with a more general sample of adults, as yet not fully analyzed, indicate that the kind of similarity and difference across age groups I will be reporting is quite widespread across the general population. The main defense I make is that I wanted to have results that could be fruitfully compared to the research others have done, both with age group differences and in general attribution research of all types, and that research has used college students almost exclusively. Thus, I decided to use college students, with the concession that they be similar within the whole sample across age groups, necessitating using continuing education rather than traditional students. Once a base of comparison has been firmly established, further forays can make the much needed extension of going beyond the captive population, highly selected group of persons interested in education.

Even with these cautions and weaknesses, the method is certainly far better than the common technique in psychology of aging and, especially, in social gerontology, that is, comparing a general senior center or housing for the elderly group to full-time college students directly out of high school or comparing nursing home residents to nursing home staff. The latter types of comparison have in fact provided quite a lot of the data on locus of control, achievement orientation, and performance that has been influential in the literature on aging. Before proceeding to the specific studies, I will briefly summarize the characteristics of the sample whose data comprise the original sections of the next three chapters.

Specific Study Participants

The participants in the research program studies, then, were selected from continuing education student lists, primarily at a major state university in the Midwest and secondarily from a community college which offered college-level courses at a private retirement community in the area. Education background of the participants ranged from "some college" to "Ph.D. level" and did not differ across age groups.

Age groups were chosen to maximize adult age comparisons while keeping the subject population to a relatively small number, because of financial and temporal exigencies inherent in a project of this type. To attain those ends, three discontinuous age groups were selected to represent young adult, middle-age, and older adult categories. The young adult subjects ranged in age from 20 to 30; the middle-aged from 40 to 50, and the older from 60 to 86. The reader should note that the latter group is a wider age range and actually includes several cohorts of young-old and old-old (Neugarten, 1974), a compromise to the original plan to use only ages 60 to 70 necessitated by the relative difficulty of obtaining an adequately large pool of potential subjects. Potential subjects were randomly drawn from the list and called to set up a time for participation, which, of course, was voluntary and for which they were paid a nominal participation fee. Seventy-five persons, fitting into age and sex categories described in more detail in the next chapter, comprised the study group.

Some of the subjects participated in more than one aspect of the study, as will be described more fully in discussions of procedures for each of the three distinct studies—questionnaire and scale responses, personality measures, and interviews about meaning.

CHAPTER 5

Perceptions of Competence:
Judging Actors by Their Ages

Type I attribution work, as noted in Chapter 4, is closely related to the classic areas of stereotyping and social perception. That is, the attributions given for outcomes of persons for whom we have minimal information other than the outcome itself and a few demographic characteristics are likely to be closely related to the broader perceptions we have concerning persons with those characteristics. Such a situation, of course, is a common occurrence when those to be judged are not well known to the judge. If, for example, there are stereotypic beliefs about differential general competencies of several groups, it may well follow that the likelihood of attributing the success or failure of a member of one of those groups to ability will be based on the orientation toward which that stereotype is biased. Alternatively, the form of the attributional schemata applied on the basis of a general feeling of competence or incompetence of "people like that" will, in turn, increase the likelihood of using consonant information to verify the stereotype, while ignoring contradictory information.

Thus, consideration of data concerning attitudes to and perceptions of older persons and consideration of data about the attributional formulae applied to people of various ages can converge to form the base for a better understanding of societal stereotypes as well as individual social perceptual age classifications and categorizations.

A wealth of data concerning attitudes toward older persons and to old age has been produced by social gerontologists at least since Tuckman and Lorge (e.g., 1953) began collecting data on attitudes toward aging by various ages and types of perceivers. Although there is a large amount of such information, most of the data collection has been devoid of theoretical grounding or conceptual clarity, and a plethora of scales have been used (see Bennett & Eckman, 1973; Kilty & Feld, 1976; McTavish, 1971; and Kogan, 1979, for several of the many reviews of these data).

Not surprisingly, given the variety of measures and samples, the results have been contradictory and uneven. For every study that shows negative attitudes to older persons there seems to be another that shows positive attitudes. For every one that shows age-of-subject differences in the direction of more positive attitudes to aging and older persons by older persons, there is another to show *less* positivity with increasing age. Again, the reader should refer to Kogan, McTavish, and others for reviews.

In any case, one particular aspect of these findings seems particularly relevant to our purposes, and that is perceptions of the competence of the members of various age groups. In this area, the data appear to be relatively consistent. Judges regularly assumed deterioration and resultant *less* competence to perform tasks on the part of the general group of old people compared to young people, especially in regard to tasks that are not heavily influenced by total amount of experience. At the same time, *specific* older targets are often not seen as differentially competent; the predominant mode in this sort of study is a finding of no differences (see Kogan, 1979). Thus, age appears to be used as a criterion for a stereotypic conception of competence, but the stereotype appears to have only a weak relationship, if any, to specific judgments.

Not surprisingly, researchers in the area of attitudes toward older persons—social perceptions by adult age groups—have begun to turn to attribution theory for a grounding the area often has lacked. This is evident in Kelly Shaver's (1978) general application of an attribution model to attitudes to older persons and Brewer's (1979) recent presentation about perceptions of older persons.

What linkages are expected? It would seem a belief in someone's relative incompetence would be tied to an attribution fitting the pattern earlier discussed as failure-oriented. That is, an incompetent person would be one whose failures are (justly) imputed to relatively stable personality factors (ability, traits) and whose successes would be less likely to be attributed to those same factors than the successes of a competent person. Alternatively, someone judged to be in a group that is generally high in competence would be judged in the pattern labeled "success-oriented"—his or her successes would be seen as related to ability and failures to extraneous, transitory factors (including, to be sure, personal, controllable ones such as mood, interest, and short-term expenditure of effort). In some sense, it can be said that observers expect them to have learned to be helpless (Abramson et al., 1978).

Whether such a set of age-differentiating attributions are used to explain the successes and failures of a person of a particular age is one of the questions addressed in the remainder of this chapter. As will be discussed, a number of researchers have been converging on this topic. Their results are verified and extended in several ways in the original research described. At the same time, other researchers have been making similar analyses based on demographic characteristics other than age, chiefly, sex of actor (e.g., reviewed in Ickes & Layden, 1978); there appear to be some major similarities in findings in age-related and non-age-related research.

Another, in some ways more developmental, question can also be asked —regardless of age of actor whose outcome is being explained, do persons of various ages characteristically use a set of attributional schemata that is in any way distinctive from the set persons of other ages use? That is, are the schemata people carry around—those presumably developed over a lifetime of experiences—universal across a wide range of ages, or are there consistent differences across age groups—either based in age or in differential experiences (cohort)? This question is being raised for the first time in this and the next chapter (this chapter concerns attributions about others—Type I attributions—whereas the next is a consideration of self-attributions—Type II attributions).

The basis for doing the research to be reported here stems in part from a need to pursue issues in the area of stereotypic perceptions of older persons by using an attribution model; however, it is important for the reader to keep in mind that the research can also be seen as focused on the much-needed expansion of attribution research to adulthood. That is, the area of age differences can be a fruitful point at which to test out more adequately some ideas that have been developed and researched within non-age-oriented attribution research. These topics include the use of attributions for ego-defensive purposes (Ross, 1977; Snyder et al., 1978) and the role of similarity to the actor in determining what attributions are selected for that actor (Snyder, 1976). This role for the research will become even more prominent in the next chapter.

RELEVANT PREVIOUS RESEARCH

As noted several paragraphs earlier, several researchers have been independently examining the notion that persons of various ages are regularly perceived as being less or more capable at a variety of tasks, and that rooted in those judgments is the consistent use of different explanations for the same outcome depending on the age of the actor. Most of the researchers have been particularly interested in the role of attribution in judgments about the competence of older persons, especially older workers. This is a salient applied social psychology area, given the movement in society away from mandatory retirement and toward ''competence testing'' of older employees (see Chapter 8 for a fuller discussion of this issue).

First of all, several researchers included a component of evaluation of older and younger others and/or generalized expectations that an actor of one or another age would be likely to be successful at a task in their research. These studies correspond most closely to the literature on attitudes toward older persons and stereotypes about them. They have found little support for the notion that people have internalized an assumption that a given older person is less competent than a younger one (note the specificity of a particular target person). Connor, Litzelman, Walsh, and Alvarez (1978), Reno (1979), Banziger and Drevenstedt (1980), and Smith (1979) all found no differences in evaluation of the general competence of old versus young actors.

In fact, Smith found differences depending on whether the task was speed- or experience-related, but the differences were not supportive of the negative stereotype of aging idea. Subjects expected that an older man would do better than a young one on the task in which experience was said to predominate, but there were no differences by age of actor on the speed task. That is, a positive stereotype of older persons (that they are more likely than young ones to do well on a task requiring much experience) was evidently internalized by the subjects, but a negative one (that older persons are slower) was not, even though it is the one expected on the basis of the literature on competence judgments of older and younger persons.

Thus, the competence difference in attitudes was not evident in these researchers' data on the attitudes of their subjects (it should be noted that all, except in Connor et al. and Banziger & Drevenstedt, were limited to college students). At the same time, most of those same investigators, in other parts of their studies, as well as several other researchers, have found systematic differences in attributions given for a particular outcome when they were told it had happened to an old versus a young actor.

Consistently, the differences have been much more apparent for failure scenarios than for success, whereas success was highly attributed to ability, regardless of age of actor.

Reno (1979) found that the hypothetical failure of an older person to get a college degree was attributed to stable personal factors more than a similar failure of a younger person, whose failure was ascribed to lack of effort; she found no differences for success. Subjects in the study by Connor et al. (1978) rated the same task (an interview situation that resulted in failure) as more difficult for an older job applicant than for a younger one. Unfortunately, their design leaves ambiguity as to whether the subjects felt this difference to be a person × task interaction (that is, answering questions of a certain type is a more difficult task for older persons) or a difference in task difficulty (that is, that the older people were actually asked harder questions). Smith (1979), using only a success outcome, found that an older worker's success on a task with a presumed negative age stereotype attached to it (a speed task) was attributed primarily to effort whereas success on a positively stereotyped task (one requiring experience) was attributed to ability. Alternatively, young actors were presumed to expend more effort on the experience-related task than on the speed-related one. Age as such was regularly used as an explanation of failure by an old actor in Banziger and Drevenstedt's study. More recently, Locke-Connor and Walsh (1980) found that their subjects (middle-aged and young adults) attributed an older person's failures more to stable factors than they did the failures of young actors.

Thus, the data produced to date show little support for a general negative attitude to older persons or lower expectations for their competence and performance, but at the same time there is a consistent finding that the failures of older persons are nonetheless more likely to be ascribed to ability or age or to other stable personal factors than the failures of others.

These studies have certainly been a welcome step in the direction of bringing attribution research of the Type I sort to bear on issues in adult development and aging, and in that regard they have been contributions to a social psychology concerned with adult development. They have illuminated some of the attributional bases for a generalized set of expectations for and attitudes about age and the limits of positing a link between those. However, all of the studies have been severely limited in scope.

Limitations in Previous Research

Each researcher has dealt with only one hypothetical situation; occasionally, only one characteristic (e.g., only success as outcome in Smith) has been used, making direct comparisons within a study impossible. One exception has been Banziger and Devenstedt (1980), who present data on attributions for old and young targets and include two situations.

A further important limitation has been the regular use of only college students as subjects. That is, researchers have tried to see if college student observers—and other people only by extension—look at older persons differently from young ones in the same way that other researchers have examined differences by race or sex of "target" actor. Few until very recently have examined whether people of various ages have different orientations or perspectives. Only Locke-Connor and Walsh (1980), Banziger and Drevenstedt (1980), and several researchers who were not explicitly examining achievement attributions (Baffa & Zarit, 1977; Bell & Stanfield, 1973; Sherman, Gold, & Sherman, 1978) have varied the age of attributor, with mixed results. None has considered more than two age groups. In that regard, most of these studies have not, in fact, been developmental studies, but analysis of college students' perceptions of varied targets; they have not even been synchronic in their approach to the processes of perception, the mechanisms of attributing across age groups.

Thus, one of the major ways in which the present study extends the previous research is by comparing young, middle-aged, and older adult attributors as they make decisions about young, middle-aged (an addition in itself), and older hypothetical actors.

On several other methodological grounds the previous studies are also inadequate and constricted. Weiner (1979; Weiner, Russell, & Lerman, 1978) and other major theorists (e.g., Frieze, 1976; Elig & Frieze, 1979) have increasingly emphasized gathering information on affects as well as attributions. Although most of the basis for this argument is in terms of Type II attribution research, it also applies to this kind of study. It is important to explore the feelings and affect attributed to actors as well as the causal implications attributed to them on the basis of the outcome. Only Banziger and Drevenstedt (1980) have included any examination of affect; theirs was very general.

Furthermore, the attribution framework, as long as it remains restricted to academic and work situations (the latter seemingly chosen to be the most similar adult analogue to the academic success and failure situations favored in the standard work on students) remains restricted to but one of a much wider range of potential situations. As will become clear, especially in the discussion of self-attributions and meaning of attributions in later chapters, it is unlikely that the same attributions would be used across a broader, more realistic set of situations. At the minimum, it is likely that use of attributions about outcomes varies as widely by type of situation in which the outcome was encountered as it does by the individual differences of the attributor or the group—stereotypic—differences of the observed actor. The few non-age studies that varied situation (e.g., Frieze, 1976) and Banziger and Drevenstedt's age comparison indicate the validity of this. Yet the research on age differences, like virtually all of the attribution research, has been restricted almost as severely in situation as in samples of subjects and types of actors.

Another severe limitation requires further explication. All the research concerned with explaining the outcomes of adult actors of various ages has used a closed-ended mode of responding. Sometimes the response choices were limited to Weiner's four categories, sometimes those plus age, and occasionally six or eight causes were available. Yet, as already discussed in Chapter 4, most researchers, including Weiner (1979), have advocated use of an open-ended technique, pointing out that the closed-ended format severely limits the potential range of attributions given. As Elig and Frieze (1975) note, there is particular danger in doing this when exploring new areas and new samples, as the research on adults is doing (although in their 1979 article they favor closed-ended response modes for certain purposes). In the original research to be discussed, I asked subjects to try to say how the hypothetical actor felt, what he or she thought about as causes, and what he or she—the actor—felt about the future for each situation. The descriptions were then categorized as described briefly below and discussed in detail in the Appendix. In this way, subjects were free to respond, to give up to three or four different causes they felt were important, and to respond to a wider variety of situations.

Several hypotheses emerging from results of the earlier age-related research, from more general achievement attribution theory, and a combination of those with generally held notions of age differences will be further explored in the Type I study. Both the research indicative of negative stereotypes about older people as a group and the studies of attributions about older persons already discussed lead to the prediction that the cause of failure given will vary by age of actor. Older persons' failures will be ascribed more to personal stable factors (ability, traits) than those of younger persons, whereas attributions for young actors' failures will be predominantly associated with lack of effort. That is, older persons will be perceived in a more failure-oriented fashion than younger ones. Attributions about middle-aged actors have not been previously examined, and thus there are no clear-cut predictions to be derived from the literature (middle-aged persons are even more ignored by personality and social psychologists than older persons are).

At the same time, in line with other success-failure research, major differences in attributions about success and failure are expected to hold for all age categories of actors. Success will be given more personal and stable attributions, whereas failure will, in general, be ascribed more to unstable and, possibly, less personal factors.

Although the conception of age-related decline in general motivation for achievement (as Neugarten, 1964; Kuhlen, 1964; and others discuss) would lead to a prediction that age of subject would be related to differential attributions, it is unlikely that such effects would generalize to attributions about others (at least not about non-old others) and it is unlikely that such effects, based in research using samples very different on education level, academic interest, and so on, as well as age, will appear in a selected sample such as the one used in this study. Thus, no age of attributor differences are expected.

METHODS AND PROCEDURES FOR TYPE I STUDY

The characteristics of the 75 participants have already been described in Chapter 4. The group consisted of old, middle-aged, and young adult men and women from continuing education programs.

Twelve hypothetical situations were given to each subject. They included variation on age category and sex of actor and success or failure outcome (although the limited validity of that latter dichotomization will be considered in detail in Chapter 7, for purposes of this portion of the study the limitations are not severe enough to obviate the analyses presented in this chapter). Each person received one each of each combination of the three factors noted. At the same time, those factors were crossed with four types of situations. The allotment of situation to a particular combination of the other factors was different in each of four lists, in which the order of presentation of the situations was also varied. That is, every person responded to every combination of age, sex, and outcome, and each of the stimuli was about one of four types of situations—a bridge contest (winning or losing a local club contest); a volunteer job situation (asked to take a paying job after working as a volunteer or told that the work was no longer needed); a mechanical repair (fixing or failing to fix one's television set); and a weight loss program (losing 12 pounds or gaining one while on a 6-week diet).

In this way, even though not every subject received every combination of situation with age, sex, and outcome, all combinations of those four factors were presented to some subgroup of subjects from all age and sex categories. The four "orders" were roughly equally distributed—two orders were given to 16 subjects each, one to 20, and one to 23. The order-situation factor will be discussed later in this chapter.

The general instructions for the 12 hypothetical situations asked subjects to put themselves in the place of the actor and to say how they thought that sort of actor would react to that outcome—what causes or reasons he or she would feel led to the result, how he or she would feel about experiencing that outcome in that situation, and what effect that experience might have on him or her in the future. It is important for the reader to note that this phrasing is somewhat different from that in the majority of Type I attribution research in several ways. First of all, it is open-ended; the kinds and number of causes or affect listed as important—and the order in which those factors come into play—were not predesignated to the respondent. Rather, the fullest possible latitude was given. As reported in the following and in the Appendix, this procedure was not without its interpretive shortcomings and required considerable time and effort to be expended on data reduction prior to most analyses, but it did satisfy the requirement to allow wide latitude to subjects so that a closer approximation to natural situations could be attained. As noted earlier, an approach that allows maximum latitude is particularly important when new populations are being approached and new sorts of situations presented. Both of those are the case in this study.

There is another important point of variance between this and the body of Type I, "attributions about" research. Subjects were asked to report how they thought the actor would feel and think, rather than reporting what they, as observers, would have concluded in those circumstances. Although this mode of presentation loses some of the flavor of a direct measure of perception of others as a separate and distinct mechanism from self-perception, I feel it is closer to the normal processes of attribution-making about others. That is, whereas stereotypes and self-distanced modes of attribution certainly come into play, major levels of perceptions of others—especially of their affect and reaction to succeeding or failing—are quite necessarily in part a matter of reducing the distance between self and other, deciding causality by recognizing or attempting to "understand" causality as experienced by the other.

Indeed, such a belief seems to underlie research which ties attributions given about others to personality variation (success-orientation and failure-orientation or achievement motivation, in the case of achievement situations). It is also related to findings, in generally Type I attribution work, that liked others and similar others (Snyder, 1976) are given attributions more similar to those given for oneself than attributions for less similar others. (See also Banziger's discussion (1979) of extension of this aspect to Type I attributions related to age correspondence of actor and observer.) This latter issue, that of self- and other-attributions, will be discussed in Chapter 6. Suffice it to say, at this point, that the use of this quasi-projective, empathic mode of response elicitation is both a stronger than usual and a weaker than usual test of Type I attributions than is found in the literature, especially in that body of it concerned with adults.

Data Reduction Procedures

As already noted, subjects in this study did not select from an experimenter-limited set of attributions and affect for a particular situation, nor did they simply rate the "strength" of each of a particular set of attributions and affect. Instead, they were asked to write down whatever they felt were the most important causes and the most likely feelings the hypothetical actor would decide were involved in the particular situation.

Although this sort of methodology certainly is appropriate, and analysis of particular patterns of attribution choice is likely to be important, the fragmented nature of the range of responses, combined with the relatively small sample sizes, especially within an age category, make statistical analysis or even category by category description on this level impossible. Several steps of coding and data reduction were necessary prior to analysis. These steps are detailed in the Appendix, but will be reviewed quickly at this point.

First of all, three coders jointly gave the response(s) (up to three per situation) of the particular subject to the particular situation. In this stage, coding was highly inclusive; that is, if there were any doubts that a response fit a preexisting category, a new category for that word or phrase was included. After this phase of coding there were 28 "attributions" listed in the Appendix. A similar, inclusive coding process resulted in 47 "affects."

As the second stage, the attributions were grouped into nine categories on the basis of similar data reductions by Elig and Frieze (1975), Weiner et al. (1978), and other attribution theorists combined with characteristics of the causal words themselves, with the help of *Roget's Thesaurus* (Dutch, 1965). The categories are:

1. *Ability-type* personal factors (ability, skill, strength, physical decline).
2. *Trait-type* personal factors (good/bad personality, will power, and "stable effort").
3. *State-type* personal factors (mood, task orientation).
4. *Current effort.*
5. *External stable* factors (task difficulty).

6. *External, nonsocial transitory* factors (luck, bad setting).
7. *Other persons, transitory* to actor (other's prejudice, interests, help or hurt).
8. *Person by task interaction* (good/bad at that sort of thing).
9. *Person by others interaction* (get along well/poorly with, etc.).

As already noted, these categories are similar to ones used by many researchers in a wide range of attribution studies of children and college students.

The affects were also clustered into nine categories, as described in the Appendix. The nine categories (and several examples of each) are:

1. Positive-activation (feeling enjoyment, joyous excited).
2. Positive-comfort (happy, satisfied).
3. Positive-enhancement (smug, humble, useful).
4. Negative-hypoactivation (exhausted, depressed).
5. Negative-discomfort (confused, sad, hurt).
6. Negative-incompetence (embarrassed, ashamed, incompetent).
7. Negative-hyperactivation (angry, panicky).
8. Negative-tension (resentful, upset, frustrated).
9. Negative-inadequacy (rejected, helpless).

The third stage of data reduction and classification of attributions and affects reduced each to several categories. Affects were simply categorized as positive or negative. The results based on those categories were not surprising in the least; positive affects predominated for success outcomes and negative affects for failures. There was, however, some crossover, particularly of ''positive'' affects associated with certain sorts of failures. This latter finding will be discussed later in the description of results.

The nine attribution categories were reduced to scores on two dimensions, corresponding to the major theoretical dimensions of achievement attribution research. One dimension, the Personal-Extrapersonal (P-E)[1] dimension, included three categories: personal (categories 1 through 4 of the ninefold classification), extrapersonal (categories 5 through 7), and mixed or interactive (categories 8 and 9). Of course, the reader must constantly keep in mind that these categorizations into dimensions are necessarily somewhat ambiguous abstractions from multifaceted continua, a point discussed in detail in the Appendix concerning coding. The dimensional classification, however, does allow for analysis along lines of the theoretical dimensions in a quantitative way, a useful first step in analysis of attributions. The Stable-Unstable (S-U) dimension was coded ''1'' for stable (categories 1, 2, and 5) and ''0'' for all other, unstable dimensions.

---

[1]This dimension corresponds roughly to that more usually labeled as internal-external. However, I feel the current naming is more precise and avoids confusion with locus of control. See Appendix for further discussion of the names.

RESULTS

Attributions for Hypothetical Others

Finally, we arrive at consideration of the data. The first question we ask is, "Do people give different causal categories of attribution for the successes and failures of persons of various ages (and do they differentiate within ages by sex)?"

Indeed, it appears that people do use age as a differentiator (at least they can do it on a questionnaire about hypothetical others for whom they have fairly minimal information, including age and sex). In fact, they are quite likely to use age to discriminate among the reasons for failure, although they do not seem to see age as a valuable predictor of causality for success. Furthermore, they are not likely to use sex of actor as a tool to decide causes for persons also differentiated by age. In other words, age is linked to certain kinds of causes of failure, and therefore, it is used stereotypically to attribute characteristics to actors of various ages; but age stereotypes of success, and sex stereotypes for any outcome, do not appear to play major roles across a broad age range of attributors.

The data to support this general statement of findings begin with the percentages of each of the nine attribution types ascribed to persons of various ages. The highest attribution for success over all subjects was to ability; furthermore, effort was virtually always in second place and trait-type factors in third. Only in the case of young subjects' and old subjects' attributions for young actors was this pattern broken; in those two groups effort was highest and ability was second. Thus, success was regularly attributed to personal causes, with stable-personal usually outpacing unstable ones.

The pattern for failure was both different overall from success and more varied within failure, with more use made of characteristics of actors and situations. Indeed, the failures of old hypothetical actors were likely to be attributed by those actors—according to our subjects—as most likely the result of lack of ability on their part, and secondarily to unstable extrapersonal but social factors (other's lack of help or actual harm; other's motives or abilities). Young actors' failures were equally attributed to effort and ability, with the social extrapersonal factor third in importance. The failures of middle-aged actors, on the other hand, were more likely to be given external causality. The most common attribution type noted was unstable, extrapersonal social factors, and the third most common (after ability) was the unstable interaction of person and task, including interference by other tasks, or not having proper equipment. The fourth most common factor for middle-aged persons' failures, too, was extrapersonal—nonsocial, unstable factors, such as luck.

These impressions from the allocation of attribution types are borne out and lent precision by the more standard tests of the dimensions. First of all, multiple analyses of variance indicated that for both locus of attribution and stability there were large inter-item differences (for P-E, $F[11, 814] = 6.87$; for S-U $F[11, 814] = 3.11$, both $p < .001$). Furthermore, a large part of the differences between questions in the multivariate analyses is the marked distinction between attributions for success and those for failure. Causes of success were more stable than causes of failure ($\bar{X}$ SU $= .42$ for success and .35 for failure; $t[74] = 2.77$, $p < .01$) and much more personal ($\bar{X}$ = 1.48 for success and 1.07 for failure; $t[74]$ = 7.54, $p < .001$). The same pattern held across all age groups of hypothetical actor.

The differentiation of success and failure, of course, is consonant with a number of studies with college students about age-unspecified actors (Weiner, 1974, 1979) and with attributions about actors of various ages by college students and others (e.g., Banziger & Drevenstedt, 1980; Locke-Connor & Walsh, 1980; Reno, 1979).

Since a finding of success-failure differences overall has almost the status of a manipulation check (it has been consistently found), the comparisons of attributions based on age are more central to the focus of this investigation. However, as will be seen shortly, the success-failure comparisons are quite crucial in regard to the age comparisons.

Repeated measures analyses of variance with age category of actor as the repeated measure indicated significant differences in attributions about actors in the three age groups. Attributions for old and young actors were higher (more personal) on the P-E dimension than they were for middle-aged actors (means were 1.34 for old, 1.19 for middle, and 1.31 for young; $F[2, 148] = 3.60, p < .05$). At the same time, there was a linear effect of age of actor on the S-U dimension (means of .45 for old, .40 for middle, and .33 for young; $F[2, 148] = 4.56, p < .05$). Older actors' outcomes were reported to be the result of more stable factors.

More important than these overall differences, valuable though they are, is the interrelationship of these differences to success and failure outcomes. All differences were considerably more apparent in descriptions of failure outcomes. In fact, as shown in Table 5.1, there were virtually no age differences in locus of attribution and a merely significant difference on stability when success outcomes were being analyzed, whereas for failure both dimensions had highly significant differences. In each case, the results verify those in the percentage analyses of the broader classification of attributions. That is, there were few differences for success, whereas there were distinct differences across all three age groups on failure. Consistently, the failures of

Table 5.1. Locus of Cause and Stability Scores by Outcome and Age of Actor

Outcome	Young	Middle-aged	Old
Success			
(P-E) Locus	1.49	1.44	1.51
(S-U) Stability	.35	.49	.44
Locus $F = 0.26$ (2, 224), $p > .05$			
Stability $F = 3.24$ (2, 224) $= p < .05$			
Failure			
(P-E) Locus	1.17	0.86	1.17
(S-U) Stability	.30	.29	.44
Locus F (2, 224) $= 6.22, p < .005$			
Stability F (2, 224) $= 6.28, p < .005$			

older actors were interpreted as relatively personal and stable, those of young actors as equally personal but considerably less stable, and those of middle-aged actors as relatively extrapersonal and unstable (the latter primarily because most extrapersonal factors are relatively unstable from the point of view of the actor, as discussed in the Appendix). The comparison of older and younger actors generally confirms the findings of others cited above, whereas the middle-aged comparisons to young and old are an important extension beyond the studies others have reported. The significance of these age differences will be considered after a brief exposition of affect findings and the effects of the factor of situations.

Attributing Affect for Various Age Actors

As described earlier and in the Appendix, the subjects were asked to say how they thought the hypothetical actor would feel about the success or failure, and those open-ended affects were classified into nine categories, or affect types. The affect responses have not been analyzed to the degree that the attributions of causality have—indeed, it is difficult to know how to proceed with analysis of affects. Others have made headway in this regard and should be consulted for potential pathways to follow in further consideration of the affects obtained (both the affects obtained and sources are described in the Appendix). However, even without detailed analysis, several interesting cross-age comparisons can be made.

As noted earlier, reporting differentiation of affect by success and failure is trivial. What is more interesting in that regard is the relatively frequent occurrence of counter-affects, especially for several situations. Relatively sizeable percentages of subjects (10–20%) reported that actors of all ages might be expected to feel affects categorized as positive-comfort after experiencing failure. These affects range from a "ho-hum, makes no difference in my life" attitude to more clearly positive feelings of calm, contentment, or relief that the task is over, pleasure at having given it a good shot, and even satisfaction at one's losing or failing effort. Alternatively, success led a subgroup of respondents to name a discomfort-related negative affect as likely. In particular, concern or apprehension at fitness for the task and about the heightened expectations others may have after the success illustrated the ambivalence success sometimes entails, especially in more open-ended, ongoing events more characteristic of life than what many studies have used. Although the numbers are not large enough to make definitive comparisons, this sort of affect reference was more predominantly applied to middle-aged and older actors (and given by middle-aged and older subjects, I might note).

Unlike attributions in relation to age, the differences among age groups in affects imputed were fairly small. However, like attributions of causes, insofar as differences were present, they were primarily for failure (except as just discussed). Discomfort was the primary affect type given for all ages of actors when they failed. However, the second highest affect varied by age category. Both old and middle-aged actors, it was felt by subjects, would be more likely to experience tension-related affect (nervousness, frustration, jealousy, upset) than young, who were more likely to experience anger or irritation (what is labeled hyperactivation). Also, old actors were more often said to be hypoactivated (exhausted, depressed) and feeling inadequate. In other words, young actors were expected to experience a more active, manic state, whereas old were expected to react to failure in a more passive, ego-deflated way.

Situational Variation

One other unusual aspect of this study deserves mention and separate analysis. Whereas attributional analyses of situations and outcomes are consistently assumed to have regular use in everyday life, in fact the range of situations for which attributions by subjects have been requested has been decidedly restricted. In fact, within the achievement attribution literature, by far the preponderance has been performance on a particular examination in a high school or college class. The research concerned with adult age differences, on the other hand, as has already been reviewed, has consistently been centered on work performance, again of a particular task. There have, of course, been exceptions to those patterns. Frieze (1976; Elig & Frieze, 1975) supplemented an academic situation with one of making friends at a party, and several other researchers have looked at specific kinds of social situations (couple relationships—Orvis, Kelley, & Butler, 1976; Harvey, Wells, & Alvarez, 1978; parole decisions—Carroll, 1979). Recently Banziger and Drevenstedt (1980) have found interesting differences—including interactions with age of actor—between two situations: a driver's test and a college course. I should note that the situational variations noted move inexorably toward life events more applicable to adults than most, yet most of the researchers—especially see Orvis et al. and Harvey et al.—have persisted in using college age subjects. This is a clear example of the strength of boundness researchers, even when examining intrinsically adult issues, have to captive populations in general and young adults in particular. This boundness, of course, has been discussed in detail in Chapter 1 and in other sources (e.g., Blank, 1978), and was recognized by the researchers themselves as restrictive in the same way Jones et al. (1972) had done earlier. Yet, it persists.

The comparative data from these few studies has been valuable. In particular, it has been quite clear that somewhat different sets of attributional possibilities and differential allocations of commonly used ones are brought into play for different situations. That is, attributions and affect ascriptions are linked in many ways to situations as much as they are to individuals who attribute and individuals whose outcomes are being explained.

I do not pretend that the data from the present study fulfill all the requirements to make situational comparisons and to fully examine the relative contributions of situation and individual difference in combination with the more standard contribution of outcome, consensus, distinctiveness, and so on. However, I believe that the availability of direct cross-situational comparisons sets in bold relief the importance of the situational variable. It opens up analysis of cause (and perhaps affect) determinations as intrinsically contextual and naturalistically ecological rather than the simple production of stored, relatively static schemata. In that way, it is likely to add to the applicability of the social psychology of attributions to adult situations and adult-made decisions and explanations of action and outcome. It is also truer, not only to a social psychology of developing adults, but to the general situationist basis of social psychology, oddly missing in attribution work.

As described earlier, each subject responded to four situations—bridge contest, weight loss, upgrading or loss of volunteer job, and television repair—across the 12 incidents in the within-subjects portion of the design. Across the four orders, every situation was linked with every combination of age and sex of actor and success and failure outcome.

Each situation, of course, is quite different from the others, although there are pairings along several dimensions. Both the TV repair and the bridge contest were fairly circumscribed, specific performances, whereas the factors underlying the volunteer job situation and weight loss were likely to be more extended temporally, more diffuse, and more processual. Thus, it may be expected that success or failure in the one-shot situations would be dependent on factors prevalent at that one limited time, and causes of success or failure at those tasks would be more specific and less processual and interactive than those for the other two situations. Perhaps surprisingly, that would lead to predictions of greater stability of causes for the short-term than for the long-term situations. The outcomes dependent on long-term factors would require a consistent confluence of a large series of interrelationships of stable and unstable factors. That connective tissue certainly has an element of instability in it that a more temporally circumscribed event may not have.

At the same time, within the specific task category lies another important distinction, a differentiation between more technical activities, represented by TV repair, and more interpretive ones, represented by the bridge contest. In this regard, it is likely that attributions for the technical activity would be high in stability (in a sense, the relation of person to object of action is in a timeless vacuum where their properties can be displayed objectively), whereas the bridge contest is an application of specific skills at one specific time and yet has a large component of transitory and random factors (luck) buffeting it and "interfering" with a pure relationship between person and object (cards, in this case).

A third dimension of difference is related to the technical-interpretive dimension just noted, but cuts across all four situations rather than merely the specific task ones. Both the weight loss and TV repair were more individual-bound than the volunteer and bridge situations, which are intrinsically social (requiring others to participate both in causality—partners, co-workers—and in definition of success itself, especially in the volunteer job situation). It might be expected that the latter two situations would be seen as more socially and interpersonally (and therefore externally) caused than the more personal pair of situations.

The kinds of considerations just noted lead to some hypotheses about the impact of type of situation on type of attribution (and affect, although those analyses have not been done). For example, the weight loss situation may be linked to personal factors (because of the third dimension just noted) that are also unstable (because of placement on the first dimension). The television repair situation is also likely to be highly personal (dimension 3), but high on stability as well (dimension 2). The volunteer job outcome would be expected to be linked with extrapersonal factors (perhaps especially social interaction ones, such as cooperation, others' help or hurt, personality conflicts, etc.). Since we have earlier and in the Appendix discussed why, from the point of view of an actor, most social causes are seen as relatively unstable, we would further expect causes for the volunteer job to be low on the stability dimension (an extension of the discussion of dimension 2 would also lean toward that direction). Finally, the bridge contest is likely to be linked with extrapersonal factors (dimension 3), including both social and nonsocial ones. Prediction of stability for this situation is rather difficult, since its one-shot character is likely to elicit stable attributions (dimension 1), whereas its interpretive characteristics would favor unstable attributions.

I am sure the reader can generate other hypotheses, based on other ways of dimensionalizing the situations and forming different linkages of those dimensions to the theories and concepts of achievement attributions. The precise nature of these predictions, in fact, is less important at this stage than the fact of the value of direct comparisons of situations, afforded uniquely by the design of this study, and the seeming theoretical import of situation differentiation even though it has been virtually ignored in the field.

What, in fact, do the data show? First of all, they complement Elig and Frieze (1975) and Banziger and Drevenstedt's (1980) findings, verifying the importance of situational differences. Further, most of the predictions just made were verified by the data, with some interesting variations. Across all occurrences of a particular situation, the predictions were consistently verified. The differentiation (labeled Dimension 1) between circumscribed and open situations held (television repair was .65 and bridge .40 on stability versus means of .25 and .31 for weight loss and the volunteer situation, respectively). The classification according to Dimension 3 was also verified. That is, the weight loss and television repair situations were significantly more highly attributed personally than the volunteer and bridge contest situations (means of 1.61 and 1.48 vs. 1.03 and 1.15).

The other level of classification, between technical and interpretive, was only partly verified. It is true that the television repair attributions were significantly higher on stability than the bridge contest (mean of .65 compared to .40). At the same time, the bridge contest mean stability was second highest overall. Of course, the ambiguity on this factor had been expected, because of the prostability element included in its highly contained character. Since it is more difficult to place the other two situations on a technical-interpretive dimension, the lack of a clear relationship on the measure is not surprising.

Although these data are certainly rather strong verification for the notions about situational influence proposed, a further breakdown of the results is even more enlightening. As with virtually all of the variables, the situational variance is considerably larger for failure outcomes than for success ones. Indeed, mean attributions for all situations resulting in success were highly personal compared to failure, whereas the stability differentiation on Dimension 1 was exacerbated, and highly stable attributions were given for success in the bridge contest (no "luck" in winning).

For failure outcomes the dimensional differentiations are particularly clear. In fact, as can be seen in the rows for failure in Table 5.2, the two situations within each hypothesized pair according to Dimension 3 are virtually identical to each other and

Table 5.2.   Mean Locus (P-E) and Stability (S-U) Scores
by Outcome and Type of Situation

Outcome	Weight loss	TV repair	Volunteer	Bridge
		Success		
P-E	1.76	1.50	1.24	1.42
S-U	.28	.57	.33	.62
		Failure		
P-E	1.46	1.45	0.82	0.82
S-U	.22	.73	.29	.18

dramatically different from the other pair. Further, the two nonsocial situations elicited virtually the same patterns in both success and failure outcomes. Also, the television repair situation is exceedingly high on stability, much higher than the stability for the more diffuse situations and the bridge contest, verifying Dimension 1 and 2 predictions.

The big surprise, and a large change from attributions for success, came in the bridge contest situation. Whereas success was explained in moderately highly personal and highly stable ways, failure was seen as not only more extrapersonally caused, but also as having extremely *unstable* nonpersonal causes. Indeed, the mean stability score for one subsegment of the situation—failure by middle-aged females—was zero! Clearly, these subjects saw those who participate in bridge contests as differentiating dramatically in locus of attribution depending on whether they end up succeeding or not, whereas the major differentiation in the other situations is a simple extension of the standard dichotomization between success and failure.

Why do the situational attributions vary as they do? I have tried to give some tentative answers early in this section, and those seem verified by the data. I will also reintroduce discussion of this point and consider some age-comparisons at several places, including Chapter 7, a discussion of similar results for different personal situations in Chapter 6, and, more briefly, in a general discussion at the end of this chapter.

One example from the data illustrates an even more basic situational variation and highlights the essential ambiguity of success and failure across situations. In fact, it indicates that the most basic aspect of an outcome—whether it is a success or whether it is a failure—is itself open to interpretation, questioning, and negotiation. The interpretation, furthermore, may be related to age, both of actor and of observer/evaluator. The example concerns the weight loss situation.

My young assistant, middle-aged assistant, and I objectified the success and failure end of trying to lose 10 pounds in six weeks as losing 12 pounds or actually gaining a pound, respectively. That dichotomy was acceptable for our young and middle-aged subjects when they were talking about young and middle-aged dieters, and for most of the older respondents when they talked about those younger dieters.

But a fairly large number of respondents, especially older ones, quite clearly labeled and reacted to the loss of 12 pounds by older dieters as at least partially a failure; they *failed* to hit the mark they had set. As best we can tell from comments, this interpretive difference is related to the kind of interpretation that can be placed on sudden weight loss in an older person, but whatever its direct explanation, it is clear that the outcome was interpreted differently both by and for older adults. A "success" is *not* necessarily a "success."

Important issues of the mixed nature of situations and the construction and negotiation of success and failure will be discussed further in Chapter 6 and, especially, Chapter 7.

Attributing by Adults

Prior to proceeding to a discussion of situations and other discussions of attributions about people of various ages, let us examine the other side of the coin, a possibility facilitated by the design of this study. What about attributions for others *by* adults of various ages? Do young, middle-aged, and older adults, with all the varied baggage of their own motivations and needs, experiences, and historical placement, use different approaches to the task of making judgments about why others succeed or fail (or, more precisely, what attributions they think others would decide upon) and about how others feel when they succeed or fail?

In a few words, the answer quite clearly is "no, they do not." These data verify the scattered negative findings about age differences in attributions found by Sherman, Gold, and Sherman (1978), Banziger and Drevenstedt (1980), and Locke-Connor and Walsh (1980). There were no significant age-of-subject effects on overall personal-extrapersonal or stability-instability scores (in fact, all F ratios were considerably less than 1.00). Likewise, there were no significant interaction effects on either measure of attribution. By the way, there was only one sex effect, of borderline significance—males were somewhat higher than females overall on stability (.42 vs. .34, $F[2, 69] = 3.46$, $p < .10$).

Furthermore, there was never a difference in direction for any of the attributions-about-others measures by age, although sometimes only one or another age group showed a significant difference on a variable. For example, only young actors' differentiation among age groups on stability was significant; the measure across all age groups was significant because of that *and* the nonsignificant differences in the same direction for middle-aged and older subjects.

The same can be said about use of affects. By and large, the categories used by all subjects were similar. The most sizeable difference was a considerably lower likelihood for older subjects to use trait-type attributions for any age group. However, the total numbers of that type of attribution are quite small (14), and thus the pattern appears to have little significance at present. Also, since trait-type attributions are usually collapsed with one or more others, including ability, to form, for example, a "personal-stable" category, and since older subjects had slightly higher percentages of attributions to ability than other subjects did, the usage differences are likely to remain minor (and uninterpretable).

A REST, A SUMMARY, AND A DISCUSSION

At this point it may be well to summarize the data presented thus far on Type I attributions and to integrate those findings on attributions about others with one another and with the findings of previous and concurrent research. Further discussion, and the application of these results to contemporary issues in attribution theory, research methods, and social concerns will be deferred to Chapters 7 and 8.

The causes of success are fairly uniformly seen as personal and stable for and by all age groups. However, older people's failures are more likely to be attributed to current ability-type factors than those of young or middle-aged actors. Even though these data were collected in a way different from other studies on several levels—for example, open-ended response mode, in which subjects were asked to project the causes which the actors would feel rather than to say what they as observers felt the causes were without reference to beliefs of the actors—the results are generally consonant with information from other studies by Banziger and Drevenstedt (1980), Connor et al. (1978), Locke-Connor and Walsh (1980), Reno (1979), and Smith (1979) in regard to comparison of young and old and are an extension of those in terms of middle age.

Like those studies, this study's finding of perceptions of older people's failures as more closely related to ability than failures of other age groups appears to support the widespread stereotypic belief that older persons are less able than younger ones. Yet, as with results from earlier studies, there is little evidence here of differences in expectations of future performance or generalized attitudes toward older persons, even though those would be expected to follow as extensions from the attribution differences. Thus, it is quite clear from a consistent set of findings that adults of all ages expect failure results to be more linked to ability when the actor is old, but that expectation neither results from nor leads to a clear negative stereotype of the ability of older persons. They are not expected to fail more, only to explain the failures they do have in terms of their ability. These results may help clarify the inconsistencies sometimes found in attitudes to aging and stereotyping research. Awareness (or perception, regardless of veridicality) of a close linkage of failure and personal stable factors among an old age group is by no means identical to the existence of negative stereotypes of aging or of old people. Insofar as the latter exist, they do not seem operative in judgments about particular old people, as the preponderance of evidence in these attribution studies and in attitudes toward aging research, as reviewed by McTavish (1971), Kogan (1979), Bennett and Eckman (1973), and others, has consistently indicated.

Secondly, these data show, more clearly than previously available data, the continuous nature of so-called stable traits such as ability. Ability is perceived as differing by stage of life, probably in absolute level, but certainly in its salience as the major component in the causal fabric of behavior.

In fact, the threefold differentiation by age indicates an interesting pattern. Observers seem to feel that actors of various ages have different beliefs about reasons for the results they have in various situations (the correspondence of the young-old comparisons to results from research that asked for perceptions of others more directly is, as noted previously, evidence for a correspondence of attributing for others by the two methods). It is as though it is assumed that young people have ability and that there is little in the outside world to stop them from succeeding, if only they have learned to apply themselves consistently; thus, their successes are seen as caused by stable personal factors and their failures mostly by lack of motivation, effort, and so on, that is, an unstable yet personal lack of application of those constantly available abilities. Middle-aged people are seen as likely to have not only ability, but also the discipline to regularly apply that ability to the task at hand. Thus, their successes, too, are resulting from application of that ability, but their failures must be explained more extrapersonally; something outside of their control must have blocked the proper exercise of that ability and effort.

However, ability is less unambiguously assumed for older persons, although it is accepted as present at their successes to almost the same degree as is assumed for younger actors. At the same time, effort or application of ability appears to be assumed, and there seems to be little tendency to look for external causes for failure. Instead, ability, since it *may* be suspect, becomes a more likely attribution for failure (in the presence of the assumed motivation). Interestingly, the latter determination is opposite to the idea that older persons lose interest in achievement or in successful performance, an issue to be considered more fully in Chapter 6.

Overall, these patterns are consonant with much in the traditional social psychological areas of attribution research. That is, success is given credit more consistently than failure is blamed on the person's stable characteristics. More interestingly, the differentiation by failure follows a typical pattern, given certain reasonable assumptions. In each case it may well be that the element least taken for granted is the one most likely to be chosen as an explanation, a pattern that fits with notions about effects of expectedness of an outcome (Wortman, 1976). The weak link for young actors is motivation, or effort, since a success-orientation and high ability level are assumed. The corresponding weak link for middle-aged persons is extrapersonal, since they are assumed to be both mature and at the peak of their abilities. The weak link, insofar as there is one (and the weakness of the assumption that there is one is evident in the results concerning expectations and success-outcome causality), for older persons is seen to be ability. That is, observers of various ages, including but not limited to older persons, apparently are less likely to take ability for granted when an older actor is involved, and therefore, are more likely to look to it as the cause for what is still a relatively unexpected occurrence—failure. A decline in ability is considered *more likely* than a loss of motivation or a decline in support from others and other external factors. When failure occurs, it is that factor most likely to be different for this age group that is used to explain that outcome. Interestingly, the factor that subjects apparently see as most likely to change between middle-age and old age is a factor usually assumed to be the most stable of all—ability. Thus, these data, and the potential for explorations like these, add a dimension to examination of issues central to Type I attributions that has been almost totally lacking in current non-age-related, college-student-focused attribution research—the ongoing, developing character of attributions, even those about other persons.

The few findings of differences in affects, too, are predominantly in regard to failure and are consonant with belief in lessened ability (or more likely to a readiness to use lessened ability to explain failure) for older persons. They are expected to react somewhat more "hypoactively"—with tension rather than active forms of agitation, whereas the latter affect could be expected to result in reattacking the task more than the former types would. In that restricted sense, as in the broader strokes of attributions, there does appear to be a tendency to expect older persons to be more failure-oriented than members of other age groups, especially young adults. The earlier caution, that these differential attributions of causal beliefs and of affects are not strongly linked to expectations of future success or to lack of motivation among older persons, must be kept in mind when adopting such an interpretation of the data.

Finally, it is clear for the first time in these original data, that the variation of causal attributions produced by differences in situation is often at least as large as variation on the basis of observer or actor characteristics. In fact, observer characteristics had only minor effects on overall attributions and they did not interact with age of actor variation. Variation of situation by characteristics such as short-term or long-term process of outcome, social or nonsocial situation type, or technical or interpretive predominance is a major factor that should be explored, but can only be fully explored by a greatly heightened emphasis on breaking out of the bounds of academic situations (and work as an extension of school work) into analysis of attributions about a wide variety of life occurrences—major and minor, social and nonsocial, technical and interpretive, knowledge-based and manual dexterity-based, pointlike and processual, clear and ambiguous. This research is a step in that direction, another step made both easier and more obviously essential by an emphasis on adulthood and on an adult-age-related approach to social psychological questions. Since it is but one step, the issues broached in this section will arise again in later discussions and will be resolved only upon further, more extensive investigation than has been part of this research program.

We will now turn to another type of attribution research, also concerned with adult development—Type II attribution work. That is, we proceed to a consideration of questions about self-attributions across age groups, centering on the following:

> Do adults of various ages perceive themselves and their own successes and failures differently?
>
> Do they react with different affects to their own outcomes?
>
> Do they place differing importance on success and failure?
>
> Do they have different orientations to achievement and performance?
>
> Are their self-attributions consonant with the Type I similarities and differences we have just discussed?

CHAPTER 6

Adults Judging Themselves: Attributions, Affects, and Expectations

In this chapter we shift gears to a set of issues that fit into the category of Type II attribution work, that is, analysis of attributions for oneself and of linkages between attributions and affects and between those and individual differences related to achievement motivation, perceived outcome experience, and self-esteem. Because of the range of issues to be discussed, the chapter is arranged into a set of interlocking subparts. Initially I shall consider self-attributions and affect in a manner similar to the last chapter's exposition of data on attributions about others. Concluding that section is a brief discussion of the sorts of situations people of various ages reported. A fuller discussion of situations will be presented in Chapter 7.

The second section is a comparison of the self-attribution responses to the responses subjects had given when projecting to others, both those similar to and those different from themselves in age group. Particularly useful are comparisons of Type II attributions to Type I attributions for one's own age group. These comparisons are of the same order as those often made between actor and observer perspectives (e.g., Jones & Nisbett, 1971; Monson & Snyder, 1977). I will, however, not use that terminology, rather using "self-other" or "Type I versus Type II" for reasons outlined below. Those problems with use of "actor-observer" lie both in methodological specifics of these studies and in the ambiguous nature of the dichotomy itself.

After that discussion, I will present data in the personality areas related to attributions among adults. This section includes a review of previous work in the areas of achievement motivation and locus of control comparisons across adult age groups and a report of data collected in the current research program, especially regarding the relationship of the personality measures to Type II attributions. The fourth section is a discussion, in more general terms, of responses subjects gave to a set of self-report questions concerning perceived changes in achievement orientation and/or success-failure ratio in the past and projected into the future, importance of success, and satisfaction with success-failure ratio. These measures will be discussed in terms of age differences and in relation to attributions across age groups. I conclude the chapter with a summary of these data and a look forward to the important issues of meaning to be discussed in detail in Chapter 7.

Prior to discussion of the data contained in this and other studies, it may be fruitful to note briefly several rather obvious points. If it is the case that attributions about the outcomes that others experience are used as basic information to influence one's attitude toward and expectations for others—and that certainly has a lot of credence even though the data are not as regularly and unequivocally supportive as one may like—then it is clear that judgments one makes about the causes and implications of his or her own failures and successes are all the more crucial for forming and maintaining a sense of self-competence (or incompetence). For one thing, attribution judgments may be almost contemporaneously linked with both general and specific affects (Frieze, 1976; Weiner, 1979; Weiner et al., 1978). The combination of outcome with attributions and with affect may then influence self-expectations and, through those and other mediators, subsequent performance.

Some of the previous data concerning these points has already been reviewed in Chapter 4, and I will not belabor them here. Suffice it to say that there is good evidence within attribution theory and in the great stress placed on feelings of self-competence and self-esteem in many personality theories (most obviously White, 1959, but by no means only in that approach) for emphasizing the importance of attributions for one's outcomes. Thus, knowledge about Type II attributions, and about their interrelationships with aspects of personality, across the broadest possible range of individual characteristics and situations is crucial to understanding not only self-conception and self-esteem, but also the processes of attribution. The aim of this chapter is to provide data to help broaden that range.

ATTRIBUTIONS AND AFFECT ABOUT ONESELF

Although much research has been done on what I have been labeling Type II attributions, that is, attributions that an actor makes for his or her own outcomes, most of the studies have suffered from the same problems as most attribution work. That is, the situations have almost invariably been limited to academic situations—and often to classroom tests within that category. Furthermore, many of the "self" attributions have really been "pseudo-self" ones; that is, persons have been asked to think about being in, or recall having been in, a situation and then to indicate how they would feel and what causes they would see as important. Alternatively, subjects have been placed into highly artificial yet ambiguous situations in which the outcome and some other factors—consensus information, for example—have been manipulated to test Kelley's (1972) and others' specific formulations. In either case, attributions have usually been measured by having subjects rate the supposed importance of a number of factors provided by the researchers.

Predominant findings in these studies have tended to support a self-defensive, ego-enhancing extension of the findings developed through the study of Type I attributions (e.g., Ross, 1977), although currently there is dispute about the specific nature of these issues (see Snyder et al., 1976; Bradley, 1978). The self-defensive notion is that people are particularly likely to favor internal stable explanations for their own success and external and/or internal-unstable explanations for their failures; both tendencies enhance self-esteem. In fact, it may be that the similar tendency in attributions for others may be caused by a generalized liking for other others (especially those ambiguous others one is normally presented with in Type I attribution studies). This notion is supported by Snyder's (1976) assertion—and Banziger's (1979) age-related extension of that idea—that liked others are treated more like oneself than disliked others are when making attributions. We will return to a discussion of the relationship of self and other-attributions shortly, after consideration of the set of personal data in and of itself.

Attribution studies in all those modes, clearly, have major limitations in terms of external validity. These problems—artificial situations, structured response modalities, and a restricted focus on academia—have been recognized by attribution researchers (e.g., Frieze, 1976; Elig & Frieze, 1979; Frieze, Bar-tal, & Carroll, 1979; Weiner, 1979) and their critics (e.g., Buss, 1979) alike. Furthermore, they are, of course, by no means limited to social psychological research on Type II attributions. Indeed, the methodological issues related to artificiality, superficiality, and restriction of responses form the core of the major critiques of social psychology discussed in detail in the first several chapters of this book and forthcoming in Chapter 12. As with my research on Type I attributions, I have attempted to meet some of these problems. For example, once again, an open-response format was used. Secondly, subjects chose actual personal experiences so as to fit major categories—e.g., important success and failure, day-to-day success and failure, and social and nonsocial types of success and failures—rather than responding to one or a few pseudo-personal, prescribed situations.

It is important and instructive to recognize that the steps taken in this research to alleviate some of those problems are both faltering and incomplete and not without a different set of interpretive morasses, which I will discuss. I believe, though, that they are at least steps in the right direction.

All of the shortcomings of Type II attributions work mentioned are, of course, exacerbated by another problem with mainstream social psychology with which we are centrally concerned; there has been virtually no research with post-college-age adults. In fact, self-attribution research has lagged far behind the fairly limited attention paid to Type I attributions across age groups. The data I will report in this chapter are the first available studies of self-attributions across adult age groups, and they also have several methodological advantages—open-ended responses and a broad, self-chosen range of situations—over most non-age Type II studies.

One study that should be mentioned prior to a discussion of these data is a study that was focused on Type II attributions of older persons. Henry McCarthy (1977) approached older people's attributions as part of a potential therapeutic plan for enhancing morale. Thus, the context and tone of his study are quite different from those of the current work on Type II attributions. However, several of his findings are germane to this discussion. McCarthy had his subjects reminisce about eight events, four of which were ''ongoing'' and four which were in the person's past. Two of each time category were to be successes and two failures. That is, McCarthy used an open-ended reminiscence format to elicit information. Unfortunately, his method for getting the causal information was not satisfactory for our purposes. Rather than asking for a set of causes, he simply had subjects allocate causality either to "their internal characteristics" or to "external characteristics of the social and impersonal environment."

He found that his older subjects made fewer external attributions for ongoing than for past events, a finding he felt was counter to expectations, but which certainly is consistent with the results of my Type i attribution comparison between old and other age groups (particularly middle-aged, a time of life that was drawn upon for many of his subjects' self-defined past events). Furthermore, he found more internal attributions for pleasing events and more external ones for troubling events, another validation of the typical differentiation between success and failure common to all age groups of attributors.

Thus, one study, using a crude measure of attributions and with a rather unsophisticated retrospective comparison design, is the sole available source of information on adult—older person—self-attributions.[1] Despite the crudeness of the outcome measure, McCarthy's study provides several interesting insights and hunches about the meaning and use of attributions in an older adult population. Those insights are clearly related to the data I will be presenting in the remainder of this section.

Attributions for Self: Percentages and Dimensional Analysis

The categorization of responses to the success experiences supports the common idea among attribution theorists that people are likely to perceive their successes as resulting from their own efforts, abilities, and other characteristics. For three of the four success situations—important, less important, and nonsocial—effort was highest and ability second highest overall and for each of the age groups. In fact, almost half (47%) of all causes were in the category of short-term effort and another third in ability-type factors. Only for the social-situation success was there less unanimity. Short-term effort, mood, personal traits, and the interactive category of Person × Social external factors were all approximately equally high and considerably higher than the ability category. Social success clearly is seen in a different, more situational and transitional light than other successes.

Also, the age groups differed appreciably only in this success situation. The rankings of responses by young subjects were: personality traits, followed by effort, ability, and Person × Social interaction, in that order. Middle-aged and older subjects rated the interaction factor higher (first and second, respectively); middle-aged subjects saw mood as the most important factor in their social successes.

As can be seen in the tabular presentation of Table 6.1, there was considerable variation in attributional explanations of failures across both age group and situation. In

---

[1] I am aware of several recently published articles (e.g., Rodin & Langer, 1977; Schulz, 1976; and later work by those authors) and several dissertations and theses (L. Green, 1980; Lindstrom, 1980) that used a broad attribution framework to investigate the value of giving control and/or success experiences to nursing home residents. These studies are both interesting and valuable (and will be fully considered in Chapter 8, at which point further references will be cited), but they have not collected self-attributions as such. Rather, they have concentrated on behavior change and differences in morale and life satisfaction. Also, Miller and Porter (1980) recently reported data from the young adult end of the lifespan on comparison of self-attributions for present and past events as well as short-term change in attributions.

Table 6.1. Ranks of Causal Categories for Failure by Type of Situation
and Age of Subjects

Young	Middle-aged	Old
	Important Situation	
Ability (33%)	Unstable-social (40%)	Ability (20%)
Unstable-social (29%)	Person X Others (24%)	Mood (17%)
Effort, Person X Task (each 24%)	Ability (20%)	Effort, Person X Others (each 15%)
	Day-to-Day Situation	
Effort (30%)	Effort (21%)	Ability (32%)
Person X Task (26%)	Ability, mood (each 17%)	Effort (27%)
Mood, unstable-social (each 20%)	Unstable-social (16%)	Person X Task (14%)
	Social Situation	
Mood (35%)	Unstable-social (48%)	Person X Others (32%)
Person X Others (25%)	Person X Others (32%)	Effort (21%)
Unstable-social (20%)	Mood, effort (each 12%)	Unstable-social (21%)
	Nonsocial Situation	
Effort (39%)	Ability (54%)	Ability (41%)
Ability (33%)	Person X Task (15%)	Person X Task (30%)
Person X Task (28%)	Mood, effort (each 11%)	Mood (24%)

fact, every situation elicited a different order of causal categories. The most similar two situations were the important failure and the nonsocial one. In both cases, ability was seen as the most important cause, followed by several external and/or interactive factors, with effort and mood only modestly involved. For the less important failure, subjects reported effort most often, then ability and an interaction of Person with Task. The social failure showed a clear tendency for failure to be ascribed fully or in part (in interaction with the person) to unstable external social factors.

Thus, the so-called defensive attribution process—attributing failure to nonpersonal causes—appears most clearly in the social situation. However, it should be remembered that the social *success* was also attributed more to social and interactive than to purely personal causes than was done for other tasks. Indeed, only in the case of nonsocial events was there a major "defensive attribution" shift, with a preponderance of personal stable attributions for success and of less personal and unstable ones for failure. Even there, within the categories of personal attributions, the shift was hardly "defensive"; indeed "ability" was the first choice for failure and was second to "effort" for success. Further, important failures, in which the need for self-defense would appear to be strongest, were attributed most to ability, whereas corresponding important successes were effort-based. These data are relevant to discussions in Miller and Ross (1975), Snyder et al. (1978), and Bradley (1978) which cannot be considered in detail at this time.

How are these differences within failure situations and between failure and success moderated or influenced by age of the actor-attributor? I believe it is rather interesting, though certainly not in a monolithic, unidirectional fashion. First of all, middle-aged subjects were much less likely to use personal attributions to explain important failures. Whereas both young and old ranked ability highest, the middle-aged subjects placed it only third, behind unstable social factors and interactional relationships between themselves and others. They also placed effort lower than the other two groups. Meanwhile, older persons' attributions were decidedly more personal than the attributions of the young. Older persons' attributions for a less important failure were close to theirs for the important failure. On the other hand, young people placed much more emphasis on effort and in the interaction of themselves with the task, with mood also fairly high, when explaining their less important failure. Middle-aged persons, who had been steadfastly nonpersonal in placing "blame" for their important failure, surprisingly, were quite likely to attribute their less important failures to themselves.

The most similar set of attributions across all ages occurred for the nonsocial situations. All age groups placed emphasis on ability and the interaction of one's ability with the task (young, however, mentioned effort considerably more frequently than middle-aged and old). The social failure, as noted earlier, was given a high preponderance of nonpersonal and interactive explanations, and this orientation held quite consistently across all age groups. Once again, a greater frequency of personal—in this case, mood—causality given by young subjects was the exception.

An analysis of the personal-extrapersonal and stable-unstable dimensions of response, similar to that discussed in Chapter 5 concerning Type I attributions, rather clearly verifies the conclusions reached from the richer, but less statistically precise data on the nine categories. As with Type I analyses, there were few significant differences on overall measures of the two dimensions collapsed across all situations. The only significant effect of age or sex on the general measure was a tendency for females to have lower stability scores (.35 vs. .42; F, 1, 69 = 4.12, $p <$ .05). However, the eight situations were different on both stability and locus, as indicated by repeated measures analyses (F ratios with 7 and 518 df were 9.40 and 3.02, respectively; $p <$ .001 and .01, respectively).

Also as had been found with Type I attributions, there was a significant tendency to give more personal attributions for success than for failure (mean P-E scores were 1.50 vs. 1.19; t [74] = 4.95, $p <$ .001). Although the pattern held for all age groups, it was of only borderline significance for the young group (see Table 6.2). Also, age groups were not discriminably different when only success situations were considered, but varied considerably in the P-E dimension for failure. Once again, middle-aged persons were least likely to use personal causes and young were most likely to do so. There were no significant differences between success and failure or among age groups on the stability-instability dimension.

Table 6.2.   Mean Locus P-E Scores for Personal Situations
by Age Category of Subject and by Outcome

	Age of Subject			
Outcome	Young	Middle-Aged	Old	All Subjects
Success	1.50	1.50	1.54	1.51
Failure	1.17	1.03	1.14	1.10

Affects

Prior to description of analysis of the relationship of these findings to Type I attributions for different age groups, I should add a note about affect categories given for personal situations. There were only fairly minor differences in types of affect reported by situation and by age group for success. The comfort category (readers should refer back to the Appendix for review of the affects contained in each category) was given most frequently in three of the four cases and was second most common in the fourth (important success). Enhancement was clearly the next most cited kind of affect for success, given most frequently for the important situation and in a strong second place for the others.

For failure, discomfort was the most frequently given type of affect overall and for all except the nonsocial failure situation, in which tension, the second most frequent negative affect overall, was highest. Feelings of incompetence were also frequently reported, especially for the important situation. Although there were variations by age of subject within each situation, the differences were generally not large or consistent across situations. For example, older persons were somewhat more likely to report incompetence-related affect for important failures than young, but were much *less* likely to use that same category for social failures and for less important ones. Young persons were, in fact, more likely to report feelings of incompetence for less important tasks even though, as the reader may recall, they were highly likely to use lack of effort as the cause for that failure, an attribution that would not be expected to be linked with feelings of incompetence. By the way, in general, subjects gave fewer affects for failure situations than they did for success.

COMPARISONS OF ATTRIBUTIONS FOR OTHERS
AND FOR ONESELF

An intriguing set of comparisons concerns the relationship of attributions for oneself to attributions one makes for corresponding success-failure outcomes of others. This is generally the already-mentioned area of actor-observer differences; as will be seen shortly, the comparisons here are compatible with the most general findings in that body of literature.

Methodological Considerations

Before I do that, however, it is important to note a number of differences between this research and most of the actor-observer studies, in addition to keeping in mind cautions about the actor-observer literature I mentioned earlier and which are discussed in the research cited earlier (e.g., Monson & Snyder, 1977; Bradley, 1978). Some of the differences between this and the other work are in the direction of greater precision and "realism" in the present study, but the variations unfortunately carry with them methodological changes that can cloud intepretation and clarity (in ways different from the problems associated with the more standard research paradigm).

Most actor-observer research has been conducted with between-subjects designs, varying instructional set or response elicitation instructions rather than type of situation. That is, some subjects have been told to report attributions for outcomes of others; other subjects—the actors—report attributions for their own outcomes. Furthermore, often the "actor" stimuli, as I noted earlier about personal attribution research in general, have been pseudo-personal in nature. Since the attributions for others have also centered on hypothetical situations, this orientation has given a consistency of situation to be judged to both sides of the actor-observer dichotomy. At the same time, it certainly can be argued that a hypothetical situation purported to be about oneself is more different from naturally occurring situations calling for causal analysis of one's own outcomes than a hypothetical situation about others is from actual observation of others. In other words, permitting subjects to choose actual life experiences to recount causally yields both the advantage of "reality" in self-attributional decisions and the disadvantage that the attributions given for self and those for another are in reaction to different types of situations. That disadvantage, of course, looms large once the wide variation by situation, exposed in the Type I data in the last chapter, is taken seriously. The other variation already mentioned—between-subjects versus within-subjects for Type I and Type II attributions—also is a mixed case. Use of a within-subjects design, such as mine, has the advantage of direct comparisons and the disadvantage of the possibility of order effects, halo (and antihalo) response patterns, and other potential confounds inherent in within-subjects repeated-measures designs (Campbell & Stanley, 1966; Baltes et al., 1977).

Third, of course, most actor-observer research has not varied age—or other characteristics—of the actor, as subject of the "observer's" attributions or of his or her own "actor's" attributions. Rather, researchers have largely limited their samples to college students and, often, males. The "actors" in the Type I portion of the research, correspondingly, have either been members of the same age-sex-race-status of the "observer" or have been left unspecified in written descriptions. Thus, the findings have been correspondingly limited in two important age-relevant ways. The comparative data available are limited to young adults, and the observer half of the equation is limited to others highly similar to oneself.

As the reader is already aware from the methods as previously described, these data have been gathered using methods quite different from the norm. Subjects have responded in a within-subjects design across types of situations, outcomes, and actor characteristics within the Type I portion of the research and across outcome and situation type within the Type II portion, as well as across those two types of situations. This design thus allows for comparison across types and for comparison of self-attributions to attributions for others who are similar to and others who are quite different from oneself.

At the same time, particularly because of the within-subjects design—and especially because self-attributions always followed attributions about others—comparisons of the two types must be made cautiously and tentatively.

There is, of course, also another factor that reduced direct comparability even as it increased richness and value of the data within types. That is, the ways that situations were elicited were by no means identical. As noted in earlier methods sections for each type of data, subjects were given particular situations about others to respond to, but they were asked to describe their own situations, only staying within some general guidelines about the characteristics of the task and outcome. The trade off between this approach and a more coordinate one—both open or both assigned situations—must be carefully considered, and its limitations must be weighed against the limitations of using hypothetical situations for both and the rarely used but important approach of having actual behavior judged by both the actor and the observer(s), as was done in the early study by Storms (1973).

Resulting Comparisons

With all these provisos and limitations kept in mind, I believe it is instructive to make cautious comparisons of the two types of data received from each person. What similarities and differences can be seen? How does the pattern of relationships vary by age?

There were no differences between Type I and Type II attribution patterns on the personal-extrapersonal dimension, a lack of difference that held for both success (1.48 for Type I and 1.51 for Type II, t [74] = 0.57) and failure (1.07 and 1.10; t [74] = 0.47). However, there were differences on the stability dimension. Subjects had considerably lower—less stable—scores on that dimension when they gave self-attributions (0.27 vs. 0.39). Interestingly, and perhaps surprisingly, the predominant difference was for success situations. For success, the means were 0.24 for Type II attributions and 0.43 for Type I (t, 74, = 5.95; $p < .001$); the difference on failure (0.29 vs. 0.35) was slightly less than necessary for statistical significance (t, 74, = 1.83; $p < .10$). In other words, subjects were likely to give attributions that were personal and unstable for their own successes even though they had given equally personal but more stable attributions for the successes of others. For failure, subjects gave external, relatively unstable attributions for both their own and others' failures, although their own attributions were slightly more stable than for others.

Various researchers, including myself, feel that people are likely to make Type I attributions for others who are similar to themselves in a fashion more similar to attributions for themselves than when asked to explain the outcomes of less similar others (see Snyder, 1976; Banziger, 1979). That is, it is hypothesized that the actor-observer differences consistently found when using a rather characterless "other" would tend to dissipate when the "other" for whom attributions were being made was particularly similar to the attributor. Since we observed age-of-actor-based differences in Type I attributions and age of self-attributor differences in Type II attributions, it is possible and important to examine more fully whether Type I attributions for same-age others are more similar to self-attributions than attributions for similar situations hypothetically occurring to actors unlike the subject in age group membership and all that we know that goes with that.

Such an analysis yields data that are slightly, but by no means unambiguously, supportive of the notion. The main differences between self and other attributions, the reader will recall, were found on the stable-unstable dimension, and it is here that the most support is found for the hypothesized relationship. Whereas overall the differences between Type I and Type II attributions for success were significant beyond the .001 level, young and old subjects did not significantly differ from their *own* age group. Middle-aged subjects, however, did differ at a high level of significance (t, 29, = 4.81; $p < .001$). For failure, also, two of three age groups did not have significantly different stability scores for themselves and their own age group, whereas they were significantly different from other age groups. In this case, however, it was old subjects who varied, giving significantly lower stability for self (t, 22, = 2.30; $p < .05$). By the way, given the emphasis on personal attributions for failure by old people both for other old actors and for themselves, the lower stability for self-failure is a particularly healthy, self-defensive attribution, moving away as it does from a more general negative stereotype of old people as personally responsible for failure in a stable, enduring, "abilitylike" way.

The interpretation of the personal-extrapersonal data in similar terms, unfortunately, is severely limited, because of the overall similarity of Type I and Type II attributions. However, insofar as degree of lack of significant differences is a reasonable measure to use to make, interpretations, these data give tenuous support to the hypotheses. That is, Type II attributions in each group were generally even more similar to Type I attributions for one's own age group than they were to Type I attributions for other age groups. The t-value for same-age comparisons was usually the smallest of the three comparisons, and the few significant differences between Type I and Type II P-E scores are in comparisons to age groups other than one's own. For example, young subjects' Type II attributions for failure on the personal dimension (mean of 1.17) were virtually identical to their attributions for other young actors (1.17), quite similar to their Type I attributions for old actors (1.26), but significantly different from their attributions for the failures of middle-aged actors (0.80; t, 21, = 2.10, $p < .05$). Similarly, middle-aged subjects' self-attributions for failure were fairly near to being significantly different from their attributions about young actors (1.03 vs. 1.29; t, 29, = 1.65, $p < .15$), but almost identical to those for their own age group; older persons' success attributions for themselves were similar to their attributions for their own age group, but nearly significantly different from their attributions for middle-aged others (1.54 vs. 1.22; t, 22, = 2.02, $p < .10$), whereas their failure attributions were virtually identical to Type I attributions they made for old actors' failures (1.14 vs. 1.12), but fairly, though not significantly, different from their attributions for middle-aged and young actors (0.87 and 0.93, respectively).

Thus, the data are certainly weak, but they give a hint at least that people in each age group tend to see their own actions, judge their own contribution to success and failure, and make self-attributions at least partially on the basis of more generally held attribution patterns for their own age group. Whether this is because general stereotypes of competence, responsibility, and so on, about others are applied to oneself or because a person typically uses his or her own attribution pattern (the "characteristic center of gravity" for self-attributions) as a basis for judgments about causal factors in the outcomes of similar others while relying on stereotypes and cultural biases for judgments about dissimilar others cannot be ascertained from these data. They are, however, important and easily researchable questions that may be more easily asked in designs that include more variation in subject (Type II-actor) characteristics and in actor characteristics (in Type I portions of the study) in a global within-subjects design than in the sort of restricted-type, between-subjects designs prevalent in the current approaches.

The discovery of such questions, which must obviously be made prior to hope of discovery of answers to them, will be facilitated by studies similar to that described thus far, even though those studies share many of the shortcomings discussed in detail in early chapters—the shortcomings of linear models, static measurement tools, and relatively low external validity. Before proceeding further in discussion of a point about importance of these studies, however, there is one more large, heterogenous set of questionnaire data to be discussed. Subjects responded to several self-report items (see questionnaire included as part of the Appendix) at the end of the session described thus far, and they also completed several personality inventories three to six months after participation in the first study. The results of those items, their relationships to data others have gathered, and their relationship to types of attribution patterns people used in other parts of their responses will be discussed in the next major section of this chapter.

PERSONALITY, ATTRIBUTIONS, AND AGE

Achievement Orientation, Motivation, and Attributional Styles

Information about several types of personality measures and their relationships to age, on the one hand, and to attributional patterns, on the other, can be particularly relevant to the issues to which this part of the book has been devoted. For example, Weiner (e.g., 1972, 1974) and others have consistently referred to an hypothesized relationship between attributional pattern and a broader personality factor—orientation to achievement. That is, there are presumed to be failure-oriented persons and success-oriented ones, with distinctly different patterns of attributions for themselves and/or for others. At the same time, those orientations should be broader approaches to performance and achievement, related in some way to achievement motivation and to nonattributional behaviors and cognitions. Measures of the orientation, on the other hand, are likely to be related to measures of test anxiety, since that appears to be based in a cognitive failure-oriented approach to tasks (see, for example, Wine, 1971; Sarason, 1976).

Indeed, Weiner and his colleagues have made several attempts to relate attributions and/or affect with achievement motivation, usually as measured by Mehrabian's (1968, 1969) scales for achievement motivation (e.g., see reviews in Weiner's 1972 book and 1979 article). As I will discuss shortly, that questionnaire—and other measures of achievement motivation and orientation available—are not at all well suited to adult age difference analyses. In this research I used a slightly different measure of achievement orientation, a set of subscales recently developed by Helmreich and Spence (1978; Helmreich, Beane, Lucker, & Spence, 1978; Helmreich, Spence, Beane, Lucker, & Matthews, 1980). In any case, the relationship of a personality measure with attributions for achievement and with outcome-related affect, using college students, has been moderately supportive of a link. Since these have been reviewed both earlier in the book (Chapter 4) and by others (e.g., Mehrabian & Bank, 1975; Weiner, 1972), I will not discuss them further at this time, except to note that one relationship that may be relevant to the relationship of attributions to age may be age-related differences in achievement orientation, self-esteem, and other personality variables.

Is there evidence for such a link? Yes and no. Social gerontologists regularly seem to assume there is (see, for example, Kuhlen, 1964; or Neugarten, 1973). They assert that older people are less achievement motivated and more concerned with "interior life," preparation for death through life reviews, and other mechanisms (to be discussed briefly in Chapters 13 and 14). The basis for these assertions, however, is primarily anecdotal and/or the interpretation of interview data in the Kansas City studies of adult development conducted in the late 1950s and early 1960s (see, for example, Cumming & Henry, 1961; Neugarten, 1973). The one available source of data directly related to achievement motivation is a study conducted by Veroff and his colleagues (Veroff, Atkinson, Feld, & Gurin, 1960). They found that there was a fairly clear linear decline over age in the percentage of high achievement motivation scores persons were given on the basis of their answers to a set of TAT-type stimuli in a national-sample survey.

I do not think it is appropriate to spend a great deal of time on analysis of that study and its results. The facts that the study was done over 20 years ago, that it used an unusual mix of TAT stimuli, a face-to-face interview, and a questionnaire response format, that it appears the data were analyzed in a fairly subjective way, and that the age groups were not balanced for education, occupation, and status—factors we have discussed previously as closely related to achievement orientation—all belie the level and confidence of interpretation that has been given the results. Those factors and the confusion of cohort and maturation involved in every cross-sectional study considered in and of itself form a slim basis, indeed, for any declaration concerning the effects of age and age-related life events such as retirement on achievement motivation. Heckhausen (1967) noted that and the need for further research along those lines almost 15 years ago, and yet no further data have been gathered.

One problem in that regard, already briefly noted, is the inappropriate nature of most measures of achievement motivation/orientation. One has the choice between TAT stimuli and an essentially clinical analysis of the stories people tell in response to those—as McClelland and others (e.g., McClelland et al., 1953) have consistently done—or an array of questionnaire measures (e.g., Mehrabian, 1968, 1969), none of which has yielded a great deal of validity or found a great deal of favor. The value of the measures, even in relation to the kinds of uses to which they are normally put, is not high. They are particularly troublesome to use in making adult age comparisons. Like much of personality and social psychology and of attribution research, they are rather specifically formulated to be appropriate to college students. Although they are theoretically concerned with motivation to achieve as a relatively general approach to performance, the specifics of the scales are usually heavily oriented toward academic achievement, on the one hand, and business success, on the other. Neither of those specific categories is likely to be appropriate for older persons or, indeed, for many adults, especially women (see Spence & Helmreich, 1978; Helmreich & Spence, 1978; Mehrabian & Bank, 1975). In fact, Mehrabian found it necessary to develop separate scales for men and women, with his clear biases toward work and business for the men balanced by stereotypic family life situations for the women. That is barely acceptable as a solution within an age group, but it becomes virtually useless across ages.

Finally, the validity of a conception of "achievement orientation" as a global, unitary factor has been seriously challenged whenever cross-cultural group differences have been of central concern (see Joe, 1971). Unfortunately, most of the criticisms apply equally to an important measure for our purposes, the test anxiety scale (Mandler & Sarason, 1952). That measure is useless for direct comparisons, since it is clearly designed for young adult college students.

As I already noted, Spence and Helmreich and their associates have developed a scale that is more useful. The scale, described in considerable detail in Helmreich and Spence (1978) and Helmreich et al. (1978, 1980), was designed to tap four separable and relatively orthogonal aspects of achievement orientation—a sense of Mastery in facing tasks, Competitiveness, Work and its importance, and Personal Unconcern with how others feel about your success.[2]

I will briefly review data I collected using the measure. The WOFO was given as part of a set of measures to the same subjects who participated in the attribution study (since five subjects could not be relocated, the N for the scales is 70 instead of 75). Further information on this part of the research is contained in an unpublished report (Blank, 1981a). I will also report here on responses to more general self-report questions concerning interest in achievement and will examine the relationships among these measures and attribution patterns. I will also compare responses of my subjects to those given to Helmreich and associates by middle-aged persons.

---

[2]The last factor and questions related to it have recently been dropped by its authors, since it showed virtually no relationship to outcome measures of interest to them (Helmreich et al., 1980; Helmreich, personal communication, January 1980). Though not directly relevant to this research, the lack of relationships is noteworthy, since the subscale was conceptually closely related to fear of success, emphasized by Horner (1972) and others (Monahan, Kuhn, & Shaver, 1974; Maccoby & Jacklin, 1974) concerned with sex differences in achievement motivation. In any case, the form used in this study was the earlier one and, therefore, includes the Personal Unconcern subscale. As you will see, no clear-cut differences on it arose in this research either.

Locus of Control

Before doing so, however, I should note one other set of personality measures that have been used fairly regularly with older subjects alone and in comparison to younger ones. The data concern locus of control, a personality factor that appears, at least on the surface, to be directly related to attributional analyses.

Obviously, locus of control, that is, the tendency of a person to feel that reinforcement for his or her behavior is controlled internally or by external forces, is conceptually closely related to the locus of causation dimension of achievement attributions. Many researchers, beginning with Rotter (1966), who devised the scale, have tried to relate scale scores to performance. Similarly, the attributional analysis of achievement orientation contains reference to an internal and an external locus for causality, and the linkages between each locus and type of outcome are the basis for discriminating between success-oriented and failure-oriented attribution styles, as described earlier.

The appearance of similarity, unfortunately, is in large part illusory and, at its worst, confusing and likely to lead to incorrect conclusions. I will not belabor the issues here, since others have considered these problems in more detail. Put succinctly, locus of control and locus of causality appear to be relatively independent of each other (Ickes & Layden, 1978); the locus of control measure does not allow for separation of locus for success and for failure events, a core concern in the attribution field (Weiner, 1972); and the scales are confusing and biasing when used for group comparison purposes (Lao, 1975; Joe, 1971; Gurin, Gurin, Lao, & Beattie, 1969). All of these reasons indicate that age comparisons of locus of control are bound to be ambiguous at best and misleading at worst, and in any case they do not tell us much about attributions and attributional pattern differences across age groups.

On the other hand, locus of control is one of the few concepts that has in fact been used regularly in social gerontology, including for therapeutic purposes. Various researchers have perceived it to be an important group differences variable between old and young (Kahana, Felton, & Kiyak, 1979; and others to be cited in the following). Generally, the assumption has been made that older people "should" (that is, would be expected by various social gerontological theories to be) be lower on internal locus of control, because they are, in fact, losing control—over source and amount of income, mobility, and so on. The data, however, have not been highly supportive of that assumption. In fact, no researchers have found indications of greater externality of locus of control in older groups. Lao (1975) and Ryckman and Malikiosi (1975) found no differences, while Kuypers (1972), Palmore and Luikart (1972), and Wolk and Kurtz (1975) all found more internality in their older samples than in their non-aged ones. Kahana and associates, in several studies reported in Kahana et al. (1979), did not compare age groups, but did find high internal locus of control among old persons. They did note, however, that the bias toward internal explanations moderated after institutionalization.

Part of the problem with their use of locus of control, and the reason for disconfirmation of hypotheses of more external feelings, clearly lies in the nature of the locus of control measure vis-à-vis attributions. That is, older persons may well be higher in internal locus, especially for failures, specifically if they see themselves losing control, the belief that the social gerontologists use as the base for their contrary notion. Of course, though, that relationship of internality and loss of control feelings should only be apparent in failure situations; the locus of control scale does not lend itself to such a separation of success and failure situations.

In any case, because the locus of control scale has been regularly used in gerontology in a way similar to attribution measures (such as discussed in social perception terms in Chapter 5), I included a locus of control measure in this study. The subjects were given a modified form of the locus of control measure (condensed and with a different response mode from the original) that had previously been used with older adults. In this way, I gathered data that can explore the relationship (if any) of that measure to what most of the researchers and therapists in gerontology are actually concerned with when they use the scale, that is, the attributions older people make for the failure outcomes they experience. It is important to explore any possible link, no matter how clouded, between the measure they have used and the concept they want to operationalize. Perhaps linking the two concerns will redirect interests of the gerontologists toward more sophisticated, less ambiguous measures of orientation to success and failure.

Study Results

Do the data I collected show relationships between achievement orientation and age and/or between locus of control and age? Do they show relationships between those personality measures and patterns of attribution, especially placement on the two major dimensions we have been considering?

After this fairly exhaustive review of those areas, the answer I am about to give is bound to be somewhat anticlimactic. The answer, in its briefest form and with several provisos to be explained below, is "no" to both sets of questions.

In this sample—and the reader must keep in mind that it is of relatively highly educated continuing education students in all age groups—there are remarkably few relationships that even approach statistical significance. As discussed further in the paper mentioned earlier (Blank, 1981a), the sole significant finding on the subscales of the WOFO is a significant effect of age on Mastery (F, 2, 64, $= 3.16, p < .05$). Older persons, particularly older women, were lower than other age groups on reported importance of and satisfaction with having mastery over tasks. There were no other significant main or interaction effects, although there was a fairly clear tendency for females, especially older ones, to score lower on Competitiveness (F, 2, 64, $= 2.95$, $p < .10$). Correlations using age as a continuous variable showed the same patterns. None of the correlations were significant, but the correlations of age with Mastery ($ - .15$) and with Competitiveness ($ - .16$) were nearly so.

Further, there were no significant age or sex effects on locus of control. Finally, there were no relationships between scale responses and types of attributions people gave (at least as could be analyzed using the dimensions). Together, these data indicate that orientation to achievement, if it varies with age, is likely to be unsystematic. Further, "age" differences, when found, may well be primarily cohort differences, a likelihood Rotter (1976) has found it necessary to attend to when making so-called developmental comparisons of successive cohorts of college students.

After reporting all that was not related to age or to attribution processes, can I report anything that was related? Yes, but only in a fairly weak fashion. As I already mentioned, subjects had been asked a series of questions about their own attribution experiences, outlook, and perceived changes in success and failure. The responses in virtually all cases were almost unremittingly optimistic and satisfied. The negative side of response possibilities were virtually never chosen. This was true of all age groups. However, within this broadly positive orientation, there was a tendency, almost always weak, but consistent across almost all measures, for the old group of subjects to be less highly optimistic, less highly satisfied, and more likely to see trouble on the horizon.

Large majorities of young and middle-aged respondents said that they "succeed *much more* often" than they fail in important situations, whereas most older respondents moderated that positive feeling to the next lower response, "succeed *more* often" than fail. This difference in frequency had a Chi-square (8 *df*) of 13.50, which was significant at $p < .10$. There were no differences in this same question for less important situations (Chi-square, 6 *df*, = 5.01). With an almost identical set of breakdowns, older persons were more likely to report that their ratio of success to failure for both important and less important situations was the same as it had been five years ago, whereas most young and middle-aged subjects said they were more successful than they had been. Again, significance tests on the Chi-square for important tasks was borderline, whereas for less important tasks it was slightly higher (Chi-square, 4 *df* = 7.83, $p < .10$, for important and 9.50, $p < .05$ for less important).

More significantly, both statistically and in relation to the future orientation of subjects and their expectations, were the similarly worded questions about estimations of future success related to the present. Older subjects had dramatically reduced expectations for the future compared to young and middle-aged ones. Whereas almost three-quarters of the young subjects and two-thirds of the middle-aged expected to better their (already very high) ratio of success to failure and the remainder in each age group felt they would stay the same, only four (17.5%) of the old felt they would be succeeding more in the future, and an equivalent number felt they would be failing more. The distributions were almost identical for less important events, and Chi-square statistical tests of significance on both were beyond the .001 level (21.12 and 20.42 with 4 *df*).

Although the direction of these effects is quite clear, and a verification of sorts of the idea that older people become less successful—and/or perceive themselves as becoming less able to succeed—several cautions are in order. First of all, as noted several times, the answers to this set of questions, and the standard personality measures, are quite positive for all age groups, conspicuously including the older one. Virtually all answers are indicative of high esteem for one's abilities and high control over one's environment and outcomes. Even the older respondents were still predominantly optimistic and predominantly success-oriented.

Secondly, most of the differences just described, clearly, are rather weak and tenuous. Except for the two questions on estimations of success five years in the future, the effects were of marginal significance by Chi-square tests of frequencies and, not previously mentioned, were not significant when studied by analysis of variance techniques (with age category and sex as independent variables).

Thirdly, answers to several other, related self-report questions showed no differences at all by age and sex. Old, equally with young and middle-aged, felt that their ratio of success to failure was at least as good as those of other people. Whereas that may not have been surprising when they were asked to compare themselves to others of their own age and sex, it is somewhat surprising that that feeling was equally strong in comparison to "people in general." Consistently, the majority of subjects in each age group felt they were equal in important tasks, day-to-day tasks, social tasks, and even physical ability with others, and, except for physical tasks, only a few subjects indicated they felt they were worse. People were less satisfied with their success compared to others in the sphere of physical activities, although even in that area most felt they were equal to or better than people in general.

Finally, there was a slight tendency for older persons and for females to rate success as slightly less important to themselves than young, middle-aged, and males in general did. However, once again, the difference did not approach statistical significance (Chi-square, 4 df, = 3.95, p = .41 for age category; Chi-square, 2 df, = 2.62, p = .27 for sex), and all subjects answered in a positive or neutral category. All subjects, showing a pattern similar to that for the importance of succeeding, were at least fairly satisfied with their ratio of success to failure and with life in general; older subjects and females in general, again, were slightly less unanimous and strong in their satisfaction, but there were no effects that approached significance in either analysis of variance or Chi-square tests.

In other words, the picture of age differences among the groups—at least, it must be remembered, among academically inclined, well-educated persons—is one of slight variation in several factors and no differences on most. Older subjects were less inclined to have feelings of mastery and more inclined to expect more failures in the future, but they, along with young and middle-aged, were generally very positive in their evaluation of their successes and failures, satisfied with their ratios and their lives, interested in doing well, motivated to achieve and to do well, highly valuing work and succeeding at what they try, and high on internal locus of control. All in all, it appears that age as such, controlling for wide variation in educational level and presumed base rate of achievement motivation—clearly a less than totally natural lack of variation, of course, in terms of present cohorts—has only minor effects on personality factors related to achievement and to attributional style.

Taken in combination with the extensive data gathered on attributions about as well as by older persons and middle-aged persons, these data indicate that people of various ages view themselves differently from how people of other ages view *them*selves, and that this variation is along lines similar to how people of all ages view their age group. At the same time, they feel the same about themselves and their successes and failures as others do. Also, all people attribute differently, not only depending on outcome, but also on type of situation, a factor seldom considered in previous research on any age group.

There are at least two major facets of this research that nonetheless militate against a sanguine interpretation of current, non-adult-oriented research. First of all, the results of this research show that, to a fairly large degree, people of various ages see themselves—their actions, outcomes, reactions, and causal responsibilities—as others (and they themselves, through societal eyes) see them (and others who are like them on a salient characteristic). Although this notion has long standing in social psychology, especially among sociological social psychologists (e.g., Cooley, 1922; Biddle, 1979), the importance of social definitions and role expectations has often been underplayed when only one group of people, with a homogeneous set of social roles, is consistently made the only object of consideration.

Thus, whereas mechanisms of attributing may be similar across a wide age and cohort range of adults, the application to oneself of the results of those mechanisms of attribution is differentiable and fairly distinctive. Each of the three age groups examined in this body of research differs from each of the others on one of the dimensions of attributing, and each has a tendency to use a particular and distinctive combination of stability and personalness of causes (and, therefore, to use one subset of the potential body of causes more than the others). Self-attributions—and presumably the effects of outcomes—are thus different for each age group.

That leads to a second, perhaps even more important, point. In a way, those who would use findings of no differences as supporting a continued disregard of age should examine more carefully the implications of that finding in combination with their own developmental model, fragmentary and relatively unexamined as it is. That is, as we discussed briefly at several points in Chapter 1 and Chapter 4, those who regularly study attributions believe that the attributions one uses at a particular time are rather direct applications of internalized schemata (Weiner, 1972; Frieze, 1976). Although those schemata are assumed to be relatively stable, they are also assumed to be the result of prior experience with success and failure when the individual has been in achievement situations. That is, the effects of attributional decisions accumulate and become bits of information added into the hopper to be used for the next causal decision. If that is the case, and if, as appears fairly obvious, people of various ages differ systematically in number of experiences with success and failure, type of past experiences, context of present experiences (e.g., work, school, retirement as defining one's primary locus of activity), and exposure to the successes and failures of others (thereby altering both consensus information and point of view when observing the performances and outcomes of others), then it is odd indeed that there is apparently as *little* variation in Type I attributions, Type II attributions, and achievement-related personality factors across such a broad range as these data indicate. Rather than proving the lack of value involved in looking across age groups, the lack of differences can and should be used as an indicator that a simple accumulation model is in fact not a proper one to describe developmental change or age group comparisons in the process of attribution. It rather points to the need for a model that *can* account for broad agreement in attributional approach *within* wide variation on exactly those factors which are readily presumed to mold attributional style and determine schemata. In other words, *both* change *and* stability must be described, explored, and explained if attribution theory is to account for the life-span use of attribution information and mechanisms.

How might such a pattern of age comparisons as has been found be explained? How might an explanation be developed from the analyses presented so far? The reader may by this point be somewhat dissatisfied with the research that has been presented. In many ways it is obviously as monochromatic and one-dimensional as the research that I have criticized, with the simple (though important) addition of age group comparisons. As I have discussed at length in the first part of the book and in the Introduction to Parts 2 and 3, I believe there is more value in such a relatively simplistic approach than some may find, including those who see group comparisons as a waste of effort and those who are sophisticated in their approach to developmental research. Even to those who are sympathetic, however, I realize that the fact remains that the research described up to this point is not nearly enough, that it is not the major advance in the direction of developmental explanation that attribution research—and social psychology in general—needs. Instead, it is concerned with a change in the veneer of social psychological research rather than the building of a new core. It is age-differences research cast in the traditional empiricist mold.

Is it of value? I argued previously in general and now in the specific that it is. Is it of sufficient value to stand on its own as the model for a social psychology of developing adults? Obviously not, but it leads toward research that is a much bolder step in that direction. It can lead to a new conceptualization of the development of social psychological aspects of adult behavior and thought and to new areas of interest within the various areas of social psychology, ones that will be useful both for developmental understanding and for static understanding of points in time and the mechanisms that define those points.

In describing the research up to this point I have gone into detail about the major effects of situation type on the pattern of attributions about others. I have said less in this chapter about the sorts of situations that persons of various ages described for themselves. Those differences will be considered in the next chapter. I believe it is in those differences that the beginnings of a more conceptually advanced, development-sensitive attribution analysis can be made. Old, middle-aged, and young persons, especially ones from a fairly homogeneous, educated, middle-class population, may indeed differ fairly little in the way they approach performances and in the way they explain outcomes. At the same time, the content—the meaning—of the outcomes and of the causes and affects themselves may change. This may be as obvious as a success by one person's definition not necessarily being seen as a success by another, as happened with the weight loss situation already described (p.102). At the same time, it may be much more subtle and much more pervasive. The perceived ratio of success to failure may stay relatively stable by having the definitions of success and failure change as one's life situation changes. The sort of outcome that is necessary to make one feel happy or angry or frustrated may not be the same at one age as at another.

In general, what our descriptive, superficial questionnaire data may be telling us is that the superficial levels we usually concern ourselves and content ourselves with (as social psychologists, not as ''lay-attributors'') may be relatively stable. But a few hints from those data may lead us to a radically different conclusion about the source of that stability. The source may be exactly in the point at which Riegel (e.g., 1978) would have us place it, and which I tried to present in Chapter 3. The stability of attributional mechanisms may be—perhaps must be—the result of constant shifting (constant tension-production and tension-reduction at the level of meanings) of *relationships*. How information about outcome is used will remain constant *only* as the definition of that outcome is constantly reconstructed to meet the changing circumstances of one's life which define where one will and will not find success or failure. Attributions may usually be stable across the adult life-span, but only as the result of constantly changing underlying patterns of the meanings of actions and of outcomes. Paradoxically, the meaning of a specific event may remain the same only as a result of the meaning of achievement changing over time, or vice versa.

At one and the same time, the decisions about causality may remain stable, not because of some stable inner controlling mechanisms, but because of reliance at all ages on external-societal definitions of behavior and its causes, that is, reliance on stereotypic *expectations* that form the basis for stereotypic *explanations*. The current data, and the interrelated nature of Type I and Type II attributions about the same age group, highlight the social nature of the attribution process, including social definitions of *both* the form *and* the content of causal decisions. Even for nonsocial tasks, even when in only the "implied presence of others"—which, we must remember, is often on a par with the actual presence of others as an important directing agent for our actions and our cognitions—attributions are, in fact, social and constructed. Attributions are *socially meaningful* or they are useless. Such a view considerably broadens the scope of attribution research and theory from its intrapsychic, individualistic, stable model.

Are these notions reasonable? Do they help explain the patterns of results I and my colleagues and others found—older people expecting to succeed less, but continuing to be satisfied with their successes; people in general attributing failure more to stable characteristics of older actors and yet not altering their expectations for those older actors (see also Connor et al., 1978, and Locke-Connor & Walsh, 1980)? Those questions, obviously, are unanswerable with the regular, normative tools of social psychology (at least when it is defined as psychological). They can, in fact, not be answered without detailed, intensive, longitudinal investigations of the phenomenology of everyday life and everyday thought (which, of course, is what Fritz Heider, 1958, sought to develop). However, perhaps some better grasp of some of those ideas, some feeble test of those notions, may take place with tools at least somewhat more useful in that regard than static, rigidly defined, artificial studies of the mental states of college students.

I have tried to produce data that can be used to make a beginning in this regard. An attempt to apply a few tools—further, qualitative analysis of the data already described and an interview centering on definitions, meaning, and perceptions of attribution processes—is the topic of the following chapter.

CHAPTER 7

The Missing Link in Attribution Theory and Research: Meaning

Our central concern in Part 2 is with attributional decisions and affective responses to success and failure. We have already discussed a considerable amount of recently gathered information from other researchers and from the set of original studies already described. Those data expand knowledge of both attributions for others and attributions for oneself across adult age groups and, thereby, expand attributional work in directions that have previously been ignored. The research makes use of traditional approaches that have been used copiously in previous research with college students.

However, in the course of my description and discussion of these data, it has often been apparent that the normal methodologies are not well suited to the kinds of analysis which are at the base of a real social psychology of developing adults. The measurements are often static; change in attribution research, as in most social psychological research, is invariably experimenter-controlled and short-term; the situations have been narrowly defined, and the emphasis has clearly been placed on an information processing model of attributions. The latter involves the implication that people carry around with them both relatively stable schemata—centers of gravity—and relatively stable, clear definitions of the vocabulary of causality and responsibility. None of those assumptions appear to be safe ones to make, especially if one's interest is in the use of the attribution conception to understand everyday thoughts and actions across a wide spectrum of individuals.

Similar points have been made recently concerning social cognition research in general, an area which certainly encompasses most attribution research including that reported upon thus far in this part of the book. In commenting upon a symposium in social knowing, Neisser (1980) roundly criticized what he perceived to be the incredible narrowness of the point of view and the range of concerns of theorists and researchers in social cognition. His general point is well illustrated in the area of attributions about achievement. Although the supposed goal is to understand the meanings that success and failure have for psychological and social life—definitions of self, expectation of future outcomes for self and others, in other words, motivation in its broadest terms (Weiner, 1979)—attribution theorists have blithely ignored the plethora of information in the mass media and popular literature about what people think of those twin concepts. A perusal of the shelves of any library or bookstore or of the pages of reference works such as *Books in Print,* in which almost four large pages of tiny print are devoted to listing books under the subject heading of ''success,'' would indicate that knowing about, thinking about, and reading about success and failure—especially how to attain the former and avoid the latter (or turn it into success, an abiding theme in books such as Sherman, 1958, or Mandino, 1978)—are major preoccupations of a large number of American adults.

Regardless of that reality, attribution theorists have ignored those sources and, indeed, have ignored the feelings, beliefs, and opinions of their subjects to a remarkable degree. Instead, they have been "more concerned with theory itself than with the phenomena that the theory was designed to explain. They see little need to investigate "social knowing" as it actually occurs in the world" (Neisser, 1980, p. 603).

Ultimately this has left attribution theory curiously devoid of meaning and any real understanding of what having a limited array of abilities and social and physical contexts, and being lucky, trying, and succeeding and failing having to do with individuals, with who and what they have been, are, and will be.

I have already discussed some of the outcomes of this perseveration and how the data I and others have begun to gather may be steps toward a more balanced, natural collection and usage of our scientific findings about achievement and attributions. I have discussed the merits, and difficulties, of using an open-ended format *and* a range of situations, even allowing subjects to generate their own situations about themselves (especially see the Appendix and Chapter 6). I have gone into detail about preliminary explorations of the relationship of age (in the current historical milieu) to reports about achievement, success, failure, and the importance of succeeding over time and to projected ideas about the effects specific incidents and outcomes may have on various sorts of adults.

In this chapter I will expand upon situational variation and refer to further analysis of data gathered in the studies described thus far. Most of the chapter, however, will consist of using some sketchy preliminary data gathered from interviews of 17 adults of various ages as tools to move toward meaningful analysis of the meaning and explanation of success and failure by these 17 persons. In the course of that consideration I will discuss in some detail a few current emphases in social psychological research on attributions, especially a controversy concerning the differentiation of cause and reason (Hamilton, 1980; Harre & Secord, 1972; Buss, 1978, 1979b; Harvey & Tucker, 1979; Kruglanski, 1979) and the interrelationship of cognitive, affective, and perceptual mechanisms underlying perception of cause and responsibility (Neisser, 1980; Newtson, 1980). One issue I wish to discuss in some detail is the concerns various theorists (Buss, 1978, 1979a, 1979b; Hamilton, 1980; Harre & Secord, 1979; Harvey & Tucker, 1979; Kruglanski, 1979) have raised concerning the differentiation, or lack thereof, of causes and reasons as attributions. I will first briefly outline the controversy, particularly using Buss's (1978, 1979a, 1979b) argument as a base, and then I will consider how the data I have gathered may be useful in illuminating aspects of the general issue. Of course, those sources cited should be referred to for a fuller discussion of the controversy.

Put simply, as Buss (1978) does at the beginning of his article, he and other "ordinary language analysis" critics of attribution theory and research assert that giving a cause and giving a reason are two logically different sorts of explanations (Hamilton refers to "explanation" and "attribution" as those terms used in legal analysis). "Causes" may be used as explanations of what happens to a person, but only "reasons'' are valid explanations of what is done *by* a person. Furthermore, it's asserted, attribution theory and research is single-mindedly devoted to only one of these types of explanation—cause. Interestingly, the ''attribution'' part of Hamilton's dichotomy (taken from Hart & Honoré's, 1961, usage in legal analysis) is the part which he asserts attribution theorists have ignored. Albeit in different terminologies, Buss and Hamilton appear to be united in their brief that attribution researchers have either avoided ''reasons'' or, worse, have completely confused the two and made them equivalent. Buss (1978) cites several examples from Kruglanski (1975) that illustrate his point. He further asserts that Heider's original formulations, even though they were the sort of ordinary language analysis Buss advocates, were lacking in this regard.

Buss proceeds to use his distinction to analyze the area of actor-observer differences. Actors, he says, always use reason explanations, whereas observers may, and, one assumes, often do, use causal ones. Again, the assertion is based on the assumption that actors and observers, although using perspective and information differences in the sense Jones and Nisbett (1971) and others I have cited earlier use it, are really different in a much more fundamental way—they are using a different logic and language of attributing, that is, explaining. Actors are likely to perceive events and outcomes as actions—intended behavior—and are thus likely to use the sort of explanation that is ''proper'' for that kind of behavioral event—a reason. Observers, on the other hand, unless given a set to reasons (that is, to account for actions) are prone to see more behavior and outcome events as occurrences. That is, actors and observers, when they differ, differ in the class of event they are explaining, not in the way they explain a similar event. ''Thus, the actor gives a reason explanation rather than a causal explanation of his or her own action'' (Buss, 1978, p. 1316).

Embedded in Buss's analysis and in Harre's (1979; Harre & Secord, 1972) similar analyses is a plea for analysis of ordinary language rather than experimental manipulation and brief questionnaire data-gathering as the methodology of choice. Two typical quotations from Buss's (1978) article and a part of Harre's (1977a) definition of the essential element of ethogenics graphically illustrate the importance placed on this approach. Early in his article, Buss states with approval the belief of ''ordinary'' philosophers that ''the major task of the philosopher should be one of clarifying how our ordinary language *actually* works and of engaging in *conceptual analysis* in order to eliminate conceptual confusion'' (p. 1313). Tellingly, Buss acts as though those two conceptually and methodologically distinct tasks are one task. We will consider this further at a later point. In his conclusion, Buss claims that attribution theorists ''need to approach the phenomenon they wish to explain (naive psychology) with less of their own restricting assumptions and more of an openness to be guided by the way lay exploration actually works'' (p. 1320). In like fashion Harre and his colleague Secord describe the cornerstone of the ethogenic methodology as involving ''the obtaining of *accounts*—the actor's own statements about why he performs the acts in question, what social meanings he gave to the actions of himself and others. These must be collected and analyzed'' (Harre & Secord, 1972, p. 10).

These points are crucial. There has been a muddiness in attribution theory, as in other areas of social psychology. This muddiness of conceptualization has been rivaled and exacerbated by a methodological restriction that avoided analyzing natural accounts of actually occurring situations, that has used "pseudopersonal," hypothetical situations to represent self-attributions instead of allowing persons to describe and analyze real-life events. Part of the muddiness has been caused by an unwillingness to separate causal analysis from reason analysis. Kruglanski (1975), as cited by Buss, 1978, is not by any means alone in his tendency to use "cause" and "reason" as equivalent terms. Indeed, in my instructions to my subjects I at times used the phrase "cause or reason," whereas at other times I asked the subject to give me reasons and at still other times referred to causes (see Questionnaire in the Appendix).

Buss's (1978) criticism did not go unnoticed or unchallenged. In 1979, the *Journal of Personality and Social Psychology* published two responses to his critique by Harvey and Tucker and by Kruglanski and a rejoinder by Buss. In these pieces the critics were quick to recognize the validity of at least a portion of Buss's argument and to question the conceptual and/or empirical validity of several of his assertions. In particular, his notion of the inability of actors to give causal explanations and of the conceptual clarity of differences between causes and reasons were directly challenged. Kruglanski, on his part, acknowledged that he had erred in originally (Kruglanski, 1975) proposing an absolute dichotomy between cause and reason explanations. In his rejoinder Buss, too, acknowledged error in his 1978 critique in regard to his proposition that actors are unable to make causal statements. He now (1979b) admits they may do so, although he proposes a sort of translation mechanism may be appropriate.

The candor and vigor of the discussions in this regard are certainly positive developments, although they seem open to Neisser's (1980) criticism of particularism. I want to add my voice to the debate, but add it on a different basis that, oddly enough, seems to have been roundly ignored by both Buss and his critics (as well as more traditional attribution researchers). None of this set of critics have directly noted several other important shortcomings we have already considered—narrowness of range of situations used and restrictions in persons used as respondents—although those sorts of criticism are certainly compatible with those they have made.

Additionally, Buss and his critical colleagues have fallen into errors of their own and have often not followed what should be their basic dictum—to collect, analyze, and try to understand how people in everyday life actually use the language of attributions. I assert, further, that the data I have gathered and analyzed, minimal and preliminary though both the gathering and analysis processes are at this point, may be quite useful in considering a number of the issues raised by Buss, Harre, Hamilton, and others.

It is interesting to me that most of the theorists whose ideas I have just briefly described place a great deal of emphasis in their description of proper methodology on the straightforward technique of asking people what they think, of gathering and analyzing everyday usage as the base for understanding any social psychological topic, especially a cognitively oriented one such as attributions.

I think it is interesting and important to note that not all of these writers would agree to this assertion. In particular, Kruglanski (1979) criticizes the "preoccupation with lay concepts" (p. 1447) and thus would appear to find description of actual usage a particularly useless enterprise. I feel there is merit in conceptual analysis as distinct from description and phenomenological, or lay, analysis, but that the latter is considerably of more import than the former in a field aimed at understanding everyday usage of language and the concepts those language elements represent. I believe Buss and most of the other critics would also feel that need (again see Neisser, 1980). I agree wholeheartedly with the emphasis on everyday usage. Yet I see little evidence of the application of that methodology in the writings of these theorists. Rather than providing their readers with descriptions of what people say about what they and others do—the subject matter of Type II and Type I attributions transformed into a Type III analysis of meanings—these writers have been content to make decisions about what lay attributions are *really* like by providing detailed theoretical, logical discussions of language as it *ought* to be. Since "reasons" and "causes" can be conceptually separated, Buss and his fellow critical analysts assume that they are kept distinct in the minds and language of the persons who share a linguistic system with them. They do not, however, proceed to query their fellows, to discover whether or not the logical distinctions are "properly" made. As Buss forthrightly declares concerning his criticism of actor-observer differences research (noted above and to be discussed in a few pages), his criticism "is conceptual rather than empirical (Buss 1978, p. 1314–1315)."

In a preliminary way, I have done what Buss, Harre, and others have exhorted me to do. As well as I could, I have asked people of various ages to tell me what they think about success, failure, and the feelings and thoughts those experiences engender; I have gathered information on how these people define not only success and failure, but "cause" and "reason." Unfortunately, at this point I only have data on open-ended questionnaire responses by 75 adults and interview data from a mere 17 of those, mostly middle-aged and older. Yet even a cursory first pass through those data is a level of analysis seldom attempted, even by these critics. The reasons, or causes, for that state of affairs are not apparent to me at this time.

In one particular case, I gathered the sort of information Buss asserted is important for understanding the reality of and explanation for so-called actor-observer differences. The reader may recall that I followed an unusual approach in my elicitation of attributions *about* other people. Rather than asking my subjects to give me the causes for what happened to the hypothetical actors in my Type I situations, I asked them to tell me what the other—the *actor*—would feel were the causes or reasons. In this way I did what Buss recommended and asked a subject to "reconstruct on the basis of the available evidence the actor's reasons for acting (p. 1316)." Thus, I have the sort of data Buss feels would be meaningful and directly comparable since both would use a similar approach, weighted toward noncausal, reason-analysis language.

What is shown by my various approaches? How do my data bear upon points concerning "cause" and "reason" and on the broader goal of Buss and Harre—to understand how people use the language(s) of causes, reasons, and affects to reveal the meanings those languages and the occurrence of success and failure events have for persons? Further, are they useful in understanding an ignored aspect of standard and nonstandard attribution analyses alike—the interplay of change and stability in those usages and meanings?

Already in the data thus far reviewed, that from the questionnaire studies, there are some answers. Interestingly, using open response modes without predetermined categories, across a fairly wide range of situations about others and about oneself, and using "observer" instructions that, Buss asserts, should produce reason explanations for both selves ("actors") and others (as "observers"), the participants in this study used approximately the same vocabularies. Further, that vocabulary was very much like that which attribution researchers have consistently found in their (to Buss, in 1978 at least) specious causal-explanation models. In fact, when asked for the cause or reason (or in some directions, merely the reason) subjects nonetheless regularly explained the result by recourse to what Buss would, it would seem, necessarily label as "causes" (preexisting conditions, nonpurposeful entities, such as ability) as well as a host of more "reasonable" explanations (motivation, interest, intentions of others, and so on). The two types of explanation seem to be almost indiscriminately applied; that is, they are often mixed in "one" explanation. They are applied in relatively equal proportions in explanations of actual personal occurrences (an illness, for example) and actions (repairing a television set) and hypothetical ones as they would be explained by the actor. There seems to be little justification in these data to expect people to give only reasons as explanations for their own outcomes or, in fact, to discriminate at all in how they refer to actions and occurrences by themselves and others.

Although there are many other meaningful ways to analyze the data gathered in the questionnaire studies—and I will in particular return to situational variance in a later section of the chapter—I want to proceed at this point to introduce the interview study to which I have referred at several points in earlier chapters and in this one, since it bears directly upon these issues.

INTERVIEW INFORMATION

After conducting the questionnaire studies described thus far, and in the process of analysis of those data, my assistants and I became increasingly convinced that, although we had in fact proceeded further than many researchers along the road to "open-ended" responses and qualitative analysis, we had not gone nearly far enough to begin to explore the natural usage of attributional language—causes *and* reasons, as well as affects associated with success and failure and with the whole concept of achievement and attainment. Toward the end of gathering at least *some* information about this, we devised a semistructured interview to try to tap meaningful levels of discourse with a subsample of our subjects. In particular, we wanted to obtain an indication of the meanings our interviewees attached to success and failure, to positive and negative feelings that go with those, to different sorts of successes and failures, and to real or perceived changes in their approach to these (and in cohort-generational differences). The reader may note that only the latter was intrinsically a developmental issue, yet I hope that I have shown how a concern with development, diversity, and change forced us to a greater concern with phenomenological and dynamic levels of meaning than we might otherwise have had. Certainly the lack of diversity in samples and situations must be part of the reason why few attribution researchers have felt uncomfortable with remaining within the boundaries of causal analysis of specific, clear-cut, experimenter-defined success and failure experiences.

All cautions I have made in the past about interpretation of data must be doubly stressed here, although they are probably hardly necessary, since most readers will note them without prompting. Our original plan was to interview 24 of the participants in the previous study—4 in each age-sex group. Obviously, that number is far too small for detailed qualitative analysis or the production of normative generalizations. Unfortunately, extraneous events (and, perhaps, we must admit, motivational ones) intervened so that in fact we have only 17 completed interviews at our disposal at the present time. We reached our quota with older persons, with 3 in each sex of middle-aged participants, but have only 2 female and 1 male younger subject. Obviously, at this stage, age comparisons are not possible.

Although I would like to have data from more participants, I make no apologies for the quality or quantity of these data. My assistant, Joyce Burr, and I have gathered a set of interviews, ranging quite well over the areas of interest outlined above, with a diversity of ages and backgrounds of participants. The data, even at a preliminary level of analysis, have yielded information and insights that should be valuable indicators of how to approach the task of understanding attributional language and usage from a small, but nonetheless only now existent, base.

Several pieces of information provide some interesting insights into the question on which I have spent a great deal of time in this chapter: the issue of "causes and reasons." It is clear that many "causal explanations" can be translated into "reasons" and vice versa (see Buss, 1979). For example, "lack of effort" may be the cause of a failure, but may be translated into "I didn't really care to succeed," that is, the lack of a goal—a reason for failure both in the sense of purposefulness and in the justificatory sense of explanation. Buss (1979b), in fact, makes this "translatability" a partial defense of his distinctions between causes and reasons.

If "causes" and "reasons" can be translated into each other, though, it seems we are back to facing the original question: are "causes" and "reasons" really two distinct and distinctive entities? The data I gathered bear upon that question in at least two places, and the answer seems to be: "If there is a difference, a considerable number of people aren't able to perceive it very well and in that case, a case can be made that, phenomenologically, it does not in fact exist."

Defining "Cause" and "Reason"

The first task we placed before our interviewees was one of definitions. We asked them to explain commonly used terms that relate to achievement as though they were describing them to someone who did not know their meaning. We left open to them the possibility of giving a normative-societal (dictionary) definition or a personal one. In fact, we found that when subjects felt there may be a difference between those two types of definition they spontaneously pointed that out and gave us both types. The words, given to a particular subject in a random order by the interviewer, included many of the words attribution theorists rather heavy-handedly assume have clear definitions. The words for which we asked definitions were: cause, reason, success, failure, ability, effort, luck, proud, satisfied, happy, sad, anger, and frustrated.

As you can see, major categories of Weiner's (e.g., 1972) attributional scheme (except "task difficulty," which seemed awkward and, in any case, is the least used category of his fourfold scheme), major positive and negative affects associated with success and failure (as reported in Weiner et al., 1978, and other sources), and several overarching concepts were included. The purpose was to gather information on the everyday language of causality.

Obviously, since I have only 17 interviews, I am not proposing detailed statements of normative definitions; nor will I catalog all the definitions given (that can be made available to interested readers). Rather, I want to use the definitions and opinions given by my few subjects as a springboard to discussion of the cause-reason debate and several other issues and as an indication of the need for further, more detailed analyses along the lines begun here.

At this time, definitions of one particular pair are of most interest. As I have discussed thus far in this chapter, Buss (1978, 1979b), Hamilton (1980), Harre and Secord (1972; Harre, 1977a,b), and Kruglanski (1975, 1979) have discussed the differer·.:s between causes and reasons, and many of them have vigorously attacked attribution researchers and theorists in general for their lack of recognition of the differences, for blurring the theoretically sharp distinctions between "cause(s)" and "reason(s)." In doing so, they have stressed the importance of precise terminology as an analytic tool in the process of evaluating the conceptual status of specific sorts of explanations.

Concurrent with this emphasis, as I have noted, has been a curious deficit on their own parts. Although the ethogenic approach and analysis of natural language usage are the methodological directives of these theorists, an important purpose of attributional analysis that would seem to be closely aligned to that methodological emphasis has been lost sight of by these philosophically inclined theorists (as well as by many of the more pragmatic empiricists, of course). This purpose, or goal, is the description of the kind of language people in ordinary discourse use to explain events such as success and failure through the direct method of asking them how they define and apply specific terms (see Harre, 1977a).

In this light, a minimal piece of information lacking in these important logical analyses is information on what people think are the similarities and differences between those two common words, "cause" and "reason," the manner and degree to which persons normally discriminate between those two ways of explaining an outcome. In our interviews, subjects were asked independently to define the two words (the order in which they arose in the larger list was roughly balanced). What did these 17 people, fairly representative of an educated adult population, do?

Some of the subjects did a good job, from Buss's (1978, 1979a,b) point of view, of giving logically separable definitions. For example, various subjects defined "cause" by referring to cause and effect or to "a series of events or conditions that lead" to an outcome. Conversely, "reason" definitions included "a mental interpretation," "an excuse you have," "a statement to justify action or explain," and "rationalizing or expressing what you believe to be the underlying cause." Clearly, some gave one of Buss's central elements of a reason—a justificatory explanation.

Others produced even purer classical definitions of a reason as "a purpose or goal, a desired effect" or as "the meaning you give to explain cause and effect." One young person neatly summarized the differences for us: "The cause is what is and the reason is why."

The above quotes indicate an awareness of the characteristic differences between cause and reason and were found both singly (one or the other definition a particular individual gave was similar to Buss's differentiations) and in a directly comparative way, as the last quoted subject did. However, this correspondence to a clear differentiation between cause and reason was not unanimously reported; indeed, it was not modal. Rather, the modal response to each item actually used the *other* term as part of its definition. That is, over half of the interviewees (9 of 17) explained "cause" at least partially by calling it a reason: "the reason something happens," "reason behind certain things happening," "reason, why things happen." One older woman noted in comparison that "reason is broader, but they are parallel." At the same time, 5 of 16 definitions of "reason" included the word "cause." Several of those went on to specifically define "reasons" as what Buss tells us are logically separate causes. For example, an older woman stated that reason was "cause" . . . circumstances that have resulted in something." An older man told the interviewer that a reason "is something that causes an event. It's more or less cause." Even more interestingly, a middle-aged male went to great lengths to differentiate the two, ending up with definitions almost on polar opposites from Buss's distinctions: "There are some subtle differences between cause and reason. Sometimes cause has a pejorative meaning, a way of putting blame on something. . . .The terms are many times interchangeable. Cause is many times used as a blaming word." To this person, "cause" seems to be that which is used to allocate blame; it is an interpretive evaluation of an action. That is, in Buss's terms (see Buss, 1978, p. 1314), it is a *reason*.

Whereas the extent of overlap and even reversals in definitions and the persistent use of one word to explain the other are open to many interpretations, it certainly does not seem that oridinary people ordinarily make logical distinctions—or, it may well be, logical choices—between causes and reasons. Thus, insofar as the goal of attribution research is to provide information about how people use concepts and words to inform themselves and others about the "whys" of events, it would appear that attribution theorists and researchers who have ignored the distinctions and blurred the boundaries may—accidentally, to be sure—have done nothing more, but nothing less, than provide a veridical picture of normal attributional processes. At the same time, they may have been inadvertently illustrating the limited value of their static-schema, stable-definition approach to attribution processes in general. Data like mine may both certify the descriptive validity of a fusion of "cause" and "reason" into "attribution" and the interpretive weakness of that same lack of clarity at the stage of analysis and theory construction.

"Before I Know Why, I Must Know . . . "

Another small piece of data leads in a similar direction in the discussion concerning the independent status of causes and reasons. As part of the interview, we approached attributions from another point of view that standard attribution theorists have ignored, but that would follow from an ethogenic approach. The interviewer described a hypothetical actor and outcome to the interviewee. This hypothetical situation gave the most minimal level of information possible—"Let's say you just heard about someone losing (winning) a competition." Rather than asking for causal statements (or reasons, for that matter), the interviewer then asked, "What sort of information of any kind would you need to know before you would be able to make a judgment about why that person failed (or succeeded)?" In other words, we asked persons to tell us the sorts of data they felt they *needed* to be *able* to make an attributional decision.

The responses, once again, do not appear to support a clear discrimination between causes and reasons that might be expected on the basis of outcome (success and failure) or perspective (an observer, in this case, giving causes) information and mode if Buss's (1978) proposed logical distinctions were operative. They do, however, support the idea Kruglanski (1975) and others have proposed and Buss briefly discussed, that "causes and reasons are both required for an adequate explanation of human action (Buss, 1978, p. 1314)." In fact, the kinds of information required match quite closely to Heider's (1958) two levels of "can"—power (ability) and environmental force (difficulty). The third component of the triad, further, is Heider's "try," that is, interest in and effort directed to the situation.

One situational thrust was a requirement to know more about the task itself; another was to know about the circumstances or conditions under which the task was undertaken (remember that the only situation we asked about was a competitive one). The situational part of Heider's "effective force" equation, however, paled in comparison to the reliance our subjects said they would place on personal factors. Only for 2 of the 32 responses given (a success and failure for each subject, with 2 nonresponses) was no personal information requested; in 18 of 32 no situational factors were mentioned as necessary.

Within the wide area of person factors both stable "personal characteristic" ones and "personal-situational" ones were apparent. Expertise, background, qualifications, and experience were often the most sought-after type of data, indicating that respondents felt such personal "cans" are crucial pieces of information. These fit more or less in the category of causes, that is, explanations based in limiting factors and, therefore, aspects that are essentially placed *upon* the person at the time of performance. I discuss this sort of externalized internal factor further in the Appendix. That is, at the time of action-occurrence of the performance and its outcome, ability, background, and qualifications are "givens" that mark the boundaries of potentiality (also see Heider, 1958, Chapter 4).

The personal factors that bear the marks of reasons, that is, factors of intentionality and exertion (again, see Heider's Chapter 4) are also prominent. Persons consistently asked for both relatively stable and relatively unstable aspects of this broad category. Examples of the former are ambition, dedication, tenacity, goals, competitive-minded nature, and characteristic ways of handling success and failure. Examples of the latter (relatively unstable) factors are feeling their best, how they approached the task, importance of the outcome, and a plan of attack.

In other words, even in the brief responses to hypothetical situations, the subjects in this sample exhibited a broad range of informational elements, one that was heavy on information that could be the basis for reason-production, but was also cognizant of the limits on performance placed upon people by their contexts—other persons, circumstances, and what are assumed to be enduring personal characteristics, such as ability and tenacity. Conspicuous in its absence, as it has also been in quantification and classification of open-ended attributions (e.g., Elig & Frieze, 1975) is "luck" as a transitory random factor. However, "circumstances" may be a relatively unstable, nonpersonal element that some subjects recognized. Information about specific task characteristics ("task difficulty"), too, was an infrequent requirement. Rather, the type of task was merely a part of the relationship among the individual, the context, and those with whom the individual was competing.

Again, the general point is that causes and reasons tend to be mixed in people's minds, leaving us with the possibility that a lack of distinction between those two types of factors is not necessarily a problem, at least descriptively, and may, in fact, reflect the thought processes, the mental arithmetic, of explanations of social actions.

Using this kind of analysis can yield data that are directly relevant to key areas of concern in attribution research at its general, nondevelopmental level of concern. The cause-reason controversy is merely one of many such areas. Another is the crucial need in achievement attribution research for a much better grasp of the meaning that success and failure, that succeeding and failing, hold for people in their everyday lives.

SUCCEEDING AND FAILING: WHAT DOES IT ALL MEAN?

As I briefly noted early in the chapter, one untapped source of such information about the meaning of success and failure is the steady stream of books on success in life, ranging from how-to books on business success to, more generally, success in being a happy human being (several examples of this almost inexhaustible source are Swell, 1977; Sherman, 1958; Mandino, 1978). Although many of these books have an almost mystical approach to the process, they contain definitions of both success and failure designed to prod the reader to the one and show him or her, in the words of one such book, *How to Turn Failure into Success* (Sherman, 1958). One particularly interesting source is a fairly recent book by Firestone (1976); it is a compilation of responses by "successful" people (mostly defined, it seems, by fame and/or money) to questions about what success means to them, how they got it, kept it, and so on.

I will not tap that resource in these pages. Instead, I will use responses in my interviews to questions about the meaning of success and failure as avenues to the understanding of meanings. These include definitions of the terms themselves, indications of areas of life in which success and failure mean the most and, last but not least, quasi-developmental data on perceived differences in orientation in comparison to other current generations (parents, children) and to their previous "selves" in a personal reminiscence. In other words, we tried to obtain "cohort" and "longitudinal" comparisons of what are admittedly the roughest possible sort.

What is success and what is failure? These questions are clearly broader than those with which attribution theorists are prepared to deal, and the answers of those interviewed clearly bears out this point. Almost invariably, researchers and theorists have sought "objectivity" in their definitions. To do so, they have dealt with quantifiables—success is getting a high score, failure is getting a low score. "Highness" and "lowness" were assumed to be immutable characteristics of the outcome or have been defined by a social-verifiability-consensus definition; that is, success is getting an A compared to others' A's, B's, C's, and so on; failure is flunking. Attribution theorists then proceed, in typical linear-model fashion, to examine the effects of success and failure on attributions and on affects and expectations. Examples of this approach abound. The corpus of work by Weiner and his colleagues, for example, was initially focused upon effects on attributions (e.g., Weiner & Peter, 1973; Weiner, 1972; Freize & Weiner, 1971). They then directed their aim toward affect as a response to attributions (attached as a third step in the linear chain) and then as both a general response to the outcome itself *and* a more specific response to the elaborated attribution (Frieze, 1976; Weiner et al., 1978).

I would assert that these endeavors—and many others that could have been highlighted, such as the plethora of research centered on specifying the effects of being an actor versus being an observer on attributions already discussed—however useful and informative, are ignoring a fundamental fact of the entire process that now comes under the label of "attributions." That fundamental fact is that success and failure are not by any means entirely characteristics of outcomes, but are *meanings* attached to events. Of course, persons *use* comparative information to decide whether some event was a success or a failure; certainly they have different feelings and different future approach-avoidance gradients depending on the meaning of the outcome. But the meaning itself—the outcome itself and its "success-failure" status—is a construction, an "objective" state negotiated on the basis of several sorts of information.

One source of information, it appears from both my interview data and even a cursory reading of many of the books noted earlier in this section, is in the way the individual *feels* after the outcome becomes a part of past experience, is past history. A primary definition of success is a feeling of happiness and of satisfaction; if one is satisfied, one has succeeded, as well as the other way around. In fact, a number of the respondents indicated that calling an event a success requires not only an affect, but a certain attribution category. That is, feeling satisfied that one did a good job on something he or she cared about and *worked* on is success; other "attainments" are, apparently considered to be what Buss (1978) would classify as occurrences. Not only do they not provide information for expectations, they simply are not perceived as successes.

Perhaps the other major definition of success and a discussion of the definitions given for failure will clarify this important point. The other major idea flowing through the definitions of success we were given was that of attainment or accomplishment of a goal. Quite clearly success outcomes are the result of actions, to refer once again to Buss's useful terms. Actions are defined by goals, therefore, success as an act is also defined by a goal. Almost invariably, that goal is clearly an internal, personal standard. Several respondents, in fact, took pains to separate the goals of the actor from external standards. Goals are personal, and therefore variable. What person A defines as success may be seen by person B as outright failure (whether it happened to person A or to person B himself/herself). What person A sees as success today, he or she may respond to as a failure tomorrow or next week or next year (I'll briefly consider perceptions of change in a few pages). A success is "something I feel to be worthwhile," it's "attaining a goal the person set for himself; ultimately, it depends on the individual," and "it must be considered in the context of the person's situation."

A fuller report of the illustration given by the last respondent quoted is a fitting transition to a discussion of definitions of failure. This older male related how his perspective was influenced by working at Goodwill Industries. "Success for them," he reported, "was very different from you and I [*sic*]." In response to a later question, concerning how you can tell if someone succeeds, he gave us a truism that includes many of the ideas discussed in this last section and once again points up the major problems in acting as though we, the researchers, are privy to the universal success or failure quality of a particular outcome. "In most situations you succeed a little and fail a little rather than have a total success or failure. You try to do something and it comes out pretty well. It could have been better but it wasn't as bad as it might have been and was better than our expectations."

If success and failure are both "spirits," if most situations or events contain elements of both (and thus could form the basis for either definition of the outcome, dependent on personal needs, relating it to personal goals), then it should be the case that failure is defined as the mirror image of success. That, we found, is in fact the case, with several provisos. Failure, first and foremost, is the nonattainment of goals; almost all interviewees had an element of that in their answer. There was, however, major disagreement in what a failure was in a deeper sense. Interestingly, the disagreement centers around the issue of action versus occurrence, once again. An overriding theme in about two-thirds of the responses was a lack of control, an inability or lack of capability to accomplish a desired end. As with success, failure is only relevant when a particular goal was desired and not attained. In that sense, both success and failure are the results of actions, whereas other outcomes in situations in which there was not striving for a goal are neither successes nor failures, despite what others may "objectively" decide. On the other hand, concerns with inability and lack of control beg for causal explanations, not reasons, and several were given: "lots of bad luck," "acts or conditions that are adverse happen to a person." Failure is the result, not of the purposive nature of the act, but of the vagaries of the world or the constitutional abilities one bears. In either case, the failure is something done *to* the individual. The initiation of action, then, will be explained with reasons, but the result with causes.

Of course, as noted previously, many explanations of failure do not fit that ideal, but include both causes and reasons among their explanations. There are two reasons for that. First, success and failure are not clean, unambiguous entities; rather events—outcomes—must be imbued with meaning before they have any psychological relevance. The information is almost never unambiguous. Second, an interesting group of respondents clearly would disagree with the definition of failures as occurrences which I just discussed. They would, in fact, see such outcomes as lacking one of the essential characteristics of failure, and that characteristic is a personal one. Not accomplishing a goal is not necessarily failure to these people, nor is accomplishing a goal in an imperfect way a success. Rather, nonaccomplishment is only a failure when it is accompanied by the ability to have attained it. Giving up, being defeated by a mistake, failing to take advantage of opportunities and using potential by getting sidetracked, not applying oneself, making poor decisions, or using bad judgment *are* the failures; the outcome is incidental to those. To these people, it appears, failure is both intensely personally and socially verifiable; it is not doing when you can rather than not succeeding when you can't. It is letting yourself down, not fulfilling your responsibilities to "be the best you can."

Does that sound familiar? It should, since it is the central maxim of third-force, humanistic psychology and of the self-help movement. It is a major way of approaching situations and outcomes used every day in management seminars and self-help groups everywhere. Failing is letting obstacles bind you. As such, this definition is alien to the "effects of" concept of the world, and particularly alien to the simple, linear model of the "passive reactor" that is immensely popular in attribution theory (see Neisser's 1980 critique). If, however, it is a working assumption of a large segment of the population (biased, probably, toward the more educated end in its verbal accessibility but, I suspect, a prevalent assumption throughout society), would it not be good for attribution theorists to recognize and deal with this conception (or, indeed, with its counterbalance, the notion that failure is inability even after giving it all you could)?

The Utility of "Success" and "Failure" Terms

By the way, another question revealed another dispute, about a side issue of potential import to attribution theorists and, especially, to those interested in achievement motivation and achievement-related attributions. Subjects were asked whether they feel terms such as success and failure are societally or personally useful. They were almost exactly split on these important questions. Those who felt the terms are useful referred to their use as a standard of comparison (the consensus use attribution theorists such as Kelley, 1972, have, of course, emphasized) and to the encouragement they give to people to strive harder for success. One person simply noted that "the labels are needed because there are both types of people." Thus, both cognitive (comparison, categorization) and motivational benefits were reported.

On the other hand, half of the respondents saw the terms as either passively or actively harmful. In particular they referred to the self-fulfilling nature of expectations based on past outcomes. These self-fulfilling prophesies, furthermore, are particularly damaging if they are shared by the individual (actor) and those who are in role relationships to the actor of both observer and supplier of subsequent opportunities, situations, and relationships. In other words, neither actors nor observers are generally perceivers; they are also constructors—of the meaning of what "happened" and of a social and personal structure in which to place outcomes and, indeed, in which to locate and define those who "act," who participate as principals in that particular drama. It is on this basis that a sizable number of my subjects felt the terms "success" and "failure" are dangerous abstractions from events and relationships.

There is a further point of danger in the use of terms noted by several respondents. They pointed out the fine line between successes as events that occur with a person or persons involved as principals—recipients sand potential causes—and successes and failures as labels given to the persons who were those principals. This is in many ways merely a larger generalization of the position just noted. Success and failure may be useless or even harmful as words to categorize and dichotomize outcomes, outcomes which are in fact likely to be intermediate between those two points and ambiguous enough to be interpreted either way, but they may be even more dangerous when coupled with the tendency to make outcomes themselves dispositional, that is to ascribe successfulness or failureness to persons. In contrast to the feeling cited above, that "the labels are needed because there are both types of people," others felt that the labels are harmful because there are *not* both types of people except insofar as they are socially conditioned to be so by the labeling-stigmatization process. I think I do not need to go into detail about that process; excellent sources such as Goffman (1963) are readily available.

Again, it is clear that the assumptions of attribution theorists, that success and failure are properties of particular events and, thus, "objective" and that, therefore, the terms are important symbols to represent those realities, are shared by a sizable percentage of those interviewed. It is also clear, however, that those beliefs themselves are by no means universally accepted, but are explicitly rejected, not only by symbolic interactionists and labeling-theory social scientists, but by persons in their naive psychologies of action, their everyday use of the language of attributions. As one pragmatic soul told the interviewer, the validity and utility of the terms will vary: "It depends on whether you're a success or a failure. . . . I think what people expect is a lot what people achieve."

"DEVELOPMENTAL" ASPECTS OF DEFINITIONS AND USAGE

Although there are many other issues that can be profitably explored in these and other such data, I wish to close this chapter with a section of analyses clustered around the "age-comparative" questions asked in the interview. Respondents were asked to compare their standards and definitions of success and failure, achievement and attainment, with others—society in general; their parents; and, when appropriate, children; or themselves 10, 20, or 50 years ago (again, when current age rendered such questions meaningful). I doubt that I need repeat the caveats mentioned earlier—that such responses are from a tiny, selective sample and that these are but the barest approximations to legitimate developmental questions whether they be longitudinal or cross-sectional cohort analyses. I hope, merely, that the data to be discussed are indications of what might be gathered, and gained, in the use of developmental and quasi-developmental social psychology.

The first question to be considered was not even developmental in the weak senses described; it merely yields a piece of interesting information about how individuals feel they relate to broad-based social definitions and how well they feel socialized to a mass definition of success and failure. Approximately one-third of the individuals said they felt their definitions were the same as "society in general," but, significantly, the majority reported having different standards and definitions. Recall, if you will, that most subjects felt that success is a personal, emotion-based recognition of matching up to internal standards of fulfilling one's potential and that failure was often characterized as either inability *or* insufficient effort to attain that feeling of satisfaction. Seldom were social comparisons made the basis for determination; even more seldom were material advantage or social position mentioned as criteria. It was in this that differences to society in general were felt. Over and over, respondents across all age groups who said they were different from society in general said that was because the "generalized other" of society was narrowly devoted to materialistic and social-position definitions whereas they themselves were more interested in goals, in "accomplishing what one starts out to do," in performing to the best of one's ability.

If most people as individuals are goal-oriented in the sense of accomplishing meaningful goals, treating others right, and attaining personal satisfaction, do "they" who think so materialistically exist? One subject had an ingenious and interesting answer, that people are similar to themselves, but the media put the stress on money, forcing us to think in those terms.

I placed this discussion in the section on "development" for a reason. The same thread runs through comparisons to people of other ages. Verifying on a small scale the consistent finding in other contexts (e.g., political socialization—Jennings & Niewi, 1974; Hess & Torney, 1967) that transmission of values through generations is generally high, the modal response, both in comparisons to parents and to children, was that the definitions, and the values they bear, were the same. Within that similarity, though, was an interesting hint of cohort and/or stage differences. All of the older respondents saw their definitions to be the same as their parents; and all but one of the six who had children felt their children's definitions were also the same. Young respondents also felt their definitions matched their parents'. The middle-aged persons, however, saw a considerable level of *dis*agreement on the level of transmission of definitions of success and failure. In fact, *none* of the six perceived their definitions to be the same as both their parents' and their children's. The four who saw differences with parents, furthermore, felt their parents had placed much more emphasis on money, security, and social status, the same variations that "society in general" had from individual respondents. Interestingly, the four who felt different from their children (two who had reported agreement with parents and two who had not) reported that their children, too, were more like society—short-sighted, materialistic, and status-oriented. In other words, middle-aged persons appear to feel themselves isolated from both older and younger generations and from society in general in their definitions. Further, they see themselves as much more likely to emphasize personal satisfaction and a "glow" of accomplishment on an individual level than those with whom they feel they differ. This is a fascinating finding, particularly in light of the widespread belief that middle-age is the height of social penetration and power for most people (evidence as disparate as Barker and Barker's, 1961, study of penetration into settings by various age groups, age stratification models, achievement motivation research, and the data on type of attributions in Chapters 5 and 6 point in that direction). A tidbit of interesting corraboration of the feeling reported by the middle-aged respondents is that the older person who felt his children (probably middle-aged at the time) were different in definition from himself reported that his children were too *nonmaterialistic*—"career success just doesn't mean as much to them."

What do we have here? Perhaps nothing at all, given the selective nature of this tiny sample. On the other hand, perhaps we see a few reflections of cohort-level patterning of definitions of success and failure. I need only note in this regard that the older respondents had all grown to maturity or were already mature during the Great Depression (Elder, 1974), that today's young adults are growing to maturity in a time of economic stagflation, teetering on the brink of both inflation and depression, and that cohorts that are now middle-aged grew up (or at least grew to maturity and entry into the work force) in a time of wartime, postwar, and cold war economic growth. Obviously, others have examined the impacts of these events in the lives and thoughts of the various cohorts; it seems long past time for attribution theorists to dig deeply into the meaning of those experiences for attribution processes and the "characteristic center of gravity" Heckhausen (1967) placed at the center of analysis of attributional weighting systems that individuals apply to particular events and the broader flow of their lives.

The responses to questions about perceived change in oneself are also useful in comparing perceived age changes to perceived current age differences. Most interviewees perceived changes in their own approach to success and failure and their meaning over their adult years. Without exception, perceived change was away from material goods and "being a success" in a narrow, socially defined (at least as they saw it) way. Several said they were now much less bound by society's definitions. In other words, that majority which felt it had changed perceived itself to be moving in the direction of the type of definition almost all of the respondents now had —internal standards, emphasis on being helpful and worthwhile, but a de-emphasis on rewards, recognition and "having things." Of course, those who felt they were the same as they had been 10 or 20 years ago simply felt they had *always* been oriented to personal satisfaction and a feeling of accomplishment (and of having given it your best even when you failed to attain a goal) rather than to a materialistic definition. Also, several who reported change also pointed out continuity. An older man said that having success means the same as it did, but getting success is different. Another indicated that although he had changed, at "both times what you achieve is important."

Such a set of findings provides some support for an idea proposed quite a while ago by Neugarten (e.g., 1964), the idea that older people become increasingly more concerned with the "interior life" and less with external matters, including social status. However, the data are really not supportive of that model for three reasons.

First of all, this "interiority" shift took place already in most of the middle-aged subjects; in fact one of the young respondents reported a shift away from monetary reward definitions in his own sphere of meanings. Certainly, if middle-aged and younger persons feel this shift to be taking place in their lives, an explanation of this in terms of interiority, life review (Butler, 1963), and preparation for death is indeed both odd and lacking in explanatory power.

Even more important in this regard, however, is a finer analysis of the situations the respondents described in the interview (and which the wider group gave in the questionnaire portion of the study). I mentioned in Chapter 7 that subjects used a wide range of personal situations as examples of successes and failures, ranging from mechanical situations to persuasion of others to the quality of life of children. I also noted that there seemed to be a tendency in the questionnaire responses for older persons to place more emphasis on social situations, such as helping others to do well or getting others won over to your point of view. This is in marked contrast to socially defined successes as they are perceived by most of these individuals, that is, money or status concerns.

This pattern with aging, as well as the overall emphasis on those sorts of situations, is both even more apparent in the interview data and even more at variance with the notion of interiority that seems to follow an emphasis on personal standards and personal goals. It is true that internal standards are used as references for defining—and perceiving, in the specific instance—success and failure; but the "internal" standard of most concern to many persons is at the same time a very social one—"how well am I doing in giving satisfaction and support to those whom I care about?"

The situations are those which are "of concern," fulfilling the action requirement and the importance of the dimension of "interest" that is highly important as a structure on which are laid those events that the person chooses to see as "success" or "failure." They are also intrinsically social. This is particularly apparent in answers to questions we asked about when success and failure are most strongly felt. The two most mentioned situations in which success is most strongly felt were those in which a real investment of self was made and those concerned with helping others. The responses were about equally split into those two categories. For example, several mentioned "overcoming an adversity," or after "a long struggle in a difficult area, in which I had to try hard." In some cases those situations were in competitions or areas of work, but often those also had a social cast.

Others were explicitly social; as "part of a group action, that has really moved things forward and been successful for a lot of people . . ., to do something for another individual where the other person gets a lot of pleasure out of it. I get pleasure from that" is the way an older woman put it. Others followed that theme, citing "in connection with my community," "helping someone else," "for the family" and "working together with others," as the most strongly felt successes.

The social cast was equally apparent in most strongly felt failure illustrations. Again, personal causation or involvement was one relevant factor, but the modal situations were clearly social. In particular the feeling of "letting others down" was acute for all, especially the middle-aged respondents (10 of 17 overall; 5 of 6 in the middle-aged group). Typical accounts stressed various aspects, ranging from very general—"let someone close down," "dealing with people especially where I'm trying to help people to change or help people to deal with a work situation or a life situation," "when I haven't done right by somebody else"—to specific relationships or contexts—"with the kids," "problems my kids have had," "where someone looked up to me for leadership," or "lovemaking."

I think it is clear from these examples that though the respondents may be tuned in to internal standards of evaluation for success and failure, they are not currently nor is there any direct or indirect evidence that they are becoming "interiorized." Instead, if anything, older persons feel they have the freedom to invest themselves and their concerns with achievement into social concerns and social situations more fully than they may have been able to do at an earlier age.

Thirdly, and as a summary for this section, I want to point out the sophisticated way in which these persons relate themselves to success and failure, to opportunities to participate in both social and nonsocial acts, and to the changing contexts of their lives. You may remember that there was no apparent shift across age toward lessened achievement motivation or intensity of orientation in the personality data reported in Chapter 6. Rather, the shift that does take place is more in the realm of emphasis. Overall, the interviewees clearly show evidence of a reasoned approach to change, one that has the effect of maintaining an equilibrium in success and failure—a relationship—in spite of changing interests, opportunities, and skills. They do this through implicit application of the dialectical model we discussed extensively in Part 1 of the book, one which sees change and stability as of one piece, not as antagonistic forces. To remain interested in achieving, in succeeding, these persons have adopted a pragmatic, flexible conception of success and failure. They have placed those meanings of events in their own control through a variety of methods. They have adjusted their actions to their expectations, not attempting areas of performance with low probability of success and using a limited range of outcomes as information for self definition. They continue to have goals and to stress attainment of them, but they are adept in calibrating those goals with their abilities.

They can do so "successfully" because they know better than attribution theorists that success and failure is a more or less proposition anyway and by making it clear that those performances they do not accomplish are not failures if they did not "put themselves on the line psychologically." Many "failures" can in fact be successes for them if (1) they didn't expect perfection to begin with and thus are "satisfied," and/or (2) they learn from them; they use them. The latter point is certainly important. A "failure" that highlights what is needed for "success" that was lacking can be used either to relabel the outcome as an occurrence—an irrelevancy—or to receive as much personal value from it (in terms of learning one's own limitations, being able not to make the mistake again) as one would have gotten from immediate "success." Since "success" and "failure" are seldom absolute and thus are open to investing them with specific meaning and definition, they are ultimately controllable; they are constructed. As long as an individual can be "in on" this construction as an active participant, not just in being an actor, but in being an interested observer/ evaluator—that is constructor—of the outcome, then success and failure are meaningful, valuable, and controllable. When those conditions are not met, one may indeed learn to be helpless and may learn to label every occurrence of negative outcome as "failure." By having failure really become uncontrollable, then, oddly, one may feel most *responsible* for failure; failure may adhere to me (Mead's me) instead of remaining a construction I negotiate with others to produce. The *relationship* has altered, and a failure becomes personal, becomes *me*.

This, of course, is pure fantasy, an extension far beyond the realms of evidence I have so laboriously and yet so superficially presented in this chapter. Yet, its relevance to current issues in attribution may be major; some aspects of that will be considered in Chapter 8. I believe, though, that the responses of these 17 persons are a piece of stone for a foundation of a meaningful understanding of attributions—as a vocabulary, as a process of labeling, as a source of some of the deepest feelings about self, and as one of the most direct and simultaneously most inferential forms of social "knowing."

I want to finally close out this rather lengthy chapter with a few slightly longer quotes from those 17 generous persons who shared their views on life with me. Rather than using pieces of response to illustrate points I will simply relate a few of the ideas that came up in the conversations.

The first set is from an interview with an older woman who had much to say throughout—and after—the interview period itself about success and failure. She points out, among other things, the way her age allows her to be more successful than before rather than making her less so.

> My ideas of what success is have varied through the years. I set less store by material things, even though I love material things—not because they're important to other people though. A successful person is someone who is in charge of his own life, and to me that's a real luxury. That's why I'm enjoying the age and stage I'm in now. It's a successful way to be. Successful means being together so one isn't running out trying to grasp something else . . . It's not having to get up in the morning until I want to, being able to do what I want to do within the boundaries of health, energy, and financial limitations. I can do pretty much anything I want to do. Enjoying things that totally passed me by earlier. A lot of people miss this because success is how many C.D.'s you have in the bank or how big an estate you can leave to your children . . . It bothers me the number of people whose idea of success tends to be more cars, more things, bigger houses, the images they project, the getting ahead that is the end of a rat race. More people, though, are getting a better perspective on values. This may come more and more as we get into energy crunches so more people will stay home and do and value the kind of things that don't take a lot of resources. I give those "flower children" a lot of credit—they had the courage to break away from established ways of doing things to get back to nature a little bit. Many of them didn't have a lot of personal resources to bring to it so many of them flopped, but it still made a break from two cars, a TV set in every room, etc. . . .
>
> Sometimes, I'm a little concerned that I haven't done more with my life, but mostly I feel that within my abilities, capacities, and interests or motivation that I've lived a fairly rewarding life. It's been rewarding for me and I don't think I've caused things to be less rewarding for other people. I feel pretty good about my life. I'm liking the latter part better than the first part. . . The things I haven't done, I haven't been motivated to or didn't really want to do it all that much.

Another older woman gave us an excellent summary statement about being a successful person:

> Anyone who has led a life where they've helped other people and not been a burden to anyone else unnecessarily—leads a decent life—or if they've had problems in their life and overcome them—that's a very strong point. It is to accomplish something worthwhile, whether it's making money or whatever else makes you happy. Everybody has their [sic] own goal that they consider success.

We had two middle-aged men in the sample who had made major career changes, one from being a pastor to being an enterpreneur in a new business, the other trying to find a place for himself in the regular work force after having retired from the Marines. Both of these men had interesting insights into the meanings of success and failure and, not surprisingly, of changes in their conception of those.

The first set of excerpts is from the ex-minister; the second from the ex-Marine.

> I don't believe in luck, in all that. I believe that, to a great extent, we are self-determining type people. What happens to us in life is to a great extent dependent on what we do. We control our destinies, in essence . . . When we do something and do it well, and we know we did it well, and we are rewarded by, perhaps what people say, or our boss or by our peers, or sometimes there's simply some kind of inner satisfaction that comes when, maybe nobody else says anything, but *you* know that what you've done was important or worthwhile or meaningful, and that it had an impact on somebody or something, therefore you feel that it was well worth the time and effort invested . . .
>
> What it means to be successful is very personal. My success might not be yours. Yours might not be mine. The little successes, the little accomplishments of children in grade school are very meaningful to them, are very good and constructive, yet we might look at them and say, Well, that wasn't much. For them, it was success, the attaining of those goals . . . (Terms like success and failure) aren't harmful necessarily, but I'm not sure that they're meaningful. I wouldn't say that they're necessarily harmful, but they're not particularly meaningful . . . The failures, those who have failed, seem to want to withdraw more and more into their own little shell and seek solace in 'My, how sad things are.' I think man was created a social being. I think when we find somebody who attempts to withdraw, it's either a protest against something, or it is an indication of some inadequacy within him/herself, or some feeling of frustration with what's going on around him. I think that by nature we want to be with other people. I think man is only complete when he shares in social relationships.

The ex-Marine, in this set of excerpts, is relating much of what he says to his current life situation, in which he has been unable to find a job he feels is of a high caliber and is, in fact, having difficulty doing well in what he feels to be a clerical job for anyone with a grade-school education.

> I just had an experience with frustration. It's an inability to indicate to anybody exactly what you're like. When I first started my job-searching I was really frus-

trated because I felt like with my background experience, education, and everything that I had, I might be a pretty good catch. If I get a new job, it won't take me very long, within two or three weeks, and I'll know what's going on. I'm not being braggy or anything, but I've been able to do it. For some reason, I didn't fit the pattern, they wanted me to . . . I think the frustration came in when, I really, the idea of starting over at the very bottom, then work back up to the top again was so distressing.

It still is. I'm very impatient. I'm a little bit discouraged. Even now, this little 90-day period that we're required to wait to get on permanent. What really bugs me is I see a lot of people who just graduated from school starting out on another level or on a different degree. A different track than what they're starting me out on. They're starting me on the track of somebody with a grade school education. It conveys to me the idea that they don't think I got it. Maybe I don't know, maybe I don't have the ability I think I do. Maybe they don't have the confidence in me that I think they should have. Maybe I'm asking too much . . . I looked for three or four months (for the job). I finally went over to the IRS and put in for this temporary thing. They called me up, and had me come over after I'd taken the test and everything. I filled out the application, and we had to take this other thing. This training period we had to go through for two weeks on CRT. I just barely passed it. Now I kind of wish I hadn't. The hours and everything are miserable. That frustration for me is very mentally distressing. It can really put you in a bind if you let it get the best of you. You can get down on yourself. You can get down on everybody around you, and you can be very tempted to just chuck it all and hit the road. I think your first inclination is to run. You kind of feel like you want to run away from it all. You say, "Nobody understands. Maybe if I go somewhere else, I'll find somebody that does." Then you say to yourself, "Just settle down." It didn't impress them very much that I had been to college. It didn't seem to impress them at all. I was really disillusioned for awhile. I told them where I should be at, and they didn't have a place for me. I told them that I was willing to start at a level that a kid coming out of college would start at. I'd be perfectly willing to do that. I think they thought I was too old to get on that track. I'm sure I was . . .

. . .if you're frustrated, upset, you can't seem to get on track. I think the frustration, like you say, you can't get on track, if you're overqualified, like I'm overqualified for what I'm doing right now. My performance is not up to par because I'm competing with young kids and I have no way to use my knowledge and experience to overcome the age factor.

Naturally, I want to be successful. I don't feel like I'm totally unsuccessful. But I don't feel like I've accomplished everything I want to. There's room to grow and places to go. I'm anxious to get on a track that leads to a job where somebody starts assessing the skill and knowledge I have, if I have any. I'm not too sure what I have to offer and I'm kind of anxious to see if I do have anything to offer.

In answer to a question to compare himself to his children, this man told us that "at this point I have a tendency to feel like they have the same ideas about success and failure as I did when I was a kid. They really don't understand what it is. I didn't really until I was 30 to 35 years old, before I even started thinking about it . . ."

The final set of excerpts comes from a younger man, in his twenties, but having been in the labor force for a number of years before and during his college years.

> I think in society being a success is driving a big car, having a nice home, wife, two kids. That's not necessarily success in being happy. Failure, might be a failure to someone else, but if that's the best that they can do, they can be considered a success. Depends on your point of reference. Where you're from, you have to realize also what your background was. What your step was from your background. If you come from a really poor, bad, deprived background and get a high school education, that could be considered very good. But if you come from a really high family, with Ph.D.'s, and you only go to high school, you're considered a failure . . .

> I don't fail very often. If it's something that I'll fail at, I usually don't do it. Maybe that's not very honest. I don't pay basketball *at all*. I like to do things I'm good at. If it's something I'll fail at, I don't do it. I try not to do it more than once unless I can correct the problem . . . I can't think of a situation really where I fail more at something than I succeed. If it's some athletic area that I'm just not good in at all, tennis, since I'm not good at it, I just don't care for it at all. I don't try to play it. I don't know whether I don't play it because I don't like it or I don't like it because I don't play it.

> I think motivation and hard work are more important than ability, luck, anything. Anybody in this country, if they're motivated, if they want to work hard enough, can get what they want, if they have average ability. People who say they can't, that's not true. Maybe it's harder for some groups than for others . . .

> I think probably my ideas are not quite the same as everyone else's. I can't really judge other people by the way I judge myself. As far as success and failure, it's nothing absolute. There are probably as many definitions as there are people.

Two valuable insights about success in life form a fitting conclusion for this chapter. Both were given by older interviewees at the end of the formal interview.

> To me the most important part of success is being willing to give of yourself. If you go down a hall and see a piece of paper, don't be afraid to pick it up. You're not too good to be a part-time janitor.

> Be kind to people, make a good living, and leave the world a little bit better than you found it.

CHAPTER 8

Uses and Abuses of Achievement and Attribution Research on Aging

In this chapter I am going to discuss the application of the data I have discussed in the previous chapters and the general attribution model to several issues in adult development and aging. I feel that the consistent concern with life-span issues and with development as an integral part of adulthood and of social behavior in general will result in direct applications of findings to issues of real concern to all of us, whether we are now old or not. I will have space to raise only a few of the topics in the manifold array of potentially useful insights that may be derived from steadfast application of a combination of adult developmental concerns and social cognitive principles and hypothesized mechanisms. A wider set has been presented as a series of researchable questions by George Banziger (1979) in a set of provocative unpublished papers. I encourage the reader to pursue that avenue for supplementation of the present discussion. I will concentrate on three issues—control and competence among nursing home residents, retirement and competence tests, and the meaning of a difficult job search process for younger and middle-aged adults. These three topics cut across clinical, industrial, and interpersonal kinds of application-oriented research and across situations that are linked both to older adulthood (the first two) and younger adulthood (the academic job search).

CONTROL AND NURSING HOME RESIDENTS

One area in which a general attribution model has been used to understand aging is that of feelings of control, especially among residents of nursing homes. In particular, Rodin and Langer (1977, 1980; Langer and Rodin, 1976) and Schulz and Hanusa (1978, 1980; Schulz, 1976; Hanusa & Schulz, 1981; Schulz & Brenner, 1977) have developed research programs concerned with the use of attribution-based techniques to induce a sense of control and competence that they feel is lacking in the typical nursing home resident. Recently, other researchers (L. Green, 1980; Lindstrom, 1980) have also used the same basic approach to enhance feelings of competence and control by giving older persons choice about scheduling of visits by younger persons.

A characteristic line of reasoning underlies most of this research. It is rooted in twin conceptions, one dominant in personality and social psychology—learned helplessness—and the other prevalent in social gerontology—the idea that nursing homes are debilitative for experience of control. As a result of the interplay of these two areas, the exploration of control and competence in nursing homebound older adults is a promising one in which to develop the linkages that are essential for social psychology to be adult-oriented and for gerontology to be opened to a cognitive-behavioral supplementation to its social structural orientation (see Chapter 13).[1]

What these social psychologists wish to analyze, and ameliorate, is a commonality of nursing home life (see the comment in Footnote): older residents of nursing homes have precious few control experiences. As a result, these researchers believe, they increasingly learn to be helpless, along the lines described by Abramson et. al. (1978). They can, however, again along the lines described by Abramson and colleagues, be retaught to be "in control."

Although most nursing home residents are voluntary admissions (in some sense, although often there are strong pressures from family, clergy, and physicians), it is hard to deny that they move into a world with few rewards for exercising control or opportunities to display competence. Decisions are made around them as to what and when they shall eat, when they will be bathed, when visitors will come, and so on. At the same time, they are rewarded for being passive and chastised for being self-determining (see those cited above and Gubrium, 1975).

These occurrences—the stifling institutional pattern—come at a time when personal competence is, in fact, likely to be failing. The etiology of this loss is multifaceted, to say the least. As people age they are increasingly likely to have physical experiences that limit their self-control. These include loss of sensitivity in sensory apparatus, slowing in nerve conduction and in muscle control, loss of strength, arthritis and other mobility-reducing illnesses, traumas from strokes, and so on. These are described in any good text on adulthood and aging (e.g., Whitbourne & Weinstock, 1979). They are also sometimes overmedicated by well-meaning but ignorant physicans and families (Butler, 1975), and the label "senile" is sometimes applied to them without relevant physiological evidence (Baizerman & Ellison, 1971; Butler, 1975). Of course, they often have severely reduced incomes, and those incomes are almost entirely derived from an opportuning, dependent relationship to the government and/or families. All of these buffetings of fortune—some with objective bases and some not—are exacerbated by life in the institution. It is difficult to escape the idea that nursing home life, even at its best, is a restricted-choice environment.

These realities fit well into the reformulated learned helplessness model proposed by Abramson et al. (1978). It is that model, and the assumptions in it that restriction in choice and/or a noncontingent, random schedule of reward and attention leads to and follows from an attributional base, on which these researchers rely. They use this

---

[1]I should point out, however, that at the same time that these important linkages have been explored, others have not as yet been made. For example, it is clear that the changes that take place with movement into a nursing home are, by and large, present in all institutions. Thus work by Goffman (1961) and many others on being institutionalized are extremely relevant. They would provide yet another cogent lifespan connection and one between two clearly different approaches to social psychology, as discussed in Chapter 12. Although the researchers have clearly embedded their work in lifespan conceptions of learned helplessness, they have not used this additional guiding framework in their formulations. They have remained consistently psychological and seem to have missed the sociological work that is relevant. In fact, as I note in the text, they have underutilized the attribution model itself.

model to make the points that cognitive placement of control over events is a central element in feelings about oneself and that attributions of certain sorts—in particular, of failure to global, stable, internal factors—negatively influence feelings of control and judgments about competence.

What, then, have these researchers found? The results have been mixed; whereas Langer and Rodin found strong effects of their manipulations, even 18 months after the manipulation (Rodin & Langer, 1977), Schulz and his associates (e.g., Schulz & Hanusa, 1978), Green, and Lindstrom have all found only relatively minor relationships. In fact, Schulz and Hanusa (1980) and Hanusa and Schulz (1981) have recently proposed that simple changes in physical environment are at least as likely to result in greater self-esteem and feelings of control as cognitive manipulations of attributions. I should add that most of the researchers have not made as extensive a use of attributional models as might be expected on the basis of their conceptions. They have only used the general idea noted above and have neither directly manipulated nor directly measured attributions as such. This weakness makes interpretation of the results of the studies in attribution terms hazy at best. The ambiguity in this regard means that other, undefined factors may be leading to the variety of results. In fact, the researchers have made extensive use of locus of control, which, you will recall, Weiner (1972) and others have criticized as inappropriate for understanding attributions. They also appear to assume personal control and personal attributions are equivalent, a position that Abramson et. al., among others (e.g., Snyder, 1976), have taken pains to point out is often unwarranted.

By the way, all have also made the unequivocal, but untested, assumption that one of the major effects of nursing homes is the negative effect of cognitive loss of a sense of control. Whereas that assumption is intuitively and stereotypically ''validated,'' in light of what we reviewed above, it is not always likely to be accurate. Such a view denies the interpretive nature of self-control. For example, many nursing home residents may feel more in control than before they went into the home because they do not have to worry as much or deal with as uncontrollable an environment. This lack of concern for a variety of interpretations of the move is odd, since the researchers all make the same sort of phenomenological approach—perception of self—a central element in their assertions that a change in cognitive orientation will result in greater feelings of control in what is essentially still an uncontrollable venue (from the point of view of having to make or being able to make constant decisions about where one should be, what one should do, etc.).

In any case, although the discussion of issues, partially in an attempt to reconcile the fairly different findings from the two major programs, is likely to continue—and the result of that discussion bears directly on the validity of an attribution-reattribution approach to that particular aspect of aging—two facts do seem to be clear. First of all, from the point of view of an observer, at least, nursing homes quite clearly are restricted environments for opportunities for success and failure experiences and are likely to compel a failure-oriented reaction, by staff in particular, to the performance of residents. Often the reward structure is oriented toward passivity, and thus provides a low level of feedback to self-initiated action (Gubrium, 1975; Goffman, 1961). Although, as I noted above, it is crucial not to take this fact too far and facilely assume that all residents are aware of or concerned with that aspect of nursing home living, it is an important fact of life in a total institutional setting and is particularly likely to be the case in a nursing home, in which certain assumptions (the truth value of which is often immaterial—see Baizerman & Ellison, 1971) about ability to care for oneself had been made as a basis for admission.

Second, from the point of view of the actor, the older individual, it is also likely that giving her control experiences may well help her to define herself in that setting and may enhance both behavior (as in Rodin and Langer's work) and at least some aspects of morale and life satisfaction (Green, Lindstrom). Although, as Schulz and Hanusa (1980) make clear, whether cognitive manipulations of attributions are or are not the most efficient method to use to engender control experiences is open to question, it is likely that, as in other areas (e.g., phobias and insomnia—Storms & Nisbett, 1970; Valins & Nisbett, 1971), attributions may be one valuable tool to be used therapeutically.

In any case, whatever the outcome of the discussion concerning the ultimate value of attributional direction in nursing homes may be, the use of an attributional model beyond college age has thus far been limited to a specific set of experiences and a specific setting that is not highly common among even aged persons (about 5% are in long-term care homes at any given time, and a particular persons has about a 20% chance of residing in a nursing home) and is obviously highly uncommon among those not categorized as elderly.

It is further clear that a sense of loss of control is by no means a necessary concomitant of being elderly nor of living in housing designed especially for older persons that is short of a nursing home atmosphere. The subjects that have been studied in my research program, by and large, see themselves as very much in control, as masters of their fate to the degree that anyone is. As I have discussed in Chapter 6, there was a tendency for the *range* of optimism and self-control to be somewhat broader in my older groups, with some indication of a failure-orientation. However, there was little basis for general statements of lower sense of control, even though the age group extended well into the eighties. Older were only rather superficially different from other age groups.

There was, of course, one particularly important difference in this regard, especially in comparing older persons to middle-aged ones. That is, older persons, even with a fairly advantaged existence compared to many of their age peers, did feel somewhat less mastery and did tend to attribute their own failures to personal but relatively uncontrollable factors, especially ones in which they may expect, if anything, a decline over the next several years—motor skills, sensory acuity, and so on. This, of course, is a mild effect, but one reminiscent of the Abramson et. al. reformulated learned helplessness model.

What does this mean in practical terms? Where might such relatively minor differences in orientation have relatively major effects? How might these findings be related to findings that concern other age groups and, in that regard, how might commonness of performance and of orientation in a general old age sample and a non-aged subsample point to one way to deal with both the attribution-orientation and the performance aspects of failure orientation?

The data gathered on attributions by and about older persons and the relatively vo-luminous data about performance differences between older and younger persons gathered by psychologists of aging (e.g., Heron & Chown, 1967; Botwinick, 1978) may be fruitfully combined, both with each other and with corresponding informa-tion about a particular segment of the younger age groups commonly studied by attri-bution researchers and other social psychologists—test-anxious students.

The peformances of older persons are, quite frequently, quantitatively and qualita-tively "poorer" than those of younger persons to whom they are directly compared. Although many of the data in this area are tainted by choice of comparison groups that are not equalized for educational experience and "intelligence," there does seem to be an "age" effect even when groups have been well controlled. In particu-lar, older persons are likely to perform more poorly as a group in situations in which there is pressure or which are unusual, unfamiliar, and/or highly artificial. That is, the deficits often found for "age" are greater in testing and experimental situations of the type commonly used by psychologists than in more naturalistic behaviors and set-tings (Labouvie-Vief, 1977; Botwinick, 1978). It may be that older persons are less tolerant of ambiguity and artificiality, and that this is related to less certainty about standards by which the actor will be judged. If standards are unclear, but presumed to be related to possible negative images of age and oldness (as Klein, 1972, and others have assumed), then older actors will be *less* effective if they take the perspective of the other than if they do not. Yet data from my studies make it clear that older persons are almost equal in their differentiations by age—differentiations that are somewhat negative in their orientation to the components of failure experiences at least—as ob-servers who are not old. Likewise, research by Kogan and Wallach (1961) and Botwinick (1966, 1969) indicates that older persons are more likely to actively seek out and use "social comparison" information about propriety and the value of certain types of performance. This all adds up to a set of social pressures toward conformity to a negative image of what the individual older person is likely to do.

More specifically related to my general point, of course, is the fact that those same sorts of conditions affect test-anxious students more than they affect nonanxious ones (Wine, 1971; Sarason, 1976). That is text-anxious persons are less certain in test situations (that, of course, includes artificiality and pressure to per-form); they show rather major decrements in those situations even when they do not do so in situations designed to be less stressful and less artificial, and they show a greater tendency to conform and to use relatively unattainable levels of performance as the standard to which to judge their own.

In other words, both test-anxious younger persons and a broader sample of elderly (especially ones less selected than the samples used in my research) appear to per-form and, also important, to think about their performance in similar ways. Further, those ways are often dysfunctional for both groups. This is the case even though they do not "feel" objectively "stupid" or "worse" when able to observe themselves in a more detached way and evaluate their "true" ability level. Artificiality and attributional tendencies may conspire to induce a poor performance in elderly and in test-anxious younger persons under certain conditions. Of course, I should note that I do not mean to imply that older persons may not at the same time be experiencing other losses—physiological, for example—that are influencing their performances in negative ways and accounting for at least some of the negative effects.

RETIREMENT AND COMPETENCE TESTING

The specific set of comparisons needed to test the above hypotheses have not yet been made, either before or during the conduct of my research program. Until that is done, the model of performance decrements as in some way related to attributional differences is obviously very tenuous. However, it may be worthwhile to proceed a bit further in considering some of the implications that it might have, what the similarity of performance of older and test-anxious younger persons might mean for several practical issues. The specific issue I will discuss is retirement policy, especially mandatory retirement based on age. For many years those concerned with retirement policy have used age 65 as some sort of magic boundary point between full employment and "retirement" as both a right and an obligation. In recent years that assumption has been challenged on many fronts, and proposals for change in so-called normal retirement age have proceeded in both directions. I will briefly mention, but not go into, some of those aspects of retirement; they are dealt with much better by social gerontologists such as J. Schultz (1976). I will then proceed to the focus of this section of the chapter.

There are several pressures pushing toward a *lower* retirement age, either as mandated or as allowable for benefits. In fact, several countries, most notably Japan, do have earlier retirement ages. The reasons given for such a change are twofold, one economic and relatively negative to older workers, the other personal and positive toward older persons. The economic reason concerns the labor force. In a time of relatively high rates of "normal" unemployment, including extremely high rates for young persons, one method of getting good cohort flow through the labor force is to have older cohorts leave the field at a relatively early age. Thus, it is considered to be a responsibility of older workers to "step aside." Although a negative image of abilities of older workers is not formally a part of the argument, it seems to be implicit and seems to follow from the policy in any case.

The personal reason is one that takes into account the idea that retirement is earned and should be savored while some vigor of youth remains. In that case, it should be available at a relatively early age so that one can "enjoy his or her golden years of retirement." Indeed, it is clear that a sizable number of workers, especially laborers and factory line workers, welcome—indeed, sometimes demand—early retirement (that is, prior to age 65).

There are also both economic and personal pressures (and ones both positive to and negative to older persons) pushing in the other direction from age 65. Business, government, and society in general are alarmed by the costs of retirement-based financial plans, especially the Social Security benefit system and pension plans. As retired cohorts live longer, they obviously take out of any system more than what was allocated into it at a time when actuarial tables had built-in expectations of earlier deaths. Corresponding to this, there have been proposals, most recently by presidential candidate John Anderson in the 1980 campaign, to raise the minimum age for Social Security benefits (his plan was a graduated step up to age 68 to soften the effect on now older workers). The effect of this, quite clearly, would be to raise the "normal" retirement age figure to that required for entry into the program. This would lead to more money being fed into the system and less being taken out. Again, I do not propose to deal in depth with the merit or demerit of the proposals.

There has been another, more clearly social psychological, policy factor concerning retirement age as well—the issue of mandatory retirement. Although the Federal government has thus far not raised the age for receiving benefits, it has raised the minimum retirement age that a private employer may use to age 70 for most occupations. (One interesting exception, of course, is academia, although it, too, is scheduled to catch up.) There are additional plans to continue to raise that age so that, in effect, age discrimination will no longer be institutionalized and legitimized. Federal government jobs already have no mandatory retirement age.

Why has the government taken these steps? One of the primary forces in that direction have been organizations that are proponents of the rights of older persons. They argue that mandatory retirement is obvious, outright discrimination by age and, further, that that discrimination is based in and strengthens false stereotypes of the abilities of older persons. They argue that the idea that somehow age 65 is a clear demarcation between being useful and being useless is an idea that has lost any of the validity it may have had in times when attaining that age was indeed becoming "very old." Certainly, those objectives to mandatory retirement are correct. Such stereotypes make little sense, and they have the effect of cutting off not only income but also a sense of occupation and worth for at least some older persons who are involuntarily retired.

In the next few pages, however, I want to consider this issue in light of some of the knowledge we have gathered about attributions and the hypothesis discussed above concerning the possibility of a general failure-orientation by and about current cohorts of older persons. I wish to discuss and examine the specific psychological and social impacts that mandatory retirement and its abolition may have because of their interplay with attributions of both major types.

It is clear that the argument against mandatory retirement is concerned partly with attributions, at least in the "attributes" sense. A negative view of older persons and of their abilities is engendered in a system that institutionalizes severing someone from his or her work tasks simply because he or she has attained a particular age. The concept draws its validity from a belief that ages beyond the mid-sixties are reliably related to loss of ability; in other words, it implies and rests upon a personal, stable attribution for the failures of older persons, but not for the failures of non-old. The Type I attribution, thus serving as a base, is verified by every case in which a person is retired because of age. The fact of retirement at the particular age, when based in the attribution outlined above and coupled with people's general tendency to believe the world is fair and just (Lerner, 1975), leads inexorably to the conclusion that declining ability as one reaches the age of mandatory retirement is an accurate depiction of reality. Thus, the attribution is indiscriminately applied to all older persons, including the many who are at least as competent and able as they were 10 years ago and as younger persons are at present. The loop is closed and the attribution-based stereotype is assumed to have been verified.   Smith's (1979) attribution work already mentioned and Rosen and Jerdee's (1976) findings of managerial decisions about not-yet-retired older workers based in negative stereotypes provide some justification for this view.

At the same time, there is some evidence, and a lot of hearsay, used by anti-mandatory-retirement groups and individuals, concerning Type II attributions as responses to the fact of being retired. It is felt that older persons who are retired by fiat feel useless and that their self-esteem is lowered. This is seen to be a direct result of having been eliminated by their company on the basis of a personal characteristic—age. Certainly, there is a clear link here, in which older persons are likely to "buy the myth" that they are no longer usable and useful members of society, even though they are told that they are to see retirement as a reward for a job well done (in the past, of course, when they could handle it). Insofar as retirement from work is preceived by older persons as a failure experience, the general tendency found in my work and that of others—that older persons are more likely than others to use personal attributions for failure—will in fact be likely to have the effect of lowering self-esteem and expectations of future success. (Or will it? Most of the data fail to show an expectation or esteem effect, even when they show an attribution effect—see Chapters 5 and 6.)

These are certainly meritorious arguments, and they have led most advocates for older persons and a large number of older persons themselves to argue persuasively against mandatory retirement policies (see Banziger [1979a] who uses Neugarten's [1974] idea of the age-irrelevant society to argue against mandatory retirement and for a flexible approach to both work and retirement). Of course, moving the age up to 70 has no absolute effect in this regard—it is no more fair or positive than the previous age limit for work— except to delay the placement by self and others into the "low ability" category. Although full abolition of mandatory retirement policies will have a sizeable effect, its impact will be smaller than what might have been expected, since a smaller percentage would want to work beyond 70 than beyond 65 (retirement as a right to be enjoyed).

However, I think it is important to consider how this plan and goal may have within it a different set of dangers, attributional ones, that should also be considered. In particular I want to consider an alternative approach to inducing cohort flow through the labor force—competence testing. Quite simple, competence testing is an organized test program to examine the ability of older workers who cannot be retired because of attaining a certain age (or other workers, although the focus is usually on older ones). The individual is given an examination of knowledge and of performance, and that test result is used to determine continued employment.

Competence Testing, Competence, and Attributions for Self

There are two aspects of competence testing that are important to consider in attributional terms.

The first concerns an issue we have mentioned several times (Chapter 4, for example): the characteristics of an attribution to age (see also Green, 1981). In many ways the attribution for losing a job because of mandatory retirement may be seen as an *external* attribution (really, a set of attributions). On its face, it is discrimination; it is prejudicial action done without regard to actual competence (although, of course, it has an underlying stereotype about general category competence). In that case, being fired because of age is really being fired because of an arbitrary system, resulting from the shortsightedness and rigid rule-orientation of superiors, even when the rules are unjust, and because of a lack of clear guidelines from government and other sources. Both older persons themselves (Type II attributions) and observers (Type I attributions) can and do make such attributions for mandatory retirement; indeed observations of that sort are at the basis of the objections to mandatory retirement—that it is arbitrary rule-following without regard for the real abilities of the individual.

This approach to the cause of retirement is a set of attributions that fits well into the middle-aged pattern of attributions for failure found in the data presented earlier. If older persons and others react in this way to the loss of a job because of mandatory retirement policy, they are likely to use that attributional information in the same way middle-aged persons in my studies did; they are not likely to blame the older person and, for him or her, to feel personally at fault for failing. This is not to imply that older workers will be happy with the result or satisfied with losing their job, but it is simply to note that their own attributions and those of other judges are not necessarily ones that would lead directly to lower self-esteem. There are, of course, concomitants other than attributions that tend in that direction, as we will consider briefly toward the end of this section.

By the same token, proceeding a step further and including the kind of information described in Chapter 7, it must be kept in mind that one person's failure is not necessarily everyone else's. If losing the job is attributed to luck or external sources, it may not be considered a failure at all (at least not a personal failure). It appeared to be the case in the research program data that older persons were more likely to see meaningful failures and successes in social interactions, in family relations and the successes and failures of their children and grandchildren, and in persuading others to their point of view. Beyond that, importance is attached to doing one's best and to internal standards of judgment about actual performances. None of those tendencies is likely to be brought into play in a situation of forced retirement solely because of age.

But what about retirement because of poor performance on a competence test? Surely that is personal; it is a direct attack on ability. One failed because he or she could not do well on the test. Both the internal-standards definition of failure just noted and the tendency already existent to attribute failure to personal stable factors are likely to be very active in such a situation (on the part of both the actor and the observers—testers—I might add). The failure is likely to be attributed quite specifically to lack of ability. Since the basis for the test is linked openly with age, it becomes a strong stable attribution to internal characteristics. *That* is likely to induce feelings of lack of control and of incompetence. Thus, abolition of mandatory retirement may, unfortunately, have a hidden attributional landmine.

Performance Deficits

A second question then becomes crucial. How likely is it that an older person will not do well on a competency test, given a level of ''competence'' adequate to do a good job on an everyday basis? Based on factors we have considered earlier in this chapter and in previous chapters, I would have to answer, "quite likely." Note the characteristics of competence testing. It is often done in an artificial setting, a test room with test apparatus. It is obviously a test situation. Often time pressure is involved, and a level of performance considerably higher than that needed for day-to-day performance in actual work contexts is required. In other words, it is a situation calling for peak performance in a high pressure setting.

It is at this point that the previous discussion of test anxiety is crucial, for the above are exactly the sort of task situations in which both older persons in general and test-anxious younger persons have been repeatedly found to show performance deficits when compared to other actors (and to themselves when more care is taken to provide a good atmosphere for performance). If older persons are somewhat more likely to use stable personal explanations for failure—a part of the failure-orientation pattern discussed in detail in earlier chapters—then the familiar effects of failure-orientation and test anxiety on performance are likely to affect their performances. Even if their work output and quality in a normal setting, with normal pacing and normal surroundings and pressure levels, may be more than adequate, they will be more likely than other persons to fail in this peculiar kind of test situation. The result—they are likely to fail, unless the test situation is job-related, familiar, meaningful, and as natural as possible (see McClelland, 1973). However, those latter characteristics are by no means necessarily going to be met in many competence testing situations.

In this complex way, the after-the-fact attribution, inescapably brought home by the situation and the outcome, is a *verification* of the "can't do it any more" mentality that is the basis for the general model favoring mandatory retirement at a particular age. It is a verification and an extension to the individual of a failure-orientation set. That, in turn, is likely to influence the later interactions of others with the individual and the expectations and self-confidence of the individual. Both of those are prime breeding ground for self-fulfilling prophesies and the sort of social breakdown syndrome Kuypers and Bengtson (1973) proposed. In other words, attributionally and in terms of labeling and role expectations, losing a job because of competence testing may very well be more devastating than losing it because of attaining a particular age. In some ways, at least, the former is more insidious and negative than the latter.

Which is better? Psychologically, at this level at least, it would seem mandatory retirement is better than a competence-testing alternative. I hasten to add that this does not mean I feel it is a good alternative nor do I mean to deny or downplay other problems with mandatory retirement, ones that are likely to outweigh the attributional issues dealt with here. The loss of income at retirement can be a major burden, to be sure. Use of mandatory retirement denies work to a wide range of older persons who may want to continue working, including those who could pass competence tests, even biased ones. Also important psychologically is the feeling of uselessness that may be brought about, with or without an attributional basis, when a person is not asked to contribute, when society is withdrawing not only its rewards, but even its demands from a person (this will be discussed further in Chapter 13).

I do not mean to downplay any of these factors; indeed, it is clear that a blind policy of mandatory retirement should be eliminated at virtually every level. I also agree that carefully considered and designed competence testing, applied uniformly across all ages of workers, may alleviate the major portion of the problems I indicated. But I do think it is important to realize and consider all sides of this important social issue. I think it is a clear case in which research of the sort discussed in the last chapters can make an impact on a broad retirement policy so that it does not harm some by promoting the greater good (and theirs) without understanding the implications of the cures. Too often social policy has proceeded without that understanding of the full implications (school busing may be one of those issues and policies). Often the policy will still be —for the sake of social justice *must* still be —followed, but it is almost certain that it will have untoward effects even as it proceeds to have positive influences in several directions.

To deny the negative impacts that the abolition of mandatory retirement may have on individuals through the mediation of their attributions and the attributions of those around them because the evils of mandatory retirement are apparent is a flawed approach. It is a denial of the complexity, quality, and contextuality of life we have stressed over and over again in this book; it is one more way to take the richness of life out of its living, changing, relational character and to impress upon it restrictions and reductions that are less than optimal. At the same time, to place total emphasis on attributions would also be wrong; to work against the abolition of mandatory retirement because of attributional implications is itself obviously incomplete and deleterious. The influence of attributions is but one part of the web of factors, influences, and effects of every direction in this complex social issue. It is important to have as much information as we can for decisions of the moment and to try to keep touch with changes in attributional perspectives with changing cohorts, changing contexts, and changing social structures—indeed, changing worlds.

Basic research in such areas as attributions cannot substitute for policy formation or for political decision-making, but it can and should have an impact on those. This is a truism, I know (see also Campbell, 1969). But it is clear that social psychology in general has not paid a great deal of attention to the linkage of knowledge and policy in any area of interest, and it is also clear that in this, as in other aspects of social psychology, adult development and aging issues have lagged behind others when social psychologists have turned their attention to such policy-relevant issues. This chapter is one brief attempt to illustrate how a social psychology of developing adults can contribute on this level, as on others, to enable social psychologists to constantly do for their discipline what all of us must do as individuals—to constantly construct and reconstruct what we are and what we have to offer, so that it can be useful for the moment—for short-term policy—and as a rough guide to how we can proceed to deal with the new realities of the new moments spreading out before us into the future.

SEEK AND YE MIGHT FIND . . . SOMETHING: ACADEMIC JOB-SEARCHING

Although I have tried to make clear throughout the book that the social psychology of developing adults I am concerned with is not merely, or even primarily, a social psychology of old people, to this point I have only concerned myself with applications to issues in aging. I want to consider in brief form one issue not concerned with aging adults, as illustrative of the application of the approach to other areas little noted by the main body of attribution researchers. The area is that of success and failure in searching for a job, specifically an academic job.

Before I discuss that issue and a set of preliminary data related to it, I must remind the reader that I am not asserting there has been no research previously that is relevant to adult developmental areas of attribution use. I have noted some of the previous work earlier—on parole decisions and marital relations. In particular I would direct you to the stimulating collection of social applications of attribution theory edited by Frieze, Bar-tal, and Carroll (1979). It includes discussions of such areas as loneliness (Peplau, Russell, & Heim, 1979; see also Shaver & Rubinstein, 1980), alcoholism (McHugh, Beckman, & Frieze, 1979), and consumerism (Valle & Johnson, 1979), as well as a report on the parole decision studies (Carroll, 1979). Wiley, Crittenden, and Birg (1979) examined a short-term version of the failure to be discussed in the next few paragraphs—rejection of an article submitted for publication.

However, what has been done thus far are initial steps, leaving many other crucial areas unexplored. One omission that seems curious to me is the use of attributions to understand reactions and approaches job seekers have to their task and to the failures and possible success that are outcomes of various stages in the process. This issue is particularly important in a time of recession and unemployment such as the United States is experiencing as these words are written. An area of employment particularly hard hit by economic and social influences toward continued recession, a constantly tight market for the foreseeable future, is the world of academia. The percentages of job aspirants to the academic life who can find what they were usually led to expect—a tenured or tenure-track position—are decreasing and will continue to do so. How do highly educated, highly motivated adults cope with a situation that is likely to be an ongoing process of many failures interspersed with occassional limited successes (a temporary job, a postdoctoral position, a tenure-track job at a less desired school)? Those processes—the approaches used, the emotional reactions, the explanations given, the constraints on future behavior—certainly are amenable to exploration in attribution terms. The immediacy and depth of the problem and its social and psychological implications for the individuals involved, their families, and the broader society (and, not least of all, the disciplines in which they were trained and the impact on disciplinary development) make it an important point at which to apply those ideas toward understanding and redirection.

Almost astonishingly, social psychologists have managed to ignore the whole issue. Although, for example, the American Psychological Association (e.g., 1980) conducts annual studies of the job situation, it deals only with broad demographic comparisons and collection of distribution data. There is no attempt to explore the social-psychological aspects one would expect psychologists to focus on. Officials and prominent educators (e.g., Kiesler, 1979; Cook, 1979; Schneider, 1980) play number games and provide vague assertions that things (a) are fine and (b) will only get better when new psychologists take their own fates into their own hands and make new kinds of primarily nonacademic jobs for themselves—an interesting, extremely dispositional attribution for failure is clearly built into their model. Likewise, the

American Sociological Association has also apparently failed to study a phenomenon close to the heart of their primary disciplinary emphasis on structures and organizations as they affect both society and individuals (see Whitt & Derber, 1979).

Ilene Staff and I, supported by a Grant-in-Aid from the Society for the Psychological Study of Social Issues, have done exploratory work on these issues using a general attributional framework similar to that I used in my other attribution studies. In particular, we are interested in getting information about the effect of job search outcomes—and the laborious process itself—on individual's lives and self-concepts and about the emphases job seekers feel are crucial to success and failure today. The latter include personal and impersonal (structural and interpersonal), and stable and unstable factors. The approach and data are reported elsewhere (Blank & Staff, 1981); I simply wish to mention the study briefly as another productive, adult-oriented one, including a sense of personal history and temporal extension of what is often treated as though it were a static entity—an outcome.

At this time we have only begun to analyze the data. They are rich and varied, indicating a broad range of reactions. As I noted briefly in Chapter 7 for the larger attribution study, also with this—a great deal of ambiguity is elicited by the situation and by either outcome. The feelings and thoughts of these persons about their searches do not fit easily into either a simple success versus failure model or a simplistic, nonprocessual point-in-time event notion. Job seekers respond ambivalently to both ''success'' and ''failure''; they revise their conceptions of what those two concepts are, and they see each event as only part of a larger picture. Also, they draw upon a rich and varied set of causal bases, many of which do not fit well into ''classic'' schemata conceptions.

CONCLUSION TO PART 2

Although the data explored in the last five chapters is only a set of beginnings in the larger path to understanding attributions as a part of the social psychology of developing adults, I hope that their variety and richness are indications of the way to proceed to understand subject matter of the field in a manner that takes into account both static, current age group differences and dynamic conceptions of the processes of self- and other-perception as historical and evolutionary. They are meant to reveal an approach that combines standard designs and standard qualitative analyses—and the strengths of those methods—with more ethogenic, phenomenological data-gathering and qualitative methods and combines basic and applied concerns in steadfastly and essentially life-span-developmental ways.

PART THREE
Environments and Activity

CHAPTER 9

Ecology, Social Activity, and Satisfaction: Age Differences and Aging

After our exhaustive consideration of the topic of attributions as one that can fruitfully be explored in a development-oriented way, we now turn to an area at first glance far removed from those considerations—ecological-environmental factors and their relationships to social activity and personal satisfaction of adults, primarily older persons. This set of concerns is closely related to Barker's (e.g., 1968) pioneering work in ecological psychology, more recent concerns (e.g., by Milgram, 1970) with urban environmental psychology, and studies of environmental cognition and the joint impact of person and environment factors on social use and social psychology. They are also related to active areas within social gerontology, as will be discussed below.

Before moving directly to discussion of the topics, I want to make several essential points concerning the apparent distance between these concerns and those of the preceding portions of the book—especially Part 2. Because of those superficial dissimilarities, several aspects of this choice for an area to illustrate and further a social psychology of developing adults may be disconcerting to some readers. I want to take a bit of time to raise and discuss several points of potential objection—to the lack of centrality of ecological concerns in social psychology, the concentration on older persons instead of a wider adult age range, and the sociological tone of many of the materials. Finally, in this preliminary section, I will briefly discuss a key unifying concept.

First of all, many researchers in enviornmental psychology have come to it from training in and because of interests in social psychology. This group includes Roger Barker (e.g., 1968) and others in the ecological psychology tradition (such as Wicker, 1979; and Bechtel, 1977) as well as more traditional social psychologists such as Milgram (1970) and Glass and Singer (1972), Altman (1975), and Sommer (1974). Further, at least some of this research—for example, studies of the effects of noise on cognitive development in children (Glass & Singer, 1972) and hearing loss in adults and Barker and Barker's (1961) ecological study, to be discussed in the following—have included a developmental component. In any case, the interrelationships of physical-environmental and individual development and the impact of physical environmental elements on social psychology and social life are certainly legitimate areas of concern for social psychology.

In particular, this sort of research is illustrative of the interlocking set of progressions (and the relationship among them) with which a social psychology of developing adults is properly and centrally concerned. That is, environmental psychology explicitly concerns the relationship of persons and personal characteristics with external factors; it is *necessarily* focused on the point of overlap of Lewin's Person and Environment. Although much of this work has proceeded without an explicit concern with Person or Environment beyond a Lewinian, main effects model and has been fuzzy on further sophistication in description of what *P* and *E* mean, without much imagination, the broad set of progressions can be fruitfully delineated. The relationship of the progressions is more clearly central in this area of social psychological interest than in many others and, thus, examination of environmental issues over time (and the changes passage of time brings about in all aspects of Person and of Environment and in their co-relations) can be useful as an illustration of a step toward a development-sensitive, relational social psychology.

The second objection—to devoting this space almost exclusively to discussion of the ecological and environmental psychology of *older persons*—likewise can be answered on grounds of both practicality and conceptual usefulness. Within ecological-environmental psychology there has been a fairly consistent concern with older persons. In fact, as will be described in a few pages, a major conceptualization of person-environment relations at all points of the life span has been formulated by a psychologist of aging and used extensively in social gerontology. Considerable data from an array of methodological and conceptual perspectives have been gathered on older persons. In part, this has been because of a direct policy need for information about effects of institutionalization of older persons (even though only about 4 or 5% of persons over 65 are in institutions), partly more indirectly to the social gerontological predilection for studying older persons in institutions and other specialized housing and the obvious fact that type of residence may have an effect on behavior and satisfaction. Partly, also, this emphasis on environmental relations of older persons has resulted from the apparent nature of the changes which take place in the inner biological progression of older persons (to be described briefly below). For these and other reasons, a considerable amount of research and, more important, a considerable amount of relatively development-sensitive theorizing have been concerned with environmental psychology of older persons and of aging processes. Measurement tools appropriate to postcollege age persons have already been developed. That makes the step from non-adult-oriented work to an adult-oriented social psychology smaller and easier than an equally large step in many other areas. Therefore, ecological-environmental effects on social behavior is an area of study quite inviting as an entry into a social psychology of adult development.

A third objection that *some* social psychologists may advance, that the approach used in the studies to be reported is sociological in tone, is a more difficult one to counter and yet one that is more tractable. I shall be relying on large-scale survey data as part of the information in both major studies to be reported. Furthermore, the interpretations of the data, in typical survey fashion, will be concerned only with a relatively limited set of variables, both as independent and as dependent factors. In particular, a sociological definition of social activity will be used when making the comparisons of different sorts of environments. These sociological characteristics might be objected to by some.

Such a tone of disciplinary chauvinism, I hope, is not to be found among my readers. If not, I need no defense for including "sociological" data as they are relevant. The information has been gathered in such a way as to facilitate comparisons among a variety of types of data—thus surveys, scales, behavioral observation, and environmental mappings have been intermixed. Each provides its own strengths and weaknesses, both of which are usually quite apparent. I think such a multidisciplinary approach is advantageous—even essential—when exploring the interplay of progressions in a coherent, systematic way.

Quite simply, it is not any more legitimate to ignore sociological variables in social psychological research than it is to ignore psychological ones. Psychological social psychologists have tried to do this, with the decidedly mixed results discussed at the beginning of this book and in many other sources cited earlier. Rather, the aim and focus of social psychology should always be upon essentially *social-psychological* understanding, on relationships and the construction of social reality, on finding stability in the constant interplay of change. To do so, one must be aware of and open to all the levels of abstraction and analysis that are at least sometimes useful in that understanding . Surely those include so-called sociological factors as well as so-called psychological ones (and so-called physical-environmental ones). Thus, the attempts to gather a variety of measures to be discussed, once again, must be recognized as only that—attempts. And yet, they may be more rather than less valuable than more narrowly focused, controlled studies would be (in a heuristic sense, though it certainly can be argued that they are less valuable in a descriptive-explanatory sense). The variety of approaches—and even the inherent weaknesses of each that will be apparent in exposition and interpretation of the studies—can be a spur to clearer, sounder, more rigorous thinking in the future.

In this particular case—and for purposes of using the research to build bridges among a range of researchers interested in adult development as a social construction process—the presence of a sociological approach strengthens the exemplar nature of the material in a specific way.

Since most of the relevant research already done in social gerontology has had a decidedly sociological cast to it, gathering of data that includes both variables familiar to those researchers and variables that are more social psychological and psychological can facilitate an effective, swift transfer of information between traditional social gerontologists who research environments and social psychologists of developing adults interested in environmental issues. As has been discussed in other contexts earlier in the book, this method of attack on the lack of interrelationships of social psychology of aging/social gerontology and mainstream social psychologies, flawed though it may be in many ways, is more likely to lead to an interactive, fully informed approach to research and application questions than narrowly focused allegiance to a more sophisticated or more comfortable approach that is likely to be alien and forbidding to many traditional researchers and interested social scientists. Even rope bridges thrown over a chasm are an advance in communication from no bridges at all.

A particular fruitful concept to link the array of psychological and sociological (and social psychological) approaches to environment together, and to relate this type of research domain with the attribution work already detailed, is that of competence and control. When we considered attributions, we often considered these two elements. Especially in our discussions of locus of control (Chapter 6) and applications of attributional work to nursing home living and to retirement (Chapter 8), it was apparent that one systematic difference between older and other-age adults appears to be a tendency for older persons today to have less of a feeling of mastery and personal control (and, possibly, competence, although the direct evidence is certainly not clearly supportive of that notion except in some nursing home samples) and more need for verification of—and assistance to insure—control over one's environment than those in other age groups.

Competence and control issues are a core of concerns that will suffuse content areas discussed in the next several chapters. We will be exploring topics such as crime; age-related reactions to a long, hot summer; cognitive mapping; the effects of institutional environments; social activity in relation to physical design; cognitive map use; and shopping behavior. In many of these discussions we will come face-to-face with an overriding difference between old people *as a general group* and non-old as a separate general group: individual biological, psychological, social and environmental factors—in other words, ones in all of Riegel's (1978) dimensions—often conspire to reduce a sense and a reality of control as people age and in the older age category at a particular point in time. As a result, as we range far and wide in a varied set of studies on "environments" (Person-Environment units, really, as I will discuss below), as we keep in mind their weaknesses and static reductions and the distance between them and more centrally social psychological—and more centrally developmental—studies, let us also attend to the possibilities of linkage—through the ideas of personal control, mastery, and environmental "competence"—between these studies and those previously discussed.

BASIC TERMS IN ECOLOGICAL ANALYSIS

Before describing specific methods and findings it may be wise to consider briefly some of the elementary terms developed by ecological and environmental psychologists, both those concerned with aging and those who have not been, so that later description can proceed more efficiently.

An obvious starting point for consideration of the relationship of persons to their environments is the considerable body of work produced by Barker and his associates (for example, Barker, 1968; Barker & Barker, 1961; Barker & Associates, 1977). Since those citations and others (e.g., Wicker, 1977; and Bechtel, 1977) are excellent sources of information concerning the approach and its uses, and since many readers are likely to be familiar with the terminology, I will only describe the most essential set of terms and their referents for those who may not be familiar with the work.

Barker has been concerned with an adequate description of the relationships of person to environment. He feels, with Brunswik (1956) and others, that to do so we must have a much better catalog of types of environments and their relevant circumstances than we have. To that end, he has described and analyzed many aspects of *behavior settings*. One aspect of a behavior setting is the inhabitants who behave within it (others include the sort of behaving which occurs there). From the point of view of settings, one could speak of whether persons of various ages are "allowed" in the setting, that is, one could differentiate behavior settings on the basis of the age distribution of inhabitants. At this point it must be made clear that "allowing" is a combination of social-cultural restrictions (e.g., roles) and physical restrictions (impossible for some type of person to enter). These "allowings" are likely to be factors in whether settings are inhabited by a particular group or not. Taken from the other point of view—that of the person—it is fruitful to consider how many settings a person uses and how far he goes to get to them (the latter is his *behavioral range*).

But habitation is clearly not a unitary factor; different people do different things in the same places (as well as doing the same thing in different places). Thus, we might ask whether older people are central or less central actors in particular settings and, alternatively, obtain an individual measure of mean *degree of penetration*. Penetration is simply a way to discuss centrality of an individual as one who defines, and controls, that place. For example, the owner of a store penetrates that setting more deeply than a customer who in turn is a more active (deeper penetrating) inhabitant than a browser or someone merely accompanying the shopper. Issues such as penetration are particularly important in terms of the control factor that is a focal point in our analysis.

In fact, Barker and Barker (1961) compared these sorts of factors across a wide age range of residents, including older persons, in two towns, one in Kansas and one in England. They found that age was indeed strongly related to both behavior range and penetration of settings. Middle-aged people were highest on both measures across the age comparisons, whereas older people were quite low, in the same range as children or adolescents. Although the results are open to interpretation at many levels (Does equality of or difference in range and penetration "mean" the same thing to different age groups? Are the differences caused by age, cohort, or something else?) and the data are 20 years old (a major shortcoming in a developmental analysis without an assumption bias in favor of transhistoricity), the research illustrates the application of basic ecological and social psychological principles to aspects of activity relevant across the entire life span. And, indeed, the differentiation of middle-aged persons from both young and old, in a way similar to the findings already discussed about attributions, points to the importance of considering that age group separately, as most representative of "those in control."

As noted earlier, several social gerontologists and psychologists of aging have researched the relationship of older persons to their environments. In particular, M. Powell Lawton and his associates (e.g., Lawton & Nahemow, 1973; Lawton, 1975, 1980) have developed several conceptual models of the relationship of older persons to their environments, and the relationship of that interaction to social activity and a limited range of social psychological issues. Lawton's competence-press model, illustrated in Figure 9.1 and described more fully in a number of sources (e.g.,

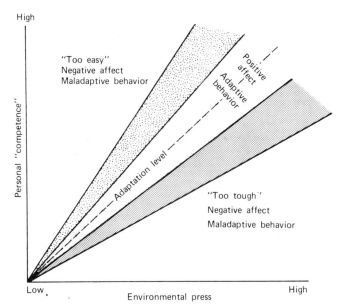

Figure 9.1   Lawton's ecological model. (Adapted from M. P. Lawton and L. Nahemow, Ecology and the aging process. In Eisdorfer, C., & Lawton, M. P. [Eds.], *Psychology of adult development and aging.* Original version, copyright 1973 by the American Psychological Association.)

Lawton & Nahemow, 1973; Lawton, 1975, 1980; Gelwicks & Newcomer, 1974) explicitly formulates that behavior, satisfaction with the environment, and successful or unsuccessful usage of the environment are the function of a relationship between a person's competence and environmental demands (which Lawton refers to as "press"). The latter may be thought of as the inverse of the environment's "competence" to be used successfully by a wide range of persons. His formulation, in turn, is conceptually similar to others concerning non-aged populations.

There are several important aspects in this model. Each of the factors—personal competence and environmental press—is a continuum. That is, an individual's ability/competence can range from virtually zero (totally incapacitated) to extremely capable, whereas the environment's press can also run from low to high, ranging from extremely simple and undemanding (a total institution) to extremely difficult and demanding at so high a level that it is intolerable to even a highly capable person (a desert, the path of a tornado).

Furthermore, the interrelationship can be either in balance or out of balance and, indeed, as with progressions and relationships in general, there is more room for imbalance than for balance. For each ability level there is only a relatively narrow range of environmental demand levels which is optimal and a small zone of a marginal relationship; except for a narrow band of environments, the range of environments will be dysfunctional for that person's competence level. This dysfunction can be in the direction of too much difficulty (the right side of Figure 9.1), in which case the environment becomes overwhelming and frustrating, or in the direction of too little challenge (the left side of Figure 9.1) in which case the environment is boring and atrophying. The adaptation level is the central point for the band of relationships that give a "fit" between the person and his or her environment (or, from the point of view of the environment, the setting and its potential inhabitants). The recognition of the relative frequency of imbalance fits in well with ideas we discussed in Chapter 3, concerning the "unusual" nature of rest, quiescence, and balance.

Shortcomings of Lawton's Model

As described up to this point, Lawton's model is useful, but it is not developmental; it does not deal with change in any way. Rather, it is a description of the relationship of Person and Environment in typically achronic terms. However, Lawton adds several reasonable developmental possibilities to the framework to make it useful for age differences comparisons and for developmental change analyses. As a person moves into late adulthood and old age it is likely that he or she moves downward on the dimension of ability (at least in some aspects of it; the ambiguity of the competence factor—and the environmental demand one—is a problematic issue which will be discussed shortly). That is, older people are likely to be less capable of dealing with a wide range of environments, because of health problems and aging-related losses in sensory processing ability, mobility, and reflexivity. The model becomes more useful with the addition of this developmental factor.

However, even with these strengths, there are major problems with Lawton's formulation as a tool for further theory and research. Although Lawton's model includes an age difference and/or aging-developmental component as outlined, it is less adequate in conceptualizing the environment as also historically developmental. But, indeed, environments do change, and change in environment is likely to be relatively important to developmental processing of environments and to developmental ecology.

Furthermore, Lawton's model is a rather clumsy attempt to reduce a wide range and variety of factors to *one* personal and *one* environmental dimension (Lawton, 1980, obviously recognizes this, and I do not mean to use the term "clumsy" in a personally pejorative sense). However, people do not age in a unitary fashion, biologically or psychologically. Certainly, at a gross level, inner biological and individual psychological progressions are distinct and often poorly synchronized and thus poorly represented by some additive conception of their relationship. Also, even within the inner biological progression, itself an abstraction—but one often assumed to have an inner unity—the processes of aging are only loosely related. Each organ system ages differentially within each person and the organ system change is not necessarily related to other psychological processes or to functional ability on anything approaching a one-to-one basis (see Heron & Chown, 1967; Botwinick, 1978; and many chapters in Birren & Schaie, 1977; and Poon, 1980, for more detailed descriptions of physiology and psychophysiology of aging). The same can be said of individual psychological progression. As we proceed further on the road to abstraction, to a single dimension of "competence," we move further and further from a usable model of relations.

The environmental dimension likewise is a conglomeration of myriad forces, each with its own progression of change and stability. Environmental demands can be purely physical (heat, cold, darkness) or perceptual (sensory deprivation or overload) or they can be social (density, discrimination, threat). They can require hard work and high energy or low but consistent levels of output. Social or cultural factors can be either bureaucratically *over*determined—taboos against use of an environment because of age stratification or other factors—or too free-form and diffuse (lack of clear roles). Each of these characteristics can lead to environmental demand or ease, but many of them are uncorrelated or negatively correlated with each other. Gubrium's (1973) socioenvironmental model goes somewhat beyond Lawton's characterization of the social environment, but is itself overly simple and less, rather than more, precise in definition of physical aspects of environmental demands.

Finally, and most important, the model is still not truly relational. As with the Lewinian model discussed earlier and the single interaction models of social psychological statistics, Lawton's model includes relationships, but it does not acknowledge and deal with the placement of the relationship itself at the center of the model or of the reality which it models. This model has little to say about the construction of both person and environment out of their relationship; rather it posits person and environment as conceptually and ontologically separate and proceeds to examine functional relationships of these presumed basic elements. Yet it is quite clear that the environment is formed and maintained by the competencies and needs of its inhabitants and that an individual's competence is meaningless without reference to environmental factors. Thus, Lawton and other users of the model tend to see change and development, but to see them as "adjustments" toward realigning the proper— static—relationship of a person to his or her environment. The adjustment notion and its attendant working assumption that the person and the environment are essentially passive receptacles of input and reactors to the characteristics of the other are maintained and assimilated wholly into this superficially relational model. And thus the model is ultimately neither developmental nor relational even if it has the appearance of both. Perhaps the use of "ultimately" as an adverb in the previous sentence is, in fact, unfair, for, as we will examine shortly, it has within it the possibility to be *both* relational and developmental. It is, however, fair to say that most descriptions of it and most uses of it in research and application have been neither relational nor developmental.

What is needed is a processual approach to the interplay of the sets of progressions as described earlier in this chapter. Environmental change and movement, individual development and progression, and social meaning of settings and of behavior (and of proper inhabitants) are no mere background to and complicating factor in clear exposition of the relationship of person and environment; they are the essential and constant rules of environmental use and environmental effects.

Yet, after all this is said and done, it is time to admit that we must return to the realities of our search for understanding—an admission we must make again and again as we proceed through the empirical sections of this book. That is, Lawton's model is flawed in several important ways, and the data to be described hardly rise above its level (in fact, they often fall below its potential). But it is a useful tool with which to examine the relationship of persons at various ages to their environments, to what is, for all practical purposes, that which is external to them.

Environmental Docility and its Meaning for Development

One additional factor in Lawton's conceptualization (1980; Lawton & Simon, 1968) is the environmental docility hypothesis. Quite simply, this hypothesis states that as a person's ability to manipulate his or her environment decreases, his or her dependence on environmental factors increases. Certainly, this notion is not surprising. As one's ability to control (or ignore) an environment *and* one's ability to escape it (and thus to maintain variety in environmental demands) are both reduced, as is the case with lessened competence to deal with the environment, the factors within the environments that remain are bound to have greater effects on behavior than they did in the past (or for a person with higher competence). Although the concept is simple, it is also an important point, especially when combined with the factors of aging in terms of individual ability already briefly noted.

The relationship of persons to their environments, always important, becomes even more crucial as people age (at least if they experience some of the age-related mobility and perception problems briefly noted before), and a general sample of older persons is likely to be more context-bound and have their behavior more environmentally determined than samples of younger or middle-aged persons. For good or ill, their behavior (and likely the cognitions and affects related to physical comfort and "fit") are heavily dependent on the kinds of environments in which older persons are located.

The fragile but pervasive interplay of all of these factors is illustrated graphically and poignantly in recent occurrences in the lower Midwest in the summer of 1980. A heat wave and drought of massive proportions—daily temperatures above 100° with nighttime "lows" often only down to about 90°—struck the region, resulting in thousands of deaths officially labeled as "heat-related." Most of the deaths were of elderly persons, caught in a complex network of environmental stressors at a variety of levels. For one thing, older persons are disproportionately found in decaying housing in center-city areas; housing with no real possibility for ventilation, but with a pervasively dangerous milieu in which to open doors or windows to get air. It was in those neighborhoods that most of the deaths occurred.

In response to the heat wave, many agencies provided relief in two forms—fans for people to use in their own homes, and air-conditioned relief centers. Yet older persons reacted to both provisions in uniquely, sadly dysfunctional ways. Many refused to leave their homes to go to relief centers, because they feared that their homes would be burglarized (we will discuss fear of crime more fully later in this chapter). And, indeed, they apparently had some justification for those fears, since, a relief worker noted, several who did go to the centers returned to find that their homes had been burglarized (Prater, 1980). Others, of course, were too fragile and mobility-impaired to get back and forth to the centers. Thus, a predominant social factor in the environment—criminals ready to ransack homes—and a psychological factor—fear of crime—combined with inner biological sensory decline to form a strong barrier to one pathway to relief.

The second path also had attendant problems, which were at least of three types. These problems resulted in a number of deaths in homes to which fans had been delivered. First of all, the fear of crime that kept many home from the centers also led them to keep windows and doors closed and locked. Second, a more purely biological factor was involved. As people get very old, they are likely to experience poor blood circulation combined with loss of sensitivity to temperature variation. As a result, many older victims apparently "felt" cold. Even though they may have "known" better, they reacted to those feelings by putting on more clothes and blankets and turning off the fans, thereby increasing their body temperatures beyond the point of no return. An inner biological factor—usually a bother but not a killer—interacted with the actual outer physical change—in temperature—to lead some older persons to think they needed to warm up. The result, of course, was disastrous.

A third, sociocultural factor completed the frustrating picture. The poor recipients of the fans, persons defined as too poor to buy a fan on their own by the provisions of the grants, were also too poor to afford to pay for the electricity to run one. Even though relief on utility bills was promised, the promises, quite simply, were not believed, partly because of experience with actual previous behavior of the social environment—promising more than it could deliver and leaving one high and dry—and, partly because of an often found tendency on the part of a sizeable number of older persons to be rigid and inflexible in their everyday thinking (Heron & Chown, 1967; Botwinick, 1978; Riley & Foner, 1968).

In any case, this very real social problem is, I think, an illustration of the richness of a detailed, relationship-oriented emphasis on the impact of environment on personal and social factors. A host of factors, across the range of person and environment competence, in a constantly varying set of combinations, formed a set of relationships with a suddenly more demanding specific environmental factor—weather—to conspire against person-environment fit for a number of persons. Those persons, in turn, were disproportionately drawn from one developmental sector, the very old (and some very young—infants—who died as well), since many of the problematic factors, the interactants with the relatively stable weather pattern, are in fact age-related even though many are not "caused" by advancing age. Included in these factors are inner biological declines in circulation and sensitivity to temperature cues; individual psychological rigidity, fear of crime, and a deeply ingrained emphasis on self-reliance; the social environmental factor of subpoverty-level incomes; and the physical environmental locus in unventiliated, cramped, inadequate housing in high crime, low service areas. The relatively specific environmental factors, as they became more crucial because of environmental docility, became less rather than more supportive, since the social supports offered had often insurmountable negative aspects. The possiblity for adequate conceptualization of these factors can be a powerful tool; it can be developed from unfortunate natural experiments such as the one just described and used to decrease the likelihood of disaster when relationships are likely to be stretched to such limits by transient environmental press. A social psychology that includes paying attention to the range and variety of factors, though obviously not a cure for such problems, may nonetheless provide information that might influence policy makers to prepare more adequately for such potential disasters.

A SOCIAL PSYCHOLOGY OF THE ENVIRONMENTAL
RELATIONSHIPS OF OLDER PERSONS

The previous discussion touched upon several crucial age differences in environment, ranging from personal through large-scale nonpersonal differences. It is at the moment-by-moment, complex interplay of those factors, as in the previous example, that we find the basis for a *social* psychology of the way persons as they develop, age, and change relate to their environments, both physical and social. These relationships—the person by environment interaction loved by social psychologists since Lewin devised his "nice" but imprecise formula—are crucial to understanding how people relate and act socially, since it is clear that context defines behavior as much as the individual does (certainly not a revelation to situationist-oriented social psychologists).

It is in this concern that a social psychology of developing adults will be particularly useful, for it is in adulthood, especially later adulthood, that the clarity and importance of the role of context and environment crystallize. Older persons, in general, are clearly more "controlled" by a host of physical environmental factors, as we have discussed when considering Barker's and Lawton's models—or hypotheses—about age changes in reliance on environmental cues and constraints. Older persons are often less mobile, and thus, more environment-bound; they are less active and penetrating, and thus they are more environment-defined. These bounds and definitions are often physical, but the *social* environment (more correctly, the sociophysical complex that is the one and only environment) also makes its presence felt more in old age—income, and thus environmental control of one important sort, is often socially not environmentally restricted; social networks of long standing and social changes in neighborhood composition can conspire to influence physical environmental use. Persons of various ages are separated from each other, often more socially than physically, making age-related differences in environmental relations that much more obvious and that much more controlling.

Thus, social psychology and environmental psychology are even closer in focus and meaning when older persons' lives are being examined than they are when persons of other ages are the focus. The social and the physical environments both exercise more control and place more constraints on certain age segments of society than others. The effects of physical barriers and physical contexts—often strong and equally often underrated and underexamined by social psychologists—on social behavior are one part of the focus of the reviews and research of the next several chapters; the origin of the definition, meaning, and location of the physical environment in the social, in the person—that is, in social psychology—is the other focus. The entry to these concerns is through the control that certain aspects of physical environments have on older persons as they change and move in those physical environments and the corresponding implications of that characteristic for personal competence and control.

These factors make a well-rounded examination of the social behavior and social cognitions of persons of various ages, especially older persons, within and about physical environments a valid and important part of a social psychology of developing adults. They provide a rationale for research oriented to this set of questions. Unfortunately, as will be discussed below, little of the research has been directed that way. As we focus more specifically on findings relating age and/or adult development to environmental use, we find a body of findings insulated from most of the concerns we have expressed, devoid of the rationale we have just developed, and instead, narrowly concerned with relatively nondevelopmental "aging" issues.

The relationship of person to environment is one that is constantly in a process of change and interdetermination, one where an understanding of relationships is crucial, yet it is also one where most research proceeds as though that is not so. Most of the theorizing and most of the research uses one or another static model, based in overabstractions from reality. Further, most of the research has been sociological; not necessarily a failing to be sure (as noted earlier), but containing in itself what might be called the "twin gods" of social gerontology—a great emphasis on adjustment and a corresponding emphasis on roles (see Chapter 13 for a fuller discussion of this characteristic of social gerontology). Thus, there has been a great deal of research on the effects of environments (note the unidirectional focus) on social activity and morale. That is, there are many descriptions of the number and types of activities of adults of various ages (their roles) coupled with measures of satisfaction and morale (their adjustment to their environments). There has been precious little research on social behavior and social cognition within various ecological milieu across time or even across age groups at one point in time.

For present purposes, both emphases are useful in a limited way, but neither is optimal. Rather, we would prefer to know about how people of various ages and over time conceive of their environments and place themselves within the ecology of their actions, how they use their environments, not just as venues for activities to display social roles, but as places in which they meet and interact with other individuals—how they react to persuasion attempts or violent acts in their environments, how they make friends or lose them based on respective placement in one's range as that range changes and is transformed, how they manipulate or are manipulated by their life spaces, or how they use public and private spaces territorially.

Unfortunately, most of the data to be discussed, not only in this chapter as a review of several active areas in environmental psychology of aging, but also in the next two chapters on original research, are limited to those areas referred to as social gerontology. Again, I want to emphasize that these are not offered as finished products, but as ways to begin to think about and operate with relationships to environments as intrinsically personal, social, and developmental, as a system of relationships. Our discussions will span the size of environment considered, and some of the studies will be more, some less, social.

The Larger Scale—Neighborhood

A striking characteristic of many of the large-scale environments that are more typical for older persons—especially in light of their old inhabitants' likely lower competence—is that the environments are *more* rather than less demanding than the environments more typical of young and middle-aged adults. We have already touched upon a number of these in discussing the deaths of elderly persons living in urban areas during a recent heat wave. Urban residency brings with it problems of deteriorating structures and streets, bad lighting and surveillance, greater concentrations of persons (leading both to larger numbers and to greater diversity with which to cope) and a likely higher incidence of crime. In fact, fear of crime is a major concern of the elderly (see, for example, Harris, 1975; Sundeen & Mathieau, 1976) probably resulting from both their physical contexts (that is, residents of central areas, regardless of age, are more fearful than others) and from their own boundness to their environments and lack of control over them because of physical and/or socioeconomic problems. Some recent research on territoriality and mastery in the elderly in relation to fear of crime (Patterson, 1978) has found that reduction in fear may accompany territoriality and feelings of mastery (less feeling of environmental docility), although the data are not unequivocal. In any case, crime (actual or feared) is a major environmental fact of life for many older persons (and, of course, for other relatively defenseless residents of similar areas), and on that basis feeds into feelings of competence.

Also, many of the non-aged residents of urban areas are of a different ethnic group or even speak a different language from the elderly residents. This replacement of members of a like ethnic group is a process that often took place during the tenure of the older person as a resident. The elderly person (who may originally have settled into the neighborhood as a "stranger in a strange land") may as a result become more and more alienated and more and more withdrawn (as would a non-aged person if he or she lived in such a setting, for example, in a foreign country).

Thus, the urban setting may militate against confortable use by older residents and/or by persons as they age. Many of these problems are likely to be related to mobility and access—an interaction of failing inner biological ability and failing environmental competence due, also, at least partially to age—but that is by no means the only factor that negatively influences penetration and comfortable use by older persons.

A comparison of older persons with some degree of mobility deficit and non-old ones with similar problems may be particularly instructive to examine this issue. Unfortunately, such cross-age comparisons, reasonable and useful though they may be, are rare in a study of older persons' relationships to their environments. One small pilot study conducted by a student in an environmental psychology of aging course I taught several years ago (Hildner, personal communication) merits a closer look.

If the environmental docility idea discussed earlier is in fact an inner-biologically based one, as Lawton (e.g., 1980) and most social gerontologists who research environment seem to feel, then older and younger persons with mobility handicaps would be expected to have similar ranges—cognitively, in terms of awareness of environ-ment and ability to map it, and behaviorally, in terms of activity range and behavior setting penetration. They would be expected to see and be affected by the same barri-ers. If, however, environmental cognition and behavioral use of environments be-tween older persons and younger normal persons are more based in cognitive, social and/or personality factors than in biological decline and loss of freedom to move about—factors of alienation, fear, and a need for safety outlined here briefly—then the approaches taken by old with mobility deficits and young with mobility deficits may be quite different. To compare these approaches, it would be productive to ex-amine the differential effects of age and level of handicap on environmental use and environmental cognitions across the entire lifespan.

Hildner's study was a preliminary effort in that direction. She compared young handicapped who were outpatients at a rehabilitation center to elderly residents of a specialized housing for older and handicapped persons. Some of the elderly persons were officially handicapped, but most simply had common age-related physical disa-bilities, but no major handicap. She used a cognitive map task and a brief question-naire concerning use of environment and attitudes toward neighborhood and commu-nity. First of all, she found that elderly persons were very uncomfortable about the request to make a map, whereas young handicapped were not. Secondly, the maps of those older persons who did the task were substantially less differentiated and less complex than those of young handicapped. Self-reported range and penetration in be-havior settings were also higher for the young handicapped. It appears from those preliminary data that older persons do withdraw in very real ways from their environ-ments (or never were well integrated with those environments) and that the pattern of that withdrawal is not explained predominantly by the actual physical limitations imposed upon those persons by advancing age. Research on the cognitive maps of all age groups from childhood to old age, some of which I am now developing, may be a very effective tool to explore the patterning of environmental knowledge and related use of environments across a variety of variables apparently differentially distributed by age in the population, such as mobility handicaps, type of neighborhood, access to transportation (especially private automobiles), social status, and feelings of confi-dence and control over the environment (related, perhaps to fear of crime).

In regard to the issues just discussed, it is valuable to remember our earlier discussions of progressions; each progression is changing, and synchronization with it means constant change in other progressions and constant reintegration. The neigh-borhood of the elderly urban dweller is alien, and yet it is familiar because it has been the locus of years of activity. Even if the older person has essentially not changed (is healthy and mobile, for example), the Person-Environment unit has changed and must change. The world, the neighborhood, and the block are *literally different* places from what they were, and yet the memories on the individual psychological level continue to reify the old places as well (Porteous, 1977, reported inclusion of no-longer-existent buildings in older people's cognitive maps). The contradictions and tensions inherent in this situation, the relationships rather than the elements, *are* the situation. Once again, change and stability are both real and yet both are merely constructions. An adult-developmental social psychology can be productive in enhancing the realization and redirection of environmental social psychology to focus upon these Person-Environment matrices rather than on static measures of separable elements. In any case, it is clear that urban areas may be less well suited to needs and abilities of many persons than other areas (although many of the perceived drawbacks, such as high density, and variety, are what make cities alive and interesting for many residents and may provide more services per unit of distance). Those potential drawbacks combine with less ability on the part of many older persons to deal with environments to give them a trapped, insecure, and psychologically uncontrollable environment. The demands for coping are high.

But it is not only urban areas that produce age-related environmental problems. Rural areas, too, are likely to place demands on people, especially demands on ability to be independent and self-contained. These demands are very different from those of the city, but they also are higher in important ways than other, more suburban areas and more likely to impact upon older residents. As a matter of fact, the relatively comfortable situation in the suburbs itself is likely to be dramatically changed by the energy crisis and its concomitants at precisely the time when larger and larger percentages of now later middle-aged persons will be growing old there. The severity of each of the progressions, and especially their combination, may produce an asynchronization between personal competence and environmental demand of major crisis proportions (see Carp, 1976, for discussion of this point). Such a development, obviously, will have major effects on social behavior and personality-social orientations of common cohorts of the elderly. Outer physical, social structural, and individual psychological progressions are likely to become increasingly disorganized and conflicting. Perhaps redirection of one or more of these progressions by research and practical effort using a change-oriented, dialectical model of person-environment relations could be of benefit in delaying or ameliorating these coming crises. Large-scale environments will be discussed further in Chapter 11.

The Smaller Scale—Place of Residence

The same kinds of arguments can be made at the smaller scale level of a single building and its interior space. Old homes—urban and rural—require greater competence on the part of the resident to do (or pay for) major repairs of structures, insulation, and so on. Especially in a time of the ''energy crunch'' and wildly rising costs, those factors, like larger scale urban problems now and suburban ones in the future, are likely to result in disequilibrium and tension.

One type of residential development which might be expected to be a productive redistribution of persons to environments that matches declining ability and less demanding environments are buildings especially designed for and solely open to older persons. These age-segregated areas themselves have a wide range of characteristics, since they vary from public high-rise buildings for elderly within age-integrated neighborhoods to fairly large cities of elderly located on the periphery of urban areas (or even in totally self-sufficient, totally separate settings) to total institutions for frail elderly. Each of these types promises amenities which could be seen as prosthetic environments to one degree or another, to enable persons of lessened personal resources to continue to have mastery over and security within their environments. In other words, they are designed with people of limited personal competence in mind. And, in fact, these settings quite apparently fill needs for just that sort of readjustment of the environment to match individual competencies. Except for nursing home residents, those who reside in specialized housing report being very satisfied with that housing (presumably compared to the alternatives they felt they had, but the comparison has seldom been that explicit). Examples of findings of satisfaction by residents are in many sources. For example, Carp (1966) found that new residents of a public housing building were very happy with it, and many other studies have shown the same pattern (Lawton & Cohen, 1974; Sherman, Magnum, Dodds, Walkley, & Wilber, 1968).

Unfortunately, many of these settings concentrate on matching to a rather simple, unitary model of competence in a rather static way, since the relational, constantly changing nature of both individual and environment are often ignored. As a result of this disregard, some important competencies may still be overly burdened or become totally unchallenged. In environmental terms, the latter may be the more likely outcome, that is, that the specialized environments are made too simple. You will recall that Lawton included the idea that too little challenge in the environment vis-a-vis competence is as bad—socially and physically—as too much challenge. In the words of nonsocial psychology, sensory deprivation (in a broader sense than merely absolute level of sensory input, including social sensation and stimulation and nonsensory physical stimulation) is as dysfunctional as sensory overload. Sometimes, older persons escaping the overload of declining urban areas, hard-to-manage old homes, and so on, find themselves in the sensory deprivation of an institution.

Indeed, an institution such as a total care nursing home takes the environmental docility maxim to its fullest. The environment is designed to be simple; further, social design includes assistance in many areas of daily living, making the environment even simpler. At the same time, that environment functionally becomes the inhabitant's whole world—a world of low demand and low expectation of competence. (Retirement communities, in turn, are likely to have environmental press characteristics somewhere between this kind of a setting and a more normal, age-integrated level of demand).

Such a world is a necessity for some persons, without a doubt—those on the low end of Lawton's personal competency—but it is actually an environmental burden to others. It can lead to atrophy of skills in inner biological and individual psychological senses, and it can lower motivation and increase dependence. All of these issues have been well documented in social gerontology and in other discussions of "institutionitis" (Sommer, 1970; Osmond, 1957; Langer & Rodin, 1976).

I have already discussed an important aspect of this lowering of competence in Chapter 8, when I discussed Langer & Rodin (1976), Rodin & Langer (1977, 1980), and Schulz's (e.g. Schulz & Hanusa, 1980) attribution-based notions and interventions. Yet these environments do not only have the potential of being too simple and undemanding. Even as they do this, they can have factors built in which discourage social activity and self-expression beyond the institutional simplicity noted above. They can be barriers to individual progress by a failure to recognize that the environmental docility of inhabitants places a greater than usual demand on these environments to be *especially* optimal and functional.

Quite a few years ago Sommer (1970; Sommer & Ross, 1958) found that such a lack of recognition can have a devastating impact on the social activity patterns of elderly residents of a nursing home (as Osmond, 1957, found to be the case with residents of another sort of total institution—a mental institution). Sommer found that the nursing home he was asked to examine had very low levels of patient interaction; he also found that the common lounge area—the only natural locus for social activity and interaction—was singularly *unsuited* to the social interaction that was avowedly of interest to the staff. Chairs were arranged around the periphery of the room in "sociofugal" fashion, that is, facing away from each other, with the effect of discouraging and disallowing coherent use of the space for social interaction. Sommer set about to redesign the room to be "sociopetal"—drawing people together by, for example, arranging chairs around small tables, and utilizing other simple devices. He found (after a period marked by disarray, when disruption of territoriality resulted from moving chairs people felt were "their own") that social activity and interaction increased dramatically. The positive effect did not end with social improvement, either; even such behaviors as reading and individual craft work, which might be expected to compete for time and energy with conversation and social activity, also showed increased levels.

With Sommer's intriguing intervention in nursing home environments illustrating the danger of complacency and sterility in design and the tremendous opportunity for enriching life in major ways by "minor" changes in environmental support that are both intrinsic to a situation in which people are reliant on the environment for *self*-definition and *self*-competence, let us end this lengthy, wide-ranging chapter. In the following two chapters, reporting primarily original research on the level of building design and neighborhood, we will consistently be returning to the general theme of the Person and his or her Environment as a unit, as a relationship that must be considered in a fully interactive way, and to the specific focus upon personal and environmental competence, control, and usefulness as essentially relational, as a constantly varying tableau of change and stability. These themes are conceptually and practically valid and necessary parts of a social psychology of developing adults.

CHAPTER 10

Design and Dysfunction: Social Aspects of Housing for the Elderly

In the last chapter we considered the viability of an ecological-environmental approach to the social psychology of older adults. We considered the potential for study of the relationship of older persons to their environments, on both larger and smaller scales, as an example of such analyses, since older persons are often more closely tied to—and thus, their behaviors are more influenced by—the physical environment. We also opened up consideration of the importance of personal competence, mastery, and control as they are related to age and raised the issue of competence of environments as well.

We considered an array of studies that have examined these relationships. We ended the chapter by discussing the work by Robert Sommer and his associates that revealed the depth and importance of environmental control of the social behaviors of residents of nursing homes and introduced the concepts of sociofugal and sociopetal aspects of living space arrangements.

In this chapter we move to consideration of original research that shows quite clearly that the sociofugal factors in design are not limited to total institutional settings, but can be found in residential settings as well. Further, the data indicate that design factors can have clear-cut effects on relatively well older persons. Individual "competence," as revealed in activity patterns and in self-reported satisfaction and morale, are intimately bound up with environmental variations at the relatively small-scale level of building design characteristics.

The research was conducted, in association with Linda Phelps, within a large-scale comparative study of retirement communities. We used a multimethod approach to examine two questions related to Sommer's work and to the broader environmental discussions of social gerontologists such as Lawton (1980) and Gelwicks and Newcomer (1974) and environmental psychologists not concerned with aging (e.g., Porteous, 1977). First of all, does design make a difference for social psychology and for social interaction of older persons residing in specialized housing for the elderly? Second, do architects (likely to be middle-aged) do a good job of concept and design to match the "special" needs of older persons, needs based in biological and social changes over time? Our approach combined unstructured field observation, systematic observation, and survey-interviews to get an idea of the social activity and social interactions, as well as of the satisfactions and perceived needs, of residents of two

HUD-sponsored, publicly managed, high-rise housing for the elderly buildings in a metropolitan area in the Midwest.

METHODS AND RESULTS OF THE STUDY

The Sites

The two sites (to be referred to as Metro Towers and Horizon Heights) were similar in many ways. Both are located in old, relatively run-down, racially mixed areas of the same metropolitan region. Both are underwritten by HUD so that low-and lower-middle-income older persons (and a few younger handicapped) pay one-fourth of their incomes for rent and utilities. Both are high-rise structures built in the early 1970's and offer studio and one-bedroom apartments. Residents of both are predominantly women (83% at both sites) and fully racial mixed with a slight balance toward blacks. Residents of Horizon Heights are somewhat older. Although the two buildings are similar on all those dimensions, there are other dimensions on which they are different. One of those is the central focus of the study, and others are considered in analysis.

The difference which will be the focus of this research is the design of the buildings. Metro Towers is designed with rooms placed around an open atrium, a design which won an award of excellence from the regional American Institute of Architects group. On the first floor the atrium is enclosed and has a small fountain and rock garden. On residential floors the rooms are arranged on the periphery of a five-foot-wide concrete hallway, separated by a waist-high metal rail from the open space above the atrium. From the hallway one can look across and over to the doors and hallways on at least three floors above and below one's own and can look down into the atrium. The purpose of the open design, in the words of materials used by the Housing Authority, is to give "all the advantages of a neighborhood block." The open atrium courtyard and inside balconies running around all four sides of each floor afford the opportunity to "see your neighbors across and up and down." That is, the design is specifically meant to increase the likelihood of social interaction, activity, and a community, neighborly feeling. These in turn are clearly means to the end of maximizing satisfaction and social behavior of the older persons who are residents.

The other structure, Horizon Heights, is a basic, one might say bland, style of construction. The first floor contains a lobby, offices, meeting rooms, and a dining-community center area. Residents' apartments are arranged along a long, dimly lit hallway stretching to each side of the elevator in a straight line, with doors on both sides of the corridor.

Research Materials

A random sample of approximately 60% of the residents at each site ($N = 164$ at Horizon Heights and 70 at Metro Towers) responded to a lengthy survey in the winter of 1977-78. In addition, lobbies, halls, and other common spaces were systematically observed, and the numbers of users and configuration of placement and spacing were recorded at 15-minute intervals.

Data

Residents at both sites said that social aspects (friendliness, community, etc.) were fairly important elements of satisfaction with living at their community (21 and 23%). However, on other measures of interaction and activity there were clear-cut, consistent differences. A larger number of Metro Towers residents reported having no interaction in each of three segments of the day—morning, afternoon, and evening (63, 65, and 76% at Metro Towers; 49, 42, and 52% at Horizon Heights). Significantly larger numbers of Metro Towers residents also reported not feeling needed (30 vs. 11%), being lonely (43 vs. 25%), and not having enough friends (19 vs. 6%). Residents also were asked to check off activities on an activity checklist that included ones that could be labeled "active" (e.g., socializing, hobbies, walking) and ones that are more "passive" (e.g., sleeping, sitting, doing nothing). At Metro Towers, 50% reported none of the active behaviors compared to 41% at Horizon Heights; at the same time, a larger percentage reported more "passive" behaviors (60 vs. 48%). Again, Horizon Heights residents seemed to be more involved in their surroundings. Also, on a more direct measure of social behavior, over one-fourth of the Horizon Heights residents (25.3%) reported two or more friends at the site, whereas only 14% at Metro Towers reported two or more on-site friends. Finally, Horizon Heights residents scored considerably higher on a measure of life satisfaction (17.4 vs. 14.6 on a modified version of the Neugarten, Havighurst, and Tobin [1961] Life Satisfaction Index).

So that we could better compare the two groups of residents to similar older persons living in their own homes, we included several questions which had been asked of the respondents in the Louis Harris-NCOA (1975) national survey of attitudes of and about older persons. To further clarify the contribution of social and environmental differences between the residents of the two sites and the national sample, we extracted a "shadow sample" of Harris respondents for each site. These "shadow samples" were matched on five variables—age, race, marital status, income, and sex (or health, when the latter was significantly different)—with the residents of a particular site, although they lived in the wider community. In this way we could "control" for such possible mediating factors as health and income which differed between the two groups.

Horizon Heights residents scored significantly higher on the life satisfaction index than their shadow sample counterparts (17.4 vs. 16.2, two-tailed $t = 2.2, p < .03$), whereas Metro Towers residents scored nonsignificantly lower (two-tailed $t = -0.69$) than their counterparts on this measure (14.6 vs. 15.2). Other questions more directly concerned with social interaction showed the same general pattern in a weaker form: Horizon Heights residents consistently scored better on the measures than their counterparts, whereas Metro Towers residents' scores were usually nonsignificantly different, varying in direction, from their shadow sample. For the questions concerning loneliness, not feeling needed, and not having enough friends, both groups scored better than their respective shadow sample members. That is, there appears to be validity to the common notion that residing in housing for the elderly results in more social interaction and less loneliness. However, as can be expected from the foregoing, the "benefits" of living in housing for the elderly appeared to be

Table 10.1.   Social "Fullfillment" Responses: Comparison of the Two Sites and of Each to a National "Shadow" Sample

	Percent agreeing it is a serious problem			
Responses	Horizon Heights	H. H. "Shadow"	Metro Towers	M. T. "Shadow"
Not feeling needed	11**	29	30	37
Loneliness	25**	48	43*	57
Not enough friends	6**	17	19	23

**Comparison of community and "shadow" significant at .01 level (one-tailed t-test)
*Comparison of community and "shadow" significant at .05 level (one-tailed t-test)

much smaller at Metro Towers. As Table 10.1 shows, Horizon Heights residents were significantly more positive than their shadow sample group on all measures, but Metro Towers residents were significantly better (at a lower level of significance) only in reported loneliness.

Overall, then, the clear indications of the survey data are that, when each group is compared to a national sample matched on health, income, and other variables, and when the residents of the two sites are compared directly to each other, residents in a building supposedly designed to promote social interactions respond less positively than do those in a less imaginative, bland design. Objections to these conclusions may already be springing to the mind of the reader based, for example, in weaknesses inherent in the choice of the samples for comparison. I will deal with those exceptions in a later section of this chapter.

Observations

Field observation at the time prior to survey administration (by the same person at both sites) had led to conclusions on the part of the observer which are in line with the survey findings. Persons at Metro Towers appeared less interested in social and other activities of the site, and neighborly interaction was at a low level. Later ecological observation of usage of common spaces confirmed and extended these observations and the survey answers. Average usage of common spaces across the entire day (in absolute numbers *and* when weighted for differences in the sizes of the two populations) is considerably lower at Metro Towers than at Horizon Heights (average of 25.2 residents [8.4/100 res.] at Horizon Heights vs. 6.0 residents [4.6/100 res.] at Metro Towers.

DESIGNS AND DESIGNERS: WHERE DID METRO TOWERS GO WRONG?

The aim of this study is to explore effects of design characteristics. Taken as a whole and in a vacuum, the data presented to this point strongly indicate that design *does* influence use and related social psychological affect and cognition, but that the value of the design of a specific building is not necessarily accurately perceived by architects.

In this case, why did a supposedly sociopetal design (the Metro Towers atrium idea) actually seem to have the opposite effect? There are several reasonable answers to that question, centering around the lack of correspondence between the "innovative" building design and the experience-based and research-based guidelines for housing for the elderly. However, prior to discussing these factors, we should consider a prior question—can the data, in fact, be stretched to such a conclusion? This leads to a consideration of mediating factors unrelated to design and of the sampling and response-mode issues noted earlier.

Possible Mediating Factors

Health and income are obviously factors which would affect a person's mobility, activity, and thus, one's social contact. Since Metro Towers residents were less healthy (as self-reported and as measured by number of days hospitalized and/or bedridden in the last year) and had somewhat lower incomes than Horizon Heights residents, it is possible that these are the "real" causes of the differences, rather than the building design. Although these factors may be at play, two separate constellations of results within the study reinforce the shadow sample results already mentioned (which included control on some of these factors). They militate against the validity of an interpretation solely or even mostly in terms of non-design factors. Rather, they point up the complex interplay of environments and persons that is more characteristic of day-to-day relationships than the simple "effects of environment or . . . " model would imply.

First of all, even though Metro Towers residents reported fewer friends within the site, they did not differ on number of total friends; that is, they reported *more* friends outside the site (41% with two or more outside vs. 24% at Horizon Heights). Along the same lines, although they reported lower levels of activity within the site, they were higher on several overall measures of activity (they had gone to *more* different places in the last year and last month), and were essentially equal in percentages of those who report being highly involved in visiting the homes of neighbors (76% at Horizon Heights and 74% at Metro Towers). They did not appear to be less mobile or less able to have social interaction because of being in generally poorer health, or having lower incomes; only *intracommunity* interaction was lower.

Second, as discussed in Chapter 9, when health and mobility restrictions (and lower incomes) are likely to lower one's territorial range, these restrictions themselves could reasonably be expected to *intensify* the effects of the near environment. Thus, those who are not in good health (especially those in fair health, who have some ability to get around—if their environment encourages them—vis-á-vis- the more truly immobilized by poor health) and those who have less adequate incomes would be expected to be *most* bound to their sites and *most* likely to draw upon and benefit from community living. Yet, when residents in the two sites were categorized by health (good, medium, poor) and by income (self-rated as adequate or as inadequate), the groups which were relatively the *worst* off at Metro Towers compared to Horizon Heights were the groups which should be benefiting the most from careful, sociopetal design—those in fair health and those who saw their incomes as inadequate. It is the large variation in those groups which resulted in significant overall community differences. Those in poor health and those in good health at the two sites did *not* differ from each other.

The same general point, of course, is made by the shadow sample comparisons—residents of Metro Towers are not nearly as positively affected by residing in housing for the elderly as residents of Horizon Heights are, when demographic characteristics including age, income, health are "held constant."

Observation bears out the survey results about health; although a greater percentage of Metro Towers residents reported mobility deficits and need for devices such as canes, walkers, wheelchairs, and so on, few such persons were in evidence at Metro Towers compared to Horizon Heights, where the lobby and halls invariably contained sizeable numbers of persons with mobility problems and aids as well as more capable residents. It appears that the design of Metro Towers was not fulfilling its social-related purpose, especially for the particular group it would be expected to benefit most.

Of course, this kind of negative evidence does not "prove" that factors other than design are minimal compared to design factors in their influence on the pattern of results. Indeed, it is folly to try to separate "design" factors from social ones and from personal competence ones, which is the whole point of our earlier discussion of Lawton's interactive model and potential extensions from it to make it developmental. It goes without saying that the interplay of personal biological and psychological factors with extrapersonal social and physical ones is more delicate than can be well reflected in superficial and ultimately static survey and observational descriptive data, no matter how many cross-comparisons and covariates are used. I do not mean this chapter to be defense of the inadequate methods we used or to be the repository for "the truth" about "how environmental design affects older persons." Rather, I mean it to be a reasonable example of the kind of research that has been done that can lead us to fill the gap in an important area of knowledge about social psychology as it is related to and interacts with characteristics of the environment. Indeed, I will soon be making the point that the crucial environmental difference between the two sites is primarily crucial in that it exerts control over the social milieu available to residents of the two sites.

In that regard, I believe these data do show that, after other reasonable mediating factors are controlled as best as they can be in such a study, most of the differences between the reported and observed behaviors and satisfactions of the residents of the two sites remain. Thus, it is at least likely to be fruitful to look for and at differences in the physical layout of the sites, to see if these aspects of residing in the two different locations may be influential in defining the social and psychological lives and experiences of the residents.

Design Factors

Given the provisos just mentioned, we may now ask, "What aspects of design are likely to be involved in this situation?" There are at least two aspects which are operative; both are recognizable to outside evaluators and obvious to residents and management. First of all, the atrium design was utilized to enhance neighborliness, openness, and a feeling that the hallway was a replacement for one's front porch. And on first glance the area appears to serve that purpose—most apartments have chairs and/or patio furniture placed outside the doors. Yet these furnishings are seldom used. Several aspects of the design and the building materials are partially responsible. The floors and ceilings of the hall areas are bare concrete, lighted by harsh bare flourescent lights, and the hall-patio is separated by an open tubular steel railing from the empty space above the atrium. The interior of the building is also bare concrete. The overall tone of the building common areas is dreary and harsh—in a word, the hallway-atrium area is ugly. Furthermore, the hall-porch space is only 5'3'' wide, hardly enough to use as a "patio" or conversation spot and still be usable as a hallway. Third, some residents reported actual fear of falling over the railing. In any case, few residents appeared to find pleasure in the architect's conception of looking out over the atrium across, up, and down. Finally, the non-climate-controlled hall and atrium area is too cold in winter and too hot in summer for pleasant use in interacting (it may actually be a deterrent to visiting someone else's apartment for those who are marginally housebound and would prefer climate-controlled, albeit barren, halls).

The common spaces, too, are rather barren, with the overriding bare concrete motif prevalent and no organized conversational circles of chairs. But perhaps more important than what the design and construction materials look like is what the design simply does not allow. All guidelines about housing for the elderly, such as those mentioned earlier, emphasize the crucial nature of good, easily accessible, sociopetal common spaces for meeting social interaction interests of the residents. For example, Gelwicks and Newcomer (1974) state that "certain spaces in a building are important because of their function as a social meeting place. Tenants with *limited physical ability* [emphasis added, related to the moderately poor health group mentioned earlier] tend to sit in public places and watch the activities even more than those who are physically able. Entrance lobbies are particularly popular" (p. 33). They also note that "management policies and the design of physical spaces should encourage social interaction between residents, between residents and staff, and residents and the community" (p. 95).

Instead, in Metro Towers the 26 by 26 foot atrium on the ground floor, and the open space above it on the other floors, insure that there are no coordinated public spaces. There is no space that serves very well as an entrance lobby, although residents do congregate on several chairs lined up near the entrance facing the elevator. Most of the people who use the areas (especially near the elevator, where an entrance lobby should be) use it merely to wait for someone to pick them up (although three or four residents sit there all day every day). One of the three aspects of interacting Gelwicks and Newcomer mention (between residents and staff) appears to be fulfilled by this design; the most active interactions of residents are directed to one of the staff: the guard, who is located immediately to the left from the door.

In contrast to this, how does the design of Horizon Heights fill the goals mentioned in the guidelines? The lobby at Horizon Heights is not a particularly attractive one—tile floors, monochromatic walls, chairs and sofas arranged in a rather sociofugal fashion around walls and pillars. Yet, there is a well-differentiated (approximately 40 x 50 feet), reasonably well-equipped lobby. Further, although it is not directly on the path to and from apartments, it is placed for easy direct line of sight by those going to and from residential units and is on the path to and from mail boxes and the community center/dining room. Thus, it is, as Gelwicks and Newcomer (1974) recommend, "directly related to the main pattern of pedestrian movement (p. 95)." This combination of proximity to traffic flow and relatively attractive space at least for sitting and for easily viewing comings and goings of others is likely to recruit participants into that process of sitting and watching. In turn, that process is quite likely to be upgraded over time from that more or less passive use of the public space to more active social interaction. The field results bear out the idea that the lobby at Horizon Heights is used more as an end in itself (i.e., as a place to go *to*), instead of merely a place to wait in to go somewhere else when transportation arrives. People sat and talked for moderate periods of time (15 minutes to 1 hour) more than at Metro Towers.

There is one other extremely important environmental outcome of the two arrangements which is also a major factor in the differences in social and psychological effects on the designs. It is especially unfortunate that the atrium design and its breaking-up of coherent common space disallows a regular congregate meal program at Metro Towers. Lawton (1975), Green et al. (1975), and other environmental psychologists, architects, and planners (and HUD [1972] itself) see on-site congregate meals as one of the prime sources of available others for social interaction as a regular event and a regular part of one's day. The effects of having or not having congregate meals on social interaction is apparent from the present data in several ways. The use of common spaces at Horizon Heights shows a huge buildup beginning about 10:15 in the morning and centered on 11–12 a.m., when the nutrition site dining room is open. The use of common space early in the morning and in mid-late afternoon is not particularly higher at Horizon Heights (in fact, as shown in Figure 10.1, after

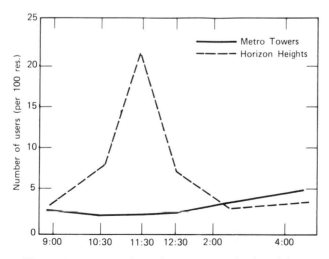

Figure 10.1   Amount of use of common spaces by time of day.

weighting for number of residents it is somewhat less), but the upsurge in use of the lobby and halls begins at about 10 a.m. and continues afer the meal until approximately 1 p.m. During this entire time the level of interaction is high and conversation is often animated. Metro Towers data do not show any large surge (there is also little evidence of any *en masse* movement to an off-site nutrition site). Reported levels of interaction and activity in the surveys bears this out—Horizon Heights residents were most distinctly positively different from Metro Towers residents in late morning and early afternoon.

Interestingly, observation at Metro Towers during a once-a-month Golden Agers club gives added evidence to the power of this interpretation. The level of interaction, including a buildup well prior to the meeting, large group during the meeting, and relatively gradual decline to baseline after the meeting, mimic the process of use which takes place at Horizon Heights five days a week.

GENERAL CONCLUSIONS

Certainly factors other than the physical design of the two buildings are involved in the survey and usage differences at the two sites, a point I have been ready to admit throughout the discussion. For example, health and income have been mentioned; although they do not appear to obviate the points made in this study to any great degree and in some ways reinforce the points about design, the obvious impact they may have in terms of competence and control cannot be ruled out.

Yet even with those provisions, the evidence that design factors do make a difference, especially for those in fair health, and that, in this case, a straightforward, rather bland design works better than an innovative one in the very areas with which the latter was designed to deal is quite strong. Further it is clear that the differences are closely tied to the lack of coherence in the design of Metro Towers and the inability of the design to provide common spaces to perform social functions recognized by researchers and practitioners as extremely important to social interaction and psychological well-being. Design with a worthy purpose is not necessarily functional; it can be actually dysfunctional if characteristics and characteristic needs of primary users of the spaces are ignored, disregarded, or misunderstood.

Specialized housing for a relatively sizeable proportion of elderly persons does appear to have benefits. Even with a sociofugal design, it brings older persons into a measure of proximity—which Lawton and Simon (1968) found to be quite important for old as well as young persons—and it includes provision of at least some on-site services and programs (e.g., Golden Agers at Metro Towers) not likely to be easily available elsewhere. Many of those services fulfill social needs and affect the social behaviors of the residents. Comparison of residents of both buildings to national shadow samples of older persons bears out that view. At the same time, the value of such housing can be enhanced or diminished by relatively fixed characteristics of design, structure, and access.

The dual nature of the last point is important and can be illustrated anecdotally. A resident of Metro Towers asked me what I was doing when I was making some observations. When I explained I was looking at design of buildings for the elderly, she told me, "I hope you don't take *this* design and make others like it." However, when I asked, "Oh, you don't like this design?" she quickly cautioned me that she really did like living there and did not want any "bad press" to upset the situation. In other words, residents recognize both the design flaws and inconveniences *and* the great value of inexpensive, more than adequate specialized housing.

It seems clear, then, that availability of various characteristics in the near environment can affect social psychology (interaction and activity patterns, friendship, and, to some degree, feelings of belonging) and larger personality (life satisfaction) aspects of individual development. The physical environment characteristics interplay with inner biological and individual psychological progressions to affect both the static here and now and the developmental course of interactions, of relationships.

One of the few studies of older persons using an approach similar to that used with younger ones (Carp, 1966) was a study of friendship formation and maintenance among persons who recently moved into specialized housing for the elderly not unlike that discussed in the preceding sections. Carp's study, in turn, was similar to Festinger, Schachter, and Back's (1950) interview and observational research in dormitories for married college students. Carp found that the mechanisms involved in the development process of establishing and maintaining a friendship were very similar across the two different settings and samples. That is, proximity was found to be a crucial factor in friendship formation for both types of housing and persons. That the operation of that principle was not apparent in the housing for the elderly Phelps and I examined illustrates once again that relatively minor design factors may have relatively major social psychological effects, especially among groups of people who are relatively environmentally docile. The effects, although exaggerated from effects for more "competent" persons (insofar as such a global, nonrelational label has any validity at all), may be either positive or negative, sociopetal or sociofugal, synchronized or asynchronized.

Prior to proceeding to the next chapter, in which I will provide a detailed analysis of several aspects of a somewhat larger scale of environment—the neighborhood—one more important point must be made. The kind of view propounded in this book—always emphasizing relationships and the interplay of change and stability (and the inevitability of development and progression as the very nature of both persons and environments)—is particularly valuable in that it clarifies the incompleteness of dichotomization between intrapersonal and extrapersonal or between static-structural and dynamic-functional. Both must always be considered. What this means, though, in the present context, is that it is not merely the individuals in a retirement community who age, who are progressing and changing. The building, the grounds, and the community in which the housing is situated are all aging and changing as well. And the very fact of aging and change within each can dramatically affect the other and the relationships between (among) them.

For example, the totality of the residents in both noninstitutional specialized housing for the elderly and total institutional nursing homes almost certainly ages from the beginning of the first cohort of residents. In the case of noninstitutional housing, more of the residents stay alive than die in a given period (unless they were selected to be terminal, but that is unlikely since those persons would not have been available for noninstitutional housing to begin with). Even in institutions, many residents are likely to live for a relatively protracted time. Thus, the cohort flow of housing for the elderly begins in a spurt—and usually with a bias toward the young end of elderly, since the old end already were likely to have not been independent. From that point the flow of new inhabitants is likely to be sporadic and fairly slow, while the original residents (and new arrivals, to be sure) continue to grow older.

Several researchers (for example, Neugarten, 1974) have afforded dramatic descriptive evidence of clear-cut differences between what may be called young-old and old-old groups (basically sixties and early seventies vs. over 75) in both needs and abilities. The differences between members of these age ranges is simply the aggregate expression of the statistically increasing inner biological progression toward disability, restriction, and reduced sensitivity with later and later points in the normal life cycle. Yet, whereas a cohort of residents can change quite drastically in 10 years (for example, if the mean age at a time of entry into the new housing was 70), the structure of the environment is not very likely to change all that much, since it opened at "maturity" with an expected life-span of 50–100 years. (It is interesting to note that buildings and other environments are not expected to have the analogous states to childhood and adolescence, but are expected to be mature and fully functioning upon completion). If the site had been built (properly) to house the young-old (and more so as it was successful in that regard), it may rather quickly become inappropriate for its aging residents.

On the other hand, a site built for or most appropriate for the old-old (e.g., a total institution) is inappropriate for most young-old inhabitants. It may age them prematurely, a case of the institutionitis described earlier as the result of an environment being too unchallenging at the same time as it becomes more inescapable.

What makes the design process even more difficult is the fact that most housing for the elderly contains *both* young-old and old-old residents (in inner biological and/or individual psychological senses) with different environmental needs and, therefore, prone to different effects of the "same" environment. Environments are seldom flexible enough to be optimal for both groups, since the people are not close together on personal competency in many areas. Thus, the environment, especially if it is not recognized to have its own progression and range, is likely to be sociofugal and incompetent for some even as it becomes sociopetal and more competent for other residents. The need for flexibility is evident, as is the need for increased understanding of influences of environmental design in relationship to age groups with different environmental abilities and to the processes of development over long segments of the life span. The original research just described was aimed toward beginning to provide that kind of information on relatively small scale factors. The next chapter details consideration of a larger scale—the neighborhood.

CHAPTER 11
Use of Neighborhood:
Older Persons Doing Their Shopping

Thus far in Part 3 we have considered some principles that may help define an understanding of the ecological placement of persons of various ages and the complex interplay of changing personal characteristics with changing environmental ones. These ecological concerns are in fact centrally social psychological—they define the individual's "place" and the uses, especially social ones, that can be made of it. In Chapter 10 we considered a set of findings that concern the heightened impact that relatively small changes in the home environment may produce in an older population as compared to a younger one. In this chapter we shift the scale somewhat—from residence to neighborhood and community—and the focus—from social activity and satisfaction to a particular sort of "nonsocial" activity, shopping. At the same time, we remain centrally concerned with understanding principles of the relationship of social and physical environments to both behaviors and thoughts (attitudes, feelings, satisfactions) and of those to each other. The methodological diversification of Chapter 10 is retained and expanded.

In this chapter, then, I wish to open a range of issues that concern the relationship of persons of various ages to what is available for their use in their own neighborhoods. This is a question of major import, not only for understanding of social and other activity patterns across age groups, but for the practical implications it contains. A major goal of urban planners and designers, especially those concerned with renewal of central city areas, is the development and maintenance of environments that support and encourage human uses for human ends (see, for example, Jacobs, 1961; Porteous, 1977; and a host of other sources in planning and design of large-scale environments). Yet, to do so quite obviously requires explicit knowledge of individual and group development, of development and change in physical environments, and of the dialectical interplay of forces that together define the Person-and-Environment entity moment by moment. It is not satisfactory to act as though any of those elements, or the relationship that is central to our concerns, is constant, for the sake of convenience, nor is it enough to make vague gestures to the processual, changing nature of the Person-and-Environment. Rather, both the elemental relationships *and* the influences—sometimes orderly, sometimes chaotic—of the constancy of development must be made central, must be at the basis of a theory of environment and design as well as a theory of individuals.

Characteristics of and flow of change within larger-scale environments impact upon social psychological processes and actions of persons at all phases of the life span. This seemingly obvious fact was overlooked by social psychologists for many years, but has been duly "discovered," noted, and elaborated upon by environmentally oriented social psychologists (or socially oriented environmental psychologists, as the case may be) in the last decade (e.g., Sommer, 1974; Altman, 1975; Bechtel, 1977; Moos, 1976). A wide array of developmental implications are relatively obvious. The sort of neighborhood in which a child is raised is likely to affect his or her social behavior and social cognition in major ways (see, for example, a fairly thorough discussion of pros and cons of urban living for children and adolescents in Porteous, 1977). Adults of all ages seek out neighborhoods that fulfill their needs and desires. Those neighborhoods, in turn, channel those needs and desires (and abilities) to match the neighborhood setting even as they (the neighborhoods) are formed and changed to fit those needs and desires (Gans, 1967). As with other areas of social psychology, the exploration of the interface of social psychology with physical environments, although growing in recent years, has lagged in its consideration of adulthood and aging. At the same time, social gerontologists have moved forward rather extensively into the area of environment and aging (see Lawton, 1980, for a comprehensive review) without benefit of a thoroughgoing social psychological perspective.

Some larger-scale factors important in this regard have already been reviewed in Chapter 9—crime and fear of crime, sense of alienation and "foreignness" within a neighborhood that has dramatically altered its perspective and, probably, its physical existence (through demolition and new construction), and physical barriers in relation to inner biological changes. A more basic research concern, that of age-related, development-related stability and change in processes of learning and using cognitive maps (internal representations of environments) will be discussed briefly in Chapter 14.

STUDYING OLDER PERSONS AS ENVIRONMENTAL USERS: SHOPPING

Rather than attempting to analyze the totality of Person-and-Environment as a definer of a wide range of social and social-related activities and cognitions, I have considerably more modest goals for this chapter. It is primarily exposition of a research program I conducted in 1978 and 1979 in Kansas City, Kansas. The central concern I had with use and meaning of neighborhood was, for purpoess of the study, reduced to an anlysis of shopping patterns and their relationship to locale, environmental characteristics, and personal needs and perceptions. This was done to make the investigation manageable at an operational level and to make the data maximally useful as input for policy and planning. I hope it also shows how an applied social psychology of developing adults is an integral part of such a social psychology.

The methods used range from a questionnaire-survey of older persons and a similar one of business owners and managers, to coding of neighborhoods and pathways in an urban area, and observation of persons as they went to and from shopping areas and used those facilities. In this chapter I will narrow my focus even further and spend most of the chapter presenting data and ideas related to the behavioral observation component of the research and the relationship of those observations to locus of the individual's housing, on the one hand, and to perceptions of ease and satisfaction with shopping, on the other. In other words, I will emphasize the way these data can be used to examine the kind of cognitive-behavioral (and ecological) social psychology of developing adults with which this book is concerned. Before I proceed to that description I once again want to warn the reader that what follows is not a polished exposition of a fully satisfactory research program or a set of findings. Rather, it is to serve as another illustration of ways to enter a social psychology of developing adults; it is a heuristic device to engender ideas and improvements by engendering interest. It is preliminary to more satisfactory approaches that are more fully social, more fully psychological, more fully ecological, and more fully developmental than time and resources allowed this to be.

Previous Research in Aging and Consumerism

It is important and interesting to note that there have been a number of studies in social gerontology and in consumer behavior research that have been concerned with this specific area. For example, Waddell (1976) compiled over 40 papers, of widely varying quality and depth, which concerned the elderly consumer; a few of those contained age comparisons. In 1978 Mason and Bearden published a review and study entitled "Profiling the Shopping Behavior of Elderly Consumers," obviously a title relevant to our concerns in this chapter. Several articles and theses in business (e.g., Bernhardt & Kinnear, 1976; Klippel, 1977; Madden, 1967) have also been focused on older persons as consumers.

Unfortunately, all the research mentioned has shared a number of characteristics that make it at best incomplete and, more importantly, tangential to the kind of analysis to be discussed in the main part of this chapter. Perhaps primary among those problems is the absolute reliance on a survey methodology, even when supposedly studying "shopping behavior." Certainly, surveys are important in this area, as in many others, to gather information on needs, desires, and satisfactions of persons, whatever age and whatever the topic. Certainly, also, it is important to try to get at the phenomenology of behavior, the perceptions people have not only of what they do, but of why they do it. Certainly, direct questions asking for self-report and demonstration of ability are necessary to explore cognitive representations of something as personal as neighborhood, or "place."

At the same time, it is awkward and misleading to use data gathered in that way to represent behavior, as though it is equivalent to observing actual behavior. Although it is clear that there are major problems of interpretation with relying on self-report data about behavior as a direct indicant of that behavior, all of the studies on aging persons have used only self-reports of frequency and time of use. This is a direct result of the locus of the work in areas that traditionally have been inimical to behavioral studies and it illustrates some of the problems of identifying areas of interests too closely with a particular method.

Secondly, the data and interpretations have been singularly nondevelopmental, even in the weak, age-comparative sense we have considered in detail in Chapter 2. None has had any intraindividual historical perspective (that is, longitudinal), and most have not made direct comparisons to the possibly varying behaviors—or needs and satisfactions—of persons in different age groups. Although the study I will report is also not strong in regard to age comparisons and has no longitudinal component, I did make observations of use of settings by all adults and have comparative data on usage patterns.

Related to the last point, about settings, is a third weakness in the previously gathered data. None of the research has been ecologically oriented, in the sense of including analysis from the point of view of setting usage rather than from the point of view of the individual consumer. In line with my belief in the importance of using a multiple set of methods to explore relationships and converge on understanding in that way and with the ecological emphasis in both social psychology (e.g., Barker, 1968; Wicker, 1979) and social gerontology (e.g., Lawton, 1980), the studies I have conducted include survey measures and the point of view of the person, but they also involve behavioral observation and a focus on settings as they are used across age groups.

The Research Program

The research program was designed both to be exploratory—to see if actual behavior of older persons corresponds to survey responses that others have reported in terms of time of shopping and so on—and to test several hypotheses about older persons' ecological behavior in relation to stores. One hypothesis in particular was tempting to consider; it proceeds from Lawton's (e.g., 1980) ideas about general use of spaces by older persons and the translation of his ideas, by himself and others (e.g., Lawton & Nahemow, 1973), into the more specific hypothesis that use of services by elderly will correspond closely to proximity to those services. The hypothesis is based on the combination of the environmental docility idea (Lawton & Simon, 1968) with findings of behavioral range limitations (Barker & Barker, 1961) and avowed less energy and mobility of individual older persons, all ideas that have been discussed previously in this part of the book (Chapter 9).

To test that hypothesis precisely, I concentrated on residents of housing for the elderly for my sample of respondents to the survey (although I also included others as will be described below) and built into the design a comparison of business districts varying on a nearness-to-elderly-housing dimension (from ones in the near-neighborhood of such housing to ones that had no such housing or other large concentrations of elderly in the vicinity). The research program included four phases. First of all, areas around the 10 specialized housing for elderly locations in Kansas City, Kansas, were examined. Initially, I should note that, unlike sites in many cities, those in this city included both inner city and more suburban locations and both public and private management. All businesses in the neighborhood of a site (approximately eight blocks were arbitrarily chosen) were located and placed on a map. Paths to the stores and services were examined for quality—presence or absence of sidewalks, curb cuts, hills, street lights, crosswalks, anything that could be either a barrier to or an aid for free movement without a great expenditure of energy.

The sites differed dramatically on these dimensions. Several of the sites adjoined or were very close to shopping areas with clear paths in between; most were relatively near to at least some important shopping, although in most cases the shopping areas did not have a full range of stores or services. Two sites were not near shopping of any sort.

Disappointingly, even those relatively close to shopping often had a barrier of some sort and degree between the housing and the stores, as did paths to buses and from buses to shopping areas. How important these barriers can be will be discussed in a few moments, but first I should reemphasize some points made a few chapters earlier. Because of slowing of refle𝓍es, loss of sensory sharpness, and, most likely, having grown up in a somewhat slower-paced society, a fairly sizeable percentage of older persons may experience as relatively serious barriers aspects of their environments which most of us would see as merely minor inconveniences. For example, a busy four-lane street is difficult to cross without a light for anyone, but for a less able person, elderly or not, it becomes frightening and dangerous to herself and to other drivers and pedestrians—a real barrier. A sidewalk crumbling and broken and with high curbs at intersections is a minor inconvenience for all, but it might make it impossible for some older persons with mobility or perception problems to use the paths, especially when carrying packages or pushing a cart of groceries. The same can be said of cluttered aisles in stores, high shelves, noise, steps into and out of buses and cars, stop signs hidden by trees, clerks who don't speak clearly, and so on. These are important factors in the environment (potential barriers to use of and satisfaction with stores) and, more generally, neighborhoods for many persons with movement or perceptual problems, which includes large percentages of older persons, percentages that become increasingly large as an older and older group is considered and as persons individually age.

The interrelationship of these environmental factors to efficient use of the environment, and policy issues related to that, will be discussed shortly, after description of other phases of the study.

Surveys

A second major portion of the research program was a survey of older persons, primarily those residing in 8 of the 10 housing for the elderly sites and members of a local AARP chapter (the latter included persons living in their own homes and residents of a ninth site). The final sample included 183 persons, of whom 27 were living in the wider community and the rest in specialized housing for older persons. In the survey, respondents were asked for description and evaluation of nearby services, perception of treatment and of needs of older persons, attitudes about satisfaction or lack of satisfaction of those needs, and transportation modes regularly used. Also, respondents were asked how government, management, and older persons themselves could improve availability of products and treatment.

I will not go into detail about this or the other survey, of 60 business owners/managers about their perceptions of older persons, what they felt they were doing for them, and so on. However, responses to several questions will be brought into later discussion of the relationship between perceptions and environmental characteristics (somewhat more information is contained in Blank, 1979b, and more detailed information and survey instruments are available from the author). I will mention that older persons were likely to report at least some problems with neighborhood stores, such as "hard to get to," "cluttered aisles," "dirty," and "rotten food."

Behaviors

The fourth phase of the study was observation of behaviors of a wide range of adults in a wide range of settings. Selected for detailed observation were all supermarket-type food stores and major drug and variety stores in the eastern half of the city, in which all 10 sites were located (the western half of the city is predominantly rural). Since the sites, as noted previously, were in a wide range of neighborhoods, the stores observed included inner city and "suburban" stores, ones in shopping centers and ones not located near other stores or services, and chains and independents. Finally, they also varied along the dimension referred to earlier. That is, they ranged from almost adjacent to elderly housing to several miles from such housing (and the latter included ones on a bus line from that housing and others that were neither on a bus line nor near elderly housing).

Cindy Piedimonte (a research assistant) and I made two sorts of observations. In the fall of 1978 we systematically sampled sites for time of day, day of week, part of month, and type of weather to make a total of 201 observations at 50 different stores. One of us entered the store, categorized all shoppers into young (25 or below), middle-aged (25–60), and older (60+) adults, and obtained counts for each category. (We also considered groupings vs. single shoppers, and other characteristics, but I will not deal with those data here.) It should be stressed that this categorization was done on the basis of visual inspection on the part of the unobtrusive observer, although the two observers, in joint sessions, had a high degree of agreement, and it is unlikely there were any systematic biases built into the observations.

The overall percentage of use by elderly was quite high: 23% young, 41% middle, and 35% old across all observations, although the 60+ portion of the adult population of the city was about 20%. In line with Lawton's proximity hypothesis, we expected that there would be a considerably larger percentage of old using stores near housing for the elderly than in other stores. Surprisingly (from that point of view, but not with some points from the surveys kept in mind) there was virtually no percentage difference of older customers near and not near the housing—36.8% near versus 34.6% not near. Proximity does *not* necessarily lead to increased usage, it seems.

Why might this be? We expected old to be more likely to need to walk and thus expected more walkers and a correspondingly greater percentage of old near housing for the elderly. And, indeed, older persons were much more likely to walk to shopping, especially in areas near housing for the elderly. Fourteen percent of all elderly shoppers walked (vs. 7.0% young and 2.5% middle-aged), and that percentage rose to 27% near the housing. These percentages are fairly close to those who said in the survey that they primarily walked to shopping. Put another way, 65% of all walkers noted were in the old category (vs. 21% young and 14% middle). Clearly, when there are barriers to walking, they are most likely to hurt elderly customers the most, even without regard to the mobility problems the older customers are more likely to have.

However, the statistics on walking must be put in the context of alternative means of transportation. For *all* age groups, including old, and at *all* locales, including near housing for the elderly, the largest percentage of shoppers arrived and left in private autos (90% young, 95% middle, and 81% old). Six to eight percent of the old used buses of various sorts (vs. 2% of the others).

In other words, most older consumers had at least limited access to at least one nonwalking mode of transportation. That alternative may not be terribly convenient and may necessitate reliance on others, but *unless* walking to the store is *very* convenient, *and* the store is decent along lines mentioned in the survey—clean, uncluttered, good selection and prices—nearby stores will not automatically have an extremely high percentage of old users even though a fairly large percentage of those who live nearby are limited to walking. If transportation were better the percentage would be likely to be lower in many cases; many of the stores very near elderly housing were not considered by the respondents from that site to be desirable. If they could—and at least most could—they went elsewhere.

The stores they both preferred (survey) and frequented (observations) could, by and large, be classified into two types. First of all, chain stores generally received a lot of complaints, whereas members of a particular local group of independently owned stores were specifically preferred by respondents to the survey, even if they weren't near, and had very high percentages of older shoppers. Several reasons are likely to be involved. The stores are more local- (neighborhood-) oriented in stocking and management, and they have a system whereby they will donate 1% of what a person spends to his or her favorite charity, which could be the resident council of housing for the elderly, the A.A.R.P. chapter, and so on. Managers of two of the five stores of this type proudly pointed out in their responses to the questionnaire that they had certificates of appreciation from senior citizens groups.

The other kind of setting for a store preferred by older persons is the cluster of stores. This makes perfect sense; since the older consumer may have more difficulty negotiating pathways, it is most clearly preferable to be as efficient as possible in terms of amount of movement. Older persons, further, have several clear needs for types of stores—food, drugs, variety, barber/beauty salon, relatively wholesome family-style restaurant, and clothing store. Most of the shopping areas near housing for the elderly have the minimum HUD-required stores, but often those are not in a nice cluster, and most of the areas do not have a complete range of places. Two shopping centers in the city are optimally clustered, and those were the two with the highest concentrations (averaging over 50%) of elderly shoppers. One is the area near the housing-for-the-elderly site which is markedly different from the others, the only site at which respondents were uniformly positive about neighborhood shopping. The other is not near housing for the elderly. It is, however, extremely desirable; it has all needed stores and services and only a few others (so distance between them is easy), is on a level site, and has covered walkways. Various means of transportation go to or near it from a number of the housing sites. There were still problems with this shopping center, especially in terms of inadequate waiting areas for transportation and some awkward routing of buses, but it was clearly a desirable shopping place for older consumers, including those who resided far away in specialized housing.

To examine the psychological importance of site placement in relation to stores and services in more detail, we recoded some of our survey data to facilitate comparative analysis of several relevant questions across sites. We categorized residents at each site by whether they said they did all their shopping by walking or not. At most sites and in the group who did not live in specialized housing over two-thirds of the respondents said they regularly used transportation besides walking; at the sites located furthest from shopping areas, in fact, no one shopped only by walking. At the site which was located adjacent to a shopping area which had all the major types of stores with a level pathway in between (a few stores were across a moderately busy street, but most had no street in between), and *at that site alone,* a clear majority of residents (14 of 21) reported doing *all* their shopping by walking. We also dichotomized the question on problems in walking to neighborhood stores, that is, we asked, whether or not they did in fact do all their shopping by walking, did they feel they *could* walk to all necessary stores if they had to? At all the special housing sites except the same one, 50% or more of the respondents reported problems. At that site, all but 1 of the 18 respondents reported there would be no difficulty walking to all needed services (70% of those not in special housing said there were no problems; perhaps significantly, the neighborhood in which those persons lived is the general area surrounding that housing site.)

PLACEMENT AND PLEASANTNESS:
DISCUSSION AND POLICY IMPLICATIONS

At this point I want to summarize the results by considering three questions. What kind of picture do these data give us of shopping behavior of different age groups? What do they mean for policy? What do they tell us about a social psychology of developing adults?

First of all, it is clear from data I did not review extensively (see Blank, 1979b) that older persons have some common needs and wants. They want more single-serving sizes of food and more coherent discount and ''specials'' policies. They need more convenient access to and within stores, including but not limited to more adequate transportation and good pathways for walking to stores and services, since many do not have immediate access to personal autos and have some problems in walking. Many of these are needs and wants found by other researchers, such as Goeldner and Munn (1976), Reinicke (1976), and Revis (1976). Indeed, the Department of Planning and Research of the city in which I did the study (1975) was cognizant of many of the general problems and the specific areas I discovered.

However, it is also clear that these needs and wants are not well met. In other words, more than simply a bit of knowledge based on surveys of older persons or on general reference sources (e.g., Lawton et al., 1976) is necessary, more than a narrowly defined "what problems can we locate and 'solve'?" approach is required. This leads directly to the second question, concerning policy. Clearly, part of the research and policy need is for direct studies of behavior. But a more important part is the need for studies of needs and wants as part of a large complex of factors and relationships. It is essential to see what the various barriers and deficits are, to be sure, but it is even more important to see those as a part of the human relationship to environment, to see the Person-and-Environment as an inseparable, changing processual relationship. At a minimum, and more along the lines of what I have been trying to do with this modest research program, the needs and wants of older persons as shoppers and consumers must be seen as part of the relationships and settings of older persons in a much broader sense. They must be considered as members of communities and neighborhoods, as living in a *place* that is literally a part of them and the meanings they have for themselves. This highlights the necessity for integrating behavioral, self-report, and phenomenological measures and information based on those. Clearly I only included the first two of these in this program. I will briefly discuss cognitive maps and perception of places in Chapter 14. Second, those needs and wants of older persons as shoppers must be considered in the light of the needs and wants of all persons, across the life span, who share those physical spaces in which, individually and in groups, older persons are likely to find themselves.

Are Older Persons Unusual Shoppers? Yes and No

I will try to be more specific about the second of those points, since I think the first has already been relatively well dealt with in Chapter 9 and as I noted, will be again in Chapter 14. It is striking that many of the needs of "older shoppers" are not part of being old in any direct sense, but rather are needs of people in general or of people with certain characteristics that set them apart from the mainstream, regardless of age (although they may well be more common among older persons, to be sure). For example, a large percentage of older persons live alone and have limited budgets; thus, they need good quality food in single-serving portions. But younger persons who live alone also want the same packaging of food. Yet few stores, including those near housing for the elderly or other concentrations of "singles," stock sufficient quantities of such packaging, except in high cost-per-unit frozen dinners. Also, elderly persons, on the average, have lower incomes and, especially, less discretionary income. Thus, they must get the best quality for the best price to make each dollar last. That is why they place importance on specials, discount programs, and high quality with as little waste as possible. At the same time, they tend to live in poorer, older areas of the city, in which stores and services move out rather than in. Lacking personal mobility and adequate transportation, they are at the mercy of those few merchants who stay. In this too they share much more with others than they are different. That is, living in neighborhoods with a poor variety and quality of stores and being less likely than those in more affluent neighborhoods to have personal transportation to escape, while at the same time needing to squeeze what they need out of the few dollars they have, are problems and needs shared with others who are in similar economic and environmental circumstances.

Older shoppers are also quite likely to have mobility problems (impaired and slow movement, poor perception) and thus they need clear, clean, safe paths to and in stores and prefer one-stop shopping to running all over for an item here and an item there (the energy situation may make all of us more like that). These characteristic needs, too, are shared with persons of all ages who have physical handicaps which limit mobility, quick reflexes, and quick response to sensory imput. One good way, perhaps, to think of the host of mobility, slowness, and convenience problems of age may be to think about shopping habits and problems of all persons with a foot of new snow on the ground. Persons will be less likely to be able to drive to the store; therefore, they will be relatively heavy users of public transportation and walking. At the same time, paths are more of a problem than otherwise and the person must slow down, will react more slowly, and be somewhat unsure and insecure about moving. And when the snow does come, persons in general behave like older persons all of the time in another way: they prefer one-stop shopping, because each move requires more energy, time, and attention than they would normally have had to give it.

Finally, like all shoppers, older persons want to be treated decently and fairly at the stores in which they spend money. They, and we, expect cleanliness; an organized, coherent display of products; courtesy on the part of fellow shoppers, employees, and management; comfort; and a basic integrity on the part of the store owners. Although these wants and desires are not surprising in themselves, I found it very instructive and important that, unless those sorts of needs are met, older persons are *not* more likely to shop near their homes than further away, even when the stores are in relatively convenient locations. They are selective about stores, strongly preferring one set of independently owned franchises to both chains and some other independents, for example. At the same time they are, to a larger degree than other shoppers, a captive population.

The combination of their preferences and needs and their relative lack of mobility means that, if a store proprietor near concentrations of older persons wants to serve a steady stream of loyal, courteous, though possibly slower, older customers, he or she must fulfill the desires and wants they share with others for courtesy, cleanliness,freshness, and so on, and the needs and wants they share with other smaller segments of the general population and the few that are relatively specific to older persons. At the same time, if managers or owners of stores near elderly housing wish to frustrate and distress those older persons who live nearby, and it appears some do, they can clutter their aisles, be rude, not stock advertised specials, and so on. They will still have large numbers of older persons shopping there, because of the lack of options for some of the residents of the housing for the elderly, but those older persons will be unhappy shoppers. They will abet and aid one of the problems they cite as making them negative about older persons; that is, older persons will try to go elsewhere whenever they can, thus they won't be as regular or loyal as they otherwise would be; they will only buy limited amounts of limited products there, and thus will be a less valuable component of the market than they would be if they were satisfied enough to do all their shopping near their housing.

The message from these data on several policy levels is quite clear. Business must recognize not only the responsibility they have to older persons as part of their customer population, with some special needs and many needs they share with other segments of the public, but they should also recognize the value older consumers are as loyal, regular customers who will use the services and buy the products if they are treated fairly and their visits are made economically sound and convenient. The message to government at various levels is clear, too. Yes, older persons want discount programs and more money from governmental sources, but they also want and very much need high quality and quantity of transportation which goes directly to and from major clusters of stores and major clusters of older persons. They *need* the elimination of those "minor inconveniences" such as unprotected bus stops, bad sidewalks, and no crosswalks which we don't see as worth the bother to fix. If the pathways are clear and the stores clustered and convenient, it can make a big difference in satisfaction and in use, as the data comparing sites showed. And, of course, these data indicate the value of taking care in original site placement of specialized housing.

The pattern of findings show promise that interventions would be not only fruitful, but also possible. To a large degree, older people are not more prone to problems caused by an uncontrollable factor—age—but caused by socially controllable ones—low income, poor stores near where they live, inadequate transportation. Even their physical changes can often be countered by prosthetic devices or prosthetic environments. They can be given control in ways at least as ameliorative as was the case with housing environments and personal attributions that affect behavior and self-concept. Indeed, better neighborhood design, better prosthetic devices and preventive medicine, and the development of better attributions, by self and others, of the causes of problems that do arise, can be potent positive interventions.

This leads to what is perhaps the most striking policy implication and the most striking value of this research as an example of a social psychology of developing adults. As noted several times before, the interrelationship of person and environment (often narrowly characterized as the effect of environmental characteristics on people) is a rich base from which to develop a relationship-oriented point of view, which considers the interplay of forces and the dynamics of the progressions. It is also an obvious point at which to consider the life span as simultaneously a continuous flow and a set of discontinuous segments. The problems, needs, and environmental relationships of older persons are differentiable in many ways from general samples of nonelderly; but the key problems, needs, and relationships are really life-spanning in nature. They have to do with a key concept we have considered previously—control over one's self and one's placement in time and space. Older persons are different in some ways from their previous selves and from other age groups, but those ways are probabalistic, not deterministic. Their behavioral settings are different from the norm (whatever fictitious "reality" that term is supposed to represent), but they are like the settings of poor nonelderly, of handicapped, of ignored and forgotten and underserved segments of society. Not just in shopping, but in the whole span of their ecology, older persons are more likely than a "normal" population to be embedded in a set of often dysfunctional and always less than perfectly predictable contexts and they are somewhat more likely to have minor biologically imposed constraints.

Getting Back to the Social Psychology

Yes, you might ask, but where is the social psychology you promised? It is there, but it is not necessarily on the surface. Of course, the nonobvious nature of the social psychological aspects of the work is partly its inadequacy on many methodological levels. Also, in part, it is the fault of a narrowly defined social psychology unwilling to admit into itself the embeddedness and contextual, relational nature of all life, making almost all actions intrinsically social. But beyond those inadequacies and surface invisibility, the social psychology is there in very concrete ways, ones traditionally oriented social psychologists should be able to recognize and find useful. It is there, because attitudes and value systems of store owners and government bureaucrats form the environments in which older persons operate; because older people are in some ways competitors with non-old in gaining and regaining mastery over their environments, whether that be home or neighborhood or city; because the organization of the physical environment and the ecologies it "produces" in constant interrelationship with individual inner-biological and psychological progressions contain and form the social relationships involved in those interactions. The type of behavioral data collected in this research is not by any means a model of precision for testing the hypotheses we considered earlier (or for description, for that matter). But it is at least behavioral when it must be and self-perceptual when that is necessary; it is a naturalistic method for exploring the way people of various ages, their needs, their abilities, and their interactions in everyday settings are in fact social psychological. The presence, absence, and attitudes of other shoppers (or users of other environments, for the approach is considerably broader than the proximate focus on shopping), clerks, transportation service providers, and others are in partnership with physical environmental factors, and individual ones, in directing and influencing the behaviors of each individual shopper.

As the data show, older persons, like others, may do what they can to transcend environments that are uncooperative and incompetent, whether those incompetencies are in physical factors (barriers to access), in explicitly social ones (discourtesy, negative attitudes to older customers, or expectations of such attitudes), or in interactions of those (lack of concern to keep aisles clear). Yet they may in fact have fewer resources upon which to draw to continue to impact upon their environments. Both the sorts of resources which may be withdrawn from them by virtue of being old—chiefly money via retirement, but also family and friends to share shopping responsibility with—and the locus of effects of an objectively more difficult environment are likely to be social and social psychological in the most central meaning of those terms. These factors include reduction in quantity of social interactions and in comfort within a particular interaction (e.g., being ignored by clerks and thus assigned less penetrating roles, in Barker's [1968] terms, or, alternatively, being treated in a systematically discriminatory fashion).

Interestingly, the discriminating treatment may include negatively toned discrimination, but it is at least as likely to be a potentially even more humiliating form of discrimination, which is positive on its surface. The latter is what might be called the "sweetie" or "old dear" syndrome. In this pattern of interaction, older persons are stripped of the role penetration and, even more so, the role choices of "prime age" adulthood. They are treated as though they share shopping characteristics with another, very different, group—also considered to be developmentally inferior to those in the "prime age" category: children. Decisions are made for them except at a trivial level, and their views and desires are often overridden by the questioner-assister who consistently compliments and patronizes the "old dear." This is reminiscent of what we discussed in Chapters 9 and 10 as institutionalization. We considered the lack of control and self-esteem even a good, positive institution may engender in its residents. Therefore, in a lesser way, any treatment of older consumers in a "positive" way negatively affects their psychological and social definitions.

An interaction that I am sure we have all observed (or could, if we shopped or did anything else where large numbers of older persons do), proceeds something like the following between a salesperson (S) and an old customer (OC):

(S).   What do you want, dear?
(OC). One of these sweaters.
(S).   What color do you want sweetie?
(OC). This green one.
(S).   Oh, no, that won't do at all. Here, this blue one would be much better. Don't you think so? (No pause.) Yes, it has to be the blue one. I'll box that for you, dear.
(As OC, slowly, reaches for money, S interrupts that process.)
(S).   Here, I'll do that for you. I'll make sure to get the proper amount.

Although that sort of interaction was not, in fact, the focus of these studies, it follows from some of the information gathered. Store managers perceived older persons as "special customers," not often on the basis of different likes and dislikes to be met by better stocking, but because they are "slow" and "need more assistance" and "can't decide what they want." At the same time, merchants did not try to train their employees to deal with those targeted special performance differences, much less concern themselves with preference or product-need differences.

Older persons have a special role, then, in the eyes of the merchants, the role of "old shopper." That role and a set of characteristics assigned to it may be either positively or negatively valenced. As with all stereotypes, it is likely to contain some group-level truth, but also likely to alter behavior toward the particular target, regardless of the truth value of the stereotype for that individual. This treatment, in turn, alters her behavior to fit the stereotype better. Both positive and negative instances lead to discriminatory behavior, in the first case to specialized service and care directed toward a shopper because of age, and in the second leading to behavior to discourage "those sorts" from disrupting the flow of traffic (in store and outside). Resistance from merchants and government officials to repeated requests at one of the sites for a demand-responsive light/crosswalk to facilitate shopping illustrated the second sort. These aspects of social perception of competency by age are, obviously, related to the Type I attribution ideas considered in detail in Chapters 4, 5, and 8.

Another social psychological aspect of all this is the perceptions older persons have of themselves, a factor related in another way to data discussed in Part 2 (especially Chapters 6 and 8). Older people perceive themselves as different. Some of that perception of difference shares the stereotypes of aging persons that the merchants have; that is, many older persons felt that old shoppers differed from others by being slow or, generally, less competent. Again, the assignment of that role to oneself can lead to stereotype-reinforcing behavior, regardless of actual ability or difference from others. At the same time, many of the older persons based the perception of their peculiarities in a different category—in special needs, for single-serving food products, for certain prosthetic devices, and for reduction of barriers. That is, it seems a more productive approach to take as well as a more accurate one. Perhaps clarification of such differences could positively offset both Type I and Type II attributions directed toward older persons.

Finally, as the data showed, physical factors can be behavior-control agents, whether those who inhabit and traverse the settings intend that or not. The siting of older persons near a set of stores that meet their needs does indeed facilitate shopping behavior, both as reported and as observed. Yet, that control is likely to be secondary to social control and psychological satisfaction—if the store treats you badly or doesn't have what you need, go elsewhere! That, in turn, leads to a different social structuring and a different set of interactions involved in the process of shopping (use of public and/or private transportation systems, family relationships, etc.). Social factors affect physical environments and vice versa.

GENERAL CONCLUSIONS TO PART 3

Both the older consumer data and the study on use of housing for the elderly common spaces as social agents illustrate the delicate, changing interplay of distinctiveness and similarity of people who are different in age. The overriding feeling one gets is that older persons are, in many ways, remarkably similar to other adults, especially if one crucial demographic, probabalistic factor is kept steadfastly at center stage: it is likely that, as people age, physical factors, particularly debilitative barriers rather than facilitative environments, are more and more likely to have more and more of an effect per unit of environment. As people grow older, they are at least somewhat likely to become restricted in range of dimensions encompassed by "environment" declines vis-à-vis their earlier selves and "newer" cohorts. In turn, their environment's competence to fully satisfy their needs and avoid becoming barriers to mobility often is reduced by decay and change. Insofar as context influences social behavior and social cognition—and it manifestly does—one's progress through life is likely to be one of an intensifying sensitivity to those controlling influences. Social activities, ranging from the more or less solitary activity of shopping to the intrinsically "group" activities of friendship and social interaction, respond at least as much as nonsocial elements of perception and cognition to that environmental control. The person finds a restricted range of options available—a smaller set of environments to choose among; less freedom as to when to change environments; fewer central, dignified roles available in any one environment—at the same time as he or she has less control over mobility and perceptual acuity to override the controls of the particular environments still available.

Social psychology, then, becomes more closely and distinctly contextual and relational. A steady state person-environment relationship *cannot* be taken for granted; rather, the distinctions become blurred and relative. A social psychology of developing adults, again, by its very existence and embeddedness in change and process, *is* an environmental psychology of social behavior. And, since behavior and cognition are but two ways of looking at human action, an environmental psychology of social behavior is one with a social psychology of behavior and cognition.

Once again, I hope that the reader, after this exhaustive consideration of another specific segment of research in a specific area of concern to at least some social psychologists, can see how these examples of synchronic analysis can serve, not as finished products to be emulated in toto, but as steps toward a social psychology of developing adults that is developmental and social, basic and applied, traditional and revolutionary. I hope the possibilities and vitality can begin to be seen shining within and through the mundane opacity of these pedestrian programs.

PART FOUR

Speculations: The Implications of a Social Psychology of Developing Adults for Psychology, Gerontology, and Related Disciplines

In Part 1, I established a rationale for the value of an emphasis within social psychology upon adult development and upon the importance of recognizing the constant intermingling of change and stability in social life. I proposed and examined two forms of a social psychology of developing adults. The one—an age-comparison-based examination of social psychological questions and issues relevant to adulthood and aging—is developmental only in a weak sense. Yet, it is an advance in many ways from the sort of antidevelopmental, achronic social psychology prevalent at present. It expands the range of social psychological theories, the areas of interest examined by social psychologists, the methods used to investigate social behavior and social cognition, and, most obviously, the sort of samples used as representatives of all persons to whom social psychological findings are to be generalized.

The second sort of social psychology of developing adults I proposed is much more revolutionary (and likely to be traumatic for many traditionally trained social psychologists). It is the replacement of stability and universality assumptions and of static methods, whether achronic, diachronic, or synchronic, whether studies of college students or of a wide range of adults, with an emphasis on the interrelationships of persons who are actors in a deep and real sense with the spatial and temporal contexts of their actions and thoughts. Beyond an emphasis on context and situationism (that is quite consistent with much of traditional social psychology) and on relationships, the polysynchronic, dialogic position places at center stage the dynamic relationships among characteristics of the persons and the situations as the interwoven texture of a set of progressions through time and space. The first section concluded with a caution lest the emphasis on change and discontinuity be purchased as the expense of a concurrently essential recognition of stability and continuity. The dialectical position requires understanding and full recognition of these essential counterpoints and, I feel, it can profit from less than fully developmental studies as long as they are examined with an eye to development and change.

In Parts 2 and 3 I changed the tone of the book considerably. They are the discussion in detail of the application of a development-sensitive, adult-oriented social psychology to areas of interest and issues explored in current social psychology without concern for adult development and adult age group differences. The exposition of research in the two areas—the patterns and use of attributions about achievement among adult age groups and the relationship of ecology and physical environmental factors to social activity patterns and usage of neighborhoods—primarily concerns on rather simple synchronic examinations. Despite this, I attempted throughout the discussion to move closer and closer to methodological and conceptual variations that can lead to a more relational and truly developmental examination of those areas. The research programs conducted thus far are only examples of several first steps to a social psychology of developing adults.

Part 4 is in several ways a return to the concerns and issues developed in Part 1 after those concerns with research. In it we move back to questions about the value and impact either or both kinds of social psychology of developing adults potentially can have on a number of areas within psychology and other social sciences. The discussions in each chapter in the section recapitulate the theoretical discussions of Part 1 and the empirical examples of Parts 2 and 3 while going beyond that recapitulation to speculation on the ways that similar, or better, investigations and conceptualizations could affect issues and current problems in social psychology of various sorts, social gerontology, lifespan development and the psychology of aging, and a range of interdisciplinary social science areas. Important concepts in current social and developmental research, such as stage, life events, interactionism, and history, will be briefly but systematically scrutinized for their value in the social psychology of developing adults.

In each of the first three chapters several researchable questions raised in a speculative instead of an empirical manner will be used as additional examples. The questions were selected to be relevant to the presentation of the social psychology of adult development contained in earlier sections. They also relate to weaknesses in the particular fields examined, weaknesses widely acknowledged and discussed by members of those disciplines with little awareness of the role a development-sensitive yet psychological social psychology of adults could play in resolution of those problems.

The final chapter is a brief exposition of the general approach developed throughout the book and an indication of the kind of conceptual framework that truly may be of value in building new bridges as well as reconstructing the established but now independent—and incomplete—islands of knowledge and ideas that bear upon the social lives, thoughts, and actions of adults who are constantly growing and changing yet consistently personally and socially identifiable as the same person over time and space.

CHAPTER 12

Competition, Cooperation, and Crises in Social Psychology: Is Adult Developmentalism a Part of the Cure?

In the first part of this book I discussed problems and deficits I see in social psychology in relation to development and adulthood. At that time I defined social psychology primarily by what is to be found in social psychology texts and journals. I showed how social psychology has been permeated by an antidevelopmental stance, and I discussed some corrective measures that could and should be taken to make social psychology development-sensitive.

During those discussions I touched upon the crises that have been defined for the field in recent years. Statements of various crises—in methods and in the assumptive bases for the enterprise—have illuminated problems and shortcomings that lie at the core of the antidevelopmentalism of the field, but even the critics, by and large, have not recognized the antidevelopmental nature of many of the problems, nor have they considered the solutions for some of the crisis issues that may lie in a social psychology of developing adults. In this chapter I will try to discuss these matters in detail, outlining how a development-sensitive, adult-oriented social psychology will naturally and decisively result in a social psychology less ridden with crisis-producing flaws.

I will also discuss another issue that may be partially resolved by developing a social psychology of developing adults—the fragmentation of social psychologies and their alienation from one another. In this context I will not discuss the "proper" classification of social psychologies into two or more types, the key elements of distinction, or the reasons for the separation; those issues have been discussed at length elsewhere (*American Sociologist,* 1977; Archibald, 1976; Blank, 1978; House, 1977; Stryker, 1977; Ventimiglia, 1979; Wilson & Schaefer, 1978). Rather, I will try to illustrate how the divisions, however deep and wide they are (and however functional they may be for intradiscipline politics), may be partially bridged by a renewed emphasis on development and change and on relationships among a number of characteristics of social life—inner-biological, psychological, sociocultural, and environmental—as central to social psychological understanding.

I might also add a note that a very different but also important kind of social psychology has been ignored by most social psychologists who have been concerned with delineation of differences and relative contributions of psychological and sociological social psychologies—that which may be labeled a social-issues approach. Social-issues social psychologists are more problem-oriented than either of the more academic, basic sciences approaches would allow. Social issues social psychologists have as their aim the solution of a social problem rather than long-term theory construction. Their areas of interest range across problems relevant to social life, whereas their methods and perspectives are those of practitioners more than of scientists. Social issues social psychologists can be found in business and industry and in social services as well as in departments of psychology, sociology, and social relations and in schools of business and social welfare. They are a group with much to contribute to resolution of the issues more scientific social psychologists have been raising and to an adult-oriented social psychology as well.

As can be seen in Table 12.1, it is clear that the three types of social psychology described above—cognitive-behavioral (psychological), social structural (sociological), and social issues—differ from one another at least to some degree in disciplinary identification, primary methods, theories, areas of interest, and, most important,

Table 12.1.   Three Types of Social Psychology

Type I Cognitive-behavioral (psychological)

Aim: To find and explore universal psychological laws about intraindividual mechanisms underlying social actions.

Focus: On individual behavior in real or imagined social situations

Method: Measure individual behavior (performance and/or verbal reports of cognitive processes), usually in laboratory settings and with experimental designs

Theories: Basic psychology-related, e.g., attribution theory is based loosely in perception, learning, and motivation

Areas of interest: Self- and other-perception, attitudes and attitude change, conformity, aggression, helping behavior, persuasion, attraction, interpersonal communication

Type II Social-structural (sociological)

Aim: To find and explore universal sociological laws about social structural, extra-individual mechanisms underlying social actions

Focus: On social structures, norms, and roles.

Method: Survey measures, aggregate analysis, correlational designs

Theories: Basic sociology-related, e.g., role theory, deviance are based in structural-functionalism and/or symbolic interactionism

Areas of interest: Normed action, role performance, interpersonal communication, group dynamics.

Type III Social issues

Aim: To solve or alleviate a social problem by research and/or application

Focus: On the social issue and its resolution

Method: Social-action based, idiosyncratic

Theories: Basically a-theoretical, but can be related to personality, community organization theories, etc.

Areas of interest: Drug use, racism and other -isms, violence, community relations and conflict, prejudice in aim and focus (I leave undiscussed, for the moment, the fact that there has been and is some degree of overlap among these—see Wilson and Schaefer, 1978, and discussion later in this chapter).

All three of those types of social psychology have been perceived by their proponents to be in danger of imminent collapse, crisis, or stagnation (e.g., Liska, 1978; Ryckman, 1976; Gergen, 1973, 1978a). All three, different though they are, share a general disregard for developmental change and individual differences (and individual direction of action beyond a hydraulic or computerlike system). Although I do not mean to imply that simply paying attention to development and to adulthood will either cure all the idiosyncratic problems within the types or heal the schisms between them, I believe that such an approach will provide invigorating possibilities for answering some of the now apparently unanswerable questions, for expanding the range of each and the degree of overlap among the types, and for making social psychology more useful as a science and as a practice.

Since the set of problems is somewhat different for each recognizable type (and the problems of one are to an interesting degree often conceived as part of the answer for another), I will discuss aspects of each separately in this chapter. The main thrust of my review, however, will concern the largest type of social psychology (and the one that probably has the longest list of problems)—what is often called psychological social psychology (or in my terms, as in Table 12.1, cognitive-behavioral social psychology).

In the last six or eight years the psychological subdiscipline of social psychology has been bombarded by a series of declarations of crises inherent in the field (Elms, 1975; McGuire, 1973; Gergen, 1978a,b, among many others).[1] Many of these "crises" are problems that have been discussed earlier in this book. Major flaws in the field as perceived by critics have been methodological and theoretical, as well as conceptual. Methodological issues have revolved around the artificiality of laboratory settings, the obsession with manipulative control and with parsimony, and the restrictiveness of subject sampling. All of these factors have coalesced into a trivialization of social psychology, an ignorance of real world phenomena and an almost total lack of humanization and relevance. Psychological social psychologists have trapped themselves in their laboratories, where aggression has been reduced to hitting a Bobo doll or shocking a "stooge," liking becomes a matter of first impressions of real (or sometimes imagined, hypothetical) strangers, attitude change is openness to persuasion to change a transitory opinion about a topic especially chosen to be noninvolving (as we considered in Chapter 1), and conflict and cooperation are what college students do in prisoner's dilemma games. Conceptual and theoretical points of crisis are centered around objections to the universality assumption of social psychology, although the objections (e.g., Sommer, 1977; Triandis, 1976, 1978) have usually been framed in spatial terms, emphasizing cross-cultural, subcultural, or natural settings expansions of the subject matter rather than the temporal ones that concerned us more in Part 1.

Obviously, both types of criticism have a range of possible solutions. But the so-

---

[1]M. Lewin (1977) provides evidence that our current stated "crisis" is by no means a new or unique phenomenon.

cial psychology of developing adults seems especially well suited to provide responses to many of the shortcomings. How then can the study of adult development and aging, of adults developing and aging, do this?

In large part, it can do it simply by being. For example, it is unlikely for several reasons that much social psychology of adult development research will take place in the laboratory. Even if middle-aged and older persons can be brought into the laboratory (which is bound to be a considerably more difficult task than getting college students in) the distracting effects of the strangeness of the surroundings that we take for granted could quickly and dramatically indicate the artificiality of the setting and influence behavior (as already discussed in Chapter 8, this is likely to blur interpretations across age groups). This could direct the investigator toward more natural settings. At any rate, it is likely to be easier to study older persons, in particular, in their more usual habitat—homes, senior centers, and so on—than to coax them into labs on campuses. Research done in settings like those could be a demonstration of the value of researching across the entire life span more regularly in more natural surroundings, especially as social psychologists become increasingly aware both of the powerful influences of physical and social contexts on all individuals and of the differential distribution of various age groups within particular contexts.

Second, study of adult development leads very naturally into study of real-world problems instead of trivialities. People who are not college students do not understand or, more likely, are not willing to put up with the artifices of a trivial problem or to grasp the "obvious" (to the researcher) relationship between, for example, hitting a Bobo doll and striking one's spouse. Furthermore, the examination of the relationship of the behavior of adults to their social stimuli can lead the investigator into important areas of research untouched by social psychologists. For example, because of the reliance on college students and corresponding ignorance of adults, cognitive-behavioral social psychologists know little or nothing at all about the social and interpersonal dynamics in such important areas of life as retirement, widowhood, marital conflicts, and parenting—a disregard discussed in detail in Chapter 1 and at other points previous to this. Yet these are real social events in the lives of many persons, not merely old ones. Furthermore, they have analogies (in many ways paler) among younger populations—unemployment, forced separation of spouses, loss of parents and grandparents. In particular, the regularity, increased incidence, and figural centrality of major social events in older persons' lives could provide the opportunity to examine the psychological effects of social transitions; this knowledge, which is valuable in itself, may also be generalized to other similar but less overwhelming events in people's lives across the life span. Just as theories specifically about aging should not be taken as general statements about transitions, likewise theories of transition effects that are limited to investigation of, for example, adolescent transitions to adulthood should be carefully labeled as being restricted. Theories which operate with data across the life span may expand the base of knowledge from either of those even for the particular age population of the more specific theory.

Another area of crisis and criticism to which a social psychology of developing adults may speak is the area of generalizability. The obvious way generalizability can be broadened is in the sheer fact of gathering and comparing data on noncollege students with the patterns found in college-student research. Simple illustrations of the obvious benefit of age differences research can, of course, be found in the work of others (e.g., Klein, 1972, see Chapter 2) and the rather dramatic differences between *each* age group in the achievement attribution findings discussed in Part 2. As data on adults across a wide age range are collected, proponents of a multitude of theories and minitheories will be able to check the generalizability of their initial findings on captive college students. Possibly, all they will discover is much needed verification of the transhistorical, transdevelopmental existence of their proposed interconnections of psychological mechanisms and social behavior and/or the behavior of oneself and the behavior of others (as appears to be the case with friendship formation and proximity—compare Festinger et al., 1950, and Carp, 1966). On the other hand, they may find discrepant information that will lead to questioning the presumed general applications of a particular result and redelineation of specific elements and of specific limits to the range of their propositions.

The latter certainly has been the case in nonsocial areas (intelligence and cognitive ability—Labouvie-Vief & Chandler, 1978) and the attribution research indicates some differences among age groups that lead to an increased understanding of limits in application of attributional rules and away from blind acceptance of equivalency of the meanings of success, failure, and so on, across broadly differing subgroups in the population. The risky shift/caution research with older adults (Kogan & Wallach, 1961; Botwinick, 1967, 1969), already discussed in Chapter 2, is another illustration of this point.

In any case, the net effect of cross-age-group and developmental investigations will be a strengthening of those theories. Similarity or differences of results can verify or disconfirm social psychological statements that are (implicitly at least) meant to be universally applicable descriptions of psychological processes, mechanisms, and determinants of behavior in social settings. Point-to-point comparisons of social behavior and cognition, even of the grossest kind, could provide the framework upon which to build more adequate theoretical and empirical structures in the way described above, even as they would also highlight the weaknesses inherent in the present system of investigation, including those age-group comparison studies themselves.

Everything I have discussed up to this point is a set of rather indirect benefits from including age comparisons and adult-oriented issues in "standard" social psychology. But, just as the approach on studying age comparisons is also an entrance to a radically different conception of the focus of social psychology and the methods to explore that relational focus; so these very general benefits are likely to be supplemented by more specific ones. Whereas the above arguments could be as easily discussed as outcomes of including other cultural groups or natural settings, what I will discuss now are aspects that are quite specific to adult development and aging.

As is both obvious and fairly well studied by psychologists interested in stresses as life events (e.g., Dohrenwend & Dohrenwend, 1974; Lowenthal, Thurnher, & Chiriboga, 1975), as persons age they become probabilistically more likely to have experienced certain social transitions than have younger members of the population at the same point in history. Adaptation to and social and cognitive structuring in response to these transitions are interesting topics of themselves and as representatives of broader categories of social transitions. Even more general than that—and more overlooked—is the obvious fact that as people age they gather an ever-greater accumulation of life experiences. Since many (most) models of social behavior are based on the accumulation of experiences as affecting social cognitions that, in turn, affect social behavior (or, in more behavioristic terms, accumulation per se is a critical factor in controlling behavior), the study of the social behavior of those with the most experience would, it would logically follow, be especially important to consider for purposes of generalizability and further theory construction. They would also be very valuable as counters to the oft-heard complaints that social psychology is irrelevant and restricted in application. Those complaints, in turn, are part of the objections and criticisms of many of those who see social psychology as at a turning point and in a crisis state. Thus, integration of examination of this valuable component of adequately testing any accumulation-based theory is of potentially great value in warding off the doom and gloom (or, sometimes, sinister glee) of those who promulgate the crisis view of current social psychology.

How adults structure their social lives, how they perceive themselves and others, and how they react to stimuli are in some ways the most valuable and valid bases for theories about those structures, perceptions, and social reactions that develop as one progresses through life experiences. Yet, as has been discussed throughout the book, little is known (in the sense of systematically organized data) about how adults of all ages form and use attributions; how they react to a request for aid or the inducement of guilt; how they behave in conflict or cooperation settings; how they make friends (or enemies) and maintain personal relationships; how they relate to other members of groups to which they belong, or into which they are thrust on an ad hoc basis; and how they participate in the construction and redefinition of reality that is at the core of social psychology. There is no significant base of knowledge in those or any other areas of social behavior. Although there are rampant stereotypic attitudes about how older persons (and middle-aged ones, of course) behave in a variety of social settings, social psychologists simply do not know if older people (or middle-aged ones) behave similarly or differently in those social situations compared to other age groups. That is, social psychologists do not know if there is a developmental aspect, beyond adolescence, to patterns and use of social mechanisms and to social behavior. However, it is obviously crucial to discover and examine these similarities and differences whenever one asserts a theory or hypothesis of general import, especially if it includes an accumulation-based component.

EXAMPLES IN COGNITIVE-BEHAVIORAL SOCIAL PSYCHOLOGY

A few examples may be important at this juncture to ground the rather abstract discussion engaged in thus far in this chapter. How might age-sensitivity and a developmental orientation answer those criticisms within specific areas of theory and research in addition to those explored in exhaustive detail in Parts 2 and 3? What benefits may accrue?

I have chosen only a few areas to examine. I had three concerns in mind when making these choices. First of all, the areas—stereotyping and prejudice, and leadership and group behavior—are important ones in social psychology throughout its history; in fact, researchers of all three types of social psychology delineated here have considered them to some degree, even though they are principally cognitive-behavioral in focus.

Second, these areas have considerable relevance to adult development and aging; that is, I believe development-sensitive, adult-oriented social psychological examinations within these areas are particularly likely to be effective, because certain aspects of them are uniquely and/or exemplarily represented in adulthood and aging. I believe these areas, when studied in the ways outlined in this book, have unique contributions to make both to adult development and aging and to the particular content area of social psychology even when aging or development are not of central concern in a particular investigation or theoretical statement.

Third, and most important in my view, I have chosen topics and areas that might be considered archetypes of both the promise, on the one hand, and the crises and constraints, on the other, that are part and parcel of present-day social psychology. That is, research in these areas has languished in many ways, because of the kinds of methodological and conceptual flaws discussed above and in the myriad other critiques. These areas have had their share and more of artificiality and the lack of generalizability that results from that artificiality and a narrowly focused selection of subjects, of disregard for historicity and process, and of ignorance of complex causality and a corresponding misplaced emphasis on linearity and simplicity in causal relationships between pairs of variables defined by the experimenter. At the same time, these areas are ones in which the interplay of stability and change, of personal and social, of structure and process, are very near the surface.

Thus, discussion of these areas from a developmental, adult framework can well illustrate the ways that adult concerns and issues may be enriched by and enrich a continuing cognitive-behavioral emphasis in psychological social psychology. As will be obvious to you as you proceed into these sections, the discussions to follow are not reviews of completed (or even in progress) research as Parts 2 and 3 were, nor are they systematic theoretical treatments of the areas. Rather, they are speculations about how each area considered—and, by extension, the whole host of areas not discussed—contains within it aspects that may be more fruitfully examined developmentally than by using restricted methods and concepts. I invite readers to use these—and similar speculations by Banziger (1979) on a variety of topics in social cognition and social behavior—as instigators of their own areas and other suitable ones, for example, altruism, helping, compliance, and persuasion.

Example: Prejudice and Stereotyping

The area I will discuss first is that of stereotyping and prejudice (and discrimination as a behavioral correlate of prejudice). I will especially concern myself with cognitive bases for and cognitive and behavioral reactions to receiving prejudice and discrimination based on stereotypic beliefs. I think we can fruitfully use aging to explore stereotyping (as we discussed concerning Type I attributions) and its more negative extension to prejudice.

This array of concerns involves situations in which the passage of time, in and of itself, devoid of differential experiences, can become crucial, in which that passage of time can become the vehicle for strong real-world manipulations of stereotyping and prejudice unparalleled by laboratory manipulation or even by other sorts of regular bases for prejudice and discrimination. It is the case that an older person, particularly a middle-class white male, may quite suddenly become a member of a derogated group, systematically discriminated against (and for) by the wider society, after a lifetime of experience as a member of a relatively valued and rewarded group. The effects of this sudden devaluation on psychological processes, personal relationships, and behavior should provide a locus for valuable research on a real-life experimental manipulation of stereotyping and prejudice which could enrich theories concerned with these important social areas (active areas of scientific investigation and social issues concerns). Alternatively, the addition of age categorization to preexistent bases for discrimination (e.g., race), leading to double or triple jeopardy (Hendricks & Hendricks, 1977), should be systematically explored in social psychological investigations.

However, age discrimination and age-based prejudice have been little explored. Those who have looked at these issues from the point of view of aging (e.g., Brewer, 1979) have been content with description of stereotypes rather than considering either prejudicial actions themselves or cognitive and behavioral effects on older persons.

Those who *have* been concerned with the cognitive mechanisms and the effects, on the other hand, have remained enmeshed in the two methodological paradigms referred to a few paragraphs ago. Many researchers (see, for example, a review by Tajfel & Turner, 1979) have tried to study stereotyping, prejudice and discrimination in the artificiality of the laboratory, attempting to isolate one or a few key factors. Although this body of work is important, it denies the possibility for the direct relevance and obvious applicability of the studies in actual, ego-integrated stereotype use and discriminatory action. These researchers have trivialized the research and pulled it further and further from both the social and interpersonal contexts in which those factors typically operate.

Other researchers (e.g., Campbell, 1967; Jones, 1972) have explored prejudice more naturally and directly, but they have consistently used immutable factors—particularly race, ethnicity, and sex—as the characteristics upon which prejudicial behavior and stereotypic attitudes are based. In this paradigm, obviously relevant variables are used and their effects are measured. Those demographically based studies, too, are valuable in research on prejudice, but use of age-based discriminators can add several highly useful dimensions to those typically considered.

First and primarily, age stereotyping and age-based discrimination are strong and real—and thus use of age combats the artificiality and limited temporal relevance of laboratory manipulations—and yet they are also quite unique within naturally occurring bases for prejudices, in that passage of time moves the individual *through* groups toward which other members of the larger society as well as the individual have distinctive attitudes and toward which they exhibit distinctive behaviors. The former was part of the investigation of achievement attributions in Part 2; as the reader will recall, there are clearly a set of stereotypic ideas about the causes for failures that occur to persons of various ages, held not only by those in different age groups from the actor, but also by those who are the members of the same group as the actor who is being judged. Those beliefs color interpretations made of outcome information. At the same time, those data showed little evidence that those stereotypes are linked to either behaviors toward the person (measured, to be sure, only very indirectly) or to other sets of attitudes, expectations, and positive regard held for and by members of the various groups. Much more direct and involving issues and aspects of stereotyping and prejudice can be found and should be explored.

One final point about age-based investigations in this area is relevant. Partly as a result of the predilections of the investigators and partly because of the type of characteristics used as the target delineators, the study of prejudicial behavior—differential action toward a person because of his or her membership in a particular group—has been almost uniformly a study of negatively toned behavior toward the minority person or group. Study of age-related "prejudice" may add a new dimension here as well. Although it is true that many actions toward older persons because they are old—job discrimination, loss of prestige—are negative, others are positive, actions Allport (1958) labeled "love prejudice." For example, older persons are given social security benefits, store discounts, reduced fares, meal programs, and many other benefits *because they are old;* few people are negative toward their receipt of those benefits (see Hickey, Rakowski, Kafer, & Lachman, 1978). That distinguishes older recipients of many social programs from other recipients, to whom labels such as "freeloaders," "welfare mothers," and "bums" are often assigned.

Yet, eligibility for the positive prejudicial action makes the category of the person obvious and thus it may make the negative components of stereotypes salient as well. This was partially explored by Katz and Glass (1979), who found a strong strain of ambivalence in positive discrimination (helping) directed toward both elderly and handicapped. Exploration of the comparative psychological and social effects of prejudice and discrimination in at least three very different contexts—a negatively toned behavior, a positively toned benefit with strong negative undertones, and a positively toned beneficial behavior with little or no negative component—is a fertile ground in which to develop a better understanding of the processes of stereotyping and prejudice. Adding to this the natural-world yet systematic, quasi-experimental nature of time passage and transitions toward an identifiable, stereotypically labeled, prejudicially treated group makes adult development and aging an attractive place, indeed, for investigation of this central content area of social psychology.

Example: Leadership in Juries

As was the case with stereotyping and prejudice, the area of group performance and leadership in naturally occurring groups is one that could profit from an adult-oriented social psychology and could advance from a current low level of interest and relevance to a higher, more central position in social psychology. The participation of older persons in groups—both those including members of other age groups and those that are age-segregated—is likely to be dependent on an interacting network of social relationships that are amenable to social psychological investigation. I will only mention one specific example, that of leadership in groups and, for added specificity, describe leadership in one particular sort of group—a jury.

The dynamics of jury decisions has been an area of great interest to group dynamics and leadership-oriented social psychologists for many years, and interest in it has particularly blossomed in the later years of the 1970s and into the 1980s. I will not attempt to review that work here; the reader is directed to many excellent sources, such as Bermant, Nemeth, and Vidmar (1976), Tapp and Levine (1977), Saks (1977), and Wrightsman (1978).

Clearly, one impetus for increased interest has been the criticisms of social psychological research as being irrelevant at the same time as relevance and application are both more consistently rewarded (by grants and by intraorganizational prestige accorded to it by social psychologists) and more needed (for example, several states have explored and are exploring or using smaller juries and nonunanimous decisions).

The potential impact of age of juries in relation to age of defendants—and the cohort factors inextricably interwoven when the generally quite old jury panels resulting from demographic and economic characteristics (often older persons do not have a job from which to take a leave of absence or children at home that need care) consider the cases of predominantly young criminals—is one unique area to consider. Another facet is choice of leader, or foreman in this case. As with many other issues, the potential influences of age of group members on choice of foreman has been little explored. Is an older, retired person more or less likely to be chosen as foreman and, thus, as titular head of the group who is likely to affect the group's later decision-making?

It would appear that several counterbalancing factors are likely to be involved. On the one hand, it is clear that tenure of group membership is a potent factor in selection of a leader—all members want a leader with experience. Both natural experiments on group formation (e.g., Shaw, 1976) and on knowledge transmission and microcultural simulation research (e.g., Weiting, 1977) make it clear that "older generations" within groups are looked to to provide guidance and direction to the group as a whole. A jury, however, is a new group, composed of strangers (perhaps that is another reason it is a popular sort of group for traditional social psychologists to study; it fits their need for a group without a history). In that case, what are the factors relied upon to choose the leader?

In the only reference to age of foremen I could find, Strodbeck, James, and Hawkins (1957) stated that older members are more likely to be chosen as foremen than others are. If that is the case, that would presumably be a halo effect of a positive stereotype of aging. That is, the belief that age brings knowledge and wisdom about the world may be used as a basis for selection, especially if it is combined with a lack of negative stereotyping, since it can be assumed that a senile person would not be kept on the jury to begin with. This combination of stereotypes is reminiscent of Smith's (1979) previously discussed finding, in a very different situation: that people may, in some circumstances at least, give more credence to a positive stereotype of age than to a negative one.

On the other hand, it is quite possible that the opposite pattern—an emphasis on negative aspects of the older member(s)—may be found. For example, occupation is usually stated in the voir dire examination. Does being retired bring to this situation the negative connotation it certainly sometimes has, especially in an era when mandatory retirement is waning and is being replaced by "competence testing" as a way to expel older workers from the work force (as we discussed in Chapter 8)? If so, would an old but still employed person have a heightened likelihood of being foreman, whereas a retired older person would be less likely to be made foreman than a younger person? Or would the middle-aged persons, apparently judged to be most "in control" of their own successes and failures (see Chapter 5), be most preferred?

These and other questions to do with age of jurors (Do these leadership choices, however they go, affect judgments?) are important and interesting ones that, once again, have been ignored by age-blind social psychologists. Indeed, most "jury studies" are of panels of young adult college students brought together in a laboratory to read real or hypothetical transcripts of trials; this procedure does little to quell cries of "irrelevance" and "artificiality." These are questions that inexorably and naturally lead social psychologists out into real-world issues and settings, into individual differences on the one hand and social structural influences on the other, as well as to adult-sensitivity and concern with developmental issues even in such a "nondevelopmental" area of behavior (because of the brief life of the jury). These issues are most amenable to little used research methodologies, such as quasi-experimental analysis of archival data, that is, by looking at court records on age of jurors, foremen, type of case, and judgment.

In any case, I hope these few cases supplement those discussed in earlier parts of the book to illustrate that psychological or cognitive-behavioral social psychology can be enriched by an adult developmental orientation and fruitfully used by defenders and critics of the current state of the field alike to further the information value of the field. Obviously, the attribution research and ecological-environmental investigations discussed in detail in previous chapters and the researchable questions posed above indicate only a few of many directions the social psychology of developing adults may take, directions which almost incidentally, yet at their core, would be fitting responses to the demands of those who eloquently described the crises and weaknesses of a social psychology without generalizability, naturalness, or relevance.

EXAMPLES IN SOCIAL STRUCTURAL AND SOCIAL ISSUES SOCIAL PSYCHOLOGIES

Thus far in this chapter I have been concerned primarily with the psychological, cognitive-behavioral brand of social psychology, criticisms of it, and examples of how a social psychology of developing adults would coordinate with it. As I said near the beginning of the chapter, that type is the largest among the social psychologies and the one with the most vociferous critics within it. But my concentration on that type should not conceal the fact that the other social psychologies, too, have had their share of weaknesses and of criticisms from within and without. And, it probably does not need to be added, they, too, have been nondevelopmental and nonadult. I will more briefly discuss each of the other major types, as I have outlined them, and give a few cursory glances at issues and problems within them that may benefit from the infusion of adult development into social psychology in general and from the emergence of a social psychology of developing adults.

Social Issues

Because a social-issues social psychological approach is intrinsically more problem-oriented, it is in some ways a more natural, almost inevitable location for a social psychology of developing adults. This is the case, since adulthood and aging are, at least as much as childhood and adolescence, times of change and times for dealing with individual problems often defined in the aggregate as social issues.

In fact, it has been within this kind of social psychology that many issues of adult development have been considered, insofar as they have been considered by any social psychologists. The *Journal of Social Issues* has recently had several issues that are directly relevant. Yet even most social issues work has centered around issues more relevant to earlier stages of the life span. Also, social issues or applied social psychology has also had shortcomings that have led interested parties to characterize it as in crisis (Helmreich, 1975; Elms, 1975; Lowe, 1976; Ryckman, 1976). Some of the problems concern ''impurity'' of applied research as perceived by more strictly scientific social psychologists. I will not concern myself too much with that basic critique, since it rests on what is in many ways an invalid dichotomization of ''basic'' and ''applied'' (see also Stang & Brothen, 1980).

On the other hand, some of the criticisms that have been directed toward social issues research are essentially that it is too *much* like basic (e.g., psychological and/or sociological) social psychology. That argument has merit and extends the criticisms of social psychology previously made (including their nondevelopmental, nonadult orientation) to this conceptually much more behavioral and situational social psychology. I will only briefly discuss this issue separately from what has already been reviewed. The topics and certain aspects of the critiques may be different, but the tone is similar to the attacks directed toward cognitive-behavioral models. Many of the conceptually broad, naturally lifespan issues of social life have been translated into laboratory studies, manipulated field events, and survey-questionnaire-scale measures. Sometimes, only college students have been researched; for example, I have already discussed the trivialization of jury research, whereas others have used marital conflict between members of a college student (and therefore, relatively newly wed) family to study marital conflict that normally takes place over a considerably wider range and history of the relationship. Intergenerational conflict has sometimes been examined by such relatively weak devices as comparing students over 26 to those under 26 (Katz & Glass, 1979) or by looking at college student-administrator issues (e.g., Alderfer, 1973). I want to stress that there is nothing invalid about those investigations—in fact, they are considerably more vital and broader in scope than much of the rest of social psychology—but rather to point out that even in areas of social psychology intrinsically real-world-oriented and intrinsically focused on problems which are life-span researchers have often succumbed to a bias against adult developmental issues. Thus, retirement and use of leisure time, grandparenting (or even parenting), long-term marital communications, and the host of so-called midlife crises are only beginning to be topics of concern to more than a few social psychologists. As social psychologists proceed to those interests, they will be less than maximally efficient if they continue to carry with them their standard tools that are not well designed for natural adult-oriented research. Those "tools" include laboratory settings, experimental manipulations, and survey designs.

Furthermore, most of that important work is as much a reaction to demands for answers as it is an intradisciplinary, conceptual, theoretical, or methodologically based initiation of interest. Again, the reactive nature of social issues research is not to be bemoaned but indeed applauded as the proper approach for this type of social psychology. Yet, as with stereotyping and prejudice, the interest areas may benefit from a more conscious effort to frame social issues concerns in developmental and generational terms, to see issues of work, unemployment, and leisure, family formation and cohesion, community relations, and other areas of interest as courses of progression through relationships, as intrinsically and necessarily developmental and historical. These points are not new (see, for example, Sherif & Sherif [1965] for an emphasis on the historical and developmental aspects of intragroup cohesion and intergroup conflict or Framo's [1979] recent offer to social psychologists of the interaction-oriented family therapy model for understanding marital, familial, and other group relations), but it appears that they bear restating, because they are regularly ignored.

A few brief examples may illustrate this broadening of focus in social issues social psychology. Many persons at one or more points in their lives are dependent upon the existence and "good graces" of public or quasi-public social service agencies staffed by bureaucracies. I have already discussed the possibilities for dependence and labeling this sort of paternalism leads to in the area of stereotyping and prejudice (and in earlier discussions of attributional implications and control), but it can also be explored as a rich locus for studies of the relationships between persons within a bureaucratic system, a concern of social issues social psychologists (e.g., Bush & Gordon, 1978). Sociologists and others have examined bureaucracy often, but few have made any attempt to trace and examine the psychological and social psychological factors in those interactions as functions of the life course and the developmental process. It is true that some researchers have found that amount of experience with agencies is a mediator of success in dealing with them, and there appear to be cohort differences in understanding of and attitudes toward social service agencies. But understanding of these issues has remained at a rather superficial level that is common in much of this area of social psychology and have seldom coalesced to form the underpinnings of a developmental, relational conception of interactions within the bureaucratic process.

As with cognitive-behavioral social psychology, so concerning this type of social psychology, speculations could be piled upon speculations. The research concerning older consumer patterns and, to a lesser degree, the applied industrial component of the achievement attribution research are both simple illustrations of many of the points made, since both include a social issues component. I will briefly review what I mean and illustrate my points by referring to the older consumer study already described (Chapter 11) and relating it more clearly to social issues—consumerism and housing placement policy.

Older persons, by virtue of being older people and/or by virtue of being in a particular cohort, have different patterns or relationships to their social and physical environments from others. A set of progressions—(1) inner biological progression toward less efficiency of movement and stamina; (2) an individual psychological orientation to neighborhood and to needs and wants; (3) the social and economic structures of site placement and concentrations of older persons, businesses, and the sources of revenue open to older persons; and (4) the current status and progression of changes within the physical environment—all are continuously interrelated to affect buying patterns and ecological usage by persons of various ages in different ways (and are likely to change those relationships in the future). Thus, policy and programming must at the minimum reflect a composite of snapshots of each element and of their correspondences, and must reflect the movement in each progression if it is to adequately inform approaches to ameliorating individual, social, and societal problems that may arise. The structure of business should not progress unaffected by the age structure of individuals who form the basis for the existence of neighborhood business. The shopping and other neighborhood use of stores and services, streets and pathways by members of any age group affect and are affected by how and when members of other age groups use those same spaces. The current situation can be directly affected by results of diachronic adult age research by social issues social psychologists, whereas the future of social issues and their social control and/or resolution should in turn be dependent upon more thoroughly developmental investigation of the issues.

Unfortunately, the research in this area is woefully inadequate. As mentioned in Chapter 11, applied researchers who wish to report about shopping behavior have consistently used a questionnaire mode of measurement; virtually all of the data are results of surveys or simple expositions of the economics of being in a particular age group at a particular time. Little attention has been paid to a sense of movement and development in the preferences reported or to the actual level of immersion of members of various age groups in the shopping milieu or to the constancy of change in an array of factors that play into the when and where and what of shopping behavior.

This illustration is meant to point out that social psychologists with primary interests in social issues and social problems resolution could fruitfully apply an adult developmental (really life-span) point of view, thereby enriching the impact of social psychological knowledge on social issues and countering the crisis of confidence shown in a social-issues social psychology that has not grappled in realistic, relevant ways with the network of development and change behind the problems of social groups. This impact can extend across the rather broad range of social groups that are of interest to those whose work fits into this classification—the large-scale level of social policy decisions and intergroup conflicts; the intermediate levels of community relations, consumerism, business, and controlled social change; and the more microlevel aspects of marital relations, energy consumption repatterning, and personal choices about birth control.

Social Structural Social Psychology

Those who have assumptions about the bases for social behavior that are intrinsically social structural—roles, norms, socialization processes—have also had their crises in recent times (see Archibald, 1976, 1978; Stryker, 1977; Burgess & Bushnell, 1969; Liska, 1977). They have found dead ends in an approach that is unable to deal adquately with social change and with the interplay of personal and individual differences with the strictures of role requirements, and that is rigidly consistent in its externalization of the sources of action. They (more properly, the disgruntled element within the group) are concerned about the inadequacies of a methodological and theoretical orientation founded on the passively reactive nature of the individual mechanically emitting role behavior in controlled settings or in response to elicitations of normative statements and descriptions of ''role activities'' as though they are produced through the individual rather than by him or her, rather than as intrinsically personally and socially constructed.

Since the perceived contributors to a crisis of stagnation in this sort of social psychology are present—sometimes in an almost caricaturelike extreme form—in what has come to be called the social psychology of aging, I will defer consideration of this issue to the next chapter, in which it will be explored in quite a bit of detail in the course of a consideration of the relationship between a social psychology of developing adults and the social psychology of aging as espoused by social psychologists such as Bengtston (1973), Bortner (1967), Havighurst (1968), and Neugarten (1964, 1968, 1973, 1977).

TOWARD INTEGRATION OF THE SOCIAL PSYCHOLOGIES THROUGH THE STUDY OF DEVELOPING ADULTS

Prior to that discussion, however, I will try to explain how I feel a social psychology of developing adults may serve a higher goal beyond answering some crisis-stage shortcomings in each social psychological type. I will briefly discuss how a social psychology that is adult-oriented and development-sensitive could help unite these disparate, often independent subtypes into a concerted effort toward a broader, deeper, more satisfying understanding of social psychological mechanisms and processes that encompasses individual, cognitive processes; structural properties and processes in the social and socially learned context of behavior; and practical issues and problems of interacting daily in a complex, demanding life space. This discussion, in fact, is actually a summary of concepts discussed earlier, especially in Chapters 2 and 3, but it is more specifically focused on how the prospect for a relational, change-oriented and development-sensitive social psychology could serve as a small force in an expanding force field directed toward an integrated social psychology. The latter is a goal many (though, clearly, by no means all) social psychologists of each type see as beneficial and realizable (see *American Sociologist,* 1977; Archibald, 1976, 1978; Armistead, 1974; Boutilier, Roed, & Svendsen, 1980; Blank, 1978; Elms, 1975; Strickland, Aboud, & Gergen, 1976; Stryker, 1977; Wilson & Schaefer, 1978; Sampson, 1979; McGrath, 1979; and others in a special edition of *SASP Newsletter* with the last two; and a symposium chaired by Latta, 1980, for a broad ranging sample of concerns in this regard, varying across dimensions from naive pro-integration through recognition of two coexisting disciplines as a goal to adamant polarization in defense against assimilation).

Two compellingly striking aspects of the current debates about crises, shortcomings, irrelevance, and disappointments about progress (or lack of it) fuel my interest in a social psychology of developing adults as a middle force toward cooperation and shared interests, toward confederation if not integration. At first glance, the two points may appear opposite, but they are really quite compatible.

On the one hand, it is clear that many of the shortcomings perceived by members of one type of social psychology are the very strengths another type wants to obtain. Although within psychology critics of their social psychology (e.g., Archibald, 1976; Gergen, 1973, 1976, 1978; Harre & Secord, 1972) feel that overreliance on an individual explanation of behavior and overuse of artificially controlled, manipulated experimental paradigms for data collection are major symptoms, if not the source, of their crisis, a number of sociologists (e.g., Burgess & Bushnell, 1969; Stryker, 1977) feel experimentation and an individual orientation are essential palliatives to their own type's rigid reliance on extrapersonal, social structural explanations based in correlational methods of data analysis. Conversely, Gergen and others (e.g., Archibald, 1976, 1978) believe that social structural context—the bailiwick of sociologists—is a crucial determinant of individual behavior and thought and that it is toward that orientation psychological social psychologists should look for real understanding of individual social psychology. Meanwhile, "basic" social psychologists look to applications and concern with social issues as avenues of escape from the dehumanized triviality of laboratory studies, whereas social issues social psychologists, especially in the roles as evaluators and policy advocates, feel their cause may be strengthened by greater emphasis on design and control of variables.

Dissatisfied adherents of each social psychology, apparently, are finding that the grass is (they hope) greener on the other side, that their brand of social psychology lacks a certain something. Whether or not they know it, that certain something is often that with which their compatriots in their own compartmentalized environments are, themselves, dissatisfied. In regard to this aspect of the current debates, it would appear that any area of interest that brings those camps together to an area neither has as part of its domain may serve several disparate purposes. It could expose members of each to the counterbalance to their own group's narrowness that they seek; perhaps surprisingly, it could also show them the despair to which those very same desired methods, concepts, and perspectives have brought others. Equally surprisingly, they may find upon closer examination some overlooked value in the approach with which they were already familiar. Studying adult developmental issues may be one of many potential pathways to this sort of "appreciation of mutual relevance," as Sheldon Stryker (1976) has labeled his version of integration (see also Blank, 1978).

The other aspect of note in the crises' descriptions, besides the complementarity implicit in the fact that the statement of the problem in one field is the statement of the solution in another, is the mutual silences in all of them. Some of those silences, of course, are the mutual disregard for development, change, and relationships. Since the corpus of this book is concerned with that aspect of social psychology, I will not discuss it in those terms again here. Rather, I will try to describe how it may be possible for a social psychology that *does* cover those aspects of social life and thought to be, in and of itself, a force for integration.

This has already been touched on. The need to reformulate and apply a particular social psychological position inevitably exposes the particular investigator to viewpoints and correspondent issues in the other social psychologies. Although exposure in and of itself is not likely to lead to greater integration and cooperation (as is well known from results in group dynamics and intergroup relations as well as from "mere exposure" research), a focused interaction that has a superordinate goal—understanding adult development as a part of social psychology and therefore understanding social psychology better—is, again as is well known in group research (e.g., the Sherifs' classic work, e.g., Sherif, Harvey, White, Hood & Sherif, 1961), likely to lead to greater positivity in cross-evaluations and greater cohesion. That is, social psychological investigators could begin to see themselves as a group devoted to a single goal and with a specific way to work toward that goal (specific in the sense it is distinct from both psychological and sociological goals and ways).

In that case, a social psychology of developing adults could join a research program Theodore Newcomb (1979) has singled out as an example of a unified, transdisciplinary social psychology of organizations (Katz & Kahn, 1976) and the syncretistic research in those areas roughly labeled as ethogenic (see Harre & Secord, 1972, and Harre, 1977a, 1979, for detailed expositions of the approach and Albert, 1980, for a coherent—and development-oriented—conceptual and empirical program using an ethogenic approach and technique). At the same time, it would add to those (as Albert's work does to some degree) a naturally processual, naturally gestaltist developmental-historical dimension.

Directed toward this concern—to understand and describe social behavior and social cognition across all the times of one's life—social psychologists could transcend collective but independent searches for similar realities and the kind of competitive relationship which that sort of uncoordinated coaction feeds; they could move in the direction of cooperation toward a higher goal, that is, they could become members of *a group*. This will and can occur, even as they remain members of other groups (departments based in disciplines, specific orientation to social psychology); being a member of several groups is nothing new.

Is such a vision likely to occur? Or is a social psychology of developing adults likely to go the way of a social psychology of aging; that is, will it become simply one more compartmentalized, narrowly defined area of interest within one or another of the still independent social psychologies (probably psychological, cognitive-behavioral social psychology)? That question cannot be answered on the basis of the bits and pieces of research that have been done. It *is* the case that most of the researchers in the examples cited have identified themselves as psychologists. But it is also the case that those psychologists are likely to be members of interdisciplinary groups (the Gerontological Society for some and the two societies closest in practice to an inter-social-psychological organization—the Society for the Psychological Study of Social Issues and the Society for the Advancement of Social Psychology—for many). That, and the willingness, indeed enthusiasm, to relate their work to social psychology of aging and other social structural approaches is encouraging, but only the future will hold a clear answer. As with other aspects of a social psychology of developing adults, taking even halting, imperfect steps in that direction can itself make our "here" a bit more like being "there."

At this point we will turn to consideration of the parochially defined social psychology of aging, both as an example of a thoroughly sociological approach to adult development and as an established, identifiable area with goals similar to many of those proposed for a social psychology of developing adults, but with several severe limitations in the pathways typically used to arrive at those goals.

CHAPTER 13

On Making Social Gerontology Social and Developmental

At several points earlier in the book I mentioned problems I see inherent in the social psychology of aging, primarily because it is part of social gerontology. I have mentioned the twin obsessions of social gerontology—a social emphasis on roles and a corresponding personal emphasis on adjustment. In this chapter I will consider these issues in more detail and discuss the social psychology of developing adults as an approach that retains the focus on adulthood and aging processes even as it abandons the worship of the two gods.

This approach may be seen by those who do not agree with the emphases endemic to social gerontology as a counterbalance, whereas those who feel adjustment to role change should be the central focus of the personality-social psychology of adult development and aging may also welcome at least some portion of it as a complement to their concerns (as Bengtson, 1973, would seem to do when he points out that it would be beneficial to the social psychology of aging to make use of concepts and theories in "mainstream social psychology"). In the latter part of the chapter I will discuss several methodological issues that must be addressed to develop a social psychology of developing adults.

I do not think I need to spend a great deal of time on description of social gerontology or on exposition of critical viewpoints. Bengtson's (1973) slim volume on social psychology of aging, Lowenthal's (1977) chapter in the *Handbook of the Psychology of Aging* (Birren & Schaie, 1977), and Neugarten's (e.g., 1973, 1977) and Rosow's (1967, 1975) writings in general are all clear illustrations of the approach, as are texts in social gerontology by Atchley (1972, 1977, 1980), Loether (1975), Hendricks and Hendricks (1977), and others. Obviously there is more to these writings than the positions I describe as problems, but it is more than fair to say that a commitment to the twin obsessions is indeed a central element in all those writings. It is also fair to say that these two obsessions have had important directive influences on the pattern and depth of social psychological-personality concerns in adult development. They have isolated this area and divorced it from the mainstreams of every social psychological orientation from which it grew—symbolic interactionism, psychological social psychology, and role theory. It has instead become a more individualized (personality theory-oriented) arm of structural-functionalism in gerontology as a whole. Thus, its lineage, historically and conceptually, is more properly Parsonian than Meadian (or Lewinian). This is not necessarily deleterious, although I will argue that it has led social gerontology into some blind alleys that make it ultimately unsatisfying.

DEVELOPMENTAL IMPLICATIONS OF A SOCIAL
PSYCHOLOGY OF ROLE ENACTMENT

First, let us consider the concept of role and the implications it has for a social psychology concerned with adults. As will become clear, one of its implications is the other obsession, with adjustment; other implications and consequences will be dealt with first, and then we will return to that aspect.

As discussed previously, the approach of sociological social psychology and, particularly, social psychology of aging has been consistently a more externalized social psychology than the more intraindividual, cognitive process-oriented social psychology dominant in psychology. Major emphases have been placed on persons as role enacters. Thus, the point of analysis often is primarily social structural. These emphases are clear in all the expositions noted above. Goffman's (1967) point about concern with moments—role enactments—rather than individuals, which I cited in Chapter 2, is echoed in Rosow's (1975) insistence on the crucial nature of roles for self-definition and in the role-counting methodology of many studies. Actions are interpreted and used to get at the ends of research, the understanding of rules and norms as they operate within a particular society.

Certainly, this emphasis is a necessary element of a social psychology of developing adults, one ignored by cognitive-behavioral social psychologists in their rush to remove their "science" from the confounds of the sociocultural base of individual behavior and thought (see Harre, 1977a,b, 1979, for one important viewpoint in that regard). It is a needed counterpoint to the kind of social psychological perspective discussed in Chapter 12. Yet the question that is relevant now is whether this approach to social behavior, to the exclusion of all else, is satisfactory. How far can we go in the direction of externalizing the locus of the causes of social behavior? To what degree can we treat the individual as a role enactor—an actor performing at the direction of societal demands—rather than as a creative participant in social process? (This question, of course, is not meant to imply that psychological social psychology has given creative participation a key role in its models; we know and have discussed that it has not done so.) In this regard, the social psychology of aging and a critical examination of it are particularly relevant, since in many ways the social psychology of aging is the extreme interpretation of social psychology in the terms just outlined. The area is suffused with notions of social support as role enactment toward the old and, especially, of aging as progressive loss of roles and movement toward a poorly socialized "roleless role" (Rosow, 1975). Very little in social psychology of aging does not have the concept of role and role enactment as central.

It can be asserted (and has been before, e.g., Marshall & Tindale, 1978) that the monochromatic perseveration on roles has resulted in a negative view of aging, even among those who assert vociferously that they wish to fight negative stereotypes of older persons (see also Kuhn's [1978] devastating critique of the Gerontological Society and Estes' important 1979 monograph, *The Aging Enterprise*). "Normal" (i.e., modal) aging is portrayed as *almost necessarily* devastating and negative, since it almost inevitably involves loss of at least some roles (such important social phenomena as retirement, widowhood, and the maturation of children are reduced thereby to loss of a role). Although the blame for loss of roles is often laid at the door of society rather than that of the individual (thus differentiating the social psychology of aging somewhat from formal disengagement theory to be discussed briefly later), the basic elements remain clear. Loss of roles is essentially equivalent to loss of the guiding forces in life, the stabilization of being a performer fitting a niche (actually, of course, a set of niches). Thus, for Rosow (1975), the "reality," as he sees it, of role loss must find its individual expression in depression, confusion, and a sense of loss of self-identity. Approximately the same time as Rosow delineated his position, Atchley (1972) entitled his landmark text in social gerontology *The Social Forces in Later Life*. That, obviously, was not an accident, but in fact was a reflection of his—and social gerontology's—focus on external "forces" as the primary influences on social behavior (though *not* necessarily as the primary influence on individual development separate from constrained behavior, as we shall consider in Chapter 14 concerning personality developmental approaches in social gerontology).

It takes little imagination to realize that retirement, having children leave home, losing a spouse, becoming unable to move freely, losing a driver's license, having a smaller behavioral range and less penetration into settings (Barker & Barker, 1961), and other concomitants of aging result in loss of roles (especially if you have previously defined those activities and the behaviors associated with each setting and relationship as roles). Thus, according to the formula, late adulthood is essentially a period of decline, retreat, and loss of control (note that this is separate from and more or less independent of the biological decline model which has infused and controlled most of the [nonsocial] psychology of aging for decades!).

And yet, the questions must be asked—is this all that obvious? Is going through life a matter of putting on and shedding roles? Is loss of role objects equivalent to loss of self-identity? Answers can be given on two levels. I will consider the first in detail in the next several pages. First of all, many people who suffer those losses continue to be personally satisfied and involved. They do not bear the marks of the traumas as deeply as they "should." To retirement they say—"no big deal; I'm tired of working anyway"; to children moving on they say—"come back and visit, but not too often." Many people suffer major "role losses" without missing a stride and with little apparent intrapersonal effect.

How can this be understood in a role approach? In several ways. Role theorists can begin a search for "new roles" or revisions of old ones which have been added to replace those that were lost. That search is the basis for the ongoing, though ultimately bloodless, debate between activity and disengagement theories. In the latter approach, "proper" aging results from individuals' sharing in the societal "conspiracy" to take away their roles, that is, by welcoming role loss prior to preparation for death (see Cumming & Henry, 1961; Neugarten's [1973] description of disengagement). In the activity theory conception, "proper" aging is a matter of one-to-one replacement of roles as they are lost, replacement by reweighting remaining roles or by finding new ones—the elder statesman, doting grandparent, and so on.

Neither of these "theories" (see Marshall & Tindale, 1978, for more detailed discussion of the illegitimacy of that label for either position) has stood up well although their work is indelibly imprinted on the field, as we will discuss again later in the chapter and in Chapter 14. Neugarten (1964, 1973, 1977; Havighurst, Neugarten, & Tobin, 1968) and others have developed a third avenue that recognizes the inadequacies of each from an empirical-justification point of view, yet retains the centrality of role. She has led a search for typologies of personality, formed early in life, that lead some to prefer to lose roles; some to tenaciously—and sometimes dysfunctionally, from the point of view of some theorists—fight to keep their no longer appropriate roles; and some to replace them with new roles, less central to society.

Yet all of these perspectives—and, indeed, many alternatives to them, such as Gubrium's (1973)—depend for their existence and validity on the belief that roles (the externalized functions one performs) are social reality; the individual, the self, springs forth from those social functions as they are judged by others. Functions, and the evaluations of functional performance by "society in general," define and give meaning to individuals.

Certainly, explanations within the general constraints of this conception are varied in texture and have both value and validity. There is strong evidence to support a belief in the relevance of roles and shifts of various sorts. In particular, the timing of events, from the point of view of life course expectations shared by the individual and by social others, is an important element in the functionality and affective tone of those life events (see Lowenthal et al., 1975; Chiriboga & Cutler, 1980, for reviews of this position). On-time events are often much less traumatic and disruptive than off-time ones, even when the event itself may be the same (outwardly, of course, not phenomenologically). Part of the reason for this is surely that on-time events allow for anticipatory socialization to a new set of requirements, a new role. That is, retirement that occurs when expected is both planned for and likely to be relatively positive. It is also the case that many older persons do try to cling to roles with which they have been identified.

Yet many researchers have noted that the most satisfied and content older persons are often the ones who refuse to submit to the rules, who, for example, fight mandatory retirement even though it is expected and thus is socializable. They relish and revel in avoiding being "typecast." Predictability in roles and clarity of social expectations are not necessarily the promise of positive adult development. However, retreat into personality typologies that "allow for" being a maverick—as a role—are both weak and tautologous.

A further point becomes important as the social psychology of developing adults moves away from such a predominant role-analysis basis. Perhaps roles are not that central in people's lives *at any point,* perhaps life only appears to be regular and well-bounded before aging dissolves that boundness and clarity. Certainly, individuals *usually* prefer relatively ordered progressions within their lives; certainly for many people being a parent or being a worker is a central pole around which social behavior and social cognition are organized. But seldom does the role one enacts take its place as the *essential* focus for individual selfhood and, certainly, for individual development, as opposed to individual stagnation, through time. Is it really the loss of the wife role which upsets a widow? Isn't it rather missing the other person, missing the relationship in all its color and movement, which is likely to be central? Even within work situations, where the role idea appears to have its most obvious application, often what is missed is the friend network of relationships centered around a particular locality and particular set of social behaviors or, quite simply, the money the job provided. "Roles" is not a bad way to refer to those behaviors, but it is not necessarily the only or even the best way to do so, since much of the social behavior that is important is not enactment of being a worker, but rather is epiphenomenal to the tasks intrinsic to working.

In the case of many losses of a locus for behaving and relating what is difficult to cope with is the time on one's hands. Again, that can be referred to as not having a clear and proper role, but the personal meaning of the experience—that it is difficult to know what to do and who to relate to and how to change so that your relationships are relatively comfortable—and explication in those terms is both less role-bound and more life spanning. Every day, relationships within a role setting are being worked out, sometimes by submission to normed behaviors that are available for use; other times by development of different relationships, new adjustments of the fabric and texture of social life. It is in this nexus of change and stability, of constrained and nonconstrained behavior, that social psychology may make a unique contribution to understanding of development, and it is in that direction social psychologists can profitably look for new perspectives. Just as an egocentric, individual psychological or inner biological analysis of the situation and the behavior is unlikely to be wholly satisfying (certainly not to a sociologist, nor to a social psychologist of developing adults), so also an externalized, role analysis is less than complete. Rather, the relationship of individuals and the construction of reality that takes place on a moment-to-moment basis and enables that relationship to be meaningful are likely to be the central interests of those who think and behave and of those who try to analyze those thoughts and behaviors.

Social psychologists, however, have done a poor job, at best, of recognizing and trying to understand this point of interplay of person and society. Most attempts have continued to be centered around either normed behavior or free, unconstrained actions; both sides have missed the point of the relationship, the interplay, as the "real" object that makes both of the sides of the interaction make sense. Pieces of research, such as work (Albert, 1980) on the character of endings to interaction, the frequency of which is estimated to be of the order of 3000 per year, is urgently needed to begin to fill those chasms in knowledge. A brief presentation/discussion/rejoinder sequence by Harre (1977a,b) and Schlenker (1977) is interesting and instructive in this regard. Although the two authors disagree in fundamental ways—Harre as a true revolutionist in the discipline and Schlenker as a traditionalist—both agree that much research and thought must go into revitalizing social psychology as a discipline so that it can better be used to understand social psychology as a personal set of life experiences. These are only slight beginnings, and they have not arisen from the social psychology of adult development and aging nor had any apparent effect upon it (and, I should add, are still relatively nondevelopmental in orientation).

In fact, it is at this point that it may be well to reiterate a point I made earlier that the social psychology of aging lacks fidelity to the fullness of sociological social psychology. Within sociological social psychology the symbolic interactionist school and adherents to that school (as well as ethnomethodologists) have long stressed exactly this aspect of reality, that it is socially constructed *by individuals*—within the framework of social structures, rules, and norms, to be sure, but dynamic and relational in and of itself. Also, nonsymbolic interactionist sociologists have also recognized individual aspects of social relations in generally the same way as psychological social psychologists have. For example, labeling theory entails an individual attitudinal, perceptual base similar in many ways to social cognition and attribution theory. Many sociological social psychologists have stressed internalization, not as a simple receiving of rules and norms, as appears to be the case in the social psychology of aging, but as an assimilation and construction of selfhood and of social relations. Generally, those aspects of SSP are not to be found in the social psychology of aging.

In any case, one major element of the social psychology of aging as a part of social gerontology has been a relentlessly role-oriented, functional approach to adult development and an externalization of individual behavior and individual self-conceptions. This role perspective is not directly related to any nonaging social psychology in this regard, except extremist role theory positions, nor does it appear to be the best way to approach an understanding of the social psychology—social actions, thoughts, feelings, and relationships—of developing adults.

An alarming aspect to the kind of role theory used in the social psychology of aging is its nondevelopmentalism. Even as the focus is labeled ''developmental'' and the active, gerundive construction ''aging'' is attached to the theory and research, the use of role enactment as *the* explanatory concept tends to entail the rejection of an active model in favor of a static one. Yes, roles change with time, and thus change is allowed into every description of aging. But each role is relatively enduring, static (until society redefines the functions of that role) and, of course, essentially nonpersonal. The people who fill the roles, except for their long-standing status as a personality *type,* are without a developmental dimension. Since they are not part of the explanation of change and of action, their development, independent of the roles they play, is either of minimal importance (as in Goffman's [1967] assertion that it is not men and their moments that is of concern, but moments and their men), or it is reduced to biology or to certain aspects of biopsychological development, as will be discussed in Chapter 14. In this sense, the social psychological role approach to aging is a stage model (also to be discussed in Chapter 14).

ADJUSTMENT AND ITS MANIFESTATIONS

Let us now turn to the other part of the social psychology of aging. If it does not adhere to the individualistic parts of the foundations of sociological social psychology, but also does not have a cognitive-behavioral, psychological focus, does it ignore individual factors totally (beyond the levels of typology already considered)? If not, where is the individual orientation to be found?

The answer, of course, is that the social psychology of aging does include an individual emphasis (or at least a pseudo-individual one, as I will argue later in this chapter). The individual factor it has is *adjustment*. This orientation, in turn, has been borrowed from psychiatry and classical personality theory.

The characteristics considered thus far—externalized social structuralism in the form of roles and the static nature of those concepts—crystallize in this overriding concern with adjustment. As I will discuss somewhat more in the next chapter, this orientation may in part be rooted in the apparently closer relationship between the Committee on Human Development at the University of Chicago with psychiatry and personality psychology than with sociology or psychological social psychology. But with or without that relationship, it is complementary to and almost an inevitable bedpartner with the approach to social psychology just discussed, a focus on norms, rules, roles, and functions within society.

The result of the wedding of structural-functional approaches to roles (and its externalization of social action and social thought) with the adjustment idea has been an extremely clear model of people—in this case, middle-aged and older adults—as *passive organisms*. This assumption runs deeply through models as disparate as Lawton and Simon's (1968) environmental docility hypothesis, Gubrium's (1973) socioenvironmental notion, social support models (e.g., Lopata, 1973) and Kuypers and Bengtson's (1973) striking, valuable social breakdown/reconstruction syndrome model of "normal aging." Furthermore, this underlying assumption of passivity of the individual—recipient of and receptacle for directions and control from societal representatives, adjustor to external circumstances—suffuses not only the disengagement theory, which at least openly espouses the view, but also the so-called activity theory. These two theories, in turn, are regularly referred to by social gerontologists and social psychologists of aging as social psychological (e.g., Bengtson, 1973; Loether, 1975; Neugarten, 1968), although they are manifestly direct translations from functionalist macrosociology to the quasi-individualistic language of personality adjustment. As discussed briefly above, the passive adjustment motif prevails in all these approaches, although its manifestation is tailored to other elements of differentiation within each model.

For example, although Neugarten, in many places (e.g., 1970, 1977), writes much and well concerning the social creativity of older persons, she at the same time considers it to be proper for older persons to move toward "interiority," toward social withdrawal. Older people are not active participants in social life because they no longer want central roles; they prefer the sidelines to center stage. This preference, presumably rooted in biological decline or in genetic programming of some sort, is seen by disengagement theorists as fortunate, since society needs them to move off to the side anyway. Those who object to disengagement theory, however, also tend to have the image of the passive organism apparent, at least by implication, in their alternative formulations.

As we have already discussed in brief, even the most ardent admirers and proponents of disengagement theory (including Cumming, 1964), have disavowed the original statement of the mutual withdrawal as universal and as essential for satisfactory aging. The linkages of individual biological and psychological development to social demands through mutual disengagement appear to be unjustified in any strong sense. Some basis for rejection, noted earlier in this chapter, is the realization that many older persons in effect choose to force asynchrony between their inner dialectics and the outer dialectics; and it is many of these "mavericks" who seem to be successful at and satisfied with growing old. Rather, theorists have emphasized the descriptive value of the "theory" for current society even as they have tried to break the link to inner biological imperatives. Although these modifications are to be welcomed, the model retains much of its emphasis on passivity of the individual in the face of social structure. Furthermore, researchers using the model have not done a good job of separating cohort, maturation, and historical moment even at the descriptive level.

Activity theory would appear on its face to be diametrically opposed to the passive organism view. "People adjust best to aging by keeping busy and active" seems to place active determination of behavior at the center of development. Yet it is clear that nothing of the sort is the result. Rather, inner processes are assumed to progress toward less energy and lower activity (Neugarten's idea of interiority is not by any means linked by her to a disengagement paradigm), and it becomes society's task as caretaker to come up with *alternative* activities—more properly, alternative *roles*—so that the older person does not feel cut off. Indeed, the goal can be fulfilled, but only if the individuals in the larger society from which older persons would be potentially cut off, are primarily receptacles for norms and players to lines the "social director" gives them. That is, older persons are given little room for self-determination, but it is the same amount given to those of other ages. All people, it is assumed, are active insofar as they perform functions in society—roles—and insofar as they maintain those roles. The individual behind the mask may age and wither, but if the roles remain (or alternate ones are given to the individual by programming—a favorite of practitioners who use the activity model), in this view, the developmental progression has remained stable.

Status Quoism

The last point leads directly to an issue referred to earlier. Neither of these approaches, nor the social psychology of aging in its other manifestations, is developmental in any real sense. For one thing, most research has been cross-sectional. In fact, most of it is completely achronic; that is, looking only at older persons at a point in time without direct comparison to other age groups. It has ignored the interrelationships of cohort and maturation and any sense of development at either societal or individual levels.

The structural-functionalist analysis of society rampant in much of social gerontology has been attacked on many levels by sociologists and sociological social psychologists (Wrong, 1961; Archibald, 1976, 1978; Gouldner, 1971; Gubrium & Buckholdt, 1977). They criticize its intrinsicially static nature, and many of them assert that it has served consistently as a prop for glorification of the status quo. The social psychology of aging, combining that external viewpoint with the internal adjustment model, is especially open to criticism in that regard; it is heavily invested in the functional model of status quoism (Marshall & Tindale, 1978).

The emphasis consistently is on functions within a relatively static (or at least orderly) social order. This emphasis is clear in the prominent role given to programming in social gerontology. That is, it is seen to be a function of society to make sure that some roles are available, even to the elderly. It is up to members of the wider society, often representatives of a governmental social order, to devise ways and means to keep (otherwise passive) older persons "active," that is, filling roles. Inability to perform is seen, on the one hand, as totally extrinsic to the person—the social structure is letting her down by not providing proper roles to this receptacle—whereas, on the other hand, it is seen as inherent in the organism, any organism, since the individual is *always* essentially passive without the guidance of rules and roles. But only an orderly, predictable social structure can fulfill those constant needs of the populace.

Survey Methods

One other point must be explicitly presented before proceeding to a discussion of the impact the social psychology of developing adults could have on the social psychology of aging, a methodological point previously made in passing. The social psychology of aging is virtually stagnating in surveys. Researchers have been concerned with relatively superficial methods to gather relatively superficial descriptions of characteristics and "needs" of older persons. They have emphasized counts (number of roles, for example, or of activities) and have ignored quality. Lowenthal and Haven's (1968) and Lopata's (1973) finding about the value of one person—a confidant—for adjustment to widowhood indicated the greater value of qualitative investigations of relationships rather than simple quantification of roles, but it is unusual in the field, and, furthermore, has been transformed rather easily into investigations comparing those who have and those who do not have someone to fill the confidant *role* for them.

Obviously, the methodological emphasis on aggregate data is proper within the scope of the approach, since the individual is considered primarily as a representative of a set of roles. In fact, even the "personal" level has been aggregate, as was done in consistent efforts to establish typologies of individuals, placing everyone into one of a few convenient categories. The question, "Is 85 year old Joe Blow going to adjust well to this setting?" is answered by a conditional response, "If he is armored defensive then. . .but if he is passive dependent then. . . ." Although such an approach may be commensurate with the kind of static, passive model, it is ill-suited to proceed beyond that model and to reveal relationships that are in fact fluid, interactive, and dialectical throughout the life span. The methodology, restricted by the model, asks questions in a perseverative way; that way of asking insures that the answers will not stray far from the narrow set of answers which fit the model well. That does not mean that either the model or the method have been verified.

Finally, social psychologists of aging have consistently eschewed anything bearing the taint of experimental design as part of their research. Certainly, experimental design has obvious and troublesome flaws which should be avoided (see Gergen, 1978, for one of many summaries of the characteristic flaws of social psychological experimentation). But a measure of understanding surely has been lost by avoiding the use of "experimental" design even as a quasi-experimental methodology, that is, by not collecting data on control groups and making detailed comparisons of groups assumed to be similar on some dimension but different on as few others as possible so as to lend precision to specific hypotheses. This consideration will become clearer in the next section of the chaper.

THE PLACE OF A SOCIAL PSYCHOLOGY OF DEVELOPING ADULTS IN THE SOCIAL PSYCHOLOGY OF AGING

How would a social psychology of developing adults relate to some of the problems of the social psychology of aging catalogued thus far in this chapter? How would it answer objections to social psychology of aging as a type of sociological social psychology area and how would it help in dealing with some of the idiosyncratic problems that set the social psychology of aging apart from both psychological and sociological approaches to social psychology in general (in particular, the emphasis on adjustment)?

Methods and Designs

Perhaps the easiest place to begin is with the last criticism mentioned, that is, in methodology of design and investigation of issues to do with data-gathering. In many areas, present understanding could be greatly enhanced by inclusion of some designed comparisons. For example, understanding of widowhood at present is based in detailed survey and interview studies of widows (e.g., Lopata, 1973). Although the descriptions are indeed rich and reveal interesting relationships of social psychological reactions to widowhood to different types of support networks available to particular widows, would it not be potentially more advantageous to examine the characteristics now defined to be those of widows with those of several other categories of persons based in several dimensions? For example, widows are likely to live alone—are their characteristics most closely related to being widowed or are they part of being alone? A comparison to always single persons living alone could answer part of that question. If widows are found to differ systematically from always-single persons of comparable age, a comparison of widowed to divorced with similar marital careers and similar time after separation from spouse may be especially productive. Also, the differential experiences of widows and widowers should be examined more carefully to specify more clearly effects of being widowed and effects of being an older female (who is alone). Although each type has been examined separately; there has been little integrative, comparative work. Thus far, comparative explorations have seldom played a part, even in extensive, costly studies of social psychological and social aspects of aging. Part of the reason for this is the antipathy sociologists—and many personality psychologists—have to exprimentation, and the resultant marked avoidance of experimental design in the field. The weaknesses of experimentation have been dangerously overgeneralized to quasi-experimental design issues that have little to do with manipulation or "control."

Also, behavioral investigations have, for the most part, been ignored even though they may be helpful. Certainly the reliance on surveys and self-reports limits the applicability of findings in the social psychology of aging. As noted in Chapter 11, several social gerontologists have talked about studies of "shopping *behavior* of elderly" when all they have are self-report data. The sort of behavioral investigations I have begun in that area and described in that chapter, manifestly modest though they are, can be productive in social psychology of aging research on diverse areas, such as social activity and friendship patterns, organizational development of senior centers and adult-oriented support groups, marital and family interactions, and others at a level that is deeper and more revealing (about behaviors at least) than self-reports or even detailed interviews. (I am by no means ignoring the inverse restrictions many mainstream social psychologists have imposed upon themselves by looking only at behavior and ignoring in-depth interviews and other means to examine the cognitive and affective components of action in society.) One fascinating area to develop, I feel, is the investigation of marital relations in the transition period from work to retirement and the major reallocation of time that event brings. Such investigations will be far richer if a combination of methods, including behavioral observation, interviews, self-reports, and even laboratory studies with experimental manipulations, are placed in a creative longitudinal combination. I discuss such a potential research program in Chapter 14.

These illustrations, however valuable they may be, are still limited to nondevelopmental issues. Developmental ones are even more challenging.

Again, widowhood may be used as an example. Although Lopata (1973) collected data on a fairly wide age-range of widows, she did little analysis relating social psychological aspects of being widowed to cohort or maturation differences. Yet, such comparisons are crucial even to begin to understand being widowed beyond detailed description of a particular cohort at a particular historical period. Also, comparisons of reactions to widowhood and to other sorts of enforced separation (e.g., one member of the dyad in the army or prison) as a function of the on-time or off-time nature of the experience can be very revealing and informative. Likewise, longitudinal exploration of marriage partners at one point in time over the continuities and discontinuities representative of various outcomes of marriage (still married, widowed, divorced, etc.), although laborious, appears to be essential. Creative methodologies designed to maximize collection of meaningful data are required, but the tasks are possible if sample size will be sacrificed for longitudinal sampling and if massive data collection of hundreds of responses from each person may be reduced to a few simple measures which are essentially naturalistic slices of both behaviors and thoughts.

A further step, both methodologically and conceptually, is a move away from the static/status quo, structural-functionalism of simplistic role analyses to the relational emphases discussed throughout this book, to understanding that social behavior, social cognition, social support, and social action are all dynamic. To refect these realities, social psychology must be equally dynamic. The age structures of societies form social norms and role differentiation, but those structures are themselves formed by attitudes, needs, and behaviors of individuals within society. Individuals use the pieces available to them—and when they are restricted to a few pieces may be when the role-adjustment model is most appropriate—to construct their world of the moment. Adjustment occurs constantly, but it is mutual. Further, adjustment is itself historical, itself only the result of continuously active processes and relationships within and between individuals. It is not produced by external manipulation of a passive receptacle; it is inhibited by that, for that transforms a relationship into a set of structures and makes the balancing act of change and stability impossible for the weaker element (usually the person, of course). Truly meaningful stability cannot be achieved with any element held constant, since the others are inexorably changed, thus changing the entire relationship. These points, of course, have been discussed in earlier chapters and in the dialectical positions of Riegel (1978, 1979) and others. In that case, the relationship can survive only as a hollow shell. Yet, the social psychology of aging is a social science of just those sorts of hollow shells.

There is little available within the social psychology of aging or, more generally, of social gerontology, to which to relate the concepts described above. One with promise as an active model of society is that of cohort flow (Riley, Johnson, & Foner, 1972). This theoretical structure is designed to transform the age stratification notion, which has usually been static, into a dynamic model. The changing individual is within a flow of cohorts, a flow changing at each historical point in time. If that kind of approach were combined with a corresponding emphasis on the dynamic nature of individual historical flow and also an open, change-oriented concept of the physical environment it may form the basis for a truly relational, dynamic concept of social interaction; one that could place the pieces of the puzzle so far collected into a larger schema. The macrolevel concerns of Riley et al. could be combined with correspondingly dynamic models of interpersonal interaction. So far, social psychologists of aging have shown little inclination to be part of that process.

The sorts of designs, methods, and approaches described thus far in this book could contain some of the necessary elements toward putting the puzzle together. A well-formed social psychology of developing adults, cognitive and behavioral in focus but systematically aware of social and physical contexts, oriented toward change and relationships (without restrictions and prohibitions against necessarily incomplete achronic representations of elements of the picture), could be a key to a redefinition of the social psychology of aging, making it developmental in both a structural and a dynamic sense. Ecological placement of behavior within changing yet stable environments, investigation of social cognitive processes such as attributions, first in relation to age differences and then in terms of meanings and relationships across time and place, serve as indications of what could be available for interrelating the social psychology of aging with the essential ideas of role and culture that sociology and anthropology find particularly useful for analysis at more aggregate levels.

Aging could be more openly and continuously considered as a part of the flow of individuals, social institutions, and physical habitats. Aging could be conceptualized in the same way as the rest of development, at the same time as that ''rest of development'' and aging alike are reformulated as intrinsically historical and relational, as a combination of change and stability, continuity and discontinuity, balance and unremitting tension and conflict. Aging and the life course of development are one, but both are less orderly and parsimonious than sociologists or psychologists interested in social psychology would like them to be. I believe the implementation of an adult-oriented, development-sensitive social psychology could do much to bring the social psychology of aging into an expanded, relational social psychology.

Where Are the Open Arms?

One big question requires discussion prior to leaving this rather rosy glow for consideration of the relationship of a social psychology of developing adults to the less-social psychology of development and aging. That is, does the social psychology of aging, as represented by those doing work identified as such, want to be part of such a social psychology of developing adults?

To answer that requires first making explicit several implications of a social psychology of developing adults. It is clearly and explicitly *not* gerontological; in fact, in a crucial way, because it is lifespan in its purview and because it is not dependent on a structural model, it is antigerontological. That is, the lifespan notions developed here are antithetical to the development of disciplines and subdisciplines on the basis of age as a subject matter. Rather, it sees aging as part of a lifelong developmental process. In fact, it emphasizes the *impossibility* of a science of an age group, since each age group is destined to be different from each other one, and every attempt to divorce one segment of a life-span from another is doomed to failure.

The social psychology of developing adults as proposed here is, like most social psychologies, an emphasis on definition of the field by content, that is, by social behavior and thought (or one or another type within that). It includes, to be sure, a critique of considering content only, devoid of the individual and societal factors that result in the multitextured nature of any and every social act, and of the inadequacies of a social psychology that is focused on social behavior and thought as simply representatives of the control of various intra-individual mechanisms. Yet, it retains an emphasis on individual actions and individual decisions and on social content that is quite different from that favored by most social psychologists of aging.

It is also methodologically at variance with the preferences of many social psychologists of aging. It is not that those researchers are ignorant of experimental methods and behavioral analysis; indeed, many social psychologists of aging are quite well informed about those. It is that they do not "like" such approaches. Again, resistance rather than embrace may come from some corners. Thus, the answer is not an unequivocal "yes." There are some indications in each direction.

Most social psychologists of aging, as noted early in the book, are deeply invested in gerontology. They publish primarily in gerontology journals; they see the social psychology of aging as part of social gerontology, and they are prominent in the Gerontological Society to a greater degree than they are in disciplinary organizations. A number of them (e.g., Lowenthal, Atchley, Bengtson) are located in major gerontology centers. Some of these social psychologists of aging may be resistant to an approach that is clearly and explicitly antigerontological.

Possible resistance because of these factors must be met head-on by proponents of the social psychology of developing adults. We must ''sell'' our view to those who may not have open arms. Hopefully, some of the indications of possibilities for advancement discussed in this book and especially in this chapter will lead to greater willingness to work together and to the mutual appreciation that is needed.

Although there is evidence of the possibility of negative attitudes, at the same time I should also emphasize the potential for a positive answer to the question. There are many indications within the social psychology of aging that emphasis on negative possibilities reflects unwarranted pessimism and lack of confidence on my part. Many within social gerontology are interested in issues which certainly fit within the purview of a social psychology of developing adults. Many social psychologists of aging are open to the sort of work described in this book. Indeed, Bengtson, in 1973, pointed out that it would be good for social psychologists of aging to pay attention to ''mainstream social psychology'' (p. 46). He then proceeded to briefly discuss role theory and several other more sociological approaches, rather than any psychology-oriented ones, but the intent of his remarks is clear and, I am quite sure, would lead to interest in more psychological approaches, such as attribution theory, as well. He, Havighurst (1968), and others have not limited their age groups to older adults. Marjorie Fiske Lowenthal (Lowenthal, 1977; Lowenthal et al., 1975), among others, has been a leader in development of life course perspectives on stress and coping and other aspects of development. Douglas Kimmel's (1980) text on adulthood and aging depends heavily on an interactionist approach that is both life-spaning and focused upon relationships. Neugarten (1977) and other social gerontological social psychologists of aging have interspersed the role-adjustment approach I have criticized heavily in this chapter with explicitly dialectical or interactionist notions.

These social psychologists of aging indeed may welcome progress on the part of ''mainstream social psychology'' toward adult developmental issues, toward topics relevant to adulthood and aging, toward methodological implementation of change-oriented and relational conceptions of social psychology. It is up to personality and social psychologists to approach them, not with heads downturned in shame at our failures nor, certainly, with a smug attitude that it is about time they use ''our'' methods and ''our'' perspective, but with new ideas, excitement, vigor, and recognition of the real need both groups have for a thoroughly polysynchronic, thoroughly humanized, constantly developing social psychology of developing adults.

CHAPTER 14

Impacts of a Social Psychology of Developing Adults on the Psychology of Aging and Other Psychological Areas

In this chapter I will deal with an interlinked set of issues centered on the relationship of a social psychology of developing adults with already established areas of psychology of adult development and aging. In that regard, I will discuss three relatively disparate segments of adult developmental psychology: personality stage theory, psychology of aging in areas other than social and personality, and life-span developmental psychology, in that order. In the final section of the chapter I will briefly consider several other specialized areas of interaction: with environmental psychology and person-environment studies, and with family studies.

STAGES IN ADULT PERSONALITY DEVELOPMENT

For several decades an active area within the psychology of aging and social gerontology has been concerned with personality development. Its central focus on adjustment, as I discussed in Chapter 13, makes it both unique and somewhat problematic for a social psychology of developing adults. I noted this in Chapter 13, but in this chapter, among other matters, I will focus on its problematic nature in some detail.

Prior to that, though, it might be well to consider why personality and adjustment have been linked so closely in adult developmental studies. One obvious reason follows from the adjustment motif—if the primary task of adults is to adjust to an increasingly uncontrollable world (and not only these personality theorists, but also others already noted, such as Lawton, 1980, in environmental psychology, and Rodin & Langer, 1980, and Schulz & Hanusa, 1980, in clinical-social psychology, take that as a major thesis), then their capacity for adjustment must be measured, monitored, and used as a guide for intervention whenever aging becomes a central problem. The personality psychology of adjustment stands ready to serve that task.

Another reason is one already discussed in Chapter 13. The backgrounds of a number of prominent theorists have been closely linked with psychiatry and classical personality theory. Indeed, a sizeable number of major theorists and researchers, including Neugarten, Havighurst, Bengtson, Kimmel, Chiriboga, and Kahana have taught and/or been trained in the Committee on Human Development at the University of Chicago. As previously mentioned, this committee has been closely aligned with psychiatry as well as with developmental and personality psychology. These backgrounds may have exerted a guiding quality, leading to a central concern with adjustment, just as much as the concern with adjustment led to interest in personality. In any case, the research and conceptual work of many prominent social gerontologists and psychologists of aging have been directed to personality processes in adulthood.

More recently, another set of researchers and theorists have become prominent in the area of personality development in adulthood. Their work (e.g., Levinson & associates, 1978; Gould, 1978; Valliant, 1977) has been very productive and has added a new dimension to adult developmental theory and research. They have used research from both cross-sectional and longitudinal case studies to verify and elaborate their psychodynamic stage theories of the psychosocial development of adults. In turn, results of their work and independent investigations and expositions by journalists such as Gail Sheehy (1976) have brought social science knowledge about adult development to a very broad lay audience.

As I will discuss below, the models that have emerged from all these sides and both these major groups have been sequential stage models that place adjustment and regularity at center stage. To be sure, the stage-based models of adult personality development both have been and are important, valuable contributions to understanding of both adults and development. They show an awareness and interest in adulthood that is sorely needed in the general area of personality development and dynamics. Conversely, the application of a general conception developed originally to refer to childhood lends a life-span flavor to the adult developmental field that it has been lacking in its achronic or synchronic ethnocentrism (age-centrism?). This life-span idea—that we can develop notions that help us understand development at all ages, individually and historically—is central to a social psychology of developing adults.

Also, Neugarten (e.g., 1977), Erikson (1976), and others who have been major figures in this area of adult personality development have continued to grow and change in their views; they have been open to development in their own lives and thoughts. This has buttressed the argument for the value of equal recognition of change with stability, of dynamics with structures, by individual example and by the evolution of their approaches toward greater and greater place given to the role of progression and the dialectical, relational nature even of stage and structure. Finally, the models have been suffused with an awareness of the social nature of personality, the interplay of self and society. These are major strengths.

At the same time, what follows will be a relatively negative critique of the class of stage models. I will be concerned primarily with exposition of deficits in this set of models as they have been and are being applied to social psychology and of the reasons why I believe a social psychology of developing adults will be very different from such models. I want the reader to remember that I am taking the role of critical analyst and of apologist for an alternative view, not because I feel those positions are worthless, but because they are influential and have worthy apologists for their defense. Obviously, also, I should note that any particular objection to stage models may be more or less true of a particular approach; they are a heterogeneous lot.

With those provisos and explanations, I will proceed to an analysis of the relationship of stage models of adult personality development to my conception of a social psychology of developing adults. Virtually all of these models have a common base and a common set of assumptions that make them rather poorly suited to be completely useful as representatives of a social psychology of developing adults. Many of the investigations have major methodological weaknesses, especially in the area of sampling; for example, Levinson's (1978) entire empirical base is case studies of 40 men. Many of the generalizations made do not seem to be grounded in even that limited data base (see Kimmel, 1980a,b; and Wrightsman, 1980, for slightly extended critiques along these lines). In this section I will leave the methodological issues for others to discuss, and instead I will concentrate on conceptual problems that I regard as deeper and more profound than would be cured by methodological and sampling advances even of major proportions.

The common base is a sound belief in the fundamental reality and phenomenological and functional importance of psychosocial stages of development. In this regard, these approaches are rather straightforward extensions of the predominant model in child personality development for many years. Why does this common base make these models less than they appear to be on the surface? Quite simply, because of it, they are only minimally developmental, and they are inbred with the belief in the essential passivity of the contribution of individuals to their own social behaviors and cognitions and, indeed to the direction of what has come to be labeled one's "personality."[1]

How this is the case has been discussed in detail by Riegel (e.g., 1978), Labouvie-Vief (1977), Kimmel (1980a), and others. I will only briefly review the issues at this point. Stage theories are built upon a base of beliefs in a set of universal phases or periods of development progressing in a unidirectional fashion toward an end state or final stage. Although many developmentalists have ignored development past entrance into adulthood, that is, have seen adulthood as the final stage (Freudian theory is an obvious example), there is no inherent problem with extending the last stage to a much later part of the life cycle, as was done brilliantly by Erikson (1959) in his extension of Freud's developmental model. Yet a clearly defined last stage *does* appear to be an essential element in any stage model. This necessity is combined with two others—that the stages be universal and in a necessary sequence, with each new one emerging from the last, and that each stage is qualitatively different from what preceded and what will succeed it. The manner of resolution of each stage sets the tone for the kind of resolutions available in and for a later stage.

There are many variants of stage model, with differentiation on such aspects as the number of stages (for example, Erikson describes eight stages over the life-span, whereas Lowenthal, Thurnher, & Chiriboga [1975] and Levinson [1978] each deal with four different stages for adulthood) and the configuration of each stage. Some emphasize rather exacting chronological counterparts for a stage (e.g., Levinson),

[1] I will not discuss here the verifiability, or lack thereof, of "personality" (see Mischel, 1968; Smith, 1980, and many sources they cite for consideration of these issues). For purposes of furthering this discussion, I will simply use "personality" to refer to the image one projects to himself or herself and others that leads them to collectively believe that the individual has a set of enduring characteristics set into a relatively idiosyncratic but relatively stable and identifiable constellation of "traits."

whereas others deemphasize any strict association between age and stage and indicate that such identification is either idiosyncratic or socioculturally determined and, thus, not universal.

The universality and unidirectionality assumptions of stage models are quite probably wrong, or at least grossly overstated, as Riegel (1978), Baltes (1980), and others have discussed. Why then do researchers in the area place such stress on regularity? How do they converge so clearly on a set of stages? It is likely that a large part of the answer to that pair of questions is the narrowness of samples just noted. Not only are the samples often tiny, but many of them (for example, in Valliant's, 1977, study) are highly biased toward professional, upper-middle-class groups (usually only males, it should also be noted). This is a severe limitation that requires more than merely the mention at the beginning of the book it is usually given. The samples from *all* the studies are from highly technologically advanced societies, societies which, it should be added, have relatively well-delineated but by no means universal age stratification structures (Riley et al., 1972). They are even from the same general cohort. Thus, the generalizability of the conclusions is suspect on several levels, not the least of which has to do with the distinct possibility that the regular, "universal" stages may indeed be regular within a very narrow band of societies, classes, and characteristics of participants, and in a very limited sociocultural point in history. The similarity of choices of samples may mimic a universality which is then not verified or even checked. These problems lie at the heart of concern with the validity of any claim to universality, to revelation of true stages of development.

A further point should be made explicit. Whereas sociologists and others may develop, and have developed, stage models that place the stages within society and social rules (and thus are at least cognizant of the culture-boundness of their stages), virtually all of the stage models of adult personality development are unambiguously based in the biological-psychological evolution of the individual. Some of these are strictly psychodynamic; others less so, but still placed in the biological-psychological domain. For example, Gutmann's (1980) article on postparental men is a clear example of a very psychodynamic model, suffused with references to "phallic young men" and "older men who seek pleasure in the pregenital direction." Also clearly psychodynamic is Erikson's stage approach. Levinson's view is less obviously psychodynamic, typified by reference to periods that are more social—"entering the adult world," "settling down," and so on, although even in this version the psychodynamic and psychiatric roots are deep and fairly obvious. Neugarten's and Lowenthal's perspectives are even less psychodynamic, although both are apparently fashioned after Erikson's earlier position.

Despite surface—and some deeper—diversity, these models all clearly share the strong assumptions that there are stages to adult life and that those stages are universal, progressive, and ultimately biological. This common grounding in biological-psychological maturation is useful in many ways, but for our purposes it is dangerous at several points. First of all, it alters the character of the role of experience in two ways from what is usually the position in social psychology and, more generally, psychology. One's past experiences are not seen as directly contributing to one's current style of life and "personality." Rather, experiences at one point in time are fundamentally irrelevant to one's stage status at a later point in time, which is determined by biopsychological maturation in some way interlinked with chronological age. By speaking of fundamental irrelevance, course, I do not mean to say that earlier experiences do not make a difference; indeed, they have profound effects. But I do mean to say that those effects are bounded *within* the constraints of stages, not transcending them. That is, *how* one deals with the demands of a stage is at least partially a function of how one has handled (experienced) an earlier stage, but *what* one deals with (e.g., the tension between integrity or despair in one of Erikson's stages) is bound by forces that are simultaneously internal (biological) and yet oddly external to the individual. They are external because they are placed upon the individual by membership in a particular species; they are without control or agency for the individual (remember our discussions of control and personal causation in Part 2).

Many of these aspects of stage models are apparent in Bühler's (1968) Erikson's (1959) approach (see also Newman & Newman, 1975; and Neugarten, 1964) and in the host of approaches to midlife development (Gould, 1978; Levinson, 1978; Valliant, 1977). Yet these aspects fly in the face of both active models of one's involvement in constructing one's personality that include the potential for profound change as a regular element of life *and* the totally experience-based continuity entailed by a nonstage accumulation model. Both certain kinds of continuity and most kinds of self-directed change are effectively disallowed. Yet those are central concerns for the social psychology of developing adults outlined in earlier sections of this book.

Second, and perhaps even more important, the stage orientation to "development" prescribes a *lack* of development at most times in one's life, that is, when one is lodged in a "stage." Only at the fringes of stages, at the transitions, is there movement beyond perturbations that are developmental only in the blandest (that is, chronological) sense of the term. Individuals are in fact "disallowed" from changing except at points in the life-span that correspond to the beginnings and ends of stages. In other words, as in social structural functionalism discussed in Chapter 13, the emphasis is on stability (within stages). A stage is essentially a plateau, during which development in a deep sense is, in fact, impossible.[2]

Also involved in stage approaches is an emphasis on linearity and unidirectionality, the embodiment of Thomas Wolfe's (1940) phrase: "You can't go home again." Indeed, there is no going back. Although this gives the models a sense of flow and change in life, its psychodynamic, unidirectional basis leads to pseudodynamic rather than fully dynamic thrusts. Further, it is highly evaluative. There is no dealing with what was "appropriately" part of an earlier stage; use of an earlier approach to a life task is usually considered to be an indication of disturbance, or re-

[2]One reader of an earlier draft has pointed out that I speak of stage theories in a generic sense, not mentioning but presumably including Piagetian theory (e.g., Piaget, 1967). He further indicates that he feels many of these objections do not apply to that stage approach. Although I believe a case can be made either way about Piaget's model, depending on which works are examined and on the predilections of the examiner, I want to make it clear at this point that I am primarily using the phrase "stage models" to refer to the set of psychodynamic/personality models specifically cited earlier and so prominent in the area of adult personality development. By that choice I am leaving consideration of and debate about Piaget's enormously successful and significant model to other times and other places.

gression, of "not acting one's age." One's personality, thus, is developed by the balance of proper and improper direction of energy at *each* stage; "proper" direction is a sign of proper progression, whereas any other direction of energy is a fixation at an earlier stage, a condition detrimental to later mental health.

This emphasis on the "one-pass" nature of experience, as in strict Freudian analyses, leads to a perseveration on the explication of typologies of personality, as exemplified by Williams and Wirth's (1965) and Neugarten's (1964, 1973) tracing of current personality functioning—and current social action—to stable personality trait-types formed at much earlier stages. It is crucial to note that such stage models of adult personality development are neither developmental in any active, interactive, constructive sense of the word nor adult. Rather, the present and the future are only the playing out of a script that was essentially completed during childhood.

This, it turns out, brings us full circle to a continuity model of adult development. Neugarten (1973), among others, appears to take pride in the verification of a stable personality structure she found in her data (although in other places, as I have noted previously, she emphasizes a more interactionist, change-oriented view). It also leads us back to the passive, adjustment approach to aging and the basis for that in (or coexistence with) a passive role conception of social psychology. Adult personality psychology is as externalized, as noninteractive, and as value-laden and normative as the social psychology of aging. It does not allow for the reality of current interaction and future changes; it does not permit the constancy of change and the locus of the "reality" of stability within that constant change that are the hallmarks of a thoroughly and vigorously developmental model.

It should not be surprising that a regular sequence of stabilities, one building upon the other, is consistently revealed by those theorists, since that is what is mandated by the rules of the model and the rules of society alike. Both are obsessed with regularity, structure, and order.

The net result of that sort of thinking has led to a personality psychology of adulthood that has not kept pace with personality theory in psychology generally or with social psychology. In the case of the former, there is little awareness of the post-Mischel (1968), situational orientation to personality, one that, together with Carson's (1971) exposition of an interactionist model, places much of the regularity of behavior and style called "personality" into a nonindividual, contextual locus. In the case of the latter, the role of social definitions of self and of the constantly constructed nature of personality, regardless of the symbolic interactionist lineage of at least some of the theorists, has also been downplayed.

A topic of central concern to both personality and social psychologists that seems to have been misplaced somewhere along the way is that of "self." As I have discussed, the typical social gerontological position on personality development leaves little room for inner direction of the trajectory of that developing personality. Instead, biological forces or social structural "forces" (Atchley, 1972, 1980) control development at all ages; the person is buffeted by inner physiological and outer environmental-social structural constraints. Self—that which is somehow a directive and reflective force in the individual, that which has been prominent and central in personality and social theory for decades (see White, 1959; Rogers, 1961; Mead, 1934, for a few obvious examples), and has regained prominence in social psychology more recently (for example, in Wicklund & Duval's 1972 monograph on self-awareness and the large body of research and conceptual development it has engendered; Smith's 1980 discussion of the self and its development; and Gergen, Greenberg, & Willis's 1980 revision and expansion of self and social exchange theory)—is intrinsically too dynamic, too truly inner-originated and inwardly controlling for a personality psychology that relegates the individual to the task of adjustment to the ravages of social and biological forces.

Even some of the findings of social gerontologists that are taken to be consonant with the passive, adjustment model of personality "development" in adulthood and aging can be the starting points for research and theory on the active, change-oriented self that appears to be at least equally characteristic of the lives of very many adults, well into later adulthood, as stability is. It may be the case that older persons see themselves as less active and controlling than before. This does not necessarily mean their self-concept has lowered, however, for the change may be seen as more extrinsic. Their activity may decline, not because of some inherent lack of movement, but because those actions defined by the larger society as activity may be decreasing. The data I gathered on attributions certainly seem to show that older persons (persons of all ages) feel themselves to be in control of their successes, at least; in fact, in some ways, older persons are seen as having more avenues of control over their failures than middle-aged persons do. More important, the kinds of experiences that define self, that give value to one's concept of self, that *mean* something in terms of self, may be quite different and distinctive at different times of life. Once again, as we have seen and discussed before, *only by altering* the bases for self-evaluation, the weightings for different actions and results, can a sense of self remain constant over the vagaries, not only of old age, but of the passage of time and the exposure to new experiences that life constantly offers to each individual.

Fortunately, there is a developing perspective in adult personality theory that has many points of correspondence with the social psychology of developing adults discussed throughout this book; one, indeed, that is an integral part of this social psychology. Increasing emphasis in adult development is being placed upon the tensions of everyday life and the basis for self-definition and other-definition in the situation and, especially, in the interaction of personal needs and experiences with the ebb and flow of changing contexts and changing societal demands. What is particularly encouraging about these developments is that they are being led and sanctioned by many of those who have in the past been identified with some varieties of stage theory. Neugarten (1977) and Lowenthal (1977) and others in the (relatively) Old Guard have increasingly made the interactionist nature of their models clear. Prominent students and colleagues of theirs, especially Kimmel (1980a,b) and Chiriboga (1980; Chiriboga & Cutler, 1980), have increasingly become closely identified with fully developed interactionist perspectives in their research and textbooks. These approaches in adult development and aging have their counterparts in the child developmental end of the discipline as well (e.g., Bronfenbrenner, 1977; Weisz, 1978).

Although these are certainly encouraging signs of a convergence of interest with the social psychology of developing adults, I think that one word of caution is in order. It may be that the sudden burst of interest in the decidedly psychoanalytic stage models about midlife (Levinson & associates, 1978; Gould, 1978; Valliant, 1977; Gutmann, 1980) may retard the development of such convergence by the stress those theorists place on a strict biological-clock, psychodynamic interpretation of the middle years. It is to be hoped that an emphasis on social behavior and social cognition as life-span, developmental phenomena—and as ultimately and intimately bound with personality, both as the product and the raw materials for the construction of social life—will lead to a personality and social psychology of developing adults that will be both descriptively and practically real, yet is neither normative nor ultimately static, antidevelopmental, and anti-individual. Toward that end both critiques of stage models, where necessary, and constant reaching out to foster convergence are essential.

PSYCHOLOGY OF AGING

Stage models of several types have also dominated another relatively distinct area of psychological interest in aging, that area regularly labeled as "the psychology of aging" (which, I have already noted and will discuss further below, sometimes does not include personality and virtually never includes social psychology). Insofar as these are stage theories, they share many of the problems just discussed, and thus there is little need to go into those issues here. I will spend most of the section describing how a social psychology of developing adults has much to offer to this psychology of aging that is at present social-less and self-less.

But first I should make clear that what I mean by "stage theories" at this point is not by any means identical to what I have meant by it up to this point (or to what is often meant by the term). Indeed, the psychology of aging presently eschews psychodynamic stage models of the sort just described. Instead, it is formed around two very different models, one of which is not strictly speaking a stage approach at all, but one which shares some "stage" components as I will note. Because of its historical precedence and relative simplicity, I will discuss that latter approach first.

For much of the history of psychological interest in aging, a straightforward biological decline model dominated all other explanations. The characteristics of the model are simple: because of biological, maturational factors, all people differentiate and gain strength in a host of processes that affect psychology as they grow into adulthood; in adulthood those abilities are at their peaks, leading to a period of stable high performance; at some later point—different for different subsystems, but converging by the later years (let us for convenience use 60 and above)—these biological substrates begin to disintegrate, following the path of least resistance toward death. The later years of the life span are inevitably a time of relatively consistent biological decline, which informs and determines declines in virtually every sphere of interest to psychologists (at least as defined by the psychologists of aging)—perception, cognition, motivation, affect, and performance.

It is important to note several aspects of this approach. Although it is overtly concerned with an accumulation of experience and accumulation of effects (of neurological traumas of various degrees, for example) this biological decline model is, in fact, a linear model that shares all but one of the major characteristics ascribed to stage models; it does *not* include a notion of qualitative differentiation of logic across stages and, thus, is not a classic stage model. However, because of the characteristics it does have, it might be labeled a ''quasi-stage'' conception, for it does involve positing a universal, unidirectional process of psychological-behavioral development, based in pan-organic, biologically determined sequences. This process is strongly age-linked and essentially irreversible. Part of natural life is to decline in capacity and ability in a linear way beginning, for the most part, in middle adulthood. Obviously, this position includes the idea of a passive, reactive individual controlled by the kind of quasi-external forces I noted earlier. It is a stage model without psychological content, except as result, and it is as normative and as restrained as other stage models already discussed.

This model in its strong form held sway in the major areas of the psychology of aging for many years and is, in fact, still useful in a range of content areas. Insofar as social processes were assumed to be subsumed under cognitive and perceptual ones (and that seems to have been totally), social psychology, too, was prey to biological decline. This view saw its fruition in the model that emphasized loss of social activity and corresponding increase in interiority with age (Neugarten, 1973). That view was explicated earlier. It should be added that there is no sense of cohort or culture and little sense of individually directed development within this model (it is *universal biological* decline). Methodologically, this was borne out in consistent use of cross-sectional designs, using subjects for the different age groups from wildly varying backgrounds (e.g., college students compared to nursing home residents). This could be comfortably done only if one assumed that virtually anyone (any ''normal'' person) of a particular age adequately represented that one point on a universal, ''externally'' determined trajectory. This assumption, of course, is that same one that has enabled social psychologists to ignore adults for so long.

Because of its methodological ignorance and its clearly overly simple conception of psychology as a slave to biology, this model has declined in popularity over the last several decades, although many examples of exactly this sort of reasoning—and even more of implicit use of designs and interpretations like these without any explicit examination of the assumptions behind that use—can be found in relatively recent work in a variety of areas of psychology of aging.

Its replacement, however, has been an even more explicit stage model, one also firmly rooted in childhood and biology and inclined to consider old age as a decline correspondent to the early-age rise, even though it is superficially very different. This is the cognitive developmental model proposed by Piaget (e.g., 1967) and totally dominant in child psychology of the last several decades. Indeed, many cognitive psychologists of aging have found new life and new direction in this model as they have applied it to aging.

But how new is it? What is implied in Piaget's model is, in fact, not substantially different from what is made more explicit in the cruder biological decline model. That is, according to Piaget, cognitive development is the crucial factor in all other development (including social development, as is most apparent in Kohlberg's 1973 extension of Piaget's model to an intrinsically social activity—moral judgments). Cognitive development, in turn, follows a universal, unidirectional sequence of stages, each embedded in those that preceded it. Although experience and contextual demands are essential to illuminate the inadequacy of one or another kind of cognitive reasoning process, the key determination of progress from one stage to another is, quite simply, ontogenetically programmed, biologically based "readiness." His model, like many others in developmental psychology, stops at emergence into adulthood as the last stage of development, with all afterwards the acting out of the controls of that previous sequence of development combined with how each previous stage had been worked out (see Piaget, 1967). Thus, it has been left to psychologists of aging to extend this perspective. When they have done so, the last stage of life has been conceived of as a decline back to the levels that had preceded it, a recapitulation back through the stages. In fact, this model has, if anything, led to a more specific conception of the decline concept. Not only is decline in a general sense to be expected, but in fact, the process of decline is the mirror image of the process of development (perhaps we should then label it as disdevelopment?). The aging person, it is expected, proceeds through the sequence in reverse fashion until, if he or she lives that long, the individual's cognitive—and therefore all—functioning is that of an infant.

This model in its strong form, that is, emphasizing the mirror image idea, has had its adherents; it has also had its detractors. In particular, many life-span developmentalists have attacked it on two grounds, both of which should be familiar to the reader by this time. Many have pointed out that the universality assumption is untested and may well not be true; they and others have pointed out that the unidirectional assumption also is not well supported. The evidence for the latter is usually the marked improvement in reasoning "stage" brought about in presumably declined older adults by relatively simple training methods and/or situational, contextual designs (see, for example, Labouvie-Vief & Gonda, 1976; and many articles and presentations by Baltes, for example, 1980). It appears that it is possible both to omit stages and to move back and forth between several stages as the task and the situation demand and constrain (Labouvie-Vief & Chandler, 1978).

A third critical point about the Piagetian model of adulthood and aging is related to the tendency to characterize later adulthood cognitive development as a mirror of child development, a decline to follow the rise. This concerns the actual equivalency or lack thereof between two behaviors that have similar surface structures. It appears that many cases of equivalent performances of children and older adults are equivalent only on a surface level that has little to do with either the reasoning processes behind the two acts or the abilities of the actors. Labouvie (1980), Baltes (1980), and others, such as Labouvie-Vief (1977), have discussed this issue in much more depth than can be addressed at this point.

This review has been perhaps too exhaustive as it is, and I will proceed to the main point. It is highly likely that both the personality-psychodynamic stage models of the Chicago aging researchers and others, including virtually all those working on middle adulthood, and the cognitive developmental stage models that have superseded the quasi-continuity biological decline model have several limitations. Both major types show a marked avoidance of dealing with multilinearity of the flow of relation-ships, with a constancy of change much deeper than mere perturbations within a rela-tively steady state, and with self-direction and self-involvement in individual devel-opment, as well as with the influences of historical flow in the larger world.

If the validity of this criticism is even partially accepted, the obvious question, of course, becomes "How will a social psychology of developing adults fit in with the psychology of aging in experimental psychology?" There are several parts to an an-swer to this. First of all, it allows for and indeed demands that attention be paid to change processes, including those of the context; thus, it is aligned with and will complement emphases on the roles of training, familiarization, and natural settings for performance in psychology of aging studies of cognition, perception, and per-formance.

But in another, quite different way, it is necessary, regardless of the sophistication of design and selection of representative contexts that have been offered to psychol-ogy of aging by life-span developmentalists (to be discussed briefly below) as pallia-tives, to emphasize the incompleteness of the psychology of aging in another regard close to the topic of this book. As we have considered in detail throughout this book, social psychology has paid precious little attention to adult development and aging; correspondingly, psychologists concerned with adult development and aging have paid little attention to the area of social psychology. The few studies of social psychological questions (e.g., Klein's 1972 conformity study) have not been pur-sued further than a very superficial level. Rather, the psychology of aging, except for the personality researchers noted earlier, has been heavily invested in the traditional experimental areas of psychology—learning, cognition, perception, psychophysics, and motor performance—while recent events and shifts in funding and social needs have led to a burgeoning clinical geropsychology. The former is well documented by reference to any of the major source books in the psychology of aging (Birren & Schaie, 1977; Botwinick, 1978; Eisdorfer & Lawton, 1973; Poon, 1980—the latter two of which were sponsored by American Psychological Associa-tion task forces on aging), all of which are very lean on social psychological topics. The more recent clinical emphasis is contained in Storandt, Siegler, and Elias (1979).

I am not the first to note this deficit. Birren and Renner (1977), in their relatively recent review of the area, remarked upon the lack of social psychological research and referred to it as one area of potential development. Riegel (1973) delineated nine cluster-areas of the psychology of aging. When he placed them in order of frequency of investigation, the area of "social variables" came in ninth place. Even with that, of course, the category includes much that is social psychology of aging and thus more sociological that psychological, as already discussed in Chapter 13. An edito-rial comment in Poon's (1980) recent volume notes Riegel's categorization, yet the volume has even less emphasis on social psychology than some of the others.

What none of these psychologists has noted or discussed is the reasons for this dis-regard and its persistence. Some of the reasons clearly lie in the experimental nature of the area, an experimentalism that has traditionally seen even "experimental social psychology" as suspect for its "softness." Another part, I believe, lies in the domain distribution issue discussed in detail at several points in this book. *The* social psychology of aging arose within social gerontology, a supposedly interdisiciplinary field that is so dominated by sociologists that it is often considered to be virtually synonymous with the sociology of aging, in which such disciplines as anthropology (Fry, 1979), political science (Binstock, 1972; Pratt, 1979), and economics (Schulz, 1976) have been making significant but peripheral inroads. Once this assignment was made—however that may have been I leave to historians of social science and those who were there at the time to decide—questions of social psychology within gerontology, including the psychology of aging, were assumed and expected to be handled by the social psychology of aging. Psychologists of aging, it appears, have not noted that a more psychological approach might be equally beneficial and more compatible with their own interests.

In any case, I believe this leaves a real vacuum to fill for a social psychology of developing adults and it gives social psychologists of adulthood a challenging point for infusion into the life of the psychology of aging. Just what has been reviewed in this book provides numerous examples of opportunities for cross-fertilization and mutual advancement converging on the problems with which psychologists of aging have traditionally been concerned. For example, the achievement attribution work has clear implications for performance, whether motor, cognitive, or social. It reveals what may be at least part of the basis for the assumed but poorly explained lower motivation levels of older adults when they are participants in performances, especially in psychology laboratories. If older persons perceive themselves in a more failure-oriented manner and know (by consensus, at least) that experimenters, testers, and evaluators have differential images of the causes of the upcoming potential failures, they are likely to perform more poorly, in fact, than they otherwise would and to give at least superficial indications of lack of motivation.

Further, those superficial indications may be no more correct about older persons than they are about test-anxious ones. In both cases there is some evidence than there may in fact be more arousal and "motivation" in both groups, but that the arousal is accompanied by and controlled by a higher anxiety level (Eisdorfer, 1968; Sarason, 1976; Wine, 1971), leading to performance that looks like that of a "normal" person when he or she is not trying very hard. That is, older persons' characteristic center of gravity for attributions may be similar to that of test-anxious persons; their behavior, as discussed in Chapter 8, appears to mimic that of test-anxious younger persons—poorer performance and more distractability when dealing with complex tasks, such as have typically been used to measure "intelligence." An attributional analysis and attribution-based interventions complement and extend the recent psychology of aging approach to the basis—and reversibility—of the differential performances of younger and older persons.

Also related to this perspective is that of self-awareness. As developed in social psychology in the 1970s (e.g., Wicklund & Duval, 1972), self-awareness theory concerns the central role of conscious self-appraisal on performance. In this regard, it would seem to be important to examine the potential that differential use of and reliance upon self-awareness processes may have as a partial explanation of differential performance. This has not yet been pursued, although Banziger (1979) has also pointed out its potential.

Both test anxiety and self-awareness are potentially closely related to the kinds of emphases apparent in the expanded, social context approaches to age differences (for example, Labouvie-Vief, 1977; Labouvie-Vief & Chandler, 1978). The sorts of social mediators that social psychologists have found to be central in social and nonsocial performance can in this way be of benefit to psychologists of aging and can serve as a bridge between their manifestly nonsocial subject matter and the latent socialness that they have been revealing within their cognition studies.

Once again, the point is that the psychology of aging, among other flaws, has ignored cognitive-behavioral social psychology even though that kind of social psychology is both operationally and organizationally closer to it than is the more sociological social psychology of aging. A social psychology of developing adults would naturally involve reliance on the methods and perspectives already current in the psychology of aging and could, thus, be directly and easily applied to issues of concern in that field.

What I am talking about here is more than a simple marriage of social psychology with the psychology of aging. In fact, as I have been discussing, the psychology of aging has often been almost as nondevelopmental as social psychology. Far too often, the behavior of college students has been taken to be a baseline from which deviation (or lack thereof) of older persons may be discovered and analyzed. There has been little sense of the relational aspects of the task and its meanings and there has also been little recognition of the intrinsic meaningfulness of behavior within *each* age group. Late adolescence-young adulthood is no more representative of ''normal'' behavior than any other age, but is simply what it is—a particular point in the life span and life cycle.

This, combined with the narrowness of social psychology in regard to methods and concepts as well as samples, makes it unlikely that a partnership of mainstream social psychology and psychology of aging would be anything more than a modest improvement on the current state of affairs. Although it is true that such a marriage may be progress of a sort—it may lead to the accumulation of information on ''social psychological'' aspects of aging and of being older—it is unlikely to be very developmental or very social psychological in the senses we have considered throughout this book, that is, in a relational, dialectical sense.

No, a simple marriage of most current social psychology and most current psychology of aging is not likely to be productive. The development of a social psychology of developing adults, as outlined in this book, however, may be particularly fruitful. Such an approach is likely to bring together the more developmental, contextual, and change- and relationship-oriented, more relevant groups within each area of interest, an approach which has been initiated in a very modest way in several recent symposia (Blank, 1980, 1981b) and several recent papers (e.g., Schulz & Hanusa, 1980; Banziger, 1979). When that is accomplished the social psychology of developing adults will be much more than a simple marriage of two subgroups in psychology. Rather, it will be an orientation to personality and social processes that involves and surrounds study of a wide range of behaviors and cognitions in an ever-widening universe of cohorts, settings, and habitats, social and cultural milieus, and individuals.

The experimental and laboratory tendencies in both areas, the achronic nature of the models and mechanisms, and the—at best—diachronic investigations of phenomena, the theoretically context-free but in reality severely context-bound nature of the data in both can be transcended by a recognition of the social in *every* behavior which psychologists of aging (or psychologists in general, for that matter) measure *and* the developmental within every individual and every context, the dynamic relationship within every experience.

Fortunately, perspectives similar to this are gaining increasing prominence in the psychology of aging and in developmental psychology of the earlier years. Examples have already been extensively cited; these include Birren and Renner (1977), Baltes (1980; Baltes & Willis, 1977), and Labouvie-Vief (1977; Labouvie-Vief & Chandler, 1978), who have all concentrated on adult development and aging, and Chandler (with Labouvie-Vief, 1978), Bronfenbrenner (1977), and Weisz (1978), who have been more concerned with child development. These developments have paralleled those in social psychology by Gergen (e.g., 1976, 1977, 1978), Smith (1980), and, I hope, myself.

I must make clear what is already likely to be obvious to the reader. The social psychology of adult development and aging will no more cure the ills of the psychology of aging than it will those of personality and social psychology or those of the social psychology of aging and social gerontology. Those ills are deep; in part that means they will be relatively intractable for a long time, even with steadfast effort applied to them. Also, in part, it means that the social psychology of developing adults is only a part of a larger set of alternative models of social behavior and social cognition, with its own imperfections and incompletenesses. What it may be, however, is a fertile ground within which to develop the seedlings; a place for planting the sorts of interrelationships which may, with time (how bound by it we are at every level of our developments) yield two harvests—understanding for the moments we have now and tools to continue to refine, redefine, and reunderstand the meanings of individual development (change and stability) in a developing yet stable world.

LIFE-SPAN DEVELOPMENTAL PSYCHOLOGY

I want to make a few comments about a group I mentioned in passing—those developmental psychologists concentrating on various points in the life-span who, nonetheless, endeavor to understand their subject matter in the perspective of the whole life-span, a group that includes most of those I referred to favorably in the last section. The focus, interests, and approaches of life-span developmentalists correspond at many points with what I have been calling a social psychology of developing adults. In many ways, in fact, this social psychology is an extension of the life-span approach to social questions, for, like the psychology of aging from which the adult developmentalists among the group have arisen, life-span developmental psychology has shown disappointingly—and surprisingly—little concern for central social psychology questions even as it has faced up to the inherently social issues of cohort, context, and the ecologies of behavior. Thus, one difference is only a difference until the subject matter is extended.

There is, however, another point of lack of correspondence in the interstice between a social psychology of developing adults as proposed here and current life-span developmental psychology. These concerns relate to methodological emphases; they have been voiced much earlier in the book (especially Chapter 2). The field that goes by the name of life-span developmental psychology has been highly determined and, in my view, constricted by the great deal of emphasis placed upon the necessity—not merely the advisability—of costly, complex methodological designs and the corresponding rejection of all lesser sorts of investigations. Because these issues have been raised and considered already, I will not proceed further on that path at this time. In any event, I think that it is obvious that a social psychology of developing adults will indeed share many goals and conceptual bases with life-span developmental psychology, even though it may part from it in a few crucial points.

TWO OTHER AREAS: ENVIRONMENTAL PSYCHOLOGY AND FAMILY STUDIES

Other areas of interest to psychologists and other social scientists will also stand to gain from the development and existence of a social psychology of developing adults. As illustrations I will briefly discuss two additional areas. Unlike the ones discussed previously in this chapter, these have been concerned neither with development nor with a cognitive-behavioral social psychology.

Environmental Psychology

As I have already mentioned in Chapter 9, environmental psychology is an area of psychology that has been growing and becoming established as a relatively distinct field within psychology. Within it are at least two differentiable kinds of investigations surrounding the common core concern with the importance of the Environmental part of Lewin's (1935) formulation, "Behavior is a function of Person and Environment" and upon the interactive aspect of that formulation (see Howard, 1979, and others for discussion of the nature of that interactive aspect).

One of those areas, roughly aligned with ecological psychology (Barker, 1968; Barker & associates, 1977; Wicker, 1979) and focused on the influence of behavior settings is, of course, fairly closely and directly associated with social psychology (as discussed in Part 3). The value of a social psychology of developing adults to this sort of research and theory has already been discussed. As persons age, their mobility, strength, and perceptual abilities are likely to go through a systematic process of change, often resulting in a dulling or lessening of overall environmental control. In turn, this is accompanied by—and constrained by—global changes in the environmental backdrop with which the person is concerned (either by aging of the current place or by transition to new environments). As also discussed previously, the net effect of those interacting processes is the stark reality of the importance of relatively minor characteristics of the environment as affecting social behavior. Some environmental psychologists have recognized environmental psychology of adult development and aging as a particularly productive area in which to examine general principles of environmental influences (e.g., Moos, 1976), since it brings to the surface the complex role of relationships that must be dealt with when flux and change are the rule in both persons and environments.

For example, biological changes are determinants of interaction, as when hardness of hearing leads to misunderstanding in an exchange with a store clerk; misunderstanding that may in turn lead to anger, frustration, and differential, discriminatory treatment not only in regard to the target interactant, but also to succeeding customers. That is, the interaction can form—or verify—negative stereotypes about the entire set of customers that share an obvious characteristic—chronological age—with the one now labeled as a "problem." (Of course, the "problem" is in the interaction, the relationship, not in either of the interactants, but the perceived —phenomenological—problem is not less real because of that.) At the same time, biological changes can quite literally also be directed by physical environments, as when a barrier-ridden environment leads to either strain and injury or atrophy, depending on inner psychological characteristics of individuals and their significant others. Thus, a social psychology of developing adults will combine forces with an environmental-ecological psychology to explore and delineate Person × Environment relationships as both "elements" change and age. In that way, the potential for revealing principles that underlie behavior setting use and influence of that use on social life will be maximized.

The other kind of environmental psychology will also be enriched, although less directly, by a social psychology of developing adults. Attention to that social psychology may bring together two groups of cognitively oriented psychologists. As mentioned earlier, psychology of aging has been heavily cognitive, as has the second main approach to environmental psychology, that of environmental perception and cognition (see Moore & Golledge, 1976, for a collection of readings in that approach). Again, as above, environmental cognitions in older persons may be a particularly effective demonstration of the wider relational principles of individual to environment and of the presumed practical side of environmental cognition—that persons with more differentiated and more "objectively correct" cognitive representations of the environment with which they must interact are more successful at those interactions. The few pieces of research done with older persons (a study mentioned by Porteous, 1977, and Hildner's pilot study discussed earlier) indicate that age (or cohort) may adversely affect cognitive ability, but this proposition has not been put to adequate test at this time.

If a relationship is found, it can be combined with other findings of the relationship of age to speed of information-processing, reaction time, and memory (as discussed in Birren & Schaie, 1977; and Poon, 1980) to reveal the potential impacts of those factors on environmental cognition in its broadest sense and across all populations.

Although that research is not intrinsically social psychological, it arises from and feeds into the environmental-ecological concerns noted above and detailed in Part 3.

How is that the case? A tenet of environmental cognition theory is that the utilization of cognitive maps and environmental knowledge allow the individual to have an "automatic pilot" guiding locomotion so that he or she can be freed to pay attention to other aspects of the environment. These other aspects, obviously, include many social elements and events. In other words, cognitive maps allow one to pay attention to changing characteristics of the environment; only deviation from "normalcy" of the more stable elements will require attention. If that thesis has validity—and it is a basic tenet of environmental cognition—then the lack of correspondence between an internal representation and the physical reality or an inability to form, store, and/or retrieve correct representations will adversely affect the ability to pay attention to the irregular, nonphysical environment. The latter, of course, is the particular locus of changing social cues and social presences. Impairment in cognitive map use, added to the more barrier-laden nature of *any* environment for a person with mobility or perceptual problems, will have an obvious adverse effect on the social psychology of those with deficits and those who interact with them. I need not remind you that the latter group includes all of us at the present, and the former group will, if we live long enough, eventually include all of us.

The interplay of cognitive and social individual changes, changes in the environment itself, and changes in social definitions of proper inhabitants and proper behavior is an intrinsically life-span, inherently social psychological relationship. A correspondence of interests in adult development and aging and the environmental cognition part of environmental psychology can enrich knowledge of environmental relationships of all ages and can point to the value of both environmental cognition and social psychological studies in the psychology of aging.

Family Studies

Within sociology, the subdiscipline of marriage and the family has by necessity included a life-span perspective (see, for example, Adams, 1970; or Framo, 1979). Marital and family therapists deal regularly with couples at various points in the life cycle and, in fact, family therapies are, of course, intrinsically intergenerational. Thus, there is a history of interest in adult development in these areas. Further, family therapists do not make the "fundamental attribution error" of overattribution to individual dispositions that many social psychologists (and especially personality psychologists) often make. Rather, they are likely to look for the problem—and for its ultimate solution—in the interactions between and among individuals. That is, they are relationists about social behavior.

Yet in many ways family studies and family therapy have been like the social psychology of aging vis-à-vis social psychology, especially psychological social psychology. That is, there has been little opportunity for conflict *or* cooperation, because there has been virtually no interaction (see Framo, 1979, for an excellent discussion of this point by a family therapist offering to social psychologists the knowledge gained—and the process, change-oriented models and methods used to gather and integrate the knowledge—from family studies).

As with many other areas we have considered, a social psychology of developing adults will not immediately wed the several disciplines and areas of interest. What it can do, however, is become a meeting place between scientific psychological social psychology and its less science-oriented and/or more practical counterparts. The family of middle-aged and older adults is an exciting venue for truly relational, process-oriented social psychology to flourish.

I will give only one speculative example, linked to an empirical research program focused on early adult marital relations, and I will briefly discuss how an expansion of that to include late marital relations, especially in light of retirement of one or both partners, could yield a variety of useful data that are unlikely to be revealed as long as a social psychology of developing adults does not exist.

The development and change of the marital dyad over long periods of time has seldom been directly explored; the impact of retirement of one or both parties on the quality of that relationship has been even less adequately considered. I make the latter statement even though there have been a number of studies that have been labeled as focused on marital relationships of retired couples and/or across retirement (Dressler, 1973; Kerckhoff, 1966). But those studies have been what I have been discussing as typical social psychology of aging. That is, analysis has been done on survey and self-report data on satisfaction and quality of adjustment, not on actual patterns of change and/or stability in marital communication. I leave undiscussed the tendency to equate retirement for couples with adjustment by both a man and his *house*wife to *his* retirement. The studies have been cross-sectional, with comparative data limited to current accounts on the one hand and retrospections of preretirement on the other. Needless to say, these restrictions in design and data-gathering, common though they are to the social psychology of aging (and psychology of aging) are likely to limit, constrain, and bias the data in ways that are troublesome, to say the least.

Fortunately, a research program developed in marriage and family studies may enable us to look at the level of analysis of dyadic interaction from a perspective in many ways similar to the approach that might be taken by a social psychologist of developing adults interested in using a cognitive-behavioral approach to understanding marital relationships and marital communication in later adult development. In the early 1970s Rausch, Barry, Hertel, and Swain (1974) conducted an extensive longitudinal study of couples as they proceeded from engagement to several years later, by which time many couples had had their first child. The investigation was a fascinating mix of methods and approaches, including extensive interviews, gathering of extensive background and demographic information, keeping of diaries of interactions, and a complex set of role-playing situations that were likely to include conflict. The participants were taped during the role-playing and their interactions later analyzed using Bales-type categorizations. For example, couples acted out a situation in which both had privately and individually (and irrevocably) made extensive but diametrically opposed plans for spending their first anniversary.

This mix of methods and variety of data are important elements of an analysis of marital relations as they may be affected by retirement. The kind of research program that could be carried out would include observation of naturalistic and quasi-naturalistic behavior, self-report on satisfaction, self- and other-perception analysis (similar perhaps to the model developed by Laing, Phillipson, & Lee, 1968, to aid in therapy with couples), and diary-keeping about emotions and relationships. All of this would be gathered across a period of time—say, two or three years—that spans retirement as it normally occurs. Comparisons to couples of similar ages, neither of which is retired, and to couples that had retired before regular retirement age would provide the necessary information to separate age (of individuals *and* of the relationship) effects from effects of retirement. Other transitions, of course, could also be used as comparisons.

This is merely one sketchy illustration of how the perspective of marital therapy and family studies may enrich and be enriched by a focus upon adult development and aging and on social psychology as a cognitive-behavioral complex of relationships. Again, as with other areas, the goal is understanding the relationships in and of themselves, rather than merely as representatives of static elements in a stable, statistically ordered interaction.

CHAPTER 15

Chronicity, Time, and Relationships: Submerging Personality and Social Psychology in the Cold Bath of Real Lives

Throughout this book I have been trying to establish the groundwork for a social psychology of developing adults. I see this kind of social psychology as both an alternative to and an extension of areas of research and theory within social psychology and developmental studies.

Such a task is obviously a major one; it has similarities to perspectives that have been and are being developed by social psychologists such as Kenneth Gergen (e.g., 1978), Paul Secord (1976), and Brewster Smith (1980); adult developmentalists such as Gisela Labouvie-Vief (1977), Paul Baltes (1980; Baltes & Willis, 1977), Orville Brim (1979), and Klaus Riegel (1976, 1977); child developmentalists such as Urie Bronfenbrenner (1977); and others within psychology and sociology (Buss, 1979; Jahoda, 1976). All those approaches and the one proposed here place much more emphasis on the interactive, multilinear, intrinsically relational nature of a wide variety of human behaviors and thoughts than has traditionally been done within psychology, in particular social psychology.

Toward this goal, I began the book with (and later returned to) a litany of flaws in the social and developmental fields central to a social psychological approach to developing adults. Some of these critical comments were directed to social psychology as it has developed in the last several generations. There are few studies of adults of any type in social psychology, which instead has had a marked preference for the period of late adolescence and entry into that hypothetical state of adulthood. There have been fewer still that have been truly adult-oriented and truly developmental. Instead, when studies have concerned adults, they often used a non-natural captive population to study—prisoners and the like—and they have in any event been synchronic tests of propositions about static mechanisms. Both the concept of development—the interplay of change and stability—and the centrality and indivisibility of relationships have been sidestepped in favor of agelessness or a simplistic positing of age group membership as a causal factor in age differences.

The concerns raised in the early part of the book were expanded in Chapter 12 to include the identification and consideration of several distinct types of social psychology—cognitive-behavioral (psychological), social structural (sociological), and social issues (applied). Each was examined to reveal its own set of flaws and crises, with a relatively idiosyncratic set of remedies that have been proposed. I asserted both that a social psychology of developing adults could and would produce reasonable and operationalizable answers to many of those type-based problems; and that a social psychology of developing adults could lead to a unification (or at least coordination) of interests, since all of them share a nondevelopmental perspective in both the traditional type and the solutions proposed to answer that type's crisis.

Social psychology was not the only discipline that has had a lack and an incompleteness in regard to a social psychology of developing adults. I pointed out and detailed how there is little social psychology in any of the various subdisciplines concerned with adult development and aging. Especially in Chapters 13 and 14 I detailed how even a field called the social psychology of aging has ignored social psychology as most (psychological) social psychologists define it. Instead, the social psychology of aging, as part of the sociological subfield of social gerontology, has perseverated on the dual obsessions of social geronotology—role performance and adjustment. The former has externalized and structuralized the bases of action, divorcing them from the individual and his or her intentions, motivations, and idiosyncracies; the latter has abetted that anti-individualism by stressing, not any positive aspects to personality direction and involvement in social behavior, but a passive, hapless reactor to the buffetings of biology and society. I explored reasons for and effects of such a set of perseverations. In particular, it is important to see how such a model is developmental only in a superficial sense; it leaves little room for individual change and, indeed, for social change.

Similar issues were raised in terms of psychology of aging. In particular, both personality psychology of adult development and, in a very different but no less pervasive way, cognitive and "experimental" psychology of aging are bound to models of development that take descriptive generalizations and make them normative, universalistic statements about strictly sequenced stages of development or linear processes of biological growth and decline. This makes them less than compatible with a social psychology of developing adults rooted in a dialectical or at least interactive conception of development at both the individual and the social level. Certain domain distribution matters, in turn, keep the psychology of aging almost completely nonsocial in orientation and subject matter.

One extremely promising area of developmental psychology, that which usually goes by the name of "life-span developmental psychology," too, has by and large ignored social psychological questions. At least part of the reason for that is, in fact, a major obstacle to a social psychology of adult development within the conceptually sophisticated, truly developmental area of life-span developmental psychology—the rigid methodological shibboleths that are placed before he (or she) who would enter therein. Legitimacy is defined by adherence to designs that, to be sure, are major advances over the potentially dreadfully misleading achronic, synchronic, and diachronic models predominant in most areas of developmental psychology and likely to be predominant in a social psychology of adult development for some time to come. Many life-span developmentalists totally spurn anything less than sequential designs. For example, Riegel (1977) concludes that the weaknesses he sees do "nothing less than invalidate all the developmental data reported in the literature" (p. 71). Baltes et al. (1977) state unequivocally that "both the simple cross-sectional and longitudinal methods show such a lack of necessary control that the data collected by application of either of them are for the most part of little validity and little use to the developmental researcher" (p. 124). I tried to deal with those concerns in Chapter 2 and at other points throughout the book, but I explained why such rigor as a *sine qua non* dooms social psychologists to proceed without any developmental sense and without being able to produce data relevant to developmental concerns they might have.

INCOMPLETENESS, IMPERFECTION, AND RELATIONSHIPS

Yes, portions of the book were a litany of shortcomings, but I hope the totality is much more than that. Perhaps a major point of this book is that incompleteness and imperfection are part and parcel of social psychology in both its scientific and its phenomenological senses. There is an inherent incompleteness and imperfection in relationships, but there is greater incompleteness and imperfection in avoidance of relationships.

The several social psychologies are, to be sure, in uneasy relationships—when there are any at all—with each other. Each has its severe limitations on several levels: conceptual, theoretical, methodological, and explanatory. Critics within each have exhaustively described the incompleteness and imperfection within that area of concern. For direction out of the morass, they have turned to aspects that another social psychology has been concerned with and, usually, found wanting in its own right. Yet there is an avoidance of meaningful relationships, replete with fears of dissolution or dissipation (*American Sociologist*, 1977). Although there have certainly been a steady stream of boundary-crossers (Wilson & Schafer, 1978; Newcomb, 1979), times of active relating are uncommon enough to be noteworthy and at the same time to be rather easily ignored by the bulk of each respective field. Since integration and even interpenetration are not likely to be easy (given, for example, the amount of reading to do to remain current even in cloistered little areas and the organizational barriers laid in the paths to the bridges) and are not going to be won without giving up something dear to each—the parochial belief that you have found the truth and now only need to work out the specifics, within the assumptions your parochialism carries with it—the tendency has been to retreat back to parochialism at the earliest opportunity. Ethnocentrism is no stranger to social psychology, certainly.

But all social psychologists seem to get together on at least one point, and that is their common ignoring of adult development and aging, another sort of incompleteness and imperfection. Social psychologists, at least those not happy with the status quo, yearn for an understanding of process and for the mechanisms toward that end, and yet they spurn the rigors that will be demanded of them if they try to think developmentally (remember Thorngate's [1976] trenchant comment that such studies are "fiendishly difficult" and "dreadfully boring"). Yet it is clear that such an emphasis on developmentalism across the whole span of life, on the interplay of individual and cultural history as individuals become and maintain themselves as social beings, is potentially a real ally in the search for more relevant, more social, more living social psychologizing.

Adult development and aging, too, is suffused with incompleteness and imperfection. There has been little that is social, at least in the sense most social psychologists mean that; instead, there has been perseveration on personality and adjustment, on stages, and on the externalized determinants of social life. I tried to discuss those incompletenesses and imperfections as fully as I did those of social psychology. As with social psychology, there are promising voices, promising yearnings within those who consider their area of interest to be adult development and/or aging. There are voices calling for a recognition of relationships—of behavior and context, of individual to social in a truly active sense, of thought to action, of social context to the inner contexts of being social. Social psychology in general, and a social psychology of developing adults in particular, can "fulfill" some of these incompletenesses and imperfections. Similar concerns were voiced and considered in other areas and aspects of psychology—environmental issues, marital relations, cognitive psychology of aging.

Suffusing all, then, is the lack of relationships. I think part of the cause for this is the fear of what will be revealed in relationships among various disciplines, just as fear of what relationships mean in real life lead some to avoid the depth that a relationship can provide. What is it that will be revealed when relationships are established and worked at? It is the constancy of imperfection and incompleteness. All will not be well, if we merely establish this or that relationship; certainly, all will not be well if we try to act as though a relationship, once formed, simply remains, a pristine object of affection. We try to avoid the frightening notion that there is no center, no stable core, whether that be society or the individual's psychodynamic or biological "state" or environmental contingencies of reinforcement. Relationships can be frightening, more frightening than living with half-truths and incomplete models and methods. The latter allow one to believe that there are whole truths somewhere, that methods can be perfected, that science can proceed in the way it *must*, by accumulating facts, piecing them together with hypotheses and theories, and then gathering more facts to be *sure*. But the former—relationships—are intrinsically dialectical; they are in and of themselves imperfect and incomplete, and yet they are the deepest veins of life, of social psychology, of development. The cardinal stable element is change. Order is made, not given; created, not revealed. It is precarious.

With this as the best we can hope for—to be forever suspended above incompleteness and imperfection, to be incomplete and imperfect—it is not surprising that we pull back from the moment of revelation. It is easier to transform the coreless relationship to an ontology of structure, of universal mechanisms; the only choice then becomes which reductionism to pursue, that of atomistic biology or that of social structure and culture.

This fear and avoidance in the social sciences that border on a social psychology of developing adults is but a mirror image of what is often the case in social psychology itself, that is, in people living as part of society and interacting with other persons. There, too, relationships are often avoided. The object of social psychology, when not an object but a phenomenon of life, is often a process of avoiding the fear-producing reality of change and instability, of trying to overcome the incompleteness and imperfection of every relationship by transforming it to a soothing set of constants. Relationships between individuals at the most intimate levels become—are safer as—marriages of convenience, where little is said because little is listened for by either party. The messiness of life is avoided by building little shells instead of real relationships. It is here, perhaps, that the role model of social psychology is at its acme of descriptive power, for it describes well the externalization of relationships that makes them seem less incomplete and imperfect (and makes them become less real).

I believe the challenge of a social psychology of developing adults is to be a source of discussion about the changing relationships of social life instead of a process of submerging them, disemboweling them, objectifying them. It must be that at every level we must teach ourselves as social psychologists, as adult developmentalists, as gerontologists, as basic researchers and as practitioners applying what we know, and, most important, as persons ourselves, to be unafraid of change, of constructing reality instead of finding it, of *relating* to each other. We can work toward models and we can come up with evidence for them—tricky though that may be, given what it is we are really studying. We can discover and relate more fully to each others' disciplines, as both stronger and weaker than those we were taught to be a part of. We can proceed unafraid of the ultimate incompleteness and imperfection and, I believe, without worrying as to whether that means we are no longer scientific or no longer based in the concrete data of life. As Gergen (1978a) also has argued, we are not abandoning science or explanation or even experimentation, but we are abandoning a blind belief in any of them as universal, as *true* and nothing else. Every task of science, of hypothesis-testing by gathering empirical data, of building theories both inductively and deductively, is *both* true and false; it is a relationship. The only order we "reveal" is the order we *must* find—for now.

To teach ourselves and others, as individuals in society, as individuals relating, to be willing to get into relationships with the knowledge we are and they are and will always be incomplete and imperfect; to work to construct, reconstruct, and sometimes to destroy our realities, our stabilities, our order is not an easy task. It is not one to be taken lightly. But it is intrinsically social, intrinsically developmental, intrinsically life-spanning. It can be therapeutic for all ages.

It is obvious, I hope, that this is not to say—in fact, it is the opposite of saying—that the social psychology of developing adults is an endpoint of social psychology. Rather, it is the freedom that can come from the recognition of no endpoint. Certainly, the data presented here are not an endpoint in any sense of the term, even if one does not deny the concept of endpoints. But I believe those data are an indication that development is everywhere; that "stable" aspects like roles and norms, age groupings, and personality types affect social cognition, self-perception, and use of environments to fulfill social and nonsocial ends. Age brings with it change, and we bring to both of those a stability we build, that is us.

Certainly, little I am saying is new, not even within social psychology and certainly not within social science in general. It is the core of dialectical analysis, the core of ethnomethodology and symbolic interaction and of many other social scientific and philosophical approaches to the meaning of being a social person. But I feel this is time for a new emphasis on the intrinsic development of all of this that is not always apparent in those other approaches and on the merging of those approaches—incompletenesses and imperfections themselves—with more traditional social psychological approaches and models (e.g., modified traditional perspectives that include universality and openness to broader investigations, such as Greenwald [1976] Manis [1975] and Schlenker [1974]). For, dialectically, the recognition of constant change and social/self construction of life must go hand in hand with the recognition of stability in society and in individuals. I hope this book can be one piece in a coalition of forces toward the goal of understanding being social throughout time.

I have tried to speak in the early chapters in general terms about a sort of social psychology that is accepting and eager to examine adults and adult issues—but not merely that; one that is sensitive to the development of the individual—but not merely that; one that is sensitive to social and physical contexts and the changing background they give to life—but not merely that. I have tried for a social psychology of developing adults. I have tried to see that stability is in change and vice versa; that they in fact do not coexist, but are part of one fabric. I hope a social psychology of developing adults will transcend age-less-ness and age-bound-ness, the hallmarks of all the areas of interest I considered.

I tried not only to talk about these approaches, but to give examples of doing them, of the few links that exist. I discussed in detail two disparate research programs I have been directing. One is identified with cognitive social psychology as it has become a central focus of mainstream psychological social psychology, whereas the other is within a more behavioral, ecological part of the broader area of social psychology. I discussed these and work of others identified as social psychologists, environmental psychologists, psychologists of aging, and social gerontologists. They are attempts at least to take age and/or change into account.

A striking and sobering characteristic of work others and I have done has been apparent in those discussions. As we proceeded to actual studies, we lost much of the emphases and many of the strengths of a developed social psychology of developing adults. That is a risk I feel is necessary—to begin somewhere, even if those attempts are crude in and of themselves and dangerously synchronic thus far. They are meant to be examples of where we are, not polished images of where we should be (where, of course, we will—can—never be).

Much of the data portion of the book and, even more so, the latter section, is purely speculative at this point. I am trying to delineate what to aim for and to give at least some examples of what it may be worthwhile to do if you, the readers, agree that a social psychology of developing adults can be a useful addition to the particular incompletenesses and imperfections that now exist. This book, obviously, will *only* be successful if and insofar as you who read it can use it as a base, a beginning, and can go beyond it conceptually, theoretically, and, particularly, empirically.

Social psychology must be open to a multitude of methods; it must be open to questions about change and development, to assumptions other than its intra-individual mechanistic base if it is to be truly practical and useful, if it is to make and keep important connections with other disciplines concerned with individuals living in society, doing and receiving social acts, conceiving of themselves as social creatures, and the like. One path—not an end—is a social psychology of developing adults.

Appendix

Coding and
Categorizing
Attributions and Affects

Anyone who conducts a social scientific endeavor must try to satisfy twin gods of value and validity who have competing demands. On the one hand, the researcher wishes to gather knowledge that is valuable as a real indicator of actual, natural social cognitions and social behaviors. On the other hand, he or she also must satisfy a second *sine qua non*, one less concerned with external values of naturalness and more concerned with amenability to interpretation of hypotheses that have been advanced for testing. That is, the researcher must tread a line between maximum usefulness of the data as social psychological indicators of reality and maximum usefulness as tests of inductively developed notions of social psychological mechanisms.

These issues, under labels of internal and external validity, or validity and generalizability, or representative design and experimental precision, have been debated and analyzed far beyond the capabilities of this author or the needs of this particular section; excellent sources include Campbell and Stanley's (1966) classic work and Selttiz, Wrightsman, and Cook (1977), among many. Some authors, particularly in many introductory texts, make arguments framed in "either-or," "one *versus* the other" terms and seek to make a hierarchical arrangement of primary usefulness—what is "really" basic and what is only secondarily important. Others, including those just cited, have stressed that both are crucial, that the researcher must not abandon one god for the other, for both are wrathful and vengeful and will wreak havoc on later usefulness of the data if not attended to sufficiently. The researcher must consistently be mindful and take care to constantly balance the sometimes conflicting judgments that follow from the two gods. Ultimately, both types of argument are resolved under the rubric of usefulness, but the synthesis is always precarious and illusive and requires limited—and limiting—decisions at every choice point.

The data-gathering methods for the set of attribution studies that form Part 2 of the body of this book provide much information on the difficulty of charting a path that has the potential to placate both of the twins. This appendix is in main part a step-by-step discussion of the development of gathering and analyzing free responses concerning attributions as an illustration of what I hope is increasing methodological usefulness at each step.

As I discuss in the body of the book, it is important to adequate understanding of the effects of success and failure on persons of widely varying personal characteristics concerned with a wide variety of experiences and situations to gather data in such a way as to reflect the richness and variety of attributional thought by allowing maximum latitude to subjects for response choice of attributions and affects. As Elig and Frieze (1975) noted, the emphasis on richness and wide latitude, always of value in attribution research, is especially crucial when exploring new avenues of type of attributor and type of situation (but also see Elig & Frieze, 1979); both of those "novelties" are involved in these studies.

Thus, I had persons respond to both personal (Type II) and nonpersonal (Type I) situations as described in the text, by simply writing down the cause(s) and affect(s) they felt were likely to be of importance in the situation. As a result, some subjects regularly reported only one attribution and/or affect; others gave three or four of each. Of course, there was also considerable variation within persons for the different situations. The subjects were given as little direction as possible concerning "proper" categories to use. Rather, they filled out a sample question (see page 1 of the attachment to this appendix, the questionnaire form for study of attributions). Their choices for that question were read over by the experimenter prior to having the subject proceed with the questionnaire itself. In this way, we insured that the subject understood the format and was responding by listing both causes and affects without forcing our dimensions upon the respondent. A similar format was used for eliciting self-relevant situational responses, with the addition that in those cases subjects were also free to choose a particular experienced situation to fit a general category; four questions crossed a dimension of high or low "importance" with success or failure, whereas the four other questions were more specifically directed to a dimension of "social" or "nonsocial" activities with success and failure.

Although I feel strongly that this approach has real advantages and provides richness, depth, and a greater degree of naturalness to the task, it, of course, has attendant problems in satisfying the second god of social psychological research—amenability to interpretation and usefulness for hypothesis testing. The rich data are analyzable in some ways, to be sure; but for most traditional analyses, especially for hypothesis testing, they must be reduced. A multistage process, allowing for data from its raw richness through intermediate levels of abstraction to categorization into dichotomous classification, seems most effective and was pursued. Even as I proceed with description of that procedure, I wish to instill in the reader a recognition of the laborious, time-consuming nature of such a process. I will, in fact, point out dead-ends as well as what I feel to be fairly successful resolutions. This appendix is concerned with data reduction itself; specific methods of data-gathering are discussed in the body of the book.

The coding team for all types and stages of categorization were myself and two research assistants, Cindy Piedimonte and Joyce Burr. As noted below, at times we worked independently, and at other times we worked as a team.

A similar process was used for both causes and affects reported; I will explain the process for attribution—cause—coding in detail first and then more briefly enumerate the levels of abstraction used for affects. The results of both processes should and can be fruitfully compared to other free attribution and/or free affect coding schemes (Davitz, 1969; Elig & Frieze, 1975; Cooper & Burger, 1980; Weiner, Russell, &

Lerman, 1978); this and each of the others has strengths and weaknesses, although I feel the categorization used here may be more widely applicable across situations, types of actors, and types of attributors than others have been. The reader must judge that for himself or herself.

I should point out one other fact about the categories that have resulted from these analyses. It will be obvious to the careful reader that many decisions resolved in a particular way are really amenable to one or more other, equally adequate, solutions. The reader must also decide between the opposing goals of fitting to a generalized model or developing a specific one tailor-made to a particular situation and design. I have tried to emphasize the nonspecific, general end of the spectrum of possibilities by having relatively broad, relatively inclusive (and thus, relatively diffuse) sets of categories.

CODING ATTRIBUTIONS: FROM MESSY FREEDOM TO CONSTRAINED ORDER

Each cause that a person listed was evaluated in several ways.[1] The first step was placement of the word or phrase into a set of causal categories. The set was based on previous taxonomies (e.g., Elig & Frieze, 1975; Weiner et al., 1978), but it was an expanding set. That is, we began with approximately 15 categories used by other researchers, expanding some too-specific ones, such as the category of "teacher's activities" used by Cooper and Burger (1980) in their analysis of teacher attributions for student success and failure, into broader categories. In the case of that particular category, we developed several categories concerned with the involvement of other persons in the success or failure—"other's intentional help or hurt," "other's personalities and interests," and "ability of those in a position of control to recognize one's value." Some of these categories had been used before, but since we were striving to develop a set that is broadly applicable across type of actor and type of situation, we were as inclusive as we could be—making a separate category for any causal statement that was not clearly subsumed in an already existent category—and as sensitive as possible to nuances—dividing a previously used category into two more precise ones when appropriate. Of course, more than one word or phrase is represented by almost every category, since some clustering is inevitable to avoid an almost infinite and extremely overlapping category set. To aid in clustering we relied on both other researchers' classifications (cited above) and *Roget's Thesaurus*

---

[1] As previously discussed, some subjects typically gave more than one cause, although only in rare instances were more than three given. At this stage, *each* attribution was separately analyzed, whether or not it stood alone or was given as part of a set for a particular situation. As noted below, at later stages of analysis multiple responses were "averaged" to get one score for each subject for each question. The significance of the lack of independence inherent in composite scores, and the different meaning accorded to a particular response by a subject when it is the *only* one noted compared to when it is part of a list, is beyond the scope of this section, or, indeed, this set of studies, although it is obviously an important question to pursue. Some additional discussion of the issue, however, is contained in a later section of the Appendix and in Chapter 7. Full consideration must await further, more directly focused research enterprises.

(Dutch, 1965) as guides for determining what synonyms or near synonyms would be given the same category designation.

Most of the process of developing categories outlined above took place during practice coding of pretest responses, although in several cases it became apparent only at the time of analysis of study responses that an additional category was required, that one ''cluster'' should be split into two. We then added a category, even though this necessitated a ''second pass'' through data from those that had already been coded. In this way, our finished classification scheme included 28 discrete causes.

Clearly, this process is both laborious and fraught with problems. If one has too broad a set of categories, legitimately synonymous responses are splintered, making analysis exceedingly vague and uncentered; if, however, one uses too narrow a set of categories, then the nuances of a causal ascription are lost. The reader must ultimately be the judge of course, although later stages of dimensionalizing the data are certainly facilitated by any scheme that begins with a broad set that can be combined or divided again as needed. Indeed, the presence of a broad set of categories available enables researchers who disagree with placement of a particular factor on a dimension (as discussed below) to reassign the cause and reanalyze the data.

The categories, including a representative selection of the set of words or phrases that were placed into each, are as follows: (the italicized word or phrase is the ''short title,'' by which it will be referred to in the remainder of the Appendix and in the body of the book):

01   General *ability,* capable/incapable, competent

02   Specific ability, *skill,* knowledge, ''good at that sort of thing''

03   *Personality,* personal characteristics (e.g., reliable, nice person)

04   *Stable effort*—hard worker, always tries

05   *Will power,* determination

06   *Physical* factors, *not age*—weakness or strength, agility, ''looks''

07   Physical factors, *age-related*

08   Poor/good *self-image,* confidence, overconfidence, fear

09   *Experience* or lack of experience, training/lack of training

10   Intrinsic motives, *interest,* task orientation

11   *Mood,* ''bad day''

12   Transitory, *specific effort*/lack of effort or concentration

13   *Task* ease or difficulty, ''hunk of junk'' syndrome

14   Extrinsic motives, *impersonal structures*

15   *Luck,* random factors

16   *Undefined external* situation

17   Ability of *others' competing* with

18   Ability of *others' cooperating* with

19   *Others' help or hurt* (intentional), prejudice

20   *Others' motives,* orientation to the task

21   *Others' personalities,* interests

22   Ability/inability of those who are in supervisory role to recognize "value," *supervisor judgments*

23   *Others' help or hurt* (unintentional), an oversight

24   *Proper*/improper *tools* or program

25   *Other activities interfered,* low priority, or other activities helped along

26   *Ability* (skill) *by Task* interaction (includes Personality × Task)

27   *Ability interaction with* characteristics or ability of *others*

28   *Personality interaction*/conflict with others, common interests

Some analysis was done on the basis of this large set of categories, although for most purposes a reduction in number of categories by a process of clustering proved to be more appropriate.

Before discussing the next step of data reduction of causes, I should mention and discuss a coordinate coding scheme we began to use and later rejected. Most researchers have proceeded directly from a set of causal categories to dimensionalizing the responses themselves. That is, "effort" was considered to be a representative of "personal" and "unstable" poles of those dimensions, task difficulty as "extrapersonal" and "stable," and so on. We tried to proceed to dimensional classification at the initial coding stage, with "independence" of causal category placement from that classification. That is, we rated each causal word or phrase on a five-step "stability" scale (from "1" equaling "very stable" to "5" equaling "very unstable") and a threefold location scale (internal, mutual or uncertain, external). In particular, we felt the dimensionalization of stability was an important step beyond other conceptualizations, since it allowed for extremity as well as direction of stability. Such capacity would be expected to be especially valuable when considering a developmental approach and/or a processual, progressive one.

Enlightened though such an approach may or may not be, we were not able to reach reasonable agreement on extremity (choice between "very stable" and "tending toward stability," for example), and we abandoned that dimension at the analysis stage. In fact, we found that it is virtually impossible to make decisions on both location and stability independently from decisions on categorization of the cause itself, and I would recommend eliminating the effort involved in trying to do this separately. Rather, it is preferable to code into causal categories only as the first step and later to reduce each of those to a specific place on each dimension as, indeed, all other researchers have done.

When this is done, the reader may protest, information is lost. Indeed, that is so; ability, effort (as Weiner, 1972, found after trying to classify it as only unstable), and virtually all of the other specific causes can *mean* different levels of stability and location to different individuals and/or for different situations. Although those points are perfectly valid and important (and I attempted to deal with them by different data-gathering methods, as described in Chapter 7), the point of loss of information is inherent in any data-gathering technique, with the possible exception of detailed probing after each causal ascription. Thus, the data, even free responses, when written succinctly, are already ambiguous and imprecise. They are not made less so by retrospective fitting into a complex classification scheme. Instead, when a word, such as "effort" clearly sometimes has modifiers or contexts that made it clear that a stable characteristic was meant and other times had modifiers and contexts indicating instability, two causal categories were made. Such was the case not only with effort, but also with "interest" (in the sense of mood or attention [unstable] and in the sense of intrinsic motivation [stable]) and for physical factors (stable disability versus unstable injury or illness). This approach is merely the application of the general attempt to be inclusive in categorization.

Categories "New" in this Coding Scheme

Several causal categories that arose in this analysis process are both unique vis-à-vis other taxonomies and interesting in relation to achievement-attributional analysis across a wide range of personal and situational characteristics.

One factor that is, of course, important in light of the focus of the research is that of "age" as an explanation of success or failure. This category (07) was not used with great frequency, and all but a few of those times it was given as an explanation for the failure of an older person. The other side of the coin, age as an indicant of wide experience and wisdom, was, however, cited several times. As will be seen at a later point in this discussion, I chose to classify age as both stable (relatively so) and personal, in that it adheres to the person across all situations. Other researchers, notably S. Green (1979), have considered "age," especially as a decline factor for older persons, as external rather than personal. Also, Banziger and Drevenstedt (1980) made "age" a conceptually and operationally distinct personal category. Although there is some merit to both sorts of arguments, I feel the constancy and personal-bodily basis for age ascriptions is predominantly personal and relatively stable, although I did make it a separate category. By the way, it was spontaneously given considerably more rarely than it was used when Banziger and Drevenstedt made it one of a limited number of categories allowed for response choice. The disagreement illustrates again the value of having a broad set of categories available for later allocation to more dimension-bound categories, rather than making assignment at the earliest stages of analysis.

By the way, one sort of ascription to "age" was not assigned to this category, but was considered to be external or extrapersonal. When it was clear that prejudice based on the age of the actor was what the attributor was signifying, then either category 19, including prejudice, or category 22, supervisor judgments, was the choice.

Another category relevant to development and age is the category that includes experience and training (09). Although this cause is sometimes seen as equivalent to ability or skill, it is clearly a more social or interactive factor than either of those. At the same time, it is a very processual, rather than strictly static or stable, factor. That is, in most cases experience can be gained by engaging in a social act; that is, by receiving training from others or experience with relevant persons (or objects). A positive reservoir of experience, on the other hand, was itself the result of a social act and is likely to require progressive and continued application.

A third personal factor that developed from the data is a category we have labeled "self-image" (08). A significant number of subjects included responses of the order that someone succeeded because they felt good about themselves or failed because they went into the situation with a negative self-image or lack of confidence. This is a factor that may in reality be either stable or unstable (although at a later stage of analysis we chose to classify it as stable). It is particularly important to distinguish this from an affective reaction to success or failure, that is, from *becoming* self-confident or losing confidence in oneself (a fairly common pair of affects, as we shall consider later and in the text itself). Rather, a preexisting state of self-perception is what is referred to in this category; a feeling of being in control that can be a major causal factor in resultant control and success or a corresponding negative self-concept that fuels the resultant failure. It is a factor that has not been distinguished in the work others have done. This is odd, since some of those others are theorists and researchers concerned with self-concept and self-confident attitudes as *results* of outcome experiences and of certain kinds of ascriptions; whereas other theorists and researchers are concerned with success-orientation and failure-orientation, with test anxiety and other self-cognitions that are increasingly seen as contributory to success or failure. That is, this category is a central one, and analysis of its use may tap the characteristic center of gravity in self-attributions, the tendency toward success- or failure-orientation.

In the course of analysis we also reconceptualized one factor that Elig and Frieze (1975) had classified as extrapersonal and developed a factor that we originally thought of as extrapersonal. However, we reconceived both of them as mutual or interactive in nature. The first is a category called "other activities interfering" (25). Although it is true that other activities or demands on attention are in many ways external, it is important to note a crucial distinction between the sorts of "interferences" that are usually discussed in psychological and social psychological research as contributory to quality of performance (usually as a factor in failure, but not necessarily, as shown by the task-facilitative effects of both social and nonsocial interference on simple tasks found by Pessin and Husband, 1933, and other researchers in social facilitation and attention and performance) and the sorts of factors people noted as causes of success and failure that could be classified as interference. The former are usually of the nature of experimenter-controlled distractions, whereas the latter are essentially matters of priority-setting and activity-selection that are in the control of the actor, at least at some decision points. The typical choices, of course, are reflective of the unreality of most traditional research. In this view, not doing a good job on a task because it is either of secondary importance in one's own current priorities or because it must be secondary because of earlier commitments (my writing this chapter may have to take a back seat to functioning as the member of a committee to which I am assigned, even though the writing is "really" more important to me) is not entirely a matter of failing because of an external cause. It is mutually determined and mutually controlled. It has to do *both* with my motivation and my interest in the task *and* with demands of others and of other activities available to me. Correspondingly, succeeding because of no distractions is also likely to be indicative of a personal choice to avoid those distractions.

A different mutual category is what we have labeled "proper tools" (24), which includes having or not having necessary equipment (e.g., for television repairs) and having or not having a proper plan of action. In both cases, that which is not had at the current time is a stable, uncontrollable factor. Depending on whether the tools are essentially internalized or external (plans vs. a voltmeter) they may be either personal or extrapersonal. Yet, in a more processual sense, having or not having "proper tools" *is* controllable and in that sense internal *and* unstable. One could, if one cared, have insured that he had proper tools to make electrical repairs, had a step-by-step manual concerning statistical analyses, or spent the time to come up with a plan of action to use in influencing others to give him or her a promotion. Advance planning and advance preparation are personal; thus, having or not having proper equipment, though it may be an extrapersonal fact at the time in which the tools or plans are needed, is of mutual location. Since it is open to readjustment for the future rather easily, it is also relatively unstable.

As others did, we identified a category that is both stable and extrapersonal and called it task difficulty (13), but it is considerably different from Weiner's paradigm for that confluence of dimensions. It contains elements of the social, but it is much less personally directed and much more task-specific than most of the social factors used by others and by us (e.g., "others' intentional help or hurt," "others' interests," etc.). Often it fit into an explanation such as "no one could fix that TV set, because it is such a hunk of junk." We added another category to the social factors cluster—ability of others in a position to control or supervise to recognize the value of the actor's contribution, in essence, to be a perspicacious supervisor (22). That category was necessary to handle the volunteer situation in particular. We also constructed an additional category that we have labeled "impersonal structures" (14). What we mean by this is that people recognize there are societal factors that are relatively stable and that greatly influence whether success or failure results, even though they are only peripherally related to task performance. A clear example of such a factor is the explanation for not being given a promotion that "we are in a recession and no one is getting promotions." The causal category shares several characteristics with task difficulty, but lacks its specificity and its "intrinsic" orientation. The task in this case may not be intrinsically difficult at all; it may not be beyond one's capabilities to perform (ability $\times$ task interaction); it may simply not be available because of impersonal structural elements in the current social situation. Those elements are not task-related, but they are task-affecting. Thus, the category of causes is quite distinctive and was made separate.

I believe this discussion of several factors illustrates the depth of analysis into the 28 causes and the approach we took in developing our list.

The "We" in Coding

Before proceeding to discussion of the next step of reduction of the causes to nine categories, I should directly discuss a major methodological issue concerning which many readers may be uncertain. I have consistently spoken of "we" when referring to the persons involved in the process of coding and categorizing without specifying exactly how I and my two research assistants proceeded. I should specify that, since it is somewhat unusual in social psychological research.

At the pretest stage, we experimented with several approaches to the data, one of which was probably the usual route that would be followed in social psychological work and another of which is the one we used in later analysis. The first approach consisted of having each of us code the causal statements independently and then checking reliability of the codes given. If this route were followed, after a period of training or coordination to ascertain we were "on the same wavelength," we could proceed by having one person code each subject's responses, while including a reliability check by cross-coding some random subset of protocols.

In the final analysis we rejected that model and proceeded with one more similar to a diagnostic group in clinical situations or, alternatively, to a proposal review panel. That is, after preliminary coding and a "write-up" of the categories by one of the research assistants, we met as a group to go over 6 to 10 protocols. We discussed the coding given by the preliminary analyst and either verified that choice or decided on an alternate that satisfied all three of us. In that way, we categorized attributions as described above and affects and future orientation to be described in the following. The panel was relatively efficient and relatively consistent (we did several reanalyses at a later time on a portion of the subject folders and virtually always reached the same conclusion as we had the first time). The procedure provided a check on such rater-based potential errors as individual biases, fatigue, and boredom (the latter because we occasionally got into lively give-and-take debates).

Clearly, such an approach is less amenable to reliability measures and strict replication. I feel the benefits outweighed (and outweigh) the problems, but the reader must decide for herself or himself.

Reduction to Two Smaller Sets

After all causal attributions had been coded (for both Type I and Type II situations—that is, answers to 20 questions by each subject) we then processed the responses to a second level of abstraction, since, obviously, the use of 28 categories for analysis is unwieldy, to say the least. We classified each "cause" into 1 of 10 categories, which corresponded to major categories found in other free-recall analyses (e.g., Elig & Frieze, 1975) and to the original Weinerian dimensions plus several interaction factors and a dichotomization of extrapersonal factors into social—other person—and nonsocial ones.

The chart below indicates the 10 categories. In it, numbers in parentheses after the brief description correspond to numbers for the 28 categories listed above, and the word or phrase in quotes is a general type for the category, one which "stands for" the range of factors grouped within that category. The title or exemplar is shorthand for the group and is the way a category at this level is referred to in the text.

Attribution Categories: A Tenfold Classification

1   Personal *ability-type* factors "Ability" (01, 02, 06, 07, 09)
2   Personal *trait-type* factors "Personality" (03, 04, 05, 08)

3   Personal *state-type* factors "Mood" (10, 11)

4   Personal *current output* factors "Effort" (12)

5   Extrapersonal, *nonsocial stable* factors "Task Difficulty" (13, 14)

6   Extrapersonal, *social stable* factors "Others' abilities and motives" (19, 20, 21, 23, if "other" is clearly a stable part of one's environment)

7   Extrapersonal, *unstable nonsocial* factors "Luck" (15)

8   Extrapersonal, *unstable social* factors "Others' efforts and help and hurt" (17, 18, 19, 20, 21, 22, 23, except as indicated in 6, above)

9   *Interaction* of Personal and *Social*-Extrapersonal factors "Personality Interaction" (27, 28)

10   *Interaction* of Personal and *Nonsocial* Extrapersonal factors "Ability-task interaction" (24, 25, 26)

Although this level of abstraction is useful for many analyses, as described in the chapters themselves, it is still below a level that permits direct analysis of hypotheses in terms of the dimensions. To proceed to that next level we simply constructed scales representing the location and stability dimensions and assigned each cause to a point on those scales. Unfortunately, as I noted above in detail, we were not successful at consistently applying a multipoint scale directly to individual causal statements and had to content ourselves for the present with rather crude measures—one a dichotomy and one a trichotomy. We retained Elig and Frieze's (1975) classifications for these purposes: each clause was rated as either stable or unstable and as personal, extrapersonal, or mutual. The reader must, of course, continually bear in mind the ultimate inadequacy of such gross classification but must also appreciate the difficulty of proceeding beyond that sort of analysis within quantitative, hypothesis-testing research and the intrinsic value of the resultant data (I hope the latter is clear from the body of the data produced). The reader also must remember that many studies of achievement attributions have data that *begin and end* at this level of analysis, whereas the data—and this appendix—are designed to allow for multiple levels of analysis for different purposes and as a set of converging operations.

For purposes of the analysis conducted on the dimensions, "ability," "personality," "mood," and "effort" were classified as personal, "task difficulty," "others' abilities and motives," "others' efforts and help/hurt," and "luck" as extrapersonal, and the two interaction categories as mutual. "Ability," "personality," "task difficulty," and "others' abilities and motives" (if the others were perceived as a consistent part of the individual's social world) were considered stable, and the other six categories were classified as unstable.

As discussed in the body of the book and elsewhere in this appendix, these classifications are, ultimately, arbitrary to some degree, and any particular choice may be open to other interpretations. In particular, the ability-task interaction, since it is an interaction of two "stable" factors, could be considered stable. However, since the likelihood of those particular two factors repeatedly being involved in situation after situation was low, we considered it to be unstable. "Personality interaction" and, in most cases, "others' abilities and motives," factors we classified as unstable for reasons similar to those just noted, under limited conditions can be quite stable. That would be the case when the "others" involved are relatively permanent fixtures of one's social environment, such as one's spouse or children or, possibly, one's boss. In those cases we classified the latter category as stable, but we always classified the personality interaction and usually classified the others' abilities and motives factor as unstable.

The possibility for differential placement is both invigorating and disturbing. It brings us nearer to the multiple reality of causality that is apparently commonplace in everyday attributing, but it obviously makes it difficult to proceed with analysis without at least a residue of ambiguity in interpretation. Our solution, an imperfect one but, I believe, a defensible one, was to consistently make one categorization and analysis, and leaving reanalysis with different categorization to other researchers and to data we have collected that is more suited to such analyses. The latter is discussed in detail in Chapter 7.

The Problem of Quantity

Prior to proceeding to a (less detailed) discussion of levels of analysis of affects and a brief note about expectations, I should discuss one other difficulty.

As noted previously, subjects' responses to situations varied in quantity. That is, some persons regularly gave one cause (and one affect), some persons regularly gave two or more, and still others varied by situation. This leads to grave difficulties in data reduction and analysis. Some responses are not totally independent. This problem, although germane at all levels of analysis, was solved differently when different levels of data were concerned. For the larger classifications (e.g., into 10 categories), the problem was solved by use of multiple response analysis. The numbers compiled and compared are totals across *all* responses, including several responses from those subjects who gave several. Although this procedure is open to criticism, to be sure, it is a commonly used analysis approach to nominal data (Nie et al., 1975).

The presence of several responses becomes more problematic when attempts are made to construct an interval scale and use standard analysis of variance techniques for analyses. We simply averaged across more than one cause when more than one was given to a particular stimulus. Thus, each person was given a location score (from 1 to 3) and a stability score (from 1 to 2) for each situation. This method has the obvious virtue of being simple. It also, obviously, has the disadvantage of ambiguity. That is, any particular score may represent several different combinations of causal types *or* a particular single cause. Citing "ability" only or "ability" and "willpower" would both result in a score of "1" on both personal and stable dimensions; using "personality interaction" only would yield the same score on the personal-extrapersonal location dimension as would reporting three causes: "ability," "personality interaction," and "luck."

We were not totally satisfied with the approach, for this and other reasons, but efforts to include intensity (e.g., having only one factor of a type as more intense than a mixed situation, but less intense than giving two or three causes, all of which were of one type) fell short of expectations and seemed even more ambiguous and flawed than the more straightforward approach.

CODING AFFECTS AND FEELINGS

As I pointed out several times previously, I will not go into nearly as much detail concerning coding of free-response affect information. Many of the step were similar to those used in coding causes. My research assistants and I worked together as a team; we initially assigned words and phrases to a rather inclusive, broad set of affects, based in part on Weiner, Russell, & Lerman (1978); we then reduced those to nine categories, and then to a simple threefold classification—positive, neutral or mixed, and negative. This section is primarily comprised of lists of those factors.

After proceeding through the pretest we arrived at 48 separable affect categories. Again, as with causes, placement of a particular word or phrase into a particular category was facilitated by use of *Roget's Thesaurus*. Also extremely helpful were taxonomic lists of other researchers, notably Davitz (1969). The list to follow contains a code number for each cluster and a word or set of words to indicate those ''affects'' that are grouped into that category. The first word is the way the set of items is referred to in the text. The affect categories were as follows:

1   Happy
2   Joyous, great, ecstatic, elated
3   Pleased
4   Good
5   Satisfied
6   Flattered
7   Successful, feeling of accomplishment
8   Relieved
9   Proud, positive self-image
10   Fun, feeling of enjoyment
11   Contented
12   Sense of well-being
13   Confident, encouraged
14   Worthwhile, accepted, useful
15   Cocky, smug, conceited, boastful
16   Humble
17   Competent, capable
18   Grateful
19   Caring, loving
20   ''No big deal,'' ho-hum
21   Surprised
22   Tired, exhausted
23   Nervous
24   Ambivalent

25   Excited
26   Confused, bewildered, puzzled
27   Embarrassed, ashamed, stupid, dumb
28   Concerned
29   —Not used—
30   Disgusted
31   Frustrated
32   Sad, unhappy, low, bad
33   Angry
34   Depressed, dejected, despondent, despairing
35   Upset, shook up
36   Guilty
37   Hurt
38   Resentful
39   Rejected
40   Scared, panicked, fearful
41   Disappointed
42   Jealous
43   Defeated, feeling of failure
44   Lack or loss of self-confidence or self-worth
45   Helpless, resigned
46   Discouraged, deflated, disheartened
47   Disturbed, uneasy, apprehensive
48   Lonely, alienated

For further analysis we reduced the list of affects to a set of nine categories. These groupings, as indicated in the following list, are based closely on Davitz's (1969) taxonomy of emotional language; they are an attempt to have clusters of affects that reflect both activation and hypoactivation aspects of each direction for emotions and to provide analyses among these and other dimensions as the vocabularies of achievement-related affect differ across groups of subjects, actors, and situations. Some detail about the application of these dimensions to analyses of the data are presented in Chapter 5 (for attributions about others' affects) and Chapter 6 (affect ascriptions to oneself).

The nine categories (with original affect category numbers included in parentheses) are:

1   Positive-activation (2, 10, 21, 25)
2   Positive-comfort (1, 3, 4, 5, 8, 20 [for success], 11, 12, 18, 19)
3   Positive-enhancement (6, 7, 9, 13, 14, 15, 16, 17)

4   Negative-hypoactivation (12, 34)

5   Negative-discomfort (20 [for failure], 26, 28, 32, 37, 41, 47, 48)

6   Negative-incompetence (27, 36, 44, 46)

7   Negative-hyperactivation (33, 40)

8   Negative-tension (23, 24, 30, 31, 35, 38, 42)

9   Negative-inadequacy (39, 43, 45)

Finally, the affects were reduced to three simple points on a positivity dimension (somewhat crossing the positive-negative dimension inherent in the above process, with 20–25 as neutral and the rest either positive or negative—I believe which of those two is the case is fairly obvious for each). By and large, analysis at this level was rather trivial—positive affects were used for success outcomes and negative ones for failure, although the fairly large number of cross-affects was somewhat surprising and intriguing. It is discussed briefly in the book, but is primarily a source for future investigations.

Other Questions

One final set of analysis tools will be discussed only briefly. The reader may remember from the text, and note in the sample questionnaire included as the final section of this appendix, that subjects were asked not only to give causes and feelings in response to outcomes in various situations, but also to say how that particular outcome would affect the actor (or did affect themselves as actors) in terms of future orientation, expectations, self-confidence, and approach to or avoidance of similar tasks in the future. We developed one global measure for these three aspects: all positive (intraresponse congruent high expectations, high self-concept, and approach), all negative (intraresponse congruent low expectations, low self-concept, and avoidance), or mixed (approach/avoidance, approach with low expectations and/or self-confidence, high expectations but avoidance), and a response that denied the possibility of making a general statement about those sorts of reactions—"it depends on the person," "some will do X, others will do Y."

As with results from the positivity dimensional analysis of affects, most of the findings in this measure are commonsensical to the point of triviality. That is, most subjects did not report positive future orientations to failures or negative orientation to success. However, there was a general tendency toward the "positive" end of the continuum and considerable use of a mixed set of reactions to both success and failure that would not be expected from much of the attributional literature. These less trivial aspects of the data are discussed briefly in the body of the book.

The above is a set of specific technical aspects to data reduction and coding of free subject responses to hypothetical situations and self-experienced reminiscences of success and failure outcomes. I think the discussion correctly emphasizes the value and the multistage, multilevel complexities and problems of such an approach and provides sufficient information for future use of the taxonomies developed within this research program by this team. I believe the categories arrived at are general enough to be useful across a broad range of actors and situations and allow for swift, direct reduction to a few dimensions for quantitative analysis. Alternatively, they are available for analysis and processing at a more open level that is meaningful in and of itself and that may be used to proceed to modifications of the clustering and categorizing we chose to use.

A sample of one of the four versions of the questionnaire, including Type I and Type II elicitors, general directions, and additional closed-response questions referred to in the body of the text (especially Chapter 6) follows.

STUDY OF REASONS FOR SUCCESS AND FAILURE

We are interested in how people react to situations in which someone succeeds or fails, and we would like to get some information from you about this issue. We are particularly interested in getting responses from people with a wide range of ages and personal situations, since most of the work related to this topic has only considered the rather unusual group of young adult college students. Your participation can help us broaden our understanding.

Some of our questions will be about other persons succeeding and failing, and other questions will ask about how you feel and react to your own successes and failures.

So that you can do this study in a group or at home at a convenient time, all the instructions and questions are written, and you are to write down your answers. However, we do not want the artificial nature of a written questionnaire to interfere with your letting us know as well as you can what you feel and think. Please try to set aside one time period (about an hour) to do the whole study in one sitting, if that is possible. And please do not ask family and friends for their opinions or talk to others who are doing the study until after your answers have been returned to us. We want *your own* views. Besides, different members of your group are receiving different versions of the study, so you do not all have the same questions on which to compare your ideas or answers.

Thank you for observing these requests and for your participation in the study. If at any point in the study you have *any* questions or are unclear about the meaning of a part of the instructions, *please* contact either Joyce, Cindy, or Tom at 276-1181, during working hours. We know there will be problems and questions because the study is all written, so we encourage you to ask them. Also, you do not have to answer any question you do not want to.

PLEASE PROCEED TO THE NEXT PAGE OF INSTRUCTIONS.

PART ONE

The first part of the study consists of a set of very brief descriptions of someone succeeding or failing in a particular situation. We would like you to "complete" each of the situations by writing down (1) *how you think* the *person* in the description *would feel,* (2) what he or she would *think about,* especially what reasons he or she would be likely to think were involved in the success or failure, and (3) what effect the results in that situation could have on that person in later similar situations. This can and should be *very brief*—(1) a few words or phrases to describe *feelings* you think the person would have, (2) a few words or phrases about *reasons* or *causes* he or she would give for the situation turning out as it did, and (3) a general idea of *future expectations* and how this all would affect his or her feelings and thoughts in the future when similar situations arise. We want clear but brief answers. You should try to answer quickly without spending a great deal of time on a particular situation.

First, I will go through a sample story with you.

I recently tried to repair a typewriter. I thought that I had it fixed, but it would not work again today.

Complete that description by putting down: (1) how you think I felt when the machine did not work, (2) why I thought I failed in getting it to continue working, and (3) what failing in that situation might lead me to feel and expect in a similar situation in the future.

Please write down an ending for that story in the space above so that we know you understand what we want for the other situations. We want to make one thing very clear—*there are no right and wrong answers* to this to which yours will be compared. We simply want to get an idea of how people think about how others react to situations. Also, you do not have to keep coming up with completely different ideas (a similar set of feelings and causes may fit with more than one) nor do you have to use the same ones for all of them. Judge each situation as independently as possible on the basis of what *you* think is reasonable, even though some of them are quite similar.

Those of you who are doing the study at home can take the rest of the booklet home and work on it as indicated on the first page. You can turn it back in at the next meeting. For those of you doing it in a group at the Institute, you may proceed to the remainder of the first part of the study. Remember to give brief words, phrases, or sentences about three aspects of each situation: (1) feelings the person would have, (2) reasons or causes he or she would think of for the result, and (3) effects of the result on expectations and interest in later similar situations.

1. A 71 year old woman, who had set a goal of 10 pounds weight loss in a six-week period, ended up actually gaining 1 pound instead.

2. A 21 year old woman won a bridge contest at her local community center.

3. A 43 year old woman failed to repair her own television set.

4. A 69 year old man was told that his volunteer work at a local hospital was not satisfactory.

Remember to give brief words, phrases, or sentences about three aspects of each situation: (1) feelings the person would have, (2) reasons or causes he or she would think of for the result, and (3) effects of the result on expectations and interest in later similar situations.

5. A 72 year old man won a bridge contest at his local community center.

6. A 23 year old man was told that his volunteer work at a local hospital was not satisfactory.

7. A 50 year old woman, who had set a goal of 10 pounds weight loss in a six-week period, ended the period with a total loss of 12 pounds.

8. A 44 year old man was successful at repairing his own television set.

Remember to give brief words, phrases, or sentences about three aspects of each situation: (1) feelings the person would have, (2) reasons or causes he or she would think of for the result, and (3) effects of the result on expectations and interest in later similar situations.

9. A 24 year old man was told that the hospital where he has been doing volunteer work wants him to take a permanent paying job there.

10. A 67 year old woman was successful at repairing her own television set.

11. A 46 year old man lost a bridge contest he thought he could win at his local community center.

12. A 26 year old woman, who had set a goal of 10 pounds weight loss in a six-week period, ended up actually gaining 1 pound instead.

PART TWO

This part of the study is quite similar to the first part, but instead of asking you tell us how you think *other* people react to success and failure, we want you to write down how *you* react to it. Also, rather than giving you a hypothetical situation about yourself, like a driver's license renewal examination, we will give you some guidelines about a certain *kind* of experience and would like you to tell us about such an experience that you have had in the recent past (the last year, if possible). For example, the first situation we ask you to tell about is an *important success* you have experienced in the last year. This may have been a promotion at work, winning a prize, getting a high grade in an important class, gaining a good friend, or a host of other things. *Whatever* you feel was an important success in the past year is what we want you to write about. We want you to say: (1) how you *felt,* (2) what *reasons* you think caused you to succeed or fail, and (3) what you felt and thought at the time it happened *about future situations* like it—did you expect success or not, did you want to try something like it again, and so on. Also, do you think the experience did affect you in these ways? Again, try to be as brief as possible while still giving us your ideas.

Again, there are no right and wrong answers and, especially for these, I want to remind you that we are not putting your name on these at all, so you do not have to worry about telling us something personal; your responses are completely anonymous. At the same time, you do not have to put down a situation you feel is too personal. Just think of another situation that fits the category or leave the space blank.

1. Tell about a success in an important situation you have had recently.

2. Tell us about a failure in an important situation which you have had recently.

3. Tell us about a failure you have had in a less important day-to-day situation that did not have a major effect on your life.

4. Tell us about a success you have had in a less important day-to-day situation.

For the next four questions, you may be able to use one of the answers you gave for one of the first four descriptions. If one of the earlier ones is appropriate, just put down the number of that earlier one. If none fits, answer the situation as you did for those earlier ones—how you felt, why you succeeded or failed, and how it affected you in similar situations.

5. Tell us about a failure you have had in a relationship with another person or persons.

6. Tell us about a situation in which you succeeded in your relations with other persons.

7. Tell about a situation related to a nonsocial task (like working with tools, repairs, physical exercise, etc.) in which you have had success.

8. Tell about a situation similar to the one in Question 7 but in which you failed.

PLEASE PROCEED TO THE LAST SECTION OF THE STUDY.

PART THREE

Now that you have told us about several incidents, we would like you to give us a few other pieces of information about yourself. We will ask for several types of general and specific information about you. Fill in the blanks or circle the best response.

1.   What is your age?_____years.
     What is your sex?   (circle)   male   female.
2.   What is your job or occupation?_____ (If you are retired, tell us what it was and that you are now retired.)
3.   To what race or ethnic group do you belong? (Circle)
     White   Black   Oriental   Hispanic   Other

Now please choose the best ending for a series of statements about your successes and failures as you see them. For some of these it may be a little hard to choose just one answer, but try your best to choose the sentence ending *closest* to how you feel and think about yourself. Circle the letter in front of the ending you feel is best.

4.   In important situations that have major effects on my life and happiness:
     a. I succeed much more than I fail.
     b. I succeed somewhat more than I fail.
     c. I succeed and fail about equally often.
     d. I fail somewhat more than I succeed.
     e. I fail much more than I succeed.
     In the last five years, I think that:
     a. I have failed more than I did five years ago.
     b. I succeeded more than I did five years ago.
     c. This relationship of success and failure has stayed the same.
     In the next five years I expect that:
     a. I will succeed more often than fail compared to what I do now.
     b. I will fail more often than succeed compared to what I do now.
     c. The relationship will be the same as it is now.
     When I am 70 or 75 years old:
     a. I will fail more often than I do now.
     b. I will succeed more often than I do now.
     c. The relationship of success and failure will be about the same.
5.   Please give the information asked about in the last set of questions, but this time about the less important, less earth-shaking, day-to-day kind of successes and failures. In less important situations:
     a. I succeed much more than I fail.
     b. I succeed somewhat more than I fail.
     c. I succeed and fail about equally often.
     d. I fail somewhat more than I succeed.
     e. I fail much more than I succeed.

In the last five years, I think that:
   a. I have failed more than I did five years ago.
   b. I have succeeded more than I did five years ago.
   c. This relationship of success and failure has stayed the same.
In the next five years I expect that:
   a. I will succeed more often than fail compared to what I do now.
   b. I will fail more often than succeed compared to what I do now.
   c. The relationship will stay the same.
When I am 70 or 75 years old:
   a. I will fail more often than I do now.
   b. I will succeed more often than I do now.
   c. The relationship of success and failure will be about the same.

6. Succeeding at what I try to do is:
   a. Very important to me.
   b. Important to me.
   c. Not too important to me.
   d. Not at all important to me.

7. In regard to comparing how often I succeed to how often I fail, I am:
   a. Very satisfied at this time.
   b. Satisfied at this time.
   c. Somewhat dissatisfied at this time.
   d. Very dissatisfied at this time.

8. In general terms, I am.:
   a. Very satisfied with my life at this time.
   b. Satisfied with my life at this time.
   c. Somewhat dissatisfied with my life at this time.
   d. Very dissatisfied with my life at this time.

9. "I am better at succeeding and doing well in interpersonal situations and social relationships (that is, in my dealings with others) than in doing nonsocial
   kinds of tasks (i.e., repairs, working with my hands, athletics, etc.)."
   a. This statement is very true about me.
   b. This statement is true about me.
   c. This statement is somewhat wrong about me.
   d. This statement is very wrong about me.

10. Finally, we want you to indicate how you think your success and failure rates
    in each of the areas we have discussed compares to the general population.
    For each area *circle* the description which fits best—the same as that of others,
    a better rate than others have, or a worse rate of success than others have.
    In important situations, mine is:
    the same   better   worse
    In day-to-day situations, mine is:
    the same   better   worse
    In relations with other persons, mine is:
    the same   better   worse
    In physical activities, mine is:
    the same   better   worse

11. Compare your rate as in Question 10, but compare your own to others about your age and your sex.

   In important situations, mine is:
   the same   better   worse
   In day-to-day situations, mine is:
   the same   better   worse
   In relations with other persons, mine is:
   the same   better   worse
   In physical activities, mine is:
   the same   better   worse

THANK YOU VERY MUCH FOR YOUR PARTICIPATION! PLEASE complete the page after this for our records. It will help us make sure that you or your group will receive the proper amount for your participation. Please put it in the separate envelope provided with your packet after you have signed it in the two spaces. It will be kept completely separate from your answers.

   THANK YOU AGAIN.

References

Abrahams, J. P., Hoyer, W. J., Elias, M. F., & Bradigan, B. Gerontological research in psychology published in *Journal of Gerontology,* 1963–1974: Perspectives and progress. *Journal of Gerontology,* 1975, **30,** 668–673.

Abramson, L. Y., Seligman, M. E. P., & Teasdale, J. Learned helplessness in humans: Critique and reformulation. *Journal of Abnormal Psychology,* 1978, **87,** 49–74.

Adams, B. N. *The American family.* Chicago: Rand-McNally, 1970.

Ahammer, I. M. Social learning theory as a framework for the study of adult personality development. In P. B. Baltes & K. W. Schaie (Eds.), *Lifespan developmental psychology: Personality and socialization.* New York: Academic Press, 1973.

Albert, S. Toward a theory of successful separation across the life cycle. In T. Blank (Chair), *Adult developmental change: New directions for personality and social psychology.* Symposium presented at the meetings of the American Psychological Association, Montreal, September 1980.

Alderfer, C. P. A video assist to student-faculty dialogue on teaching and learning. *Social Change,* 1973, **3**(2), 6–8.

Allport, F. H. *Social psychology.* Boston: Houghton Mifflin, 1924.

Allport, G. W. *The nature of prejudice.* Garden City, NY: Doubleday Anchor, 1958.

Allport, G. W. The historical background of modern social psychology. In G. Lindzey & E. Aronson (Eds.), *The handbook of social psychology,* 2nd ed., Vol 1. Reading, MA: Addison-Wesley, 1968.

Altman, I. *The environment and social behavior: Privacy, personal space, territory, and crowding.* Monterey, CA: Brooks/Cole, 1975.

American Psychological Association. *Preliminary results of the 1979 doctoral employment survey.* Washington, DC: Author, 1980.

American Sociologist. Exchange: The dissipation of sociological social psychology. *American Sociologist,* 1977, **12,** 1–23.

Ames, C., Ames, P., & Felker, D. W. Informational and dispositional determinants of children's achievement attributions. *Journal of Educational Psychology,* 1976, **68,** 63–69.

Angyal, A. *Foundations for a science of personality.* Cambridge, MA: Harvard University Press, 1941.

Archibald, W. P. Psychology, sociology, and social psychology: Bad fences make bad neighbours. *British Journal of Sociology,* 1976, **27,** 115–129.

Archibald, W. P. *Social psychology as political economy.* New York. McGraw Hill, 1978.

Armistead, N. (Ed.). *Reconstructing social psychology.* Baltimore: Penguin, 1974.

Atchley, R. C. *The social forces in later life.* Belmont, CA: Wadsworth, 1972.

Atchley, R. C. *The social forces in later life,* 2nd ed. Belmont, CA: Wadsworth, 1977.

Atchley, R. C. *The social forces in later life,* 3rd ed. Belmont, CA: Wadsworth, 1980.

Atkinson, J. W. *An introduction to motivation.* Princeton, NJ: Van Nostrand, 1964.

Atkinson, J. W., & Feather, N. T. (Eds.). *A theory of achievement motivation.* New York: Wiley, 1966.

Baer, D. M. The control of the developmental process: Why wait? In J. R. Nesselroade & H. W. Reese (Eds.), *Lifespan developmental psychology: Methodological issues.* New York: Academic Press, 1973.

Baffa, G. A., & Zarit, S. H. Age differences in the perception of assertive behavior. *Gerontologist,* 1977, **17,** 36.

Baizerman, M., & Ellison, D. L. A social role analysis of senility. *Gerontologist,* 1971, **11,** 163–169.

Baltes, P. B. Plasticity of lifespan human development: Promise or despair? Paper presented at the meetings of the Eastern Psychological Association, Hartford, CN, April 1980.

Baltes, P., & Labouvie, G. Adult development of intellectual performance: Description, explanation, and modification. In C. Eisdorfer & M. P. Lawton (Eds.), *The psychology of adult development and aging.* Washington, DC: American Psychological Association, 1973.

Baltes, P. B., Reese, H. W., & Nesselroade, J. R. *Lifespan developmental psychology: Introduction to research methods.* Monterey, CA: Brooks/Cole, 1977.

Baltes, P. B., & Schaie, K. W. On the plasticity of intelligence in adulthood and old age: Where Horn and Donaldson fail. *American Psychologist,* 1976, **31,** 720–725.

Baltes, P. B., & Willis, S. L. Toward psychological theories of aging and development. In J. E. Birren & K. W. Schaie (Eds.), *Handbook of the psychology of aging.* New York: Van Nostrand-Reinhold, 1977.

Banziger, G. Applications of social cognition to aging, Parts I, II, and III. Unpublished manuscript, Marietta College, 1979.

Banziger, G., & Drevenstedt, J. Achievement attributions by young and old judges as a function of perceived age and performance history. Unpublished manuscript, Marietta College, 1980.

Banziger, G., & Drevenstedt, J. Achievement attributions as a function of perceived age and performance history. In T. O. Blank (Chair), *Attributions and attributes: Advances in adult development and aging.* Symposium presented at the meetings of the Eastern Psychological Association, New York, April 1981.

Barker, R. G. *Ecological psychology.* Stanford, CA: Stanford University Press, 1968.

Barker, R. G., and associates. *Habitats, environments, and behavior.* New York: Harper and Row, 1977.

Barker, R. G., & Barker, L. S. The psychological ecology of old people in Midwest, Kansas, and Yoredale, Yorkshire. *Journal of Gerontology,* 1961, **16,** 144–149.

Baumgardner, S. R. Critical studies in the history of social psychology. *Personality and Social Psychology Bulletin,* 1977, **3,** 681–687.

Bechtel, R. B. *Enclosing behavior.* Stroudsburg, PA: Dowden, Hutchinson, and Ross, 1977.

Bell, B. D., & Stanfield, G. G. The aging stereotype in experimental perspective. *Gerontologist,* 1973, **28,** 491–496.

Bem, D. J. Self-perception theory. In L. Berkowitz (Ed.), *Advances in experimental social psychology,* Vol. 6. New York: Academic Press, 1972.

Bengtson, V. L. *The social psychology of aging*. Indianapolis: Bobbs-Merrill, 1973.

Bennett, R., & Eckman, J. Attitudes toward aging. In C. Eisdorfer & M. P. Lawton (Eds.), *The psychology of adult development and aging*. Washington, DC: American Psychological Association, 1973.

Berger, P. L., & Luckmann, T. *The social construction of reality*. New York: Doubleday, 1966.

Berkowitz, L. *An introduction to social psychology*. Chicago: Dryden, 1975.

Bermant, G., Nemeth, C., & Vidmar, G. *Psychology and the law*. Lexington, MA: Lexington, 1976.

Bernhardt, K. L., & Kinnear, T. C. Profiling the senior citizen market. In F. E. Waddell (Ed.), *The elderly consumer*. Columbia, MD: Human Ecology Center, Antioch College, 1976.

Berry, J. W. The cultural ecology of social behavior. In L. Berkowitz (Ed.), *Advances in experimental social psychology,* Vol. 12. New York: Academic Press, 1979.

Biddle, B. J. *Role theory: Expectations, identities, and behavior*. New York: Academic Press, 1979.

Binstock, R. H. Interest group liberalism and the politics of aging. *Gerontologist,* 1972, **12,** 265–280.

Birren, J. E. *The psychology of aging*. Englewood Cliffs, NJ: Prentice-Hall, 1964.

Birren, J. E., & Renner, V. J. Research on the psychology of aging: Principles and experimentation. In J. E. Birren & K. W. Schaie (Eds.), *Handbook of the psychology of aging*. New York: Van Nostrand-Reinhold, 1977.

Birren, J. E., & Schaie, K. W. (Eds.). *Handbook of the psychology of aging*. New York: Van Nostrand-Reinhold, 1977.

Blank, T. O. Two social psychologies: Is segregation inevitable or acceptable? *Personality and Social Psychology Bulletin,* 1978, **4,** 553–556.

Blank, T. O. Adulthood and aging in social psychology texts. *Teaching of Psychology,* 1979, **6,** 145–148. (a)

Blank, T. O. Older people doing their shopping. In D. Baugher (Chair), *Growing old in America: Psychological and policy issues*. Symposium presented at the meetings of the American Psychological Association, New York, September 1979. (b)

Blank, T. O. (Chair). *Adult developmental change: New directions for personality and social psychology*. Symposium presented at the meetings of the American Psychological Association, Montreal, September 1980.

Blank, T. O. Achievement orientation as a personality factor in young, middle-aged, and older adults. Unpublished manuscript, Lehigh University, 1981. (a)

Blank, T. O. *Attributions and attributes: Advances in adult development and aging*. Symposium presented at the meetings of the Eastern Psychological Association, New York, April 1981. (b)

Blank, T. O. Meaning and motivation in adult self-perceptions of causality. In T. O. Blank (Chair), *Attributions and attributes: Advances in adult development and aging*. Symposium presented at the meetings of the Eastern Psychological Association, New York, April 1981. (c)

Blank, T. O., & Staff, I. The search: Attributions about a close-to-home process. Unpublished manuscript, Lehigh University, 1981.

Bortner, R. W. Personality and social psychology in the study of aging. *Gerontologist,* 1967, **7,** 23–36.

Botwinick, J. Cautiousness in advanced age. *Journal of Gerontology,* 1966, **21,** 347–353.

Botwinick, J. *Cognitive processes in maturity and old age.* New York: Springer, 1967.

Botwinick, J. Disinclination to venture responses versus cautiousness in responding: Age differences. *Journal of Genetic Psychology,* 1969, **115,** 55–62.

Botwinick, J. *Aging and behavior,* 2nd ed. New York: Springer, 1978.

Boutilier, R. G., Roed, J. C., & Svendsen, A. C. Crises in two social psychologies: A critical comparison. *Social Psychology Quarterly,* 1980, **43,** 5–17.

Bowers, K. S. Situationism in psychology: An analysis and a critique. *Psychological Review,* 1973, **80,** 307–336.

Bradley, G. W. Self-serving biases in the attribution process: A reexamination of the fact or fiction question. *Journal of Personality and Social Psychology,* 1978, **36,** 56–71.

Brewer, M. B. Cognitive model of stereotypes for the aged. In M. B. Brewer (Chair), *Perceptions of the aged: Basic studies and institutional implications.* Symposium presented at the meetings of the American Psychological Association, New York, September 1979.

Brim, O. G. On the properties of life events. Paper presented at the meetings of the American Psychological Association, New York, September 1979.

Bronfenbrenner, U. B. External validity in the study of human development. Unpublished manuscript, Cornell University, 1976.

Bronfenbrenner, U. Toward an experimental ecology of human development. *American Psychologist,* 1977, **32,** 513–531.

Brunswik, E. *Perception and the representation design of psychological experiments.* Berkeley: University of California Press, 1956.

Buck-Morss, S. The Adorno legacy. *Personality and Social Psychology Bulletin,* 1977, **3,** 707–713.

Bühler, C. The developmental structure of goal setting in group and individual studies. In C. Bühler & F. Massarik (Eds.), *The course of human life.* New York: Springer, 1968.

Burgess, R., & Bushnell, D. (Eds.). *Behavioral sociology.* New York: Columbia University Press, 1969.

Bush, M., & Gordon, A. C. (Eds.). People and bureaucracies. *Journal of Social Issues,* 1978, **34,**(4), 1–136.

Buss, A. R. Causes and reasons in attribution theory: A conceptual critique. *Journal of Personality and Social Psychology,* 1978, **36,** 1311–1321.

Buss, A. R. *A dialectical psychology.* New York: Irvington, 1979. (a)

Buss, A. R. On the relationship between causes and reasons. *Journal of Personality and Social Psychology,* 1979, **37,** 1458–1461. (b)

Butler, R. N. The life review: An interpretation of reminiscence in the aged. *Psychiatry,* 1963, **26,** 65–76.

Butler, R. N. *Why survive? Being old in America.* New York: Harper and Row, 1975.

Campbell, D. T. Stereotypes and the perception of group differences. *American Psychologist,* 1967, **22,** 812–829.

Campbell, D. T. Reforms as experiments. *American Psychologist,* 1969, **24,** 409–429.

Campbell, D. T., & Stanley, J. C. *Experimental and quasi-experimental designs for research.* Chicago: Rand-McNally, 1966.

Carlson, R. Where is the person in personality research? *Psychological Bulletin,* 1971, **85,** 203–219.

Carp, F. M. *Future for the aged: Victoria Plaza and its residents.* Austin: University of Texas Press, 1966.

Carp, F. M. Housing and living environments of older people. In R. H. Binstock & E. Shanas (Eds.), *Handbook of aging and the social sciences.* New York: Van Nostrand-Reinhold, 1976.

Carroll, J. S. Judgments made by parole boards. In I. H. Frieze, D. Bar-tal, & J. S. Carroll (Eds.), *New approaches to social problems.* San Francisco: Jossey-Bass, 1979.

Carson, R. C. *Interaction concepts of personality.* Chicago: Aldine, 1969.

Chiriboga, D. A. Life events and personal change: A consideration. In T. O. Blank (Chair), *Adult developmental change: New directions for personality and social psychology.* Symposium presented at the meetings of the American Psychological Association, Montreal, September 1980.

Chiriboga, D. A., & Cutler, L. Stress and adaptation: Lifespan perspectives. In L. W. Poon (Ed.), *Aging in the 1980's.* Washington, DC: American Psychological Association, 1980.

Christie, R., & Geis, F. L. (Eds.) *Studies in Machiavellianism.* New York: Academic Press, 1970.

Connor, C. L., Walsh, R. P., Litzelman, D. K., & Alvarez, M. G. Evaluation of job applicants: The effects of age versus success. *Journal of Gerontology,* 1978, **33,** 246–252.

Cook, S. W. Do we train psychologists only to fill jobs—or also to create them?: Response to Thomas Blank. *American Psychologist,* 1979, **34,** 447–449.

Cooley, C. H. *Human nature and social order.* New York: Scribner, 1922.

Cooper, H. M., & Burger, J. M. How teachers explain students' academic performance: Categorization of free response academic attributions. *American Educational Research Journal,* 1980, **17,** 95–109.

Crandall, V. C., Katkovsky, W., & Crandall, V. J. Children's beliefs in their own control of reinforcement in intellectual achievement situations. *Child Development,* 1965, **36,** 91–106.

Cronbach, L. Beyond the two disciplines of academic psychology. *American Psychologist,* 1975, **30,** 116–127.

Cumming, E. New thoughts on the theory of disengagement. In R. Kastenbaum (Ed.), *New thoughts on old age.* New York: Springer, 1964.

Cumming, E., & Henry, W. E. *Growing old: The process of disengagement.* New York: Basic, 1961.

Davitz, J. R. *The language of emotions.* New York: Academic Press, 1969.

deCharms, R. *Personal causation.* New York: Academic Press, 1968.

Dohrenwend, B. S., & Dohrenwend, B. P. *Stressful life events: Their nature and effects.* New York: Wiley, 1974.

Dressler, D. M. Life adjustment of retired couples. *International Journal of Aging and Human Development,* 1973, **4,** 335–339.

Dutch, R. A. (Ed.), *Roget's thesaurus.* New York: St. Martin's Press, 1965.

Eisdorfer, C. Arousal and performance: Experiments in verbal learning and a tentative theory. In G. A. Talland (Ed.), *Human aging and behavior.* New York: Academic Press, 1968.

Eisdorfer, C., & Lawton, M. P. (Eds.). *The psychology of adult development and aging.* Washington, DC: American Psychological Association, 1973.

Elder, G. H. *Children of the Great Depression: Social change and life experiences.* Chicago: University of Chicago Press, 1974.

Elias, M. F., Elias, P. K., & Elias, J. W. *Basic processes in adult developmental psychology.* St. Louis: Mosby, 1977.

Elig, T. W., & Frieze, I. H. A multi-dimensional scheme for coding and interpreting perceived causality for success and failure events: The Coding Scheme of Perceived Causality (CSPC). JSAS *Catalog of Selected Documents in Psychology,* 1975, **5,** 313.

Elig, T. W., & Frieze, I. H. Measuring causal attributions for success and failure. *Journal of Personality and Social Psychology,* 1979, **37,** 621–634.

Elms, A. C. The crisis of confidence in social psychology. *American Psychologist,* 1975, **30,** 967–976.

Erikson, E. H. Identity and the life cycle: Selected papers. *Psychological Issues,* 1959, **1,** 50–100.

Erikson, E. H. Reflections on Dr. Borg's life cycle. *Daedalus,* 1976, **105,** 1–28.

Eskilson, A., & Wiley, M. G. Whatever happened to significant others? The limitations of causal cues in attribution research. Unpublished manuscript, University of Illinois at Chicago Circle, 1979.

Estes, C. L. *The aging enterprise.* San Francisco: Jossey-Bass, 1979.

Falbo, T., & Beck, R. C. Naive psychology and the attributional model of achievement. *Journal of Personality,* 1979, **47,** 185–195.

Festinger, L. *A theory of cognitive dissonance.* Stanford, CA: Stanford University Press, 1957.

Festinger, L., Schachter, S., & Back, K. *Social pressures in informal groups.* New York: Harper, 1950.

Firestone, R. *The success trip.* New York: Playboy Press, 1977.

Framo, J. L. Family psychology and intimate contexts: Neglected areas in social psychology. In P. Minuchin (Chair), *Social and developmental implications of family systems therapy.* Symposium presented at the meetings of the American Psychological Association, New York, September 1979.

Fried, S. B., Gumppert, D. C., & Allen, J. C. Ten years of social psychology: Is there a growing commitment to field research? *American Psychologist,* 1973, **28,** 155–156.

Frieze, I. H. The role of information processing in making causal attributions for success and failure. In J. S. Carroll & J. W. Payne (Eds.), *Cognition and social behavior.* Hillsdale, NJ: Erlbaum, 1976. (a)

Frieze, I. H. Causal attributions and information seeking to explain success and failure. *Journal of Research in Personality,* 1976, **10,** 293–305. (b)

Frieze, I. H., Bar-tal, D., & Carroll, J. S. (Eds.). *New approaches to social problems.* San Francisco: Jossey-Bass, 1979.

Frieze, I. H., & Weiner, B. Cue utilization and attributional judgments for success and failure. *Journal of Personality,* 1971, **39,** 591–606.

Fry, C. L. (Ed.). *Aging in culture and society: Comparative viewpoints and strategies.* New York: Bergin, 1979.

Gans, H. J. *The Levittowners*. New York: Pantheon, 1967.

Gelwicks, L. E., & Newcomer, R. J. *Planning housing environments for the elderly*. Washington, DC: National Council on the Aging, 1974.

Gergen, K. J. Social psychology as history. *Journal of Personality and Social Psychology*, 1973, **26**, 309–320.

Gergen, K. J. Social psychology, science, and history. *Personality and Social Psychology Bulletin*, 1976, **2**, 373–383.

Gergen, K. J. Stability, change, and chance in understanding human development. In N. Datan & H. W. Reese (Eds.), *Lifespan developmental psychology: Dialectical perspectives*. New York: Academic Press, 1977.

Gergen, K. J. Experimentation in social psychology: A reappraisal. *European Journal of Social Psychology*, 1978, **8**, 507–527. (a)

Gergen, K. J. Toward generative theory. *Journal of Personality and Social Psychology*, 1978, **36**, 1344–1360. (b)

Gergen, K. J. The emerging crisis in lifespan developmental theory. In P. B. Baltes & O. G. Brim (Eds.), *Lifespan development and behavior*, Vol 3. New York: Academic Press, 1979.

Gergen, K. J. Toward intellectual audacity in social psychology. In R. Gilmour & S. Duck (Eds.), *The development of social psychology*. New York: Academic Press, 1980.

Gergen, K. J., Greenberg, M. S., & Willis, R. H. (Eds.). *Social exchange: Advances in theory and research*. New York: Plenum, 1980.

Glass, D. C., & Singer, J. E. *Urban stress*. New York: Academic Press, 1972.

Goeldner, C. R., & Munn, H. L. The significance of the retirement market. In F. E. Waddell (Ed.), *The elderly consumer*. Columbia, MD: Human Ecology Center, Antioch College, 1976.

Goffman, E. *Asylums*. Hawthorn, NY: Aldine, 1961.

Goffman, E. *Stigma: Notes on the management of spoiled identity*. Englewood Cliffs, NJ: Prentice-Hall, 1963.

Goffman, E. *Interaction ritual*. New York: Doubleday Anchor, 1967.

Goldstein, J. H. *Social psychology*. New York: Academic Press, 1980.

Gould, R. *Transformations: Growth and change in adult life*. New York: Simon and Schuster, 1978.

Gouldner, A. W. *The coming crisis of Western sociology*. New York: Basic Books, 1971.

Green, B., Parham, I. A., Kleff, R., & Pilisuk, M. (Eds.). Old age: Environmental complexity and policy interventions. *Journal of Social Issues*, 1980, **36**(2), 1–94.

Green, I., Fedewa, B. E., Deardorff, H. L., Johnston, C. A., & Jackson, W. M. *Housing for the elderly: The development and design process*. New York: Van Nostrand, 1975.

Green, L. *The effects of predictability and attitudinal training on the institutionalized aged*. Unpublished master's thesis, University of Missouri-Kansas City, 1980.

Green, S. K. Stereotyping, behavioral expectancies, and age as a causal variable. In M. B. Brewer (Chair), *Perceptions of the aged: Basic studies and institutional implications*. Symposium presented at the meetings of the American Psychological Association, New York, September 1979.

Green, S. K. Senility versus wisdom: The meanings of old age as a cause for behavior. In T. O. Blank (Chair), *Attributions and attributes: Advances in adult development and aging.* Symposium presented at the meetings of the Eastern Psychological Association, New York, April 1981.

Greenwald, A. G. Transhistorical lawfulness of behavior: A comment on two papers. *Personality and Social Psychology Bulletin,* 1976, **2,** 391.

Gubrium, J. F. *The myth of the golden years.* Springfield, IL: Charles C. Thomas, 1973.

Gubrium, J. F. *Living and dying at Murray Manor.* New York: St. Martin's Press, 1975.

Gubrium, J. F., & Buckholdt, D. R. *Toward maturity: The social processing of human development.* San Francisco: Jossey-Bass, 1977.

Gurin, P., Gurin, G., Lao, R. C., & Beattie, M. Internal-external locus of control in the motivational dynamics of Negro youth. *Journal of Social Issues,* 1969, **25,** 29–53.

Gutmann, D. L. The post-parental years: Clinical problems and developmental possibilities. In W. H. Norman & T. J. Scaramella (Eds.), *Mid-life: Developmental and clinical issues.* New York: Brunner-Mazel, 1980.

Hamilton, V. L. Intuitive psychologist or intuitive lawyer? Alternative models of the attribution process. *Journal of Personality and Social Psychology,* 1980, **39,** 767–772.

Hanusa, B. H., & Schulz, R. Situational constraints on changing attribution patterns of the aged. In T. O. Blank (Chair), *Attributions and attributes: Advances in adult development and aging.* Symposium presented at the meetings of the Eastern Psychological Association, New York, April 1981.

Harre, R. The ethogenic approach: Theory and practice. In L. Berkowitz (Ed.), *Advances in experimental social psychology,* Vol. 10. New York: Academic Press, 1977. (a)

Harre, R. Automatisms and autonomies: A reply to Professor Schlenker. In L. Berkowitz (Ed.), *Advances in experimental social psychology,* Vol. 10. New York: Academic Press, 1977. (b)

Harre, R. *Social being: A theory for social psychology.* Totowa NJ: Rowman and Littlefield, 1979.

Harre, R., & Secord, P. F. *The explanation of social behavior.* Oxford, England: Blackwell, 1972.

Harris, L., and associates. *The myth and reality of aging in America.* Washington, DC: National Council on the Aging, 1975.

Hart, H. L. A., & Honore, A. M. Causation in the law. In H. Morris (Ed.), *Freedom and responsibility.* Stanford, CA: Stanford University Press, 1961.

Harvey, J. H., Ickes, W. J., & Kidd, R. F. (Eds.). *New directions in attribution research,* Vol. 1. Hillsdale, NJ: Erlbaum, 1976.

Harvey, J. H., Ickes, W. J., & Kidd, R. F. (Eds.). *New directions in attribution research* Vol 2. Hillsdale, NJ: Erlbaum, 1978.

Harvey, J. H., & Smith, W. P. *Social psychology: An attributional approach.* St. Louis: Mosby, 1977.

Harvey, J. H., & Tucker, J. A. On problems with the cause-reason distinction in attribution theory. *Journal of Personality and Social Psychology,* 1979, **37,** 1441–1446.

Harvey, J. H., Wells, G. L., & Alvarez, M. D. Attribution in the context of conflict and separation in close relationships. In J. H. Harvey, W. Ickes, & R. F. Kidd (Eds.), *New directions in attribution research,* Vol. 2. Hillsdale, NJ: Erlbaum, 1978.

Havighurst, R. J. A social psychological perspective on aging. *Gerontologist,* 1968, **8**(2), part 2, 67–71.

Havighurst, R. J., Neugarten, B. L., & Tobin, S. S. Disengagement and patterns of aging. In B. L. Neugarten (Ed.), *Middle age and aging.* Chicago: University of Chicago Press, 1968.

Heckhausen, H. *The anatomy of achievement motivation.* New York: Academic Press, 1967.

Heckhausen, H., & Weiner, B. The emergence of a cognitive psychology of motivation. In B. Weiner (Ed.), *Achievement motivation and attribution theory.* Morristown, NJ: General Learning Press, 1974.

Heider, F. *The psychology of interpersonal relations.* New York: Wiley, 1958.

Helmreich, R. Applied social psychology: The unfulfilled promise. *Personality and Social Psychology Bulletin,* 1975, **1,** 548–560.

Helmreich, R. L., Beane, W. E., Lucker, G. W., & Spence, J. T. Achievement motivation and scientific attainment. *Personality and Social Psychology Bulletin,* 1978, **4,** 222–226.

Helmreich, R. L., & Spence, J. T. The Work and Family Orientation Questionnaire: An objective instrument to assess components of achievement motivation and attitudes toward family and career. JSAS *Catalog of Selected Documents in Psychology,* 1978, **8,** 35 (MS 1677).

Helmreich, R. L., Spence, J. T., Beane, W. E., Lucker, G. W., & Matthews, K. A. Making it in academic psychology: Demographic and personality correlates of attainment. *Journal of Personality and Social Psychology,* 1980, 896–908.

Hendricks, J., & Hendricks, C. D. *Aging in mass society: Myths and realities.* Cambridge, MA: Winthrop, 1977.

Heron, A., & Chown, S. *Age and function.* Boston: Little, Brown, 1967.

Hess, R., & Torney, J. V. *Development of political attitudes in children.* New York: Irvington, 1967.

Hickey, T. H., Rakowski, W., Kafer, R., & Lachman, M. Aging opinion survey. Paper presented at meetings of the Gerontological Society, Dallas, November 1978.

Higbee, K. L., & Wells, M. G. Some research trends in social psychology during the 1960's. *American Psychologist,* 1972, **27,** 963–966.

Homans, G. C. *Social behavior: Its elementary forms.* New York: Harcourt, Brace, and World, 1961.

Horn, J. L., & Donaldson, G. On the myth of intellectual decline in adulthood. *American Psychologist,* 1976, **31,** 701–719.

Horner, M. S. Toward an understanding of achievement-related conflicts in women. *Journal of Social Issues,* 1972, **28**(2), 157–176.

House, J. S. The three faces of social psychology. *Sociometry,* 1977, **40,** 161–177.

Hovland, C., Janis, I., & Kelley, H. H. *Communication and persuasion.* New Haven, CN: Yale University Press, 1953.

Howard, J. A. Person-situation interaction models. *Personality and Social Psychology Bulletin,* 1979, **5,** 191–195.

Ickes, W., & Layden, M. A. Attributional styles. In J. H. Harvey, W. J. Ickes, & R. F. Kidd (Eds.), *New directions in attribution research,* Vol. 2. Hillsdale, NJ.: Erlbaum, 1978.

Jacobs, J. *Death and life of great American cities.* New York: Random House, 1961.

Jahoda, G. Critique: On Triandis's "Social psychology and cultural analysis." In L. H. Strickland, K. E. Aboud, & K. J. Gergen (Eds.), *Social psychology in transition.* New York: Plenum, 1976.

Jakobson, R. *Child language, aphasia, and phonological universals.* The Hague: Mouton, 1972.

Jennings, M. K., & Niemi, R. G. *Political character of adolescence.* Princeton, NJ: Princeton University Press, 1974.

Joe, V. C. Review of the internal-external control construct as a personality variable. *Psychological Reports,* 1971, **28,** 619–640

Jones, E. E., Kanouse, D. E., Kelley, H. H., Nisbett, R. E., Valins, S., & Weiner, B. (Eds.). *Attribution: Perceiving the causes of behavior.* Morristown, NJ: General Learning Press, 1972.

Jones, E. E., & Nisbett, R. E. *The actor and the observer: Divergent perceptions of the causes of behavior.* Morristown, NJ: General Learning Press, 1971.

Jones, J. M. *Prejudice and racism.* Reading, MA: Addison-Wesley, 1972.

Kahana, E., Felton, B., & Kiyak, A. Assessing internal locus of control among older persons. In B. Chodorkoff (Chair), *New approaches to clinical psychological assessments of the aged.* Symposium presented at the meetings of the American Psychological Association, New York, September 1979.

Kanouse, D. E., & Hanson, L. R. Negativity in evaluations. In E. E. Jones et al. (Eds.), *Attribution: Perceiving the causes of behavior.* Morristown, NJ: General Learning Press, 1972.

Katz, D., & Kahn, R. L. *Social psychology of organizations,* 2nd ed. New York: Wiley, 1978.

Katz, I., & Glass, D. C. An ambivalence-amplification theory of behavior toward the stigmatized. In W. G. Austin & S. Worchel (Eds.), *The social psychology of intergroup relations.* Monterey, CA: Brooks/Cole, 1979.

Kelley, H. H. Attribution in social interaction. In E. E. Jones et al. (Eds.), *Attribution: Perceiving the causes of behavior.* Morristown, NJ: General Learning Press, 1972.

Kerckhoff, A. C. Family patterns and morale in retirement. In I. H. Simpson & J. C. McKinney (Eds.), *Social aspects of aging.* Durham, NC: Duke University Press, 1966.

Kiesler, C. A. The job market: Response to Thomas Blank. *American Psychologist,* 1979, **34,** 447 (Comment).

Kilty, K. M., & Feld, A. Attitudes toward aging and toward needs of older people. *Journal of Gerontology,* 1976, **31,** 586–594.

Kimmel, D. C. *Adulthood and aging,* 2nd ed. New York: Wiley, 1980. (a)

Kimmel, D. C. Current theoretical issues in adult social and personality development. In T. O. Blank (Chair), *Adult developmental change: New directions for personality and social psychology.* Symposium presented at the meetings of the American Psychological Association, Montreal, September 1980. (b)

Kirscht, J. P., & Dillehay, R. C. *Dimensions of authoritarianism: A review of research and theory.* Lexington: University of Kentucky Press, 1967.

Klein, R. L. Age, sex, and task difficulty as predictors of social conformity. *Journal of Gerontology,* 1972, **27,** 229–236.

Klein, D. C., Fencil-Morse, E., & Seligman, M. E. P. Learned helplessness, depression, and the attribution of failure. *Journal of Personality and Social Psychology,* 1976, **33,** 508–516.

Klippel, E. Marketing research and the aged consumer: The need for a new perspective. *Journal of the Academy of Marketing Science,* 1974, **2,** 242–247.

Kogan, N. Beliefs, attitudes, and stereotypes about old people: A new look at some old issues. *Research on Aging,* 1979, **1,** 11–36.

Kogan, N., & Wallach, M. A. Age changes in values and attitudes. *Journal of Gerontology,* 1961, **16,** 272–280.

Kohlberg, L. Stages and aging in moral development: Some speculations. *Gerontologist,* 1973, **13,** 497–502.

Krauss, R. M., & Glucksberg, S. Social and non-social speech. *Scientific American,* 1977, **236,** 100–105.

Kruglanski, A. W. The endogenous-exogenous partition in attribution theory. *Psychological Review,* 1975, **82,** 387–406.

Kruglanski, A. W. Causal explanation, teleological explanation: On radical particularism in attribution theory. *Journal of Personality and Social Psychology,* 1979, **37,** 1447–1457.

Kuhlen, R. G. Developmental changes in motivation during the adult years. In J. E. Birren (Ed.), *Relations of development and aging.* Springfield, IL: Charles C. Thomas, 1964.

Kuhn, M. E. An open letter. *Gerontologist,* 1978, **18,** 422–424.

Kuypers, J. A. Internal-external locus of control and ego functioning, and personality in old age. *Gerontologist,* 1972, **12**(2), Part 1, 168–173.

Kuypers, J. A., & Bengtson, V. L. Social breakdown and competence: A model of normal aging. *Human Development,* 1973, **16,** 181–201.

Labouvie, E. W. Identity versus equivalence of psychological measures and constructs. In L. Poon (Ed.), *Aging in the 1980's.* Washington, DC: American Psychological Association, 1980.

Labouvie-Vief, G. Adult cognitive development: In search of alternative interpretations. *Merrill-Palmer Quarterly,* 1977, **23,** 222–263.

Labouvie-Vief, G., & Chandler, M. Cognitive development and lifespan developmental theories: Idealistic versus contextual perspectives. In P. B. Baltes (Ed.), *Lifespan development and behavior,* Vol. 1. New York: Academic Press, 1978.

Labouvie-Vief, G., & Gonda, J. N. Cognitive strategy training and intellectual performance in the elderly. *Journal of Gerontology,* 1976, **31,** 327–332.

Laing, R. D., Phillipson, H., & Lee, A. R. *Interpersonal perception.* New York: Springer, 1966.

Langer, E. J., & Rodin, J. The effects of choice and enhanced personal responsibility for the aged: A field experiment in an institutional setting. *Journal of Personality and Social Psychology,* 1976, **34,** 191–198.

Lao, R. C. The developmental trend of the locus of control. *Personality and Social Psychology Bulletin,* 1975, **1,** 348–350.

Latta, R. M. (Chair). *Integrating psychological and sociological social psychology.* Symposium presented at the meetings of the Eastern Psychological Association, Hartford, CN, April 1980.

Lau, R. R., & Russell, D. Attributions in the sports pages. *Journal of Personality and Social Psychology,* 1980, **39,** 29–38.

Lawton, M. P. *Planning and managing housing for the elderly.* New York: Wiley, 1975.

Lawton, M. P. *Environment and aging.* Monterey, CA: Brooks/Cole, 1980.

Lawton, M. P., & Cohen, J. The generality of housing impact on the well-being of older people. *Journal of Gerontology, 1974,* **29,** 194–204.

Lawton, M. P., & Nahemow, L. Ecology and the aging process. In C. Eisdorfer & M. P. Lawton (Eds.), *The psychology of adult development and aging.* Washington, DC: American Psychological Association, 1973.

Lawton, M. P., Newcomer, R. J., & Byerts, T. O. (Eds.). *Community planning for an aging society.* New York: Halsted, 1976.

Lawton, M. P., & Simon, B. The ecology of social relationships in housing for the elderly. *Gerontologist,* 1968, **8,** 108–115.

Lerner, M. J. The justice motive in social behavior. *Journal of Social Issues,* 1975, **31,** 1–19.

Levinson, D. J., and associates. *The seasons of a man's life.* New York: Knopf, 1978.

Lewin, K. *A dynamic theory of personality.* New York: McGraw-Hill, 1935.

Lewin, M. Kurt Lewin's view of social psychology: The crisis of 1977 and the crisis of 1927. *Personality and Social Psychology Bulletin,* 1977, **3,** 159–172.

Lindstrom, A. *Personal control, depressive symptoms, and causal attributions for success and failure in the aged.* Unpublished doctoral dissertation, University of California-Santa Barbara, 1980.

Lindzey, G., & Aronson, E. (Eds.). *Handbook of social psychology, 2nd ed. (5 Vol.).* Cambridge, MA: Addison-Wesley, 1968.

Liska, A. E. *The dissipation of sociological social psychology. American Sociologist,* 1977, **12**(1), 2–8.

Locke-Connor, C., & Walsh, R. P. Attitudes toward the older job applicant: Just as competent but more likely to fail. *Journal of Gerontology,* 1980, **35,** 920–927.

Loether, H. J. *Problems of aging,* 2nd ed. Belmont, CA: Dickenson, 1975.

Lopata, H. Z. *Widowhood in an American city.* Cambridge, MA: Schenkman, 1973.

Lowe, R. H. Survey of social psychological methods, techniques and designs; A response to Helmreich. *Personality and Social Psychology Bulletin,* 1976, **2,** 116–118.

Lowenthal, M. F. Toward a sociopsychological theory of change in adulthood and old age. In J. E. Birren & K. W. Schaie (Eds.), *Handbook of the Psychology of Aging.* New York: Van Nostrand-Reinhold, 1977.

Lowenthal, M. F., & Chiriboga, D. Social stress and adaptation: Toward a life-course perspective. In C. Eisdorfer & M. P. Lawton (Eds.), *The psychology of adult development and aging.* Washington, DC: American Psychological Association, 1973.

Lowenthal, M. F., & Haven, C. Interaction and adaptation: Intimacy as a critical variable. *American Sociological Review,* 1968, **33,** 20–30.

Lowenthal, M. F., Thurnher, M., Chiriboga, D., & associates. *The four stages of life: A comparative study of women and men facing transitions.* San Francisco: Jossey-Bass, 1975.

Maccoby, E. E., & Jacklin, C. N. *The psychology of sex differences.* Stanford, CA: Stanford University Press, 1974.

Madden, E. S. *A survey of grocery buying behavior of an aging low-income population in a housing development in Washington, D.C.* Unpublished master's thesis, University of Maryland, 1967.

Mandino, O. *The greatest secret in the world.* New York: Bantam, 1978.

Mandler, G., & Sarason, S. B. A study of anxiety and learning. *Journal of Abnormal and Social Psychology,* 1952, **47,** 166–173.

Manis, M. Comments on Gergen's "Social psychology as history." *Personality and Social Psychology Bulletin,* 1975, **1,** 450–455.

Marshall, V. W. Bernice Neugarten: Gerontologist in search of a theory. In *Concerning theory in aging.* Symposium presented at the meetings of the Gerontological Society, New York, 1976.

Marshall, V. W., & Tindale, J. A. Notes for a radical gerontology. *International Journal of Aging and Human Development,* 1978–79, **9,** 163–175.

Mason, J. B., & Beardon, W. O. Profiling the shopping behavior of elderly consumers. *Gerontologist,* 1978, **18,** 454–461.

McCarthy, H. Time perspective and aged persons' attributions of their life experiences. Paper presented at meetings of the Gerontological Society, San Francisco, 1977.

McClelland, D. C. Testing for competence rather than for intelligence. *American Psychologist,* 1973, **28,** 1–14.

McClelland, D. C., Atkinson, J. W., Clark, R. A., & Lowell, E. L. *The achievement motive.* New York: Appleton-Century-Crofts, 1953.

McGhee, P. E., & Crandall, V. C. Beliefs in internal-external control of reinforcement and academic performance. *Child Development,* 1968, **39,** 91–102.

McGrath, J. E. Togetherness for the two social psychologies: Why can't we just be friends? *SASP Newsletter,* December 1979, 5–6.

McGuire, W. J. The yin and yang of progress in social psychology: Seven koan. *Journal of Personality and Social Psychology,* 1973, **26,** 446–456.

McGuire, W. J. Toward social psychology's second century. In T. Newcomb (Chair), *Centennial symposium: Social psychology—What have we learned?* Symposium presented at the meetings of the American Psychological Association, New York, September 1979.

McHugh, M., Beckman, L., & Frieze, I. H. Analyzing alcoholism. In I. H. Frieze, D. Bartal, & J. S. Carroll (Eds.), *New approaches to social problems.* San Francisco: Jossey-Bass, 1979.

McMahan, I. D. The relationship between causal attributions and expectation of success. *Journal of Personality and Social Psychology,* 1973, **28,** 109–114.

McTavish, D. G. Perceptions of old people: A review of research methodologies and findings. *Gerontologist,* 1971, **11**(4), Part II, 90–101.

Mead, G. H. *Mind, self, and society.* Chicago: University of Chicago Press, 1934.

Mehrabian, A. Male and female scales of the tendency to achieve. *Educational and Psychological Measurement,* 1968, **28,** 493–502.

Mehrabian, A. Measures of achieving tendency. *Educational and Psychological Measurement,* 1969, **29,** 445–451.

Mehrabian, A., & Bank, L. A manual for the Mehrabian measures of achieving tendencies. Unpublished manuscript, University of California, Los Angeles, 1975.

Meyer, J. P. Causal attributions for success and failure: A multivariate investigation of dimensionality, formation, and consequences. *Journal of Personality and Social Psychology,* 1980, **38,** 704–718.

Meyer, W. V. *Selbster Antwortlichkeit und Leistungsmotivation.* Unpublished doctoral dissertation, Ruhr Universität, 1970.

Milgram, S. The experience of living in cities. *Science,* 1970, **167,** 1461–1468.

Miller, D. T., & Porter, C. A. Effects of temporal perspective on the attribution process. *Journal of Personality and Social Psychology,* 1980, **39,** 532–541.

Miller, D. T., & Ross, M. Self-serving biases in the attribution of causality: Fact or fiction? *Psychological Bulletin,* 1975, **82,** 213–225.

Mischel, W. *Personality and assessment.* New York: Wiley, 1968.

Monahan, L., Kuhn, D., & Shaver, P. Intrapsychic versus cultural explanations of the "fear of success" motive. *Journal of Personality and Social Psychology,* 1974, **29,** 60–64.

Monson, T. C., & Snyder, M. Actors, observers, and the attribution process: Toward a reconceptualization. *Journal of Experimental Social Psychology,* 1977, **13,** 89–111.

Moore, G. T., & Golledge, R. G. (Eds.). *Environmental knowing.* New York: Halsted, 1976.

Moos, R. *The human context: Environmental determinants of behavior.* New York: Wiley, 1976.

Neisser, U. On "social knowing." *Personality and Social Psychology Bulletin,* 1980, **6,** 601–605.

Neugarten, B. L. *Personality in middle and later life.* New York: Atherton, 1964.

Neugarten, B. L. Adaptation and the life cycle. *Journal of Geriatric Psychiatry,* 1970, **4,** 71–87.

Neugarten, B. L. Personality change in late life: A developmental perspective. In C. Eisdorfer & M. P. Lawton (Eds.), *The psychology of adult development and aging.* Washington, DC: American Psychological Association, 1973.

Neugarten, B. L. Age groups in American society and the rise of the young-old. *The Annals of the American Academy of Political and Social Sciences,* 1974, 187–198.

Neugarten, B. L. Personality change and aging. In J. E. Birren & K. W. Schaie (Eds.), *Handbook of the psychology of aging.* New York: Van Nostrand Reinhold, 1977.

Neugarten, B. L. (Ed.). *Middle age and aging.* Chicago: University of Chicago Press, 1968.

Neugarten, B. L., & Datan, N. Sociological perspectives on the life cycle. In P. B. Baltes & K. W. Schaie (Eds.), *Lifespan developmental psychology: Personality and socialization.* New York: Academic Press, 1973.

Neugarten, B. L. Havighurst, R. J., & Tobin, S. S. The measurement of life satisfaction. *Journal of Gerontology,* 1961, **16,** 134–143.

Newcomb, T. M. Organization as an open system: A case of scholarly miscegenation. *SASP Newsletter,* December, 1979, 9–10.

Newman, B. M., & Newman, P. R. *Development through life.* Homewood, IL: Dorsey, 1975.

Newtson, D. An interactionist perspective on social knowing. *Personality and Social Psychology Bulletin,* 1980, **6,** 520–531.

Nie, N. H., Hull, C. H., Jenkins, J. G., Steinbrenner, K., & Bent, D. H. *Statistical package for the social sciences,* 2nd ed. New York: McGraw-Hill, 1975.

Orvis, B. R., Kelley, H. H., & Butler, D. Attributional conflict in young couples. In J. H. Harvey, W. J. Ickes, & R. F. Kidd (Eds.), *New directions in attribution research,* Vol. 1. Hillsdale, NJ: Erlbaum, 1976.

Osmond, H. Function as the basis of psychiatric ward design. *Mental Hospitals,* 1957, **8,** 23–30.

Palmore, E., & Luikart, C. Health and social factors related to life satisfaction. *Journal of Health and Social Behavior,* 1972, **13,** 68–80.

Patterson, A. H. Territorial behavior and fear of crime in the elderly. *Environmental Psychology and Non-Verbal Behavior*, 1978, **2,** 131–144.

Peplau, L. A., Russell, D., & Heim, M. The experience of loneliness. In I. H. Frieze, D. Bartal, & J. S. Carroll (Eds.), *New approaches to social problems*. San Francisco: Jossey-Bass, 1979.

Pessin, J., & Husband, R. W. Effects of social stimulation on human maze learning. *Journal of Abnormal and Social Psychology*, 1933, **28,** 148–154.

Phares, E. J. *Locus of control in personality*. Morristown, NJ: General Learning Press, 1976.

Piaget, J. *Six psychological studies*. (Translated by A. Tenzer). New York: Random House, 1967.

Planning Department, City of Kansas City, Kansas. *Survey of elderly residents and their needs*. Author, 1975.

Poon, L. W. (Ed.). *Aging in the 1980's*. Washington, DC: American Psychological Association, 1980.

Porteous, J. D. *Environment and behavior*. Cambridge, MA: Addison-Wesley, 1977.

Prater, J. Elderly residents die as heat rises. *Kansas City Times*, July 17, 1980.

Pratt, H. J. Politics of aging: Political science and the study of gerontology. *Research on Aging*, 1979, **1,** 155–186.

Psathas, G. (Ed.). *Phenomenological sociology: Issues and applications*. New York: Wiley, 1973.

Rausch, H. L., Barry, W. A., Hertel, R. K., & Swain, M. A. *Communication, conflict, and marriage*. San Francisco: Jossey-Bass, 1974.

Reinicke, J. A. Retailing and social responsibility: The case of the elderly. In F. E. Waddell (Ed.), *The elderly consumer*. Columbia, MD: Human Ecology Center, Antioch College, 1976.

Reno, R. Attribution for success and failure as a function of perceived age. *Journal of Gerontology*, 1979, **34,** 709–715.

Revis, J. S. Transportation for the elderly: The state of the art. In F. E. Waddell (Ed.), *The elderly consumer*. Columbia, MD: Human Ecology Center, Antioch College, 1976.

Riegel, K. F. On the history of psychological gerontology. In C. Eisdorfer & M. P. Lawton (Eds.), *The psychology of adult development and aging*. Washington, DC: American Psychological Association, 1973.

Riegel, K. F. The dialectics of human development. *American Psychologist*, 1976, **31,** 689–700.

Riegel, K. F. *Psychology, mon amour*. Boston: Houghton Mifflin, 1978.

Riegel, K. F. *Foundations of a dialectical psychology*. New York: Academic Press, 1979.

Riegel, K. F., & Riegel, R. M. Development, drop, and death. *Developmental Psychology*, 1972, **6,** 306–319.

Riley, M. W., & Foner, A. *Aging and society*, Vol. 1: *An inventory of research findings*. New York: Russell Sage Foundation, 1968.

Riley, M. W., Johnson, M., & Foner, A. *Aging and society*, Vol. 3: *A sociology of age stratification*. New York: Russell Sage Foundation, 1972.

Rodin, J., & Langer, E. J. Long-term effects of a control-relevant intervention with the institutionalized aged. *Journal of Personality and Social Psychology*, 1977, **35,** 897–902.

Rodin, J., & Langer, E. Aging labels: The decline of control and the fall of esteem. *Journal of Social Issues,* 1980, **36**(2), 12–29.

Rogers, C. *On becoming a person.* Boston: Houghton Mifflin, 1961.

Rose, A. M. The subculture of aging: A framework for research in social gerontology. In A. M. Rose & W. A. Peterson (Eds.), *Older people in their social world.* Philadelphia: Davis, 1965.

Rosen, B., & Jerdee, T. H. The influence of age stereotypes on managerial decisions. *Journal of Applied Psychology,* 1976, **61,** 428–432.

Rosenbaum, R. M. *A dimensional analysis of the perceived causes for success and failure.* Unpublished doctoral dissertation, University of California, Los Angeles, 1972.

Rosow, I. *Social integration of the aged.* New York: Free Press, 1967.

Rosow, I. *Socialization to old age.* Berkeley: University of California Press, 1975.

Ross, L. The intuitive psychologist and his shortcomings: Distortions in the attribution process. In L. Berkowitz (Ed.), *Advances in experimental social psychology,* Vol. 10. New York: Academic Press, 1977.

Rotter, J. B. Generalized expectancies for internal versus external control of reinforcement. *Psychological Monographs,* 1966, **80,** (Whole Number 609).

Rotter, J. B. Some problems and misconceptions related to the construct of internal versus external control of reinforcement. *Journal of Consulting and Clinical Psychology,* 1975, **43,** 56–67.

Rubinstein, S. L. *Grundlagen der allgemeinen Psychologie.* Berlin, Volk und Wissen, 1958. Summarized in T. R. Payne, *S. L. Rubinstein and the philosophical foundations of Soviet psychology.* New York: Humanities Press, 1968.

Ryckman, R. M. Applied social psychology: Haven for the comfortable radical pussycat. *Personality and Social Psychology Bulletin,* 1976, **2,** 127–130.

Ryckman, R. M., & Malikiosi, M. X. Relationship between locus of control and chronological age. *Psychological Reports,* 1975, **36,** 655–658.

Saks, M. J. *Jury verdicts: The role of group size and social decision rule.* Lexington, MA: Lexington, 1977.

Sampson, E. E. The sociohistorical siting of psychological facts. *SASP Newsletter,* December, 1979, 6–7.

Sarason, I. G. Anxiety and self-pre-occupation. In I. G. Sarason & C. D. Spielberger (Eds.), *Stress and anxiety,* Vol. 2. Washington, DC: Hemisphere, 1976.

Sarason, S. B. *Work, aging, and social change.* New York: Free Press, 1977.

Schaie, K. W. A general model for the study of developmental problems. *Psychological Bulletin,* 1965, **64,** 92–107.

Schaie, K. W. Quasi-experimental research designs in the psychology of aging. In J. E. Birren & K. W. Schaie (Eds.), *Handbook of the psychology of aging.* New York: Van Nostrand-Reinhold, 1977.

Schaie, K. W., & Baltes, P. B. Some faith helps to see the forest: A final comment on the Horn and Donaldson myth of the Baltes-Schaie position on adult intelligence. *American Psychologist,* 1977, **31,** 720–725.

Schaie, K. W., & Labouvie-Vief, G. Generational versus ontogenetic components of change in adult cognitive behavior: A fourteen year cross-sequential study. *Developmental Psychology,* 1974, **10,** 105–120.

Schlenker, B. R. Social psychology and science. *Journal of Personality and Social Psychology*, 1974, **29**, 1–15.

Schlenker, B. R. On the ethogenic approach: Etiquette and revolution. In L. Berkowitz (Ed.), *Advances in experimental social psychology*, Vol. 10. New York: Academic Press, 1977.

Schneider, S. F. Positions of psychologists trained for research. *American Psychologist*, 1980, **35**, 861–866.

Schulz, J. H. *The economics of aging*. Monterey, CA: Brooks/Cole, 1976.

Schulz, R. The effects of control and predictability on the psychological and physical well-being of the institutionalized aged. *Journal of Personality and Social Psychology*, 1976, **33**, 563–573.

Schulz, R., & Brenner, G. Relocation of the aged: A review and theoretical analysis. *Journal of Gerontology*, 1977, **32**, 323–333.

Schulz, R., & Hanusa, B. H. Long-term effects of control and predictability enhancing interventions: Findings and ethical issues. *Journal of Personality and Social Psychology*, 1978, **36**, 1194–1201.

Schulz, R., & Hanusa, B. H. Experimental social gerontology: A social psychological perspective. *Journal of Social Issues*, 1980, **36**(2), 30–46.

Secord, P. F. Transhistorical and transcultural theory. *Personality and Social Psychology Bulletin*, 1976, **2**, 418–420.

Selltiz, C., Wrightsman, L. S., & Cook, S. W. *Research methods in social relations*, 3rd ed. New York: Holt, Rinehart, and Winston, 1976.

Shaver, K. G. *Introduction to attribution processes*. Cambridge, MA: Winthrop, 1975.

Shaver, K. G. Attributional error and attitudes toward aging: A view of the NCOA National Attitude Survey. *International Journal of Aging and Human Development*, 1978, **9**, 101–113.

Shaver, P., & Rubinstein, C. Childhood attachment experience and adult loneliness. In L. Wheeler (Ed.), *Review of personality and social psychology*, Vol. 1. Beverly Hills: Sage, 1980.

Shaw, M. E. *Group dynamics: The psychology of small group behavior*, 2nd ed. New York: McGraw-Hill, 1976.

Sheehy, G. *Passages: Predictable crises of adult life*. New York: Dutton, 1976.

Sherif, M., Harvey, O. J., White, B. J., Hood, W. E., & Sherif, C. W. *Intergroup conflict and cooperation: The robber's cave experiment*. Norman: University of Oklahoma Book Exchange, 1961.

Sherif, M., & Sherif, C. W. Research on intergroup relations. In O. Klineberg & R. Christie (Eds.), *Perspectives in social psychology*. New York: Holt, Rinehart, and Winston, 1965.

Sherman, H. M. *How to turn failure into success*. Englewood Cliffs, NJ: Prentice-Hall, 1958.

Sherman, N. C., Gold, J. A., & Sherman, M. F. Attribution theory and evaluations of older men among college students, their parents, and grandparents. *Personality and Social Psychology Bulletin*, 1978, **4**, 440–442.

Sherman, S. R., Magnum, W. P., Dodds, S., Walkley, R. P., & Wilber, D. M. Psychological effects of retirement housing. *Gerontologist*, 1968, **8**, 170–175.

Smith, M. B. *Humanizing social psychology*. San Francisco: Jossey-Bass, 1974.

Smith, M. B. A dialectical social psychology? Comments on a symposium. *Personality and Social Psychology Bulletin,* 1977, **3,** 719–724.

Smith, M. B. Attitudes, values, and selfhood. In H. E. Howe & M. Page (Eds.), *Nebraska Symposium on Motivation, 1979.* Lincoln: University of Nebraska Press, 1980.

Smith, S. H. Performance expectations and causal attributions for older and younger workers. Paper presented at American Psychological Association meetings, New York, September, 1979.

Snyder, M. The self-monitoring of expressive behavior. *Journal of Personality and Social Psychology,* 1974, **30,** 526–537.

Snyder, M. Attribution and behavior: Social perception and social causation. In J. H. Harvey, W. J. Ickes, & R. F. Kidd (Eds.), *New directions in attribution research.* Hillsdale, NJ: Erlbaum, 1976.

Snyder, M., Stephan, W. G., & Rosenfeld, D. Egotism and attributions. *Journal of Personality and Social Psychology,* 1976, **33,** 435–441.

Snyder, M., Stephan, W. G., & Rosenfeld, D. Attributional egotism. In J. H. Harvey, W. J. Ickes, & R. F. Kidd (Eds.), *New directions in attribution research,* Vol 2. Hillsdale, NJ: Erlbaum, 1978.

Sommer, R. Small group ecology in institutions for the elderly. In L. A. Pastalan & D. H. Carson (Eds.), *Spatial behavior of older people.* Ann Arbor: Institute of Gerontology, University of Michigan and Wayne State University, 1970.

Sommer, R. *Tight spaces.* Englewood Cliffs, NJ: Prentice-Hall, 1974.

Sommer, R. Toward a psychology of natural behavior. *APA Monitor,* 1977, **8**(1), 1, 7.

Sommer, R. & Ross, H. Social interaction in a geriatrics ward. *International Journal of Social Psychiatry,* 1958, **4,** 128–133.

Spence, J. T., & Helmreich, R. L. Comparison of masculine and feminine personality attributes and sex-role attitudes across age groups. *Developmental Psychology,* 1979, **15,** 583–584.

Stang, D., & Brothen, T. (Eds.). Towards a more applied social psychology. *SASP Newsletter,* 1980, **6**(2), 1–10.

Stone, G. P. & Farberman, H. A. (Eds.). *Social psychology through symbolic interaction,* 2nd ed. New York: Wiley, 1981.

Storandt, M., Siegler, I., & Elias, M. (Eds.). *The clinical psychology of aging.* New York: Plenum, 1979.

Storms, M. Videotape and the attribution process: Reversing actors' and observers' points of view. *Journal of Personality and Social Psychology,* 1973, **27,** 165–175.

Storms, M. D., & Nisbett, R. E. Insomnia and the attribution process. *Journal of Personality and Social Psychology,* 1970, **16,** 319–328.

Streib, G. F. Are the aged a minority group? In A. W. Gouldner (Ed.), *Applied sociology.* New York: Free Press, 1965.

Strickland, L. H., Aboud, F. E., & Gergen, K. J. *Social psychology in transition.* New York: Plenum, 1976.

Strodbeck, F., James, R., & Hawkins, C. Social status in jury deliberations. *American Sociological Review,* 1957, **22,** 713–718.

Stryker, S. Developments in "two social psychologies": Toward an appreciation of mutual relevance. *Sociometry,* 1977, **40,** 145–160.

Sullivan, H. S. *The interpersonal theory of psychiatry*. New York: W. W. Norton, 1953.

Sundeen, R. A., & Mathieu, J. T. The fear of crime and its consequences among elderly in three urban communities. *Gerontologist*, 1976, **16**, 211–219.

Swell, L. *Success: You can make it happen*. New York: Simon and Schuster, 1977.

Tajfel, H., & Turner, J. An integrative theory of intergroup conflict. In W. G. Austin & S. Worchel (Eds.), *The social psychology of intergroup relations*. Monterey, CA: Brooks/Cole, 1979.

Tapp, J. L., & Levine, F. *Law, justice, and the individual in society*. New York: Holt, Rinehart, and Winston, 1977.

Thorngate, W. "In general" versus "it depends": Some comments on the Gergen-Schlenker debate. *Personality and Social Psychology Bulletin*, 1976, **2**, 404–410.

Triandis, H. C. *Interpersonal behavior*. Monterey, CA: Brooks/Cole, 1976.

Triandis, H. C. Some universals of social behavior. *Personality and Social Psychology Bulletin*, 1978, **4**, 1–16.

Triandis, H. C., & Lambert, W. W. *Handbook of cross-cultural psychology*, Vol. 5: Social psychology. Boston: Allyn and Bacon, 1980.

Tuckman, J., & Lorge, I. Attitudes toward old people. *Journal of Social Psychology*, 1953, **37**, 249–260.

U. S. Department of Housing and Urban Development (HUD). *Management of congregate housing: A HUD guide*. Washington, DC: Author, 1972.

Valins, S., & Nisbett, R. E. *Attribution processes in the development and treatment of emotional disorders*. Morristown, NJ: General Learning Press, 1971.

Valle, V. A., & Johnson, E. J. Consumer response to product quality. In I. H. Frieze, D. Bar-tal, & J. S. Carroll (Eds.), *New approaches to social problems*. San Francisco: Jossey-Bass, 1979.

Valliant, G. E. *Adaptation to life*. Boston: Little, Brown, 1977.

Ventimiglia, J. (Ed.). Interfacing the two social psychologies. *SASP Newsletter*, December 1979.

Veroff, J., Atkinson, J. W., Feld, C., & Gurin, G. The use of thematic apperception to assess motivation in a nationwide interview study. *Psychological Monographs*, 1960, **74** (12, Whole No. 499).

Vygotsky, L. S. *Thought and language*. Cambridge, MA: MIT Press, 1962.

Waddell, F. E. (Ed.). *The elderly consumer*. Columbia, MD: Human Ecology Center, Antioch College, 1976.

Weiner, B. *Theories of motivation: From mechanism to cognition*. Chicago: Markham–Rand-McNally, 1972.

Weiner, B. (Ed.). *Achievement motivation and attribution theory*. Morristown, NJ: General Learning Press, 1974.

Weiner, B. A theory of motivation for some classroom experiences. *Journal of Educational Psychology*, 1979, **71**, 3–25.

Weiner, B., & Peter, N. A cognitive-developmental analysis of achievement and moral judgments. *Developmental Psychology*, 1973, **9**, 290–309.

Weiner, B., Russell, D., & Lerman, D. Affective consequences of causal ascriptions. In J. H. Harvey, W. J. Ickes, & R. F. Kidd (Eds.), *New directions in attribution research*, Vol. 2. Hillsdale, NJ: Erlbaum, 1978.

Weisz, J. R. Transcontextual validity in developmental research. *Child Development,* 1978, **49,** 1–12.

Weiting, S. G. Microcultural generations. Unpublished manuscript, University of Iowa, 1977.

Whitbourne, S. K., & Weinstock, C. S. *Adult development: The differentiation of experience.* New York: Holt, Rinehart, and Winston, 1979.

White, R. W. Motivation reconsidered: The concept of competence. *Psychological Review,* 1959, **66,** 297–334.

Whitt, J. A., & Derber, C. Problems of professional nomads need attention. *ASA Footnotes,* 1979, **7**(8), 2.

Wicker, A. W. *An introduction to ecological psychology.* Monterey, CA: Brooks/Cole, 1979.

Wicklund, R. A., & Duval, S. *The theory of objective self-awareness.* New York: Academic Press, 1972.

Wiley, M. G., Crittenden, K. S., & Birg, L. D. Why a rejection: Causal attribution of a career achievement event. *Social Psychology Quarterly,* 1979, **42,** 214–222.

Williams, R. H., & Wirths, C. *Lives through the years.* New York: Atherton, 1965.

Wilson, D. W., & Schafer, R. B. Is social psychology interdisciplinary? *Personality and Social Psychology Bulletin,* 1978, **4,** 548–552.

Wine, J. Test anxiety and the direction of attention. *Psychological Bulletin,* 1971, **76,** 92–104.

Wolfe, T. *You can't go home again.* New York: Harper & Row, 1940.

Wolk, S., & Kurtz, J. Positive adjustment during aging and expectancy for internal control. *Journal of Clinical and Consulting Psychology,* 1975, **43,** 173–178.

Worchel, S., & Cooper, J. *Understanding social psychology,* Revised ed. Homewood, IL: Dorsey, 1979.

Wortman, C. Causal attributions and personal control. In J. H. Harvey, W. Ickes, & R. Kidd (Eds.), *New directions in attribution research,* Vol. 1. Hillsdale, NJ: Erlbaum, 1976.

Wrightsman, L. S. *Social psychology,* 2nd ed. Monterey, CA: Brooks/Cole, 1977.

Wrightsman, L. S. The American trial jury on trial: Empirical evidence and procedural modifications. *Journal of Social Issues,* 1978, **34**(4), 137–164.

Wrightsman, L. S. Personal documents as data in conceptualizing adult personality development. Presidential address of Division 8 presented at the meetings of the American Psychological Association, Montreal, September 1980.

Wrong, D. H. The oversocialized conception of man in modern sociology. *American Sociological Review,* 1961, **26,** 183–193.

Zajonc, R. B. Preface and postscript to "Birth order and intellectual development." In L. H. Strickland, F. E. Aboud, & K. J. Gergen (Eds.), *Social psychology in transition.* New York: Plenum, 1976.

Zuckerman, M. Actions and occurrences in Kelley's cube. *Journal of Personality and Social Psychology,* 1978, **36,** 647–656.

Author Index

Page numbers in *italics* refer to complete references as author and/or editor.

Subject Index

Ability:
  as attribution for self, 110
  as category archetype, 69
  and competence testing, 158
  differing by stage of life, 104
  and environmental use, 171
  inferred from experience, 14
  interaction with social factors, 188
  major attribution, 65, 69, 96
  as power, 136
  and success- and failure-orientation, 79
Accumulation model:
  of attributions, 14, 138
  of cognitive development, 252
  of development, 11, 12, 216
  of personality development, 245–247
  and psychology of aging, 250, 251
Achievement, 137–141
  attribution research and theory, 78–80
  dictionary of terms, 78
  and performance in aging, 254
  shortcomings in research, 127
  see also Achievement motivation;
      Achievement orientation; Attribution
Achievement motivation:
  assumed age-related decline in, 92,
      118
  inadequacy of scales of, 119
  related to attribution variation, 107
  and Type II attribution, 73, 74
  see also Achievement; Achievement
      orientation
Achievement orientation:
  age-group differences, 118–123
  research on, 55
  and Type II attributions, 74
  see also Achievement; Achievement
      motivation; Work and Family
      Orientation Questionnaire

Achronic social psychology, 39–40
  of attributions, 82
  of environmental psychology, 171
  and psychology of aging, 256
Activity theory, 30, 42, 231–232, 235
Actor/observer differences:
  and cause vs. reason, 129, 131–132
  ego-defensive attributions, 75, 89
  information-processing explanation, 74–76
  and Type II attributions, 113–117
Adjustment:
  central in personality and social psychology
      of aging, 30, 229, 234–236, 240,
      243–248
  in marital relations, 260
  to normative demands, 28
  and passivity, 248
  in Person-Environment fit, 172
Adolescence, 19, 194
Adult development:
  and environmental relations, 194
  research on, 55–57
  and social psychology of aging, 28, 248
  and stage model, 29, 247
  in traditional social psychology, 5, 262
Adulthood:
  and attributions, 80–82, 106
  as final stage, 245
  and personality studies, 244
  as research topic, 19
Affect:
  ascribed to others, 94, 98, 99
  categories of, 95, 280–282
  data-gathering and coding, 270, 280–282
  and definition of success and failure,
      138
  differences by attributor, 103
  and feelings of incompetence, 113
  and locus of causality, 66, 69, 79

Psychology and Psychiatry in Courts and Corrections: Controversy and Change
    by Ellsworth A. Fersch, Jr.
Restricted Environmental Stimulation: Research and Clinical Applications
    by Peter Suedfeld
Personal Construct Psychology: Psychotherapy and Personality
    edited by Alvin W. Landfield and Larry M. Leitner
Mothers, Grandmothers, and Daughters: Personality and Child Care in
Three-Generation Families
    by Bertram J. Cohler and Henry U. Grunebaum
Further Explorations in Personality
    edited by A. I. Rabin, Joel Aronoff, Andrew M. Barclay, and Robert A. Zucker
Hypnosis and Relaxation: Modern Verification of an Old Equation
    by William E. Edmonston, Jr.
Handbook of Clinical Behavior Therapy
    edited by Samuel M. Turner, Karen S. Calhoun, and Henry E. Adams
Handbook of Clinical Neuropsychology
    edited by Susan B. Filskov and Thomas J. Boll
The Course of Alcoholism: Four Years After Treatment
    by J. Michael Polich, David J. Armor, and Harriet B. Braiker
Handbook of Innovative Psychotherapies
    edited by Raymond J. Corsini
The Role of the Father in Child Development (Second Edition)
    edited by Michael E. Lamb
Behavioral Medicine: Clinical Applications
    by Susan S. Pinkerton, Howard Hughes, and W. W. Wenrich
Handbook for the Practice of Pediatric Psychology
    edited by June M. Tuma
Change Through Interaction: Social Psychological Processes of Counseling and Psychotherapy
    by Stanley R. Strong and Charles D. Claiborn
Drugs and Behavior (Second Edition)
    by Fred Leavitt
Handbook of Research Methods in Clinical Psychology
    edited by Philip C. Kendall and James N. Butcher
A Social Psychology of Developing Adults
    by Thomas O. Blank